# Inflation Stabilization

The World Institute for Development Economics Research (WIDER) of the United Nations University was cosponsor of the conference "Inflation Stabilization: The Experience of Israel, Argentina, Brazil, Bolivia, and Mexico" along with the Ford Foundation, the Rockefeller Foundation, and the Fundacion Ortega y Gasset.

# Inflation Stabilization

The Experience of Israel,
Argentina, Brazil, Bolivia,
and Mexico

edited by
Michael Bruno
Guido Di Tella
Rudiger Dornbusch
Stanley Fischer

The MIT Press
Cambridge, Massachusetts
London, England

This book was set in Palatino by Asco Trade Typesetting Ltd. in Hong Kong, and printed and bound by Halliday Lithograph in the United States of America.

Library of Congress Cataloging-in-Publication Data

Inflation stabilization.

Papers and comments presented at the conference titled: "Inflation stabilization" held in Toledo, Spain, June 1987, cosponsored by the World Institute for Development Economics Research (WIDER) of the United Nations University, the Ford Foundation, the Rockefeller Foundation, and the Fundacion Ortega y Gasset.

Includes index.
1. Inflation (Finance)—Latin America—Case studies—Congresses. 2. Inflation (Finance)—Israel—Congresses. 3. Latin America—Economic policy—Case studies—Congresses. 4. Israel—Economic policy—Congresses. I. Bruno, Michael. II. World Institute for Development Economics Research.
HG660.5.154   1988        332.4'1'098        88-2768
ISBN 0-262-02279-6

# Contents

Preface    vii
Editors' Note    xiii

## I    Israel

**1    Israel's Stabilization: A Two-Year Review**    3
Michael Bruno and Sylvia Piterman

**2    The End of High Israeli Inflation: An Experiment in Heterodox Stabilization**    48
Alex Cukierman

**Comments**    95
Peter M. Garber, Nissan Liviatan, Elhanan Helpman
Reply by Alex Cukierman

## II    Argentina

**3    Stopping Hyperinflation: The Case of the Austral Plan in Argentina, 1985–87**    111
Jose Luis Machinea and Jose Maria Fanelli

**4    Inflation Stabilization or Hyperinflation Avoidance? The Case of the Austral Plan in Argentina, 1985–87**    153
Alfredo J. Canavese and Guido Di Tella

**Comments**    191
Daniel Heymann, Juan Carlos de Pablo, Carlos Alfredo Rodriguez, Sylvia Piterman

## III Brazil

**5 The Cruzado First Attempt: The Brazilian Stabilization Program of February 1986**   215
Eduardo M. Modiano

**6 Price Stabilization and Incomes Policies: Theory and the Brazilian Case Study**   259
Mario Henrique Simonsen

**Comments**   287
Eliana A. Cardoso, Roberto Macedo, Guillermo Ortiz, Miguel Urrutia

## IV Bolivia

**7 Inflation Stabilization in Bolivia**   307
Juan-Antonio Morales

**Comments**   347
Gail E. Makinen, Joseph Ramos

## V Lessons from Mexico

**8 Lessons from Mexico**   361
Francisco Gil Diaz and Raul Ramos Tercero

**Comments**   391
Herminio Blanco

## VI How to Restore Growth

**Three Views on Restoring Growth**   395
Domingo Cavallo, Manuel Guitián, Rosemary Thorp

Contributors   409
Index   411

# Preface

The contributors to this book offer descriptions and critical analyses of the disinflation programs introduced in Argentina, Bolivia, Brazil, and Israel in 1985–86 and a discussion of the possibility of such a program in Mexico.[1]

The collection of essays and comments is of interest for at least four reasons. First, several of the authors were among the actual architects of the programs and hence are closely acquainted with the strategy, details, and focal points of the programs they describe and evaluate. This places them in a particularly good position to assess which aspects were economically and politically most important in getting the programs accepted and where the reasons for subsequent difficulties and failures must be looked for. Second, the collection makes possible a comparative evaluation of the successes and failures of the programs. There are strong similarities among the programs in different countries—for example, Argentina, Israel, and Brazil—but evidently major differences in the outcomes. The inclusion of Bolivia makes it possible to contrast different styles of stabilization, for example, Bolivia and Argentina. Third, there is an interest in judging whether any of the experiences might be applicable to other countries that still face the task of stabilizing, for example, Mexico, where inflation is rising to above the 100% mark. Finally, these programs are interesting and important for reasons of political economy. If policymakers can find a way of stopping inflation without recession, as was the case in Israel, then something dramatically new has been learned in the field of macroeconomics. And if these programs are particularly dangerous in the hands of a reckless government, then that too is important information.

The broad issue raised in this book is apparent from table 1, which shows monthly rates of inflation. The stabilization program in Argentina was implemented in June 1985, that of Israel in July 1985. Bolivia stabilized in August 1985, and Brazil followed in February 1986. Mexican inflation is

**Table 1**
Inflation rates (percent per month, except 1984)

| Year | Argentina | Bolivia | Brazil | Israel | Mexico |
|------|-----------|---------|--------|--------|--------|
| 1984[a] | 627 | 1281 | 197 | 334 | 66 |
| **1985** | | | | | |
| I | 19.9 | 81.3 | 11.3 | 6.9 | 5.4 |
| II | 27.4 | 32.6 | 7.8 | 10.8 | 3.2 |
| III | 11.2 | 56.4 | 11.2 | 12.8 | 3.4 |
| IV | 0.8 | 14.5 | 10.9 | 2.9 | 4.4 |
| **1986** | | | | | |
| I | 0.6 | 14.4 | 13.2 | 1.2 | 6.4 |
| II | 2.6 | 2.5 | 2.6 | 2.1 | 5.2 |
| III | 6.3 | 1.8 | 0.7 | 1.0 | 6.2 |
| IV | 6.0 | | 1.9 | 2.0 | 6.5 |
| **1987** | | | | | |
| I | 5.7 | | 11.5 | 1.8 | |
| II | 1.3 | | | | |
| III | | | | | |
| IV | | | | | |

Source: IMF, *International Financial Statistics* (Washington, D.C.: International Monetary Fund, 1987).

still (in the fall of 1987) below the levels of the other countries when they stabilized.

As the inflation data show, only Israel and Bolivia have succeeded in keeping inflation low. By mid-1987 Argentinian inflation was already well above 100% per annum, and inflation in Brazil, in the aftermath of a second program, reached 27% per month before yet another freeze was instituted. A chief aim of this book is to document not only the initial steps in stabilization but also the reasons for failure. It is said that two out of three stabilizations fail.[2] Each of the four countries had attempted to stabilize before 1985 and failed. So far, two of the four countries that tried in 1985–86 have failed. The chief reason for failure, as the various contributors amply demonstrate, is a failure to push fiscal consolidation early and vigorously. Particularly in cases in which extensive freezing of wages and prices suspends or suppresses the warning signals, the lack of fiscal control is most obviously responsible for the rapid unraveling of the initial stabilization.

Rather than review in detail the contents of the book, we want to provide here a brief overview of the chapters, not even touching on the various comments that round out, complement, and sometimes critically qualify them. The book starts with the experience in Israel. Bruno and Piterman (chapter 1) not only describe the Israeli experience but also lay out the key issue of the exchange rate. There is a need in a stabilization for a nominal anchor, and in the open economy the exchange rate can play that role. Whether the exchange rate should be rigorously fixed is an important issue. If the exchange rate is the keystone of the program, then failure to hold it may lead to the rapid return of inflation. But if the government permits itself some flexibility on the exchange rate, it reduces its initial credibility. Cukierman (chapter 2) blends analytical modeling with an examination of how the program has fared. He develops a model with long-term wage contracts (in high inflations these need only be of the order of several months) and examines the interaction of money, wages, prices, and activity under rational expectations that take into account the government's policy objectives. The different predictions, depending on the exchange rate rule, are then evaluated in the light of Israeli experience. Cukierman, like Bruno and Piterman, highlights the challenge to policy-makers in Israel today, namely, how to shift from stabilization to the revival of sustained growth.

The Argentine stabilization is discussed by Machinea and Fanelli (chapter 3) and by Canavese and Di Tella (chapter 4). The Argentine chapters are of particular interest not only in their careful description of the details of stabilization but also in raising wider issues about high-inflation economies and stabilization. Two of these issues are particularly interesting. One focuses on the fact that inflation is endemic in Argentina,[3] which has developed an entire defense mechanism against the costs of inflation—which in turn generates even higher rates of inflation. The other deals with the implications of a sudden increase in the external debt-servicing burden, which increases the budget deficit and may set off an inflationary process, perhaps leading even to hyperinflation.

The discussion of Brazil by Modiano (chapter 5) and Simonsen (chapter 6), beyond covering the details of stabilization, raises two interesting questions. First, the Brazilian system of overlapping, six-month labor contracts brings with it special features for the inflation process and for stabilization. A pure wage freeze would leave some workers at the trough of the real wage cycle, whereas others would be at their peak. Thus a freeze has to find an equitable way of dealing with relative wage differentials arising from the contract timing. Second, the inflationary erosion of real wages comes to an end with stabilization, and hence there is a need to adjust the base wage so as to avoid an increase in the real wage. Simonsen, beyond discussing these wage issues, develops an ambitious game-theoretic rationalization of incomes policy as a coordinating device for imperfectly competitive economies. He argues that, in an economy of price setters, stabilization cannot be expected to lead *instantaneously* to the classical equilibrium with full employment and zero inflation because the actions of each price setter depend on the assumptions about other price setters' decisions. The gap left by the missing Walrasian auctioneer needs to be filled by a set of rules, such as a wage, price, and exchange rate freeze.

Cagan defined hyperinflation as a rate of increase of prices in excess of 50% per month. Bolivia, which is discussed by Morales in chapter 7, did reach hyperinflation. Moreover, this was not the first inflationary explosion. In 1958 there was a stabilization under much the same conditions as today.[4] In an economy in which all pricing was already geared to the dollar, Morales shows how stabilizing the exchange rate, without a wage or price freeze, achieved stabilization once the crucial steps on the budget had been taken. The Bolivian case is especially interesting because it forcefully raises the question of whether there were any substantive differences between the program in, say, Israel, where wages and prices were frozen, and that in Bolivia, where (relative) prices were liberalized. Is Bolivia a case where Sargent's analysis applies, namely, that once the budget is stabilized, inflation comes to a dead end by the sheer force of credibility? Or is exchange rate fixing *the* essential step? Or is the Sargent analysis applicable only when economic dislocation has proceeded so far that the public understands the existing situation cannot continue?[5]

Mexico today faces the challenge of dealing with high inflation. Stopping inflation with recession is ruled out on political grounds, and gradual disinflation is implausible because wages, the exchange rate, and public sector prices are not plausible candidates for initiating the disinflation. That leaves incomes policy as the alternative. Could an incomes policy—based program work in Mexico? This is the question Diaz and Tercero address in chapter 8.

This volume concludes with a panel discussion on growth. It is difficult enough to stop inflation but, as this discussion shows, the restoration of growth is so hard because it requires reconstructing institutions and incentives that have been eroded in more than decade of economic disintegration.

The papers and comments brought together in this volume were first presented at the conference "Inflation Stabilization" in Toledo, Spain, in June 1987. We are indebted to the Ford Foundation, the Rockefeller Foundation, the WIDER Foundation, and the Fundación Ortega y Gasset for their support and sponsorship of this undertaking. Our special thanks go to Carol McIntire, who organized the conference and this book, and to Simon Johnson, who helped edit it.

## Notes

1. This book does not cover, regrettably, the experience in Peru, where a heterodox program was implemented in August 1985 by the government of Alan Garcia. A good starting point for the Peruvian experience is *El Peru Heterodoxo*, by D. Carbonetto et al. (Lima: Instituto Nacional de Planificacion, 1987).

2. See L. Yeager and Associates, *Experiences with Stopping Inflation* (Washington D.C.: American Enterprise Institute, 1981), and R. Dornbusch and S. Fischer, "Stopping Hyperinflation" (*Weltwirtschaftliches Archiv*, April 1986, Band 122, Heft 1, 1–47) for a review of some earlier experiences.

3. The Israeli inflation was relatively short-lived; it entered the double-digit range in the early 1970s and the triple-digit range in 1979. By contrast, Argentina has suffered from recurrent bouts of near triple digit inflation

4. See J. Eder, *Inflation and Development in Latin America* (Ann Arbor, Mich.: University of Michigan Press, 1968) and Yeager et al., *Experiences with Stopping Inflation*.

5. See T. Sargent, "The Ends of Four Big Inflations," in *Inflation*, R. Hall, ed. (Chicago, Ill.: University of Chicago Press, 1982), 41–96; the discussion in R. Dornbusch, "Stopping Hyperinflation: Lessons from the German Experience in the Twenties," in *Essays in Honor of Franco Modigliani*, R. Dornbusch, S. Fischer, and J. Bossons, eds. (Cambridge, Mass.: MIT Press, 1987), 337–366; and E. Helpman and L. Leiderman, "Stabilization in High Inflation Countries: Analytical Foundations and Recent Experience," in *Carnegie Rochester Conference Series*, K. Brunner and A. Meltzer, eds. (Amsterdam: North-Holland, forthcoming), vol. 28.

# Editors' Note

Throughout this volume "seigniorage revenue" denotes the real value of money printed by the government; "inflation tax" denotes the loss in real value of money (or, more generally, all nominal assets) held by the public. Authors use these terms interchangeably only in steady state, where real money balances are constant.

# I    Israel

# 1

# Israel's Stabilization: A Two-Year Review

## Michael Bruno and Sylvia Piterman

After more than a decade of continuously escalating inflation and recurrent balance of payments crises, which since 1973 had caused the virtual stagnation of economic growth, Israel launched a comprehensive stabilization program in July 1985. The new policy achieved a drastic slowdown of inflation together with an improvement in Israel's external position without causing a significant rise in unemployment.

The program's success lies in a dramatic cut in the government deficit, but it is also due to the appropriate initial credible synchronization of the most important nominal variables. At the same time it was supported by favorable external circumstances—improved terms of trade, depreciation of the dollar, and emergency aid granted by the United States.

Viewed close to its second anniversary, the stabilization program can be credited with remarkable achievements, but recent developments have also brought out several problems that Israel's policymakers will have to address. The first of these is that inflation continues to run at 20% per annum and has so far not declined to the rate prevailing in Western countries. In part, this may be a by-product of stabilization itself. In its wake came excessive wage demands and higher private consumption. Also, both a sharp fall in private savings (which may be temporary) and a real appreciation of the shekel were considerable setbacks to the current account in 1986 and early 1987; the capital account continued to provide the surplus in the overall balance of payments. At the same time business profits were at their lowest historical level and there was only a moderate increase of gross domestic product and productivity in 1986, although a significant improvement was visible toward the end of 1986 and in early 1987. In the course of stabilization a series of structural difficulties have come to the surface in several sectors. Although inflation was running at a high rate, these problems were obscured by various financial and accounting devices. These problem areas, notably in the agricultural and construction sectors, have required special government intervention in the form of loan conversions and other measures. Finally, the program has not dealt with the most important long-term structural problem of Israel's economy, centering on an oversize public sector.

In order to cope with some of the long-term problems, the government has recently planned several reforms intended to reduce distortions in the capital and credit markets and in the tax system. Within this framework some preliminary measures were adopted in April 1987.

At the present juncture a permanent reduction in inflation hinges on a more flexible wage policy and continued budget balance. The government's abstinence from further debt issue is also a key to the success of the capital market reform. It still remains to be seen whether the recent acceleration of economic activity will be sufficiently export oriented and investment inducing to turn the economy toward a self-sustaining growth path. Once started, more rapid growth and more fundamental structural reforms could then reinforce each other.

We review here various aspects of the stabilization program. In section 1.1 we describe the background of its adoption in July 1985 and the supplementary policy measures taken in 1986 and in early 1987. In section 1.2 we discuss developments in the real economy in 1986, with special emphasis on the untoward trend of wages and private consumption. We deal with monetary developments and dilemmas relating to the objectives of monetary policy and its management in the process of disinflation in section 1.3, and in section 1.4 we review the development of the various nominal variables in relation to the exchange rate and discuss synchronization and the policy choice between a crawl and an exchange rate peg. We discuss some real microeconomic effects of disinflation in section 1.5, and in the last section we briefly address the renewal of long-term growth.

## 1.1   The Stabilization Program: Background, Implementation, and Complementary Policy Measures

Until the adoption of the stabilization program in July 1985, the Israeli economy went through more than a decade of recurrent balance of payments crises, each of which escalated inflation as the government tried to solve the crisis by resorting to price-shock-inducing policy measures (big devaluations and sharp increases in prices of subsidized goods and services). Underlying these developments were continuous high budget deficits, mounting public debt, and an accommodating monetary policy. Not every balance of payments crisis was caused by an increase in the government deficit, but no countercyclical policy was conducted with regard to the balance of payments that might have prevented the deterioration of the foreign payments position to the point of crisis.[1] This process severely impaired economic growth: For more than a decade GDP and productivity virtually stagnated.

In the two years preceding the stabilization program and following a policy of slowing devaluation (in 1982–83), the Israeli economy ran into a severe financial crisis. At the end of 1983 the government resorted to a price shock: a large nominal devaluation accompanied by raising controlled prices of goods and services so as to reduce outlays on subsidies. This together with the decrease in wealth resulting from the partial collapse of bank shares brought about a large increase in saving and a considerable improvement in the external current account, but it proved inadequate for arresting the financial deterioration. First, the "bank share arrangement" of October 1983 (in which the government, in order to avoid the total collapse of these shares, guaranteed their value at a level considerably above their real value) greatly increased the domestic debt and caused apprehension with regard to the government's ability to meet its obligations. Second, the rate of inflation jumped to 15% per month, a rate at which the existing indexation mechanisms could no longer function adequately. Third, the tax system broke down, particularly with regard to nonwage income; the breakdown was due partly to banks' ceasing to pay income tax as their profits turned negative and partly to the tax arrears caused by the acceleration of inflation. The decrease in tax revenue further undermined the public's confidence in the government's ability to meet its payments on the public debt. This caused an increase in speculative purchases of foreign currency in 1984, despite the improvement in the external current account. Attempts to put a halt to capital outflow by devaluations and price shocks caused price inflation to rise to more than 20% per month in September and October of 1984.

Between November 1984 and July 1985, when the stabilization program was adopted, several tripartite agreements (so-called package deals) among the government, the trade unions, and the employers' organizations were concluded. The agreements imposed price freezes and stipulated agreed wage increases. The exchange rate was not frozen, and the shekel continued to be devalued rapidly. In the transition from one package deal to the next, prices were adjusted and subsidies were cut, and the 1985–86 budget adopted during this period included a substantial reduction in the government's deficit.

The package deals slowed inflation temporarily and resulted in a real devaluation, a rise of the relative price of the subsidized goods, and a substantial improvement in the current account (see figure 1.3 and table 1A.1). In this sense they formed a background and provided some lessons for the subsequent adoption of the stabilization program. However, toward mid-1985 the continuing acceleration of inflation and the renewal of speculative acquisitions of foreign currency made it evident that the package deals were inadequate to bring about a sustainable stabilization of the economy. A more drastic and comprehensive program was therefore called for.[2]

The stabilization program launched in July 1985 had the dual objective of an abrupt reduction of inflation and a simultaneous significant improvement in the balance of payments. This two-pronged attack on *both* inflation *and* the balance of payments problem—coming after more than a decade of trying to attack one of these objectives at the expense of the other—was also intended to lay the ground for a structural change in the economy and for the eventual renewal of growth.

The program's design was the combination of a drastic cut in the deficit with the synchronized fixing of several nominal anchors (the exchange rate, wages, and bank credit). The cut in the deficit was primarily designed to stabilize the balance of payments and facilitate a credible pegging of the exchange rate (after an initial devaluation). The anchoring of prices to several nominal variables was intended to ensure that inflation (and expectations) would be brought down rapidly without throwing too much weight on a single anchor, which might have led to excessive real costs. For example, if bank credit is set as the only nominal anchor, the cost in unemployment and growth may become politically intolerable. Similarly, if the exchange rate is set as a single anchor, the loss of competitiveness and the deterioration in the balance of payments would eventually bring about the end of the program.

The time span foreseen for the implementation of the program as a whole was originally set at one year, of which the first three months were declared an economic emergency period. The principal measures of the program were as follows.[3]

*The Budget*
For the real part of the program the original objective was to put a halt to any further increase in the public debt, both domestic and foreign. This would have implied cutting the government deficit by $2–$2.5 billion, 10% of GDP, from its level in the 1984–85 budget (or by 5% of GDP as

compared to the planned 1985–86 budget). The deficit reduction actually incorporated in the stabilization program was lower, as a result of a compromise on the intended cut in public spending, and was put at 6% of GDP by comparison with the 1984–85 budget. The deficit was to be reduced primarily by cutting subsidies and raising taxes. As will be seen, the cut of the deficit eventually turned out to be deeper, in both the 1985–86 budget and the 1986–87 planned budget. By the end of fiscal year 1986 the government had indeed not increased its domestic and foreign debt over the preprogram level.

*Devaluation and the Freezing of the Exchange Rate*
With the launching of the stabilization program on July 2, the shekel was devalued by 25% (including some minor adjustments a few days earlier) and its exchange rate against the US dollar was stabilized at IS1,500 or NIS1.5.[4] At the same time, effective exchange rates for imports and exports were partially unified.

*Multiple Nominal Anchors*
When the program was launched, the government declared its intention to freeze all nominal variables denominated in local currency; the freeze on the exchange rate was made conditional on maintaining an appropriate level of nominal wages, which was still to be negotiated with the Histadrut (the General Federation of Labor) and the employers' organizations. (These negotiations were concluded only two weeks later, on July 15.) The Bank of Israel undertook to restrict bank credit by raising the reserve requirements and the real interest rates on the discount-window loan to commercial banks. In addition, the prices of most goods and services were frozen and subjected to administrative control.

*The Capital Market*
With regard to the capital market, the principle was adopted that long-term savings were to be safeguarded and the liquidity of indexed assets reduced. The measures taken included a ban on converting shekels into residents' foreign currency demand deposits. Existing deposits of this type, which since 1978 had provided an indexed money substitute, became a one-way street: They could be converted into shekels, but their acquisition for periods of less than a year was prohibited. Another decision provided for gradually making government bonds tradable in order to create a basis for a more effective management of monetary policy in the future.

*Wage Policy*

The tripartite wage agreement among the government, the Histadrut, and the employers' organizations was signed two weeks after the official launching of the stabilization program and came at the end of some strikes and demonstrations. The agreement provided for a temporary suspension (until October 1) of the existing cost-of-living allowance agreement, which stipulated an 80% compensation for price increases. From October 1, the threshold for payment of the cost-of-living allowance was set at 4% of the cumulative price increases in the preceding period[5] (or after three months, if less than 4%), instead of 12% under the previous agreement. An initial compensation of 14% was paid with July wages for the 28% price rise that month; in addition, it was agreed in advance that in December, January, and February wage increases of 4%, 4%, and 3.5%, respectively, would be paid.

There was some concern about the implications of the subsequent increase in indexation and the nominal consecutive monthly adjustment beginning in December. However, this was the price that had to be paid in the bargain with a partner (the Histadrut) that was facing a sharp immediate drop in real wages with no guarantee that the government, given its poor previous track record, could deliver on promised price stability.

Even in its first few months, the program achieved considerable success.[6] Inflation, which had run at an average monthly rate of 15% before the program, fell to 3–4% per month in the first three months and then declined to about 1.5% per month, a rate that has continued until recently (figure 1.1).

The improvement in the balance of payments showed in the country's liquidity. The favorable turn in the terms of trade (the fall in prices of oil and other raw materials) and the US emergency aid of $1.5 billion payable over two years supported the amelioration of the balance of payments position, but it is noteworthy that during this period the country's foreign currency reserves increased cumulatively by an amount approximately equal to the US emergency grant. The main contribution that this special aid thus made was in providing a safety net for the stabilization of the exchange rate. There is also no doubt that the confidence the public accorded the program (as well as high domestic interest rates; see section 1.3) played a role in the repatriation of considerable amounts of capital, which had earlier leaked abroad.

The substantial and continuous contraction of the domestic budget deficit lies behind these developments. The deficit decreased from 12–15%

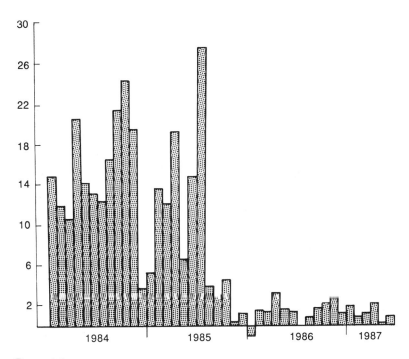

**Figure 1.1**
Consumer price index, January 1984 to June 1987 (monthly change in percent). Source:
Bank of Israel, *Annual Report 1986*, chapter 3.

of GDP in the decade before the program to no more than 2–3% of GDP.
As can be seen from figure 1.2, the dramatic decrease in the deficit was
mainly due to the increase in taxes but also to some reduction of expenditures. These results are partly due to the disinflation process itself (see
section 1.5).

Finally, the minimal (and only temporary) rise in unemployment should
be emphasized. Economic activity rose above the preprogram level by the
second half of 1986. These developments and those of relative prices
(primarily real wages, the real exchange rate, and real interest) are discussed
in greater detail in the following sections. For the moment we need only
mention a series of supplementary corrective and supportive measures
taken during the last two years. These can be regarded as part of the
program's continued implementation.

We have already mentioned that the 1986–87 budget, which became
operative in April 1986, reflected the continuation of the fiscal restraint

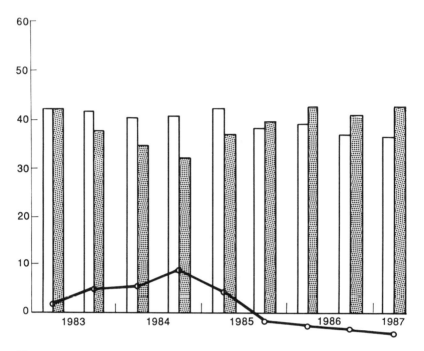

**Figure 1.2**
Real expenditure, revenues, and deficit of the public sector, 1983 (first quarter) to 1987
(second quarter) (percent of GDP). Source: Bank of Israel, *Annual Report 1986*, table VIII-4.
Connected circles, excess demand; white bars, expenditure; shaded bars, revenues.

that preceded it. A highly restrictive fiscal policy permitted a degree of
easing up on monetary restraint. However, in the wake of successive cuts
of the free market interest rate (from 880% and 560% per annum in July and
August 1985, respectively, to 53% per annum in April 1986), bank credit
expanded rapidly. Further cuts in the interest rate were therefore halted,
and the level of real interest remained high. In the second half of 1986 there
was a substantial rise in demand, mainly in the form of private consumption, which in turn led to a still more rapid expansion of credit. In order
to counter these trends, the prime rate was raised again, by 3% per annum
in October 1986 and by 12% per annum in February 1987. The interest
rate was lowered gradually from February to July 1987. There has been a
large gap between the marginal domestic and the foreign interest rates
that has been maintained by restrictions on capital imports. The gap
was reduced recently, in July 1987, by the imposition of a 3% tax on
capital imports.

Until August 1986 the policy was to keep the exchange rate stable against the US dollar; in August this was replaced by pegging the shekel to a five-currency basket, with the main foreign currencies weighted according to their share in Israel's foreign trade. During the period of high inflation that preceded the program, the US dollar had been widely accepted as a stable yardstick; the continued peg of the shekel to the dollar therefore reinforced the perception that the stabilization program was successful. The European currencies, however, continued in this period to appreciate against the dollar, with the result that from July 1985 until August 1986 the shekel effectively depreciated against the currency basket at a monthly rate of about 1%. This partially compensated for the excessive wage rise in the business sector in early 1986 (see table 1.1), which had impaired the competitiveness of exports. However, the continuous depreciation at the same time pushed up import prices. This may at least in part help to explain why inflation failed to drop further during 1986—a point to be taken up again in section 1.4.

Wage costs in the business sector continued to remain high throughout 1986. Employers were partially compensated for this by cuts in wage taxes and National Insurance contributions. A corrective devaluation of 10% against the currency basket in January 1987 further helped to restore the level of profitability of exports to its average 1986 level. The January devaluation was accompanied by a fresh tripartite agreement among the government, the Histadrut, and the employers' organizations that provided for a partial waiver of the cost-of-living allowance.

Finally, it should be mentioned that the detailed price control system imposed with the start of the program, was relaxed considerably. Since March 1986 price controls have remained in force for 40% of all goods and services (as against 25% in normal times and 90% at the beginning of the program). It seems that price controls were at no stage in the program's implementation effective in repressing inflation; their main role was to create a favorable atmosphere for the program and to enlist the support and agreement of the social partners in the overall process of stabilizing expectations.

A follow-up economic program was adopted by the government in early 1987, when the 1987—88 budget was drafted. This program, directed at continuing stabilization and reviving growth, is composed of several partial reforms affecting the capital and credit markets and the tax system. These are reviewed at the end of this chapter.

## 1.2    Real Wage Overshooting and the Private Savings Squeeze of 1986

The measures taken with the implementation of the program brought about a squeeze in demand and a considerable expansion in supply. This outcome was important for the success of the program because it supported rapid disinflation and enabled the price freeze to function immediately without pressures [see Blejer and Liviatan (1987)]. Nevertheless, this downward pressure on domestic prices did not last long. Already by the end of 1985—during the second quarter of the program—demand and supply started to return to their former levels and then overshot in 1986.

Several events immediately become visible when reviewing the economy's performance in 1986: (1) a substantial rise of real wages[7] much in excess of the increments foreseen in the wage agreement, (2) a fall in real interest rates, and (3) a real appreciation of the currency. These developments are clearly revealed in figure 1.3, which also shows the sharp rise in private consumption. As can be seen from table 1.2, the increase in private consumption outweighed the decline in other components of domestic demand (public consumption and investment) and the rise in exports. Despite this expansion of demand, there was only a slight rise in real GDP, mainly toward the end of the year. The import surplus grew significantly, although its absolute level is still low by comparison with 1982 or 1983 (figure 1.3).

These developments are obviously interrelated, but the question remains of whether some of them can be regarded as leading the others or whether they have another cause. The explanation presented here looks at both supply-side factors and demand-side factors. The excessive rise of gross wages in early 1986 resulted in diminished profitability and curbed GDP growth. At the same time the massive increase of net wage earnings (including transfer payments), combined with the increase in wealth, the decline in interest rates, and the expansion of credit (see section 1.3), resulted in a huge increase in demand for private consumption goods and services. The upswing of private consumption helped to generate the real appreciation of the currency and the increase in the import surplus and was consistent ex post with the real wage increases at the beginning of the year.

The first question that arises is therefore, What caused this high wage rise? The explanation seems to be a combination of factors. First, there seems to have been a widespread feeling that the state of the economy had improved, particularly with regard to the balance of payments, so that

**Figure 1.3**
Changes in main macroeconomic indicators, 1980–87. (a) Gross business sector product
and private consumption, 1980 to 1987 (first quarter); 1981 = 100 based on 1980 prices.
(b) Relative price of exports, 1980 to 1987 (second quarter); 1981 = 100. (c) Real wages
in business sector, 1980 to 1987 (first quarter); 1982 = 100. (d) Real cost of nondirected

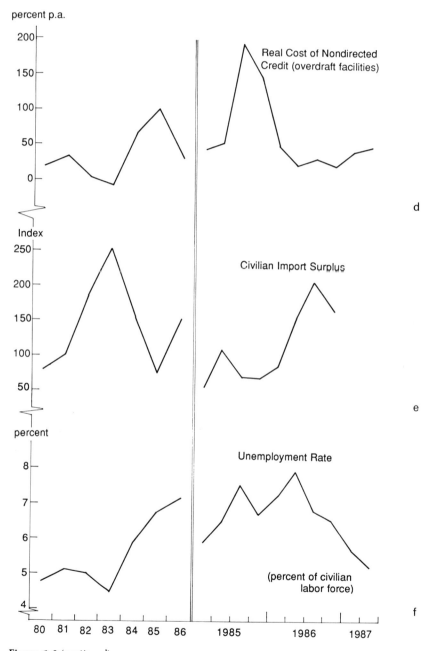

percent p.a.

Real Cost of Nondirected
Credit (overdraft facilities)

d

Index

Civilian Import Surplus

e

percent

Unemployment Rate

(percent of civilian
labor force)

f

80  81  82  83  84  85  86      1985        1986        1987

**Figure 1.3** (continued)
credit (overdraft facilities), 1980 to 1987 (second quarter); percent per annum. (e) Civilian
import surplus, 1980 to 1986; 1981 = 100 at 1980 prices. (f) Unemployment rate, 1980
to 1987 (second quarter); percent of civilian labor force. Source: Bank of Israel, *Annual
Report 1986*, chapters 2, 4, 7, and 8.

continued austerity was no longer justified. This may have reinforced wage demands, which came on top of the agreed-to wage increases (see section 1.1). This interpretation finds support in the wage increases in industries that remained depressed in 1986 (construction and agriculture); in these sectors wages had fallen sharply in previous years but rose in 1986 despite the continuing fall in employment.

Second, firms and workers apparently did not expect price stability to last; in early 1986 firms therefore agreed to sign expansionary wage contracts. Both firms and workers, in other words, expected devaluation and a renewal of inflation and therefore set nominal wage increases at excessively high levels.

Finally, increases in various wage components that had been agreed to before the stabilization program were postponed until the first opportune moment. Moreover, the cost-of-living compensation for fringe benefits was not included in the cost-of-living allowance agreement, and fringe benefits were therefore not nominally fixed. This, together with the higher wage demands, led to full compensation for the abrupt price rise at the start of the program, and fringe benefits increased considerably in real terms.

The wage increases found support in an expansionary monetary policy, manifested in cuts of interest rates and an expansion of bank credit. Because prices were at the same time frozen, firms could not promptly shift wage increases onto higher prices. The "comfortable" liquidity situation, however, enabled them to finance the wage hike and to wait until the devaluation, which was firmly expected to come.

Even though the government might initially have had no intention to devalue, it could reasonably be assumed, on the basis of more than a decade of experience in this regard, that the government would not be able to resist for long the pressure of exporters and of potential unemployment for devaluation. There was therefore little risk in yielding to wage demands. Nor should it be overlooked that the program never committed itself to keep the exchange rate absolutely stable under all circumstances. In fact, official policy always made the stability of the exchange rate conditional on wage stability. The stance of official policy itself was therefore not rigidly anti-inflationary.

The currency was, in effect, devalued only much later, in January 1987, but the relative appreciation of the European currencies during 1986 meant that the shekel gradually depreciated against the currency basket (until August 1986, when the shekel was pegged to the basket instead of to the dollar). This depreciation, together with tax reductions for employers, partially compensated for the erosion of export profitability resulting from the large wage increases. (For a further discussion, see section 1.4.)

**Table 1.1**
Wages, employment and the consumer price index, 1986 (%)

| Sector | Wage rise in excess of public sector wages[a] | Increase in number of employed persons | Average annual change in CPI component over the change of the currency basket |
|---|---|---|---|
| Business sector, total | 4.3 | 2.1 | 13.0 |
| Agriculture, forestry, and fishing | 4.8 | − 1.3 | 50.2 |
| Industry (manufacturing and mining) | 2.2 | 4.2 | 6.1 |
| Electricity and water | − 3.1 | − | − 11.8 |
| Construction | 7.8 | − 6.5 | − 1.3 |
| Transport, storage, and communication | 4.3 | 0.5 | 6.4 |
| Financing and business services | 6.1 | 0.4 | } 36.0 |
| Commerce, restaurants, and hotels | 6.5 | } 3.8 | |
| Personal and other services | 12.7 | | |

Sources: Bank of Israel, *Annual Report 1986*, tables IV-10, IV-14, and V-2.
a. The 8% rise in public sector wages was approximately the real wage increase planned for 1986 within the framework of the stabilization program.

The explanation that the excessive rise in business sector wages was due to union demands and errors in expectations may have been valid at the beginning of the year but not for the whole year, during which employers had the opportunity to adjust their wage costs, for example, by slowing the wage drift. The employment statistics lend support to this argument. They show that in the first half of 1986 the unemployment rate rose in tandem with the wage increase. In the second half of the year, by contrast, real wages rose while the unemployment rate declined (see figure 1.3). The data on wages by sectors (table 1.1) show that the exceptional wage hikes were concentrated in sectors in which price rises were high and in which employment increased. Moreover, in sectors producing a large proportion of tradables, such as manufacturing industry, wages rose at the rate that was in fact planned for 1986. Against this, in sectors having a lower proportion of tradables (various services, for example) wages rose steeply. The only exceptions are construction and agriculture, both of which are depressed sectors. As mentioned earlier, the wage increases in these two sectors reflect the demands of workers whose wages had in earlier years been eroded much more sharply than in the rest of the economy. These two sectors account for less than 10% of total employment, so they did not dominate wage developments in 1986. Nevertheless, the wage increases in these two sectors may indicate that in depressed industries money wages are inflexible downward, particularly when the general state of the economy is improving, and therefore changes in relative wages have to take place through a rise of money wages in sectors with rising activity and demand for labor.

Thus the wage increases of early 1986 seem to have been autonomous, but the maintenance of a high level of real wages throughout 1986 seems to be a combination of a pull of aggregate demand for labor and downward inflexibility of wages in depressed sectors. This raises the question of which factors caused the increase in aggregate demand in the course of the year. For an explanation we must look at what led the substantial expansion of private consumption. First of all, the wage rise made itself felt in the increase in consumption. Taking into account a built-in limit on taxes and an increase in government transfer payments, the increase in real disposable income of wage earners was estimated at 11% per capita, whereas private consumption rose by 12%. Wage income (including wages imputed to the self-employed) accounted for some 80% of total disposable income, and no doubt had an even larger share in the increase of private consumption, particularly in the short run. Second, the fall in the real interest rate certainly had a direct effect on the increase in private consumption mainly by bolstering the acquisition of durables (which the statistics record as private consumption). However, current consumption was apparently also affected by the greater availability of consumer credit. This is taken up again in section 1.5. Third, the rise of private consumption may in fact be a symptom of the very success of the stabilization program. It seems that the improvement in the economy's financial position—overcoming financial difficulties in the balance of payments, rehabilitation of the tax system, and halting inflation—brought about an increase in the public's perceived wealth and hence a rise in private consumption. Finally, the increase in private consumption may have been boosted by the continued price freeze (including that on imported goods) and the gradual relaxation of price controls during 1986, which fanned expectations of price rises.[8]

The large increase in private consumption leads to the question of how this affected GDP and demand for labor, but before going into this matter, we should say something about the other components of aggregate demand and possible changes in the composition of demand between imports and domestic output.

As profitability declined in line with the rise in wage costs and as GDP started to grow at the end of 1986, no revival of investment in equipment and structures was in sight; nor was there, as population growth had ceased, any increase in residential construction. At the same time there was a substantial increase in stocks of imported final products and raw materials, which were being replenished as interest rates fell. Civilian public consumption contracted between 1984 and 1986 by 1% of GDP, and defense consumption fell by 3% of GDP. The cut in defense expenditure was mainly achieved by the reduction of procurement from defense-related industries, which shifted increasingly to producing for export. Therefore a substantial part of the 15% rise in exports of manufactures was accounted for by industries normally producing for the defense ministry (exports of industrial products other than those of the highly defense-oriented in-dustries of electric and electronic equipment and transport goods increased in these two years by a mere 5%). Total use of resources rose by 7% over 1984 and 1985, with most of the increase resulting from the rise in private consumption (table 1.2.)

Private consumption generally has a higher component of domestic product than exports or investment in equipment and machinery. In 1986 the composition of demand nevertheless tilted toward imports as a result of the massive increase in purchases of durable consumer goods and of the substantial increase in stocks. When the real increase in GDP, imports, and other uses is estimated without these two components, we still obtain a higher rise of imports than of the GDP, although its increase amounts to only 5%. The increase in the acquisition of consumer durables and of stocks therefore explains the lion's share of the rise in imports of goods and services by comparison with their level in 1985 or even 1984. In com-parison with 1984, imports increased by 11%, whereas the business sector product rose by 8%. The change in 1986 compared with 1985 is remark-able: Imports rose by 15%, whereas the business sector product rise for 1986 amounted to only 4%.

The upshot of the foregoing analysis is that, when purchases of durables and increases in stocks are excluded, demand did not expand significantly and exhibited only a moderate preference for imports. Moreover, there was a decline in stocks of domestic products (see table 1A.2 in the appendix), which apparently reflects an unplanned liquidation of stocks. This may help to explain the pressures on the domestic price level that led to a real appreciation of the currency in the second half of the year and is consistent with the revival of economic activity toward the end of the year.

However, it does not yet explain the discrepancy between the expansion of resource uses and the sluggish increase of GDP in 1986, unless we turn to factors that affected aggregate supply. The sharp fall in inflation, which

**Table 1.2**
Resources and uses,ª 1973–86

| Resource or use | Value at current prices in billions of new shekels (1986) | Real change (%) | | | | | |
|---|---|---|---|---|---|---|---|
| | | Average 1973–85 | 1983 | 1984 | 1985 | 1986 | 1984–86 |
| **Resources** | | | | | | | |
| Gross domestic product | 41.0 | 3.2 | 2.7 | 1.8 | 2.8 | 2.2 | 5.1 |
| Civilian imports | 21.4 | 4.0 | 11.1 | −3.6 | −3.9 | 15.1 | 10.6 |
| Total resources | 62.4 | 3.4 | 5.8 | −0.3 | 0.3 | 6.8 | 7.1 |
| **Uses** | | | | | | | |
| Private consumption | 26.1 | 4.3 | 8.0 | −7.3 | −0.4 | 14.0 | 13.5 |
| Public consumption | 11.2 | 2.5 | 1.7 | 1.0 | −0.8 | −4.8 | −5.6 |
| Gross domestic investment | 8.0 | −1.6 | 12.0 | −7.5 | −13.6 | 8.1 | −6.6 |
| Gross domestic investment excluding changes in stocks | 7.2 | −1.0 | 14.0 | −11.7 | −9.9 | −5.5 | −14.9 |
| Domestic use of resources | 45.4 | 2.5 | 7.2 | −5.3 | −3.2 | 7.8 | 4.4 |
| Exports at local prices | 17.0 | 6.0 | 2.1 | 13.9 | 8.6 | 4.7 | 13.7 |
| Total use of resources | 62.4 | 3.4 | 5.8 | −0.3 | 0.3 | 6.8 | 7.1 |
| Gross domestic product of the business sector at market prices^b | 28.4 | 2.8 | 3.1 | 1.8 | 3.8 | 3.7 | 7.6 |

Source: Bank of Israel, *Annual Report 1986*, table II-1.
a. Excluding direct defense imports.
b. Gross domestic product excluding product of public services and private nonprofit organizations and excluding housing services.

raises productivity, and the improvement in the terms of trade augmented aggregate supply in 1986, even if the fall in oil prices was only partially passed on to firms and households, as the government effectively increased the indirect taxation of fuel by reducing its price by less than the fall in its import price. Against this there were factors that curbed aggregate supply. The first and perhaps most important factor on the supply side was the wage increases, which reflect the downward inflexibility of wages in sectors confronted with declining demand and still higher real wage rises in sectors where demand expanded. Second, there are institutional and occupational barriers to labor mobility that prevent a shift of labor from declining industries to those in which demand expanded. This also has a contractionary effect on the aggregate supply schedule or causes it to be steeper than it would otherwise be.[9] Finally, aggregate supply decreased as indirect taxes were raised sharply, mainly by the cut in subsidies but also as a result of the disinflation process itself, which eliminated the gain from tax arrears.

To sum up this discussion we present figure 1.4, which combines the hypothetical shifts of the aggregate demand and supply curves during the period under review. The figure shows the position of the economy in the period 1983–86, where one axis measures the business sector product and the other measures the domestic price level relative to prices of tradable goods.[10] We have also plotted aggregate demand curves, deriving their position from data on the economy's resource use.

Points $A_{83}$, $A_{84}$, and $A_{85}$ show an increase of business sector product together with a real depreciation, whereas the transition from $A_{85}$ to $A_{86}$ shows a modest rise in business sector product together with a real appreciation. Our interpretation of these developments is that the shift between 1983 and 1985 is due to a decrease in demand and to a substantial expansion of aggregate supply coming from the erosion of real wages in 1984 and 1985 and the decrease in prices of imported raw materials and energy in 1985. The transition from 1985 to 1986 represents the combination of supply contraction together with a demand expansion.[11] This interpretation is also consistent with the improvement in the import surplus from 1983 to 1985 and with its worsening from 1985 to 1986.

By looking at the developments during 1985 and 1986, we can further articulate this interpretation of events. More detailed data indicate that a large increase in aggregate supply was achieved in the second half of 1985, but GDP remained low because demand had contracted dramatically. These developments were associated with the initial stage of the stabilization program. In the first half of 1986 both aggregate supply and demand

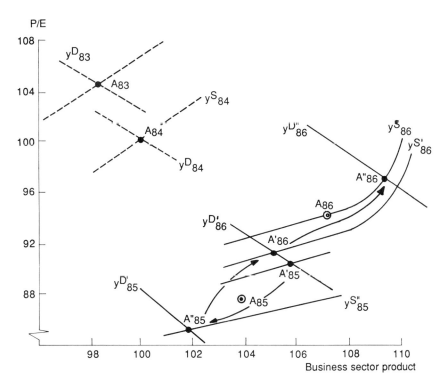

**Figure 1.4**
Business sector product and relative domestic prices, 1983–86. Domestic prices relative to export prices using currency basket exchange rate. Business sector product, 1984 = 100.

returned to almost the level of the first half of 1985, before the stabilization program. (As stated before, the rise in real wages in the first half of 1986 was offset on the supply side by improved terms of trade and the gain from disinflation.) In the second half of 1986 aggregate supply declined further (real wages continued to rise), but the prominent change was the substantial increase in aggregate demand, causing a rise in GDP, a decline in unemployment, a real appreciation, and a rising import surplus. In both periods there was a real appreciation of the currency, but, according to the argument presented here, its source differed between the first and the second halves of the year; this difference stems from wage increases in the first half and from the upsurge of domestic demand in the second.

The change in the import surplus may be considered by examining the respective changes in imports and exports, but for our purposes it is also

**Table 1.3**
The import surplus by components, 1983–86 (% of GDP, annual averages, at constant prices)

| Component | Change over previous year (percentage points of GDP) | | | Cumulative change | |
|---|---|---|---|---|---|
| | (1) 1984 | (2) 1985 | (3) 1986 | (4) 1983–86 [(1) + (2) + (3)] | (5) 1984–86 [(2) + (3)] |
| **Decline in investment** | 2.3 | 3.7 | − 1.2 | 4.8 | 2.5 |
| **Increase in savings** | 6.1 | 3.0 | − 4.8 | 4.3 | − 1.8 |
| Private savings | 16.3 | − 6.1 | − 12.3 | − 2.1 | − 18.4 |
| Public savings[a] | − 10.2 | 9.1 | 7.5 | 6.4 | 16.6 |
| Increase in net taxes | (− 8.2) | (7.8) | (3.6) | (− 3.2) | (11.4) |
| **Decline in the import surplus[b]** | 8.4 | 6.7 | − 6.0 | 9.1 | 0.7 |
| Exports (increase) | 5.0 | 2.7 | 1.2 | 8.9 | 3.9 |
| Imports (decrease) | 3.4 | 4.0 | − 7.2 | 0.2 | − 3.2 |

Source: Central Bureau of Statistics, *National Accounts, 1983–1986.*
a. Domestic surplus less net expenditures abroad not including defense imports.
b. Excluding direct defense imports.

useful to review it from the perspective of the investment-savings balance, particularly because of the important role played in this period by public savings. Table 1.3 shows that in 1985 the increase in public savings more than made up for the fall in private savings, but private savings fell in 1986 so drastically that the current account was affected adversely despite the continued decline in the government deficit.

However, as shown in columns 4 and 5 of table 1.3, the import surplus was still at a much lower level than that of 1983 and was similar to that of 1984. The country's other foreign currency receipts make it sustainable at this level, but the present trend is of a rise in the import surplus, which has continued despite the January 1987 devaluation. However, most of the recent increase in imports is accounted for by intermediate production inputs, together with the beginnings of higher imports of capital goods. This may reflect an incipient upswing of economic activity and an expansion of capacity.

This increase in the import surplus has nevertheless not recreated the country's foreign payments difficulties because of the increase in the foreign currency reserves and the stability of the exchange rate, which resulted from the public's confidence in the success of the program and also

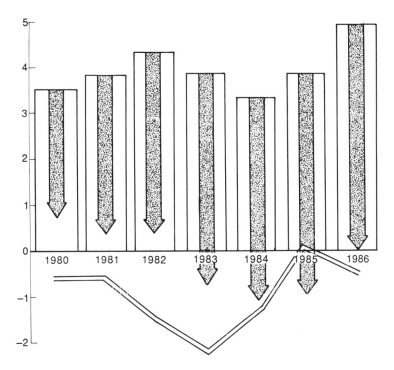

**Figure 1.5**
Foreign currency reserves (white bars), net current debt (shaded arrows), and private
sector current account deficit (double line), 1980–86 (billions of US dollars). Source:
Bank of Israel, *Annual Report 1986*, ch. 7.

from the gap between domestic interest rates and the expected returns on
foreign currency. These factors, in addition to the special US grants-in-aid,
led to capital inflows. The improvement in the country's net foreign asset
position can be seen in figure 1.5, which represents the financial facet of the
real appreciation; we return to this again in the following sections.

If it is concluded that a rise in wages and in private consumption and a real
appreciation of the currency are partly the endogenous result of successful
stabilization programs, then the corollary is that they contain a built-in
mechanism that partially offsets the success of the program. There are
several reasons for this. First, such programs are devised in a period of
crisis; even if the real exchange rate appreciation reflects a change in the
composition of resource uses (for example, from tradable to nontradable
goods), the authorities hesitate to risk a significant real appreciation. Such

a fall may impair the balance of payments position; the authorities are inclined to carry out nominal devaluations in order to correct the path of the real exchange rate. These devaluations upset the price stability that has been achieved.

Second, if the authorities take a firm stance on the nominal side and, regarding the balance of payments as still solid, allow the real appreciation of the currency, the real exchange rate will generally overreact. Possible external shocks to the economy will then require an abrupt climb-down from a tall ladder, which may have disastrous results. Developments in Chile in the early 1980s are an outstanding example of such a situation. Even in the absence of external shocks overreaction of the exchange rate makes it necessary to return to a more reasonable exchange rate. Only if prices are flexible downward is it easy to achieve the real devaluation required for this purpose. When prices are inflexible downward, such a process entails high unemployment and loss of output unless the authorities carry out nominal devaluations that, in turn, have the inflationary effect noted.

Finally, the increase in private consumption can be curbed by monetary restraint—a major component of policy that operates through effects on both wealth and liquidity. However, when there are strong pressures for cutting interest rates and policy has the aim of promoting the renewal of economic growth, a restrictive monetary policy is difficult to maintain for a protracted period.

Stabilization programs are therefore a problematic policy instrument. They require that fiscal restraint and an incomes policy be upheld for a long time, within the framework of recurrent package deals. It is obviously difficult to persuade the trade unions to waive wage demands when the economic situation looks favorable, but the failure to achieve wage restraint imposes the need for periodic nominal adjustments of the exchange rate, with the consequence that the economy will be condemned to an inflation rate higher than those in Western countries.

## 1.3   Stabilization and the Problem of Monetary Control

Among the outstanding events on the money and capital markets was the rapid rise, since the adoption of the stabilization program, in the real balances of shekel-denominated assets at the expense of indexed assets. Bank credit to the public also expanded rapidly, especially from mid-1986, and average real interest rates fell substantially compared to their level

**Table 1.4**
Real value of monetary aggregates and bank credit to the public, 1985−87 (in billions of new shekels)[a]

| Date | M1 | M2 | M4 | Total bank credit to the public |
|---|---|---|---|---|
| Before the stabilization program | | | | |
| (June 1985) | 510 | 1,682 | 8,307 | 5,962 |
| **Indexes** | 100 | 100 | 100 | 100 |
| After the stabilization program | | | | |
| December 1985 | 133 | 181 | 96 | 93 |
| June 1986 | 195 | 192 | 99 | 101 |
| December 1986 | 245 | 260 | 103 | 112 |
| June 1987 | 247 | 312 | 121 | 130 |

Source: Bank of Israel, *Annual Report 1986*, ch. 8.
a. M1 is cash in circulation and demand deposits; M2 is M1 plus local-currency time deposits and CDs; M4 is M2 plus residents' foreign currency deposits and negotiable indexed bonds.

in 1985. Nonetheless, interest on nondirected credit in local currency remained at a relatively high level. (In addition to this category of credit there is bank credit in foreign currency, the volume of which is restricted by ceilings, and directed credit for exports; interest rates on these types of credit are close to international rates.)

As can be seen from table 1.4, until the end of 1986 M1 and M2 increased in real terms by about 2.5 times, whereas a broader aggregate, M4, which is composed to M2 plus residents' foreign currency deposits and negotiable bonds held by the public, increased by only 3%.[12] This portfolio change of course reflects the decline in inflationary expectations. The adjustment process has been fairly slow[13] and is apparently not yet concluded. As time goes on, the public is also becoming more disposed to hold shekel assets for longer terms. Thus the share of local-currency deposits for more than a month, which in June 1986 had accounted for 10% of total shekel assets, had by March 1987 increased to 26%.

Behind the real expansion of monetary aggregates there is an even larger nominal expansion because inflation was not brought down completely. This, together with the fall in real interest rates, shows that monetary policy in 1986 has been expansionary. However, for a better understanding of that policy, we must consider the targets assigned in the program to the Bank of Israel, the policy instruments, and the fact that in 1986 the marginal interest rate remained high by international standards (see table 1.5).

A program that succeeds in stabilizing price inflation cannot possibly keep the quantity of money unchanged because lower inflation generates a higher demand for money. The authorities in Israel decided to accommodate this increase, even though this could be interpreted as an expansionary policy [see Fischer (1984)]. It was, however, possible to restrain the expansion of credit, because disinflation as such does not significantly affect its real interest rate [see Fischer and Frenkel (1982) and Frenkel et al. (1984)]. It was assumed that individuals would therefore obtain the quantity of money they demanded by converting foreign currency assets or indexed assets they held as near-money before inflation slowed down and not by expanding bank credit.

In the program the role of the central bank was to permit the accommodation of bank credit to the price shock of July 1985 less ten percentage points and to prevent any further nominal expansion in the subsequent period. This was a difficult task for several reasons. First, when fiscal and incomes policy is aimed chiefly at a reduction of private disposable income, the public tends to offset this policy by borrowing, especially if the policy is perceived as temporary. Second, the steep decline in the expected return on foreign currency was anticipated to lead to higher capital inflows, which would offset the policy to a considerable extent. Third, a sharp improvement of bank liquidity was expected as indexed bonds and residents' foreign currency demand deposits (on which the reserve requirement was 100%) were converted into shekel deposits with lower reserve requirements.

In order to prevent credit expansion despite these forces, the Bank of Israel raised the reserve requirements on shekel deposits and maintained an extraordinarily high interest rate on its discount-window loans. This was reflected in the real interest rates on overdraft facilities, which reached more than 320% per annum in August 1985, following the implementation of the program, and an average of 168% per annum in the whole six-month period following the program (see table 1.5).

The nominal (and real) interest rate was gradually lowered during the second half of 1985 and until March 1986, even though credit expanded in excess of the target. The actual fall in interest rates was therefore due to heavy political pressure by the government and the various sectors in the economy. There was also the feeling in the Bank of Israel itself that such a high real interest rate was damaging to the economy and was paradoxically leading to an *increase* in the credit balance, rather than to a decrease, as firms had to finance their enormous interest payments.

**Table 1.5**
Real annual cost of bank credit to the public, 1984–86

| Type of credit | 1984 | 1985 | 1986 | 1985 (second half) | 1986 First half | Second half |
|---|---|---|---|---|---|---|
| Overdraft facilities | 67.0 | 100.4 | 31.1 | 168.3 | 37.2 | 25.2 |
| Indexed local-currency credit | 21.2 | 16.8 | 11.6 | 88.3 | 11.6 | 11.7 |
| Nondirected foreign currency credit (subject to ceilings) | 47.3 | 13.7 | 9.4 | 18.8 | 14.9 | 4.2 |
| Other foreign currency credit | 27.6 | −6.5 | −11.6 | −5.2 | −8.8 | −14.2 |

Source: Bank of Israel, *Annual Report 1986*, table VIII-10.
All figures are annualized interest rates.

As the Bank of Israel abandoned the original target, it began to set its policy by taking into account the performance of the economy: the inflation rate, the expansion of demand, the external current and capital accounts, etc. Nevertheless, it continued its efforts to achieve some restraint in the expansion of credit and to this effect halted the process of declining interest rates in March 1986. In any event, in the second half of 1986 a boom in demand and a deterioration in the private sector's current account together with a rapid increase in credit caused the bank to raise the prime rate by 3% per annum (see section 1.1) even though its real level was still high.

In retrospect, two years later it seems that the choice of the volume of bank credit as the target of monetary policy was inappropriate. First, in the context of a fixed exchange rate regime, more attention has to be paid to the *total* domestic sources of monetary expansion—credit to the government and to the public from the Bank of Israel and the commercial banks continued despite the restriction of bank credit to the public. This means that nominal targets based on some definition of *net domestic credit* rather than bank credit to the public alone would seem to be more suitable. Second, if bank credit is nevertheless set as the nominal target of monetary policy and therefore if the central bank wants to allow accommodation to the rising demand for money without any expansion of credit, the bank must supply money by increasing the monetary base and at the same time raise the reserve ratio so as to prevent any credit expansion. This would imply very high reserve requirements. If, on the other hand, the central bank is reluctant to increase the reserve requirements, it must permit some growth in credit. In other words, the higher demand for money must be accommodated partly by growth of the monetary base and partly by credit expansion.

As can be seen from table 1.6, the actual accomodation in the second half of 1985, with M2 growing by 17.7% of GDP, was due mainly to the expansion of the money base by 10% of GDP,[14] whereas the expansion of bank credit was 8% of GDP in this period despite the sharp increase in reserve requirements. In contrast, during 1986 the increase in local-currency assets was mainly fed by the expansion of bank credit. Credit expansion in this period was due to the bank's policy of trying to reduce the money base by bond sales and simultaneously lowering reserve requirements. However, the Bank of Israel was concerned with the rise in credit, and in the second quarter of 1986 the decline in interest rates was halted.

## 1.4   Exchange Rate Policy and the Synchronization of Nominal Anchors

One of the most important components of the stabilization program was the establishment of a set of several nominal anchors, with the intent of stabilizing prices without throwing all the weight on a single anchor. These anchors were the exchange rate, wages, bank credit, and the price freeze imposed on a wide range of goods and services. These nominal anchors function properly only if they are at sustainable real levels at the outset of the program; if this is not done, the stabilization program itself must contain real changes in these variables so as to allow them to reach a reasonable level.

The program was initiated by a general hike of prices before they were frozen, a sharp rise in the exchange rate, an erosion of real wages, and a low level of credit resulting from unprecedentedly high real interest rates. Because the nominal exchange rate was frozen and it was clear that some prices would rise at the outset of the program, the real exchange rate was planned to be eroded in the first few months. In addition, the agreement concluded with the Histadrut provided for a real wage erosion for some months and for wage increments to be paid in several installments until the first quarter of 1986. The real rate of interest was also cut gradually and more or less stabilized from the first quarter of 1986. It was therefore natural that, following decline at the outset of the program, a real expansion of credit would be induced by the fall in interest rates (for more details, see section 1.3).

**Table 1.6**
The government deficit, its sources of finance, bank credit to the public, and unindexed financial assets of the public, 1981–86 (% of GDP)

| Component | 1981 | 1982 | 1983 | 1984 | 1985 | 1986 | 1985 (second half) | 1986 First half | 1986 Second half |
|---|---|---|---|---|---|---|---|---|---|
| 1. Government deficit | 11.6 | 10.0 | 6.0 | 12.1 | 9.0 | 2.6 | 5.7 | 2.9 | 2.3 |
| **Financing of the deficit** | | | | | | | | | |
| 2. Increase in net domestic debt | 8.1 | 6.2 | −1.0 | 0.8 | −1.2 | −0.4 | −6.1 | 2.6 | −3.4 |
| 3. Sales of foreign currency to private sector | 1.9 | 2.6 | 6.3 | 8.6 | 4.8 | 2.5 | 2.2 | 2.4 | 2.6 |
| 4. Change in money base, net | 1.6 | 1.2 | 0.7 | 2.7 | 5.4 | 0.5 | 9.6 | −2.1 | 3.1 |
| 5. Expansion due to banking activity (mainly bank credit) [(6) − (4) = (5)] | 2.7 | 5.3 | 5.0 | 5.7 | 8.3 | 7.5 | 8.1 | 6.2 | 8.7 |
| 6. Change in M2 | 4.3 | 6.5 | 5.7 | 8.4 | 13.7 | 8.0 | 17.7 | 4.1 | 11.8 |

Source: Bank of Israel, *Annual Report 1986*, Table VIII-6.

These real changes, which by necessity had to follow from the exceptional initial level of the nominal anchors, must be taken into account when evaluating the performance. The nominal changes in wages, import prices, and bank credit relative to the consumer price index are shown in figure 1.6, which assumes a certain initial real level for each of these variables.

The intention of the authorities was to fix nominal wages and nominal bank credit after their initial adjustment to support the fixed exchange rate regime. As can be seen in figure 1.6, all the nominal variables tended to increase prices. The fact that wages and bank credit exceeded their planned nominal path has already been discussed, but it is interesting to note that import prices were also clearly on an upward trend during 1986, despite the absence of inflation abroad and the adoption of a fixed exchange rate regime, and they were an additional factor pushing prices up, although wages and credit grew faster.

This leads to the question of what drove up import prices and whether inflation would have fallen more rapidly if import prices had remained stable. For a year after the adoption of the stabilization program the shekel remained pegged to the US dollar. This peg, at a time when the dollar depreciated rapidly against European currencies, effectively caused the shekel to depreciate against the currency basket, which reflects the composition of Israel's foreign trade better than the dollar. Thus the exchange rate for the export basket[15] (excluding diamonds) depreciated by 15% between the third quarter of 1985 and the last quarter of 1986. It seems, therefore, that the continuous price rise until the third quarter of 1986 was pushed by the depreciation of the shekel against the relevant currency baskets, in addition to wages and credit.

In August 1986 the shekel was pegged to a five-currency basket instead of the US dollar.[16] If the exchange rate had been fixed to the currency basket (at its level in the third quarter of 1985) instead of pegged to the dollar and if we assume that the resulting lower depreciation would have been passed on fully to the CPI, then inflation in 1986 would have run at only 13% per annum (instead of the actual rate of 20%). In this case the nominal dollar exchange rate and export prices would have fallen. Moreover, for a slower depreciation to be passed on as a lower rate of inflation, wages and the domestic prices of the relevant industries would have to fall. Given the downward inflexibility of money wages, inflation would have fallen by less, real wages would have risen by more, and the real exchange rate would have fallen by more. This would have cut more sharply into the

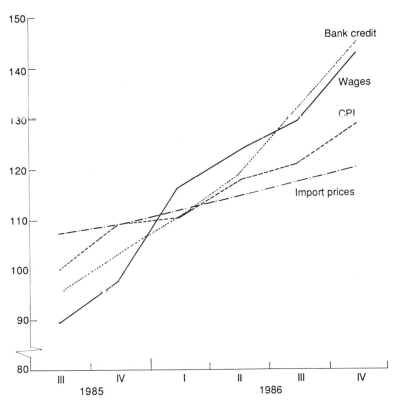

**Figure 1.6**
Wages, import prices (excluding fuel and diamonds), CPI, and bank credit, 1985 (third quarter) to 1986 (fourth quarter). The base level for the nominal variables was chosen on the following assumptions: (1) that the program was designed to bring real wages in the first quarter of 1986 back to their level in the first half of 1985 (which was also the 1982 level); (2) that the adjustment of prices to the July 1985 devaluation had been concluded by the third quarter of 1985; and (3) that the adjustment of the real interest rate was concluded in the first quarter of 1986, as was the adjustment of the real credit balances. Source: Bank of Israel Research Department, Main Israeli Economic Data.

profitability of exports, with consequent implications for GDP, employment, and the import surplus.

It would therefore seem that, taking into account the changes in the cross rates of foreign currencies and international relative prices, the dollar peg operated in favor of the economy because it made reductions in prices and wages in some sectors less necessary, thereby easing pressures that might have adversely affected the stabilization program. Higher inflation was the price that was paid for the easing of these pressures.

The contraction of public consumption, the subsidy cuts, and the very process of disinflation call for a shift of production factors between industries and for changes in wages and relative prices. With prices and wages being inflexible downward, such structural changes tend to be inflationary, so that a rigid anti-inflationary policy may have a high cost in terms of unemployment and foregone output. Does it follow that a crawling peg would be more appropriate to stabilization programs than a fixed exchange rate? In the circumstances of the Israeli economy a fixed exchange rate and a price freeze made it easier to reach an accord with the workers, without which the rapid stabilization that has been achieved would not have been possible. Viewed in this light, it is possible that the creeping depreciation that was accidentally forced on Israel because of the changes in foreign exchange rates has made it possible for the economy to benefit from the best of two worlds: On the one hand, the freeze of the exchange rate bought stability, whereas the effective depreciation until August 1986 facilitated the gradual adjustment of relative prices.

The one-time corrective 10% devaluation of January 1987 was accompanied by a fresh agreement between employers and workers, in which the workers agreed to waive half of the 5.4% cost-of-living allowance due to them in March 1987 as a result of the devaluation. For the other half, employers were compensated by a reduction of their National Insurance contributions by 2.7%. In the first quarter of 1987 prices, particularly those reflected in the CPI, actually rose less than had been expected: The CPI rose at a monthly average rate of 1.5% and 1.3% in the first and second quarters of 1987, respectively, as against 2.3% in the last quarter of 1986. The wholesale index of industrial output rose faster and reflected the price increases expected to result from the devaluation: After a slowdown of wholesale price rises to 1% per month in the second half of 1986 (which may be attributed to the switch to pegging the shekel against a currency basket), the rise in this index accelerated to 2.3% per month in the first quarter of 1987 and decreased to 1% in the second quarter of 1987. This amounts to a cumulative 5% rise following the 10% devaluation. At the time of writing it is not yet clear what the price indexes will show in the rest of the year. It is hoped that wage agreements, due to be signed soon, will be restrained and will make it possible to hold on to a stable exchange rate. Inflation may in that case taper off to below the average rate of 1986.

The devaluation was successful in increasing export profitability, but it upset the equilibrium in the assets market. During the months following the devaluation there was a capital inflow of about $1 billion. This capital inflow began as a result of the sharp decline in the cost of foreign currency credit after the devaluation, when it became certain that another devaluation was not to be expected in the near future. It could have caused monetary expansion, an additional increase in demand, pressure on domestic prices, and a rapid real appreciation. However, the policy of absorbing money prevented a rapid choking off of capital imports while restraining demand and moderating price increases following the devaluation. Price increases were lower and spread over a longer period than had been expected. The moderate price rises immediately following the devaluation were highly valuable in reinforcing the public's expectations that price stability would be maintained.

## 1.5   Miscellaneous Benefits and Costs of Rapid Disinflation

Inflation is a nominal phenomenon that has far-reaching effects on the real economy. It determines the real return on money, thereby affecting the payments system, the forms in which assets are held, and consumption patterns. Some of these effects have been dealt with already. In this section we review some salient events that have occurred since the stabilization program was put into effect. These events are related to the rapid deceleration of inflation and to the particular manner in which the program was implemented. The specific effects of each of these factors are difficult to quantify.

Government Revenue and Expenditure

One important effect of the stabilization process was its impact on real government revenue and expenditure. So long as inflation ran at a high rate, revenues and expenditures could be timed so as to effect substantial real changes. With a monthly inflation of 15% it is clearly possible to increase real expenditure by 15% in excess of the volume planned in the budget by concentrating outlays in the beginning of the month. Equally, by delaying tax payments to the end of the month, their real amount can be reduced by 15%. Merely changing the timing of payments might therefore double the government's deficit. When inflation ran at 15%, these possibilities were in time taken into account and the budget was in many ways adjusted to inflation. However, its nominal component still left considerable opportunities to maneuver (the disbursement of allocations to government ministries a month in advance was one example). So long as inflation runs at a steady rate, even if that rate is high, the increase in real expenditure and the decrease in real revenue is of constant size. The great changes occur when there is a sharp acceleration or deceleration of inflation. Therefore the cuts in public spending carried out in the framework of the stabilization program were twofold: First, there was a planned contraction of expenditures, and, second, the advantages of timing outlays to the beginning of the month were eliminated. This resulted in larger than planned expenditure cuts.

The substantial increase in real government revenue as a result of disinflation appears in the literature (the Tanzi effect). The Israeli experience confirms this phenomenon even under conditions of a partially indexed tax system. The program, in addition to the changes it brought about on the expenditure side, also incorporated measures to rehabilitate the tax system, which came under serious stress in 1984. These measures, combined with the real effects of disinflation itself, caused the overall tax level to overshoot its target (see table 1.7). This effect of disinflation on government expenditure and tax revenue helped to reduce the deficit and bolstered stability. In certain sectors, however, it led to financial crises, particularly in government budget-dependent organizations and enterprises such as the

**Table 1.7**
Gross taxes and transfer payments by the public, 1980–86

| Year | % of GDP |
| --- | --- |
| 1980 | 45.2 |
| 1981 | 44.3 |
| 1982 | 48.0 |
| 1983 | 48.5 |
| 1984 | 40.0 |
| 1985 | |
| First half | 46.5 |
| Second half | 50.5 |
| 1986 | 52.3 |

Source: Bank of Israel, *Annual Report 1986*, table V-2.

universities, the Histadrut sick fund, and hospitals. In the period of high inflation these entities had managed to maintain a given level of real activity. The slowdown of inflation deprived them of potential financial profits and caused them to run into much more severe financial difficulties than those implied by the intended budget cuts.

The Business Sector

The disinflation process also affected the functioning of firms. Under high inflation, financial operations dominated their activities. With nominal interest rates at 20% per month, errors in timing are costly for business firms, and thus considerable resources are allocated to financial operations, improved management of debt collection, and the timing of payments for goods and services. With disinflation real activity again took a more important place. Industries in which real activity was depressed, such as the construction industry, had been able to survive under high inflation by financial management appropriate to such conditions, but with disinflation this option disappeared. Moreover, the conventional accounting rules made it possible to show profits even when there were real losses. Financial statements that seemed to show profits made it possible for the banks to continue extending credit to these firms. Disinflation exposed their real situation. Thus only the slowdown of inflation revealed that Solel Boneh, Israel's biggest construction firm, had been sustaining real losses for many years. Although the crisis in the construction industry was no doubt partly worsened by the unprecedented rise in real interest rates at the start of the stabilization program, it seems that the slowdown of inflation itself played a considerable role.

In agriculture, in particular, a severe crisis affected Israel's two most important organizational branches, the kibbutzim (collective settlements) and the moshavim (cooperative settlements). Their financial crisis was caused by a combination of bad financial investments made during the period of high inflation, overinvestment in real assets serving consumption in the time when financing was subsidized, and high real interest rates in the early stages of the stabilization program. Bad financial investments were a particularly aggravating cause of the difficulties of the kibbutzim. However, because the kibbutzim have come to be based increasingly on manufacturing industry and because their movement has built-in mechanisms of mutual help, they have been able to mount a comprehensive recovery program. The government and the banks have cooperated in this mainly by debt consolidation. The moshavim, by contrast, remain in deep

**Table 1.8**
Employment and number of branch offices of the banking institutions, 1984–86
(percent change over previous year)

| Year | Number of branch offices | Number of employees in the five large banks |
|------|--------------------------|---------------------------------------------|
| 1984 | −4.3 | −9.8[a] |
| 1985 | −1.1 | −5.3 |
| 1986 | −2.3 | −6.3 |

Source: Bank of Israel, Examiner of Banks, *Annual Banking Statistics, 1982–86*, table A-1.
a. The change from September 1983 to December 1984.

crisis, mainly because they have no mutual assistance system similar to that of the kibbutzim. It is doubtful that they will be able to extricate themselves from their difficulties without massive government assistance.

A final observation is that the effects of the shift from financial to real activity as inflation comes down will make its effects felt primarily in the banking system by the reduction in foreign currency and securities transactions. The banking system ended 1986 with small profits, mainly because of a sharp increase in the provision for bad debts that were partly due to the extremely high interest rates at the beginning of the program. Against this there were several factors that increased bank profits. First among these was the switch of the public from residents' foreign currency deposits (on which the banks' margin is negligible) to local-currency deposits on which the margin is higher. Second, the financial margins on shekel operations were exceptionally high in the early phases of the stabilization program, when the central bank conducted a highly restrictive monetary policy. In the future the liberalization of the capital market is likely to reduce the banks' financial margins, so that with low inflation and less financial activity in the economy the banks will have to shrink their size and scope of activities further and release resources for productive activities.

The cutback in the size of the banking system started with the bank shares crash in 1983; although the process was slowed down in 1985, renewed contraction took place in 1986 (see table 1.8). Although it is not clear how much of the 1986 contraction is due to the slowdown of inflation as such, it probably played some part.

Consumer Credit

In the first quarter of 1986 a spurt of increased consumer credit made its appearance in the chain store networks. These credit campaigns concerned the authorities because they were regarded as encouraging private consumption and putting pressures on the price level and the balance of payments.

One explanation for such an expansion of credit when inflation comes down is that under high inflation, when it is not worthwhile to hold money or even short-term financial instruments that have a negative real yield, consumers tend to keep a relatively large stock of consumer goods. When the inflation rate falls, the optimal level of stocks also declines; the holding of stocks is shifted to the distributors, who pay high real interest rates. The distributors then make efforts to induce the consumers to return to holding larger stocks by launching campaigns of discount sales and by extending credit for a longer term.

The extension of credit for a longer term can also be viewed from a different aspect. The chain stores used to give their customers credit for a week or two (through the use of credit cards) even before the slowdown of inflation. Before the stabilization program the cost of credit for two weeks was about 10%, and this cost was of course reflected in the price level. At the end of the first quarter of 1986, 10% was the cost of credit for two and a half months. For the chain stores it was therefore optimal to lengthen the term of credit, and it is reasonable to assume that their suppliers also extended the term for which they granted credit.

Such an extension of the term of credit means a one-time rise in credit balances, and this may in part explain the rapid increase of credit during 1986 even though the real interest rate was still high. The gradual fall of nominal interest rates from high levels postponed this rise in credit balances until early 1986 and thereby acted as a stabilizing factor.

## 1.6 From Stabilization to Growth?

The stabilization program, together with favorable external factors, has been remarkably successful in its two main objectives: putting a halt to inflation and improving the country's external position. However, the goal of reducing inflation to present world levels has not yet been achieved, and economic policy cannot yet be conducted without a constant close watch over possible new balance of payments difficulties. We have also seen that the stabilization process has brought to the surface a number of serious structural problems that call for solutions. But over and above these issues there hangs a much more important question mark. This has to do with the prolonged stagnation that has afflicted the economy as a consequence of the crises of the 1970s. The question is whether the conditions have already been created for a renewal of rapid growth under continued relative stability.

As stated, economic activity had picked up and unemployment had come down by the end of 1986 and into early 1987. Data on investment are not yet available, but imports of capital goods have recently started to rise again. These changes may herald a certain change in the economy's growth trend—a change that is expected as a result of disinflation, the contraction of public spending, the fall in energy prices, the decline in real interest rates, and the reduced need for public borrowing.

A stagnant economy in which capacities are underutilized can increase its product for a short time as demand rises even without additional investment, so long as the balance of payments position permits such an expansion of output. In general, however, the process of capital formation must be renewed for real and sustained growth to be revived. The net stock of capital in Israel's business sector has almost ceased to grow, as investment has fallen off rapidly in recent years. A solidly based revival of the capital formation process (as distinct from one artificially nourished by the injection of public funds) depends on two principal variables: (1) the real return to investment for the economy as a whole and for the individual producer and (2) the real cost of investment finance on the capital market.

Data for the return on new investments are not available. The only overall indicator at hand to indicate what difficulties lie in the path of renewing investment is the average gross rate of return on the capital stock of the business sector, as estimated from the functional distribution of GDP between wage income and income from capital. Figure 1.7 provides a historical series of gross returns to labor, and figure 1.8, which is almost its mirror image, shows the series of returns to capital. The figures bring out clearly what has happened to Israel's economy since the end of the prosperity period of 1968–75. The share of wages in domestic income has risen to 75–80% of the total, and in 1986 even to 85%, reflecting the rise in wage costs in excess of the increase in productivity. This development had the consequence that the gross return to capital in 1986 fell to its lowest level since the 1966 recession.[17]

In reality, however, the situation as regards profitability was even worse in 1985–86. For the individual producer it is the net after-tax return that counts, and in this respect the success of the stabilization program in raising the tax revenue from the business sector at the same time implied a deterioration in after-tax profitability. A partial indicator for this is provided by the data on the drastic change in the distribution of tax revenue from wages and taxes on unearned income:

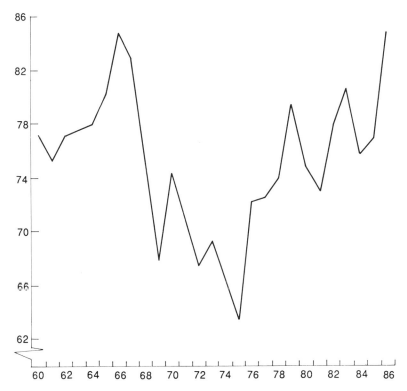

**Figure 1.7**
Gross returns to labor, percent of domestic income of the business sector, 1960–86.
Calculations by Yaacov Lavi, Bank of Israel Research Department.

Share of income tax from wage income in 1980    44.8
1984    53.3
1985    43.5
1986    37.4

This leads to the question of what mechanisms can be used to correct these trends. The halting of inflation and the modifications in the functioning of the business sector may also facilitate a rise in productivity. There are indications that in manufacturing industry, for example, output per person hour began to rise rapidly in the second half of 1986. The crucial question is, What will happen to wage costs when growth is renewed? This brings us back to the structure of the labor market, the ability of the trade unions to dispense with automatic general wage escalator mechanisms, and their readiness to let the labor market determine more flexible adjustments of

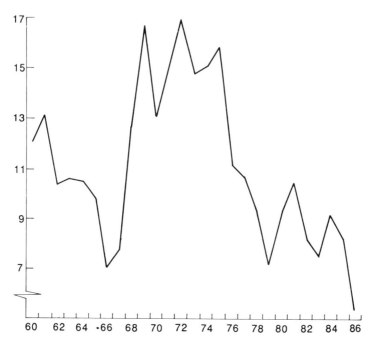

**Figure 1.8**
Gross before-tax returns per unit of capital in business sector, 1960–86 (percent).
Calculations by Yaacov Lavi, Bank of Israel Research Department.

wages in accordance with the conditions in different industries. Direct and indirect taxes on wages are another central component of wage costs.

Israel has one of the highest overall rates of taxation in the world (see table 1.7). It is almost twice as high now as it was during the period of rapid growth in the 1960s. A major part of the rise in the gross tax rates is the consequence of the considerable increase in transfer payments, subsidies, and a wide range of various tax exemptions. This means that the rate of net taxation is much lower than the gross tax rates. This situation calls for a tax reform that will on the one hand reduce the gross tax rates in order to increase the motivation to work and invest and, on the other hand, expand the tax base and reduce transfers so as not to lower the net rate of taxation too much and to enable the government to finance its other expenditures.

The marginal individual income tax rate was reduced in April 1987 from 60% to 50%, and corporation taxes were reduced at the same time. The planned reductions of tax exemptions have not yet been negotiated; these are essential because an income tax cut as the exclusive measure of the tax reform will increase the deficit, which may destabilize the economy again.

In the long run tax cuts within the framework of a tax reform depend on a continuous reduction of the share of public expenditure in GDP. Politically this is a thorny issue.

As regards the financing of new investment, Israel's capital market has always been characterized by a high degree of government intervention, as a result of the large financing requirements and because of the desire to allocate the remaining savings to preferred purposes. The recent substantial decline in the need to finance the deficit on the one hand and the lesser administrative intervention on the other will enable the private sector to allocate savings more efficiently.[18]

The measures adopted in a partial reform of the capital market since April 1987 go in this direction: (1) the share of investment in government bonds that is obligatory as cover for long-term deposits (saving schemes, provident and pension funds) has been reduced; (2) the tax discrimination in favor of interest on government bonds over private securities has been abolished; and (3) the requirement of government approval for private capital issues has been eliminated, and such issues are now only subject to approval by the supervisory authorities of the Stock Exchange. Issues of bonds by banks, however, are still restricted in order to prevent them from using their monopolistic power on the capital market. The restrictions on capital movements with the rest of the world have also remained in force.

The real yield of private capital issues, it may be noted, had fallen substantially toward the end of 1986 and in the beginning of 1987—from 10–11% to 7–8% per annum. For the long run this is still a higher than desirable interest rate, but it may indicate an improvement in the financing possibilities of private investment. As with the need to reduce the rate of taxation, future developments in the private capital market depend on budget balance. If the recent favorable budgetary trends can be maintained, it may become possible to reduce the ratio of domestic debt to GDP (which at present stands at 1.4) and thus also the cost of recycling the debt. Continued stability and the further strengthening of the country's foreign payments position may also make it possible to raise external funds for investment at reasonable interest rates. Rising productivity and a policy of restraint and flexibility for wages may increase the business sector's profitability.

The reforms of the tax system and the capital market are still in the early stages of implementation, as are the structural changes required in order to return to rapid growth. Only time will tell if the third goal of the recovery program, that of reviving economic growth, will indeed be achieved in significant measure.

# Appendix

**Table 1A.1**
Main Economic indicators, 1980–1987

| Economic indicator | Mean 1980–84 | 1984 (during year) | 1985 Jan.–July | Aug.–Sept. | Oct.–Dec. | 1986 Jan.–Mar. | Apr.–June | July–Sept. | Oct.–Dec. | 1987 Jan.–Mar. | Apr.–June |
|---|---|---|---|---|---|---|---|---|---|---|---|
| **Prices, exchange rates, and wages** (monthly percentage change rates) | | | | | | | | | | | |
| Consumer prices | 8.7 | 15.2 | 14.0 | 3.5 | 2.1 | 0.5 | 2.1 | 1.0 | 2.2 | 1.5 | 1.3 |
| Wholesale prices | 9.1 | 15.2 | 12.4 | 1.8 | 2.4 | 1.2 | 1.7 | 0.9 | 1.0 | 2.4 | 1.1 |
| $ Exchange rate | 8.8 | 15.9 | 13.6 | 0.2 | −0.1 | 0.0 | 0.0 | 0.0 | 0.0 | 2.8[g] | −0.3 |
| Five-currency basket exchange rate | 7.5 | 15.3 | 15.3 | 0.7 | 2.0 | 1.5 | 0.5 | 0.0[f] | 0.0 | 3.8[g] | −0.1 |
| Nominal wage | 9.0 | 16.5 | 11.0 | 0.3 | 4.5 | 6.4 | 4.3 | −1.7 | 3.0 | 0.3 | – |
| **Money and credit** (monthly percentage rates) | | | | | | | | | | | |
| Total bank credit | 8.6 | 16.1 | 13.0 | 4.8 | 1.7 | 2.9 | 2.4 | 3.7 | 3.3 | 4.6 | 3.1 |
| Quasi-money (M3)[c] | 10.7 | 15.9 | 13.0 | 3.5 | 1.9 | 2.3 | −1.0 | 3.2 | 3.3 | 4.3 | 1.5 |
| Means of payment (M1) | 8.0 | 13.4 | 11.8 | 16.2 | 6.7 | 15.7 | 0.9 | 7.0 | 4.2 | 2.4 | 0.5 |
| Interest rate (end-of-period level) | | 16.1 | 21.0 | 14.1 | 7.2 | 4.0 | 3.6 | 3.5 | 4.0 | 4.9 | 4.1 |
| **Relative price levels** (1980 = 100) | | | | | | | | | | | |
| Real exchange rate (new basket)[a] | 94 | 92 | 103 | 110 | 105 | 103 | 98 | 96 | 93 | 98 | 95 |
| Real wage (gross) | 108[b] | 116 | 116[c] | 95 | 95 | 108 | 113 | 114 | 117 | 115 | |
| Real wage (after tax) | 109[b] | 114 | 116[c] | 99 | 103 | 117 | 120 | 121 | 124 | 123 | |

| | | | | | | | | | | | |
|---|---|---|---|---|---|---|---|---|---|---|---|
| **Budget deficit** (% GDP) | 10.2[b] | 15.0 | 12.0[c] | 5[d] | 4 | 3 | 1 | 3 | 0 | 0 | 1.7 |
| **Unemployment rate** (%) | 4.9[b] | 5.9 | 6.0[c] | 7.8[d] | 6.6 | 7.2 | 7.9 | 6.8 | 6.6 | 5.7 | |
| **Balance of payments: Basic balance** | | | | | | | | | | | |
| (uncorrected; billions of dollars) | −0.2[b] | −0.3 | −0.7[c] | 0.6[d] | 1.2 | −0.1 | 0.0 | 0.3 | 1.3 | | |

a. Relative wholesale prices of major trading partners (new basket of five).

b. Mean, 1980–83.

c. Mean, January to June 1985.

d. Mean, July to September 1985.

e. Money and liquid assets; includes foreign currency demand deposits.

f. Data for August and September. On August 1, 1986, a new basket was adopted. (The figure for July was 2.0.)

g. In January the new shekel was devalued by 11% relative to the five-currency basket.

**Table 1A.2**
Import component and changes in stocks, 1985–86

| Component | Change, 1986 over 1985 at 1986 prices |
| --- | --- |
| 1. Total use of resources, excluding direct defense imports and changes in stocks | 2,586 |
| 2. Actual direct imports | 967 |
| 3. Total demand for domestic product [(1) − (2) = (3)] | 1,619 |
| 4. Imports of intermediate goods at 1985 weights in input-ouput table | 586 |
| 5. Total demand for GDP [(3) − (4) = (5)] | 1,033 |
| 6. Actual GDP | 782 |
| 7. Change in domestic stocks [(6) − (5) = (7)] | −251 |
| 8. Total change in stocks | 994 |
| 9. Change in stocks of imported intermediate goods [(8) − ⟨7⟩ = (9)] | 1,245 |
| 10. Total imports of intermediate goods, including services [(4) + (9) = (10)] | 1,831 |
| 11. Total imports of goods and services | 2,798 |

Source: Bank of Israel.

## Notes

We wish to express our gratitude to members of the Research Department of the Bank of Israel for many useful discussions on the topics with which this chapter is concerned and for many helpful comments on an earlier draft, particularly, Mordechai Frenkel, Shmuel Amir, Rafi Melnik, Akiva Offenbacher, and Zalman Shiffer. We are also grateful to Meir Merhav for translating and editing this paper and to Yossi Margoninski for research assistance.

1. For an analysis of the inflationary process in Israel, see Bruno and Fischer (1986), Liviatan and Piterman (1986), and Liviatan (1986, 1987).

2. For a discussion of the package deals, see Liviatan (1986, 1987).

3. For a detailed description of the measures, see Bruno (1986b). See also Blejer and Liviatan (1987), Dornbusch and Fischer (1986), Dornbusch and Simonsen (1987), and Helpman and Leiderman (1987) for a comparison of different stabilization programs, including that of Israel.

4. The new shekel, which dropped three zeros from the old shekel (NIS1 = IS1,000), was introduced only in August 1985; the final replacement of the old currency by the new took place in January 1986. This was no more than a belated change of the numeraire.

5. The cumulative price rise in October and November 1985 in fact exceeded 4%, as a result of seasonal factors, and payment of the cost-of-living allowance was renewed on December 1. In the new wage agreements signed in April 1986 by the Histadrut and the employers' organizations, the threshold was raised to a cumulative price rise of 7%.

6. For the implementation of the various components of the program and its results in the first six months, see Bruno (1986b).

7. Labor costs (wages deflated by producer prices) increased even more sharply.

8. An additional argument relying on Deaton (1977; see comments in chapter 2 on the Bank of Israel's annual report for 1986) refers to the individual's lack of discrimination at times of change in the inflation rate between changes in relative prices and changes in the general price level. When inflation accelerates, the rate of saving tends to be higher than normal and, conversely, when inflation decelerates, the rate of saving tends to be lower. In the reality of Israel's economy the test of this hypothesis is exceedingly difficult because in years of accelerated inflation, such as 1980 and 1984, when the savings rate rose, the phenomenon may be explained by the changes in disposable income and private wealth. If the Israeli savings rate rises with continuing stability after the decrease caused by the deceleration of inflation, this may lend support to the validity of this argument.

9. Formally the derivation of the upward-sloping commodity supply schedule (figure 1.4) in this case consists of profit maximization by firms subject to both a

real wage and a minimum labor input constraint with only raw materials being a truly variable factor.

10. The index of wholesale prices of industrial products for domestic uses (excluding food, mining, and quarrying) divided by the exchange rate of the shekel against the currency basket and the wholesale price index abroad. For the use of this diagram for the analysis of economic developments from 1965 to 1982, see Bruno (1986a).

11. However, as can be seen in figure 1.4, the aggregate supply curve in 1986 lies to the right of the 1983 curve, despite the higher real wages in 1986. This is due to the terms of trade improvement and perhaps also to the sharp decrease in inflation, which raises productivity (see section 1.5).

12. The rapid expansion of M4 in the first half of 1987 is related to the increase in domestic currency value of foreign currency deposits after the devaluation of January 1987 and to the large capital inflow in this period. We refer to this phenomenon in section 1.4.

13. As was actually expected from econometric estimations; see Bank of Israel (1985).

14. This large increase in the money base, compared with its expansion in 1981–84, was mainly due to a decrease in sales of foreign currency to the private sector and to a decline in net domestic debt, both of which offset the reduction of the government deficit to a considerable extent.

15. The exchange rate for the import basket rose more rapidly, but, if the price fall of raw materials is taken into account, the actual price change of the import basket is similar to that of the export basket. We have therefore taken the export basket as an indicator of the shekel's depreciation.

16. The basket is made up of the following five currencies (percentage weights in brackets): US dollars (60), deutsche marks (20), pounds sterling (10), French francs (5), and yen (5).

17. It should be observed, however, that this is the average return on the capital stock that does not necessarily represent the return to new investments. The revival of the stock market and of new share issues in the first half of 1987 may indicate that the expected rates of return are higher.

18. For a survey of government intervention in the capital market and outlines for a reform, see Blum and Piterman (1987).

## References

Bank of Israel. 1985. *Economic Review* 60. Jerusalem: Bank of Israel.

Blejer, M., and N. Liviatan. 1987. *Stabilization Strategies in Argentina and Israel, 1985–86.* Working Paper. Washington, D. C: International Monetary Fund.

Blum, L., and S. Piterman. 1987. "Government intervention in the Israeli capital market— Survey and reform outlines." *The Economic Quarterly* 131:855–864. (In Hebrew; English translation available from authors.)

Bruno, M. 1986a. "External shocks and domestic response: Macroeconomic performance, 1965–1982," in *The Israeli Economy: Maturing through Crises*, Y. Ben-Porath, ed. (Cambridge, Mass.: Harvard University Press), 276–301.

Bruno, M. 1986b. "Sharp disinflation strategy: Israel 1985." *Economic Policy* 2:379–402.

Bruno, M., and S. Fischer. 1986. "The inflationary process: Shocks and accommodation," in *The Israeli Economy: Maturing through Crises*, Y. Ben-Porath, ed. (Cambridge, Mass.: Harvard University Press), 347–371.

Deaton, A. 1977. "Involuntary saving through unanticipated inflation." *American Economic Review* 67: 899–910.

Dornbusch, R., and S. Fischer. 1986. "Stopping hyperinflation: Past and present." *Weltwirtschaftliches Archiv* 122:1–47.

Dornbusch, R., and M. H. Simonsen. 1987. *Inflation Stabilization with Incomes Policy Support*. New York: Group of Thirty.

Fischer, S. 1984. *Real Balances, the Exchange Rate and Indexation: Real Variables in Disinflation*. Working Paper. Cambridge, Mass.: National Bureau of Economic Research.

Fischer, S., and Y. Frenkel. 1982. "Stabilization policy for Israel." *The Economic Quarterly* 114:246–255. (In Hebrew.)

Frenkel, M., S. Piterman, and M. Sokoler. 1984. "Principles for a plan for rapid disinflation." *The Economic Quarterly* 123:334–343. (In Hebrew.)

Helpman, E., and L. Leiderman. 1987. "Stabilization in high inflation countries: Analytical foundations and recent experience." Tel Aviv University.

Liviatan, N. 1986. *Inflation and Stabilization in Israel: Conceptual Issues and Interpretation of Developments*. Working Paper WP/86/10. Washington, D.C.: International Monetary Fund.

Liviatan, N. 1987. "The evolution of disinflationary policies in Israel 1980–86." *The Economic Quarterly* 131:902–913. (In Hebrew; English translation available from authors.)

Liviatan, N., and S. Piterman. 1986. "Accelerating inflation and balance-of-payments crises, 1973–1984," in *The Israeli Economy: Maturing through Crises*, Y. Ben-Porath, ed. (Cambridge, Mass.: Harvard University Press), 320–346.

Yariv, D. 1986. *An Estimate of Inflationary Expectations in Israel under the Disinflation Programs of 1984–1985*. Discussion Paper 86–11. Jerusalem: Bank of Israel. (In Hebrew.)

# 2

# The End of the High Israeli Inflation: An Experiment in Heterodox Stabilization

## Alex Cukierman

In July of 1985 a comprehensive stabilization program was introduced by the Israeli government. This followed approximately six years of inflation at more than 100% per annum and at more than 400% in 1984. The officially announced aims of the program were to eliminate hyperinflation and to decrease the deficit in the balance of payments. The program immediately and persistently reduced annual inflation from the 400% range to around 20% and was, on this count, an instant success. The program combined traditional contractionary fiscal and monetary measures with less orthodox measures, such as a temporary price and wage freeze and pegging of the exchange rate.

I discuss the developments that led to the implementation of the program, its main features, and the experience so far, with particular emphasis on the more general lessons that can be drawn from the program's performance.[1] A major thesis here is that the speedy and almost complete success in reducing inflation is due to the heterodox nature of the program, which combined a big decrease in the budgetary deficit and monetary contraction with a temporary precommitment of the paths of all major prices in the economy, including, in particular, the exchange rate. My view is that unorthodox measures alleviate dynamic inconsistency problems that arise as a result of the interaction of government and unions in the presence of staggered wage contracts with high inflationary expectations inherited from before the stabilization. This is demonstrated by means of a precise theoretical example in section 2.3.

Section 2.1 contains a discussion of the conditions that preceded the stabilization program and a description of its main features. The experience with the program to date is summarized in section 2.2. Further assessment of the Israeli stabilization and its particular features appear in section 2.4. This is followed by concluding comments and several observations about what lies ahead.

## 2.1    Immediate Preconditions and Main Features of the July 1985
## Stabilization Program

Immediate Preconditions

The rate of inflation in Israel penetrated the 100% mark in 1979 and remained in the 100–140% range until the third quarter of 1983. Thereafter it jumped to a substantially higher level, reaching more than 500% in mid-1984 (details appear in table 2.1). Until the end of 1983 inflation was high by Western standards, but neither the public nor the government seemed overly concerned. Widespread (although not full) indexation alleviated the redistributional effects of an uncertain price level, and, most important, the policies of Treasury Minister Aridor brought an unprecedented increase in private consumption and the real wage rate, which increased by almost 16% between 1980 and 1983. Under those circumstances the public was willing to tolerate high but relatively stable inflation, making it unnecessary for the government to embark on the arduous recessionary path leading to price stability. Those policies caused a tremendous increase in net foreign debt (from about 50% of GNP in 1980 to about 80% in 1983) and severely limited Israel's borrowing ability. In the autumn of 1983 the emphasis of policy shifted to improving the balance of payments and checking the increase in foreign debt. The rate of devaluation was stepped up dramatically, as was the rate of change in the prices of controlled goods.[2] Because of the high (but not complete) degree of wage indexing and the large number of prices that were quoted in dollar terms, wages and prices in the free sector of the economy reacted with a short lag. This made it necessary to devalue and increase the price of controlled goods again in order to maintain both a real devaluation and a decrease in the budgetary burden of direct subsidies. As a consequence, the desired changes in relative prices were brought about only at the cost of accelerating inflation.[3] This mechanism and the insistence of the policymakers on improving the balance of payments combined to produce the tremendous acceleration of inflation in 1984. The accommodative response of money and of domestic credit enabled this process to hold center stage.

A noteworthy development was the increase in the budgetary deficit during 1984. This was due mostly to a decrease in tax revenues (columns 6, 7, and 9 of table 2.1) triggered by the acceleration of inflation in 1984. Several features of the tax structure combined to produce this effect. Of particular importance was the fact that a shekel has the same value for tax purposes at any time during the tax year.[4] This effect, known as the

**Table 2.1**
Rates of inflation, the rate of expansion of short-term credit,[a] taxes, subsidies, budgetary deficit and its financing, and velocity

| Period | (1) Inflation at yearly rates (%) | (2) Inflation at quarterly rates | (3) Rate of devaluation with respect to dollars | (4) Inflation in free sector | (5) Rate of change in total bank credit to the public | (6) Total taxes (% of GNP) | (7) Direct taxes (% of GNP) | (8) Direct subsidies to domestic products (% of GNP) | Deficit and items financing it (% of GDP)[e] | | | | |
|---|---|---|---|---|---|---|---|---|---|---|---|---|---|
| | | | | | | | | | (9) Deficit in domestic government budget[d] | (10) Increase in domestic debt | (11) Sale of foreign exchange to private sector | (12) Net seigniorage[f] | (13) Yearly velocity of circulation of M1[g] |
| 1976 | 38.0 | 8.4 | | | | | | 3.2 | | | | | 13.2 |
| 1977 | 42.5 | 9.3 | | | | | | 3.1 | | | | | |
| 1978 | 48.1 | 10.3 | | | | | | 3.2 | | | | | |
| 1979 | 111.4 | 20.6 | | | | 43.4 | 23.7 | 3.3 | | | | | |
| 1980 | 133.0 | 23.6 | | | | 42.2 | 25.2 | 2.6 | | | | | 23.1 |
| 1981 | 101.5 | 19.1 | | | | 41.3 | 25.1 | 6.1 | 11.6 | 8.1 | 1.9 | 1.7 | 28.3 |
| 1982 | 131.5 | 23.4 | | | 23.5 | 45.1 | 25.1 | 4.3 | 10.0 | 6.2 | 2.6 | 1.2 | 33.2 |
| 1983 | | | | | | 45.9[b] | 24.7[b] | 3.8 | 6.0 | −1.0 | 6.3 | 0.8 | 40.2 |
| I | 118.6 | 21.6 | 17.6 | 22.5 | 12.2 | | | | | | | | |
| II | 134.9 | 23.8 | 20.1 | 23.9 | 16.1 | | | | | | | | |
| III | 137.2 | 24.1 | 34.1 | 24.7 | 27.0 | | | | | | | | |
| IV | 486.2 | 55.6 | 69.2 | 51.9 | 44.7 | | | | | | | | |
| 1984 | | | | | | | | 4.6 | 12.1 | 0.8 | 8.6 | 2.7 | 58.6 |
| I | 311.2 | 42.4 | 42.2 | 41.3 | 41.2 | 41.6 | 23.5 | | | | | | |
| II | 495.3 | 56.2 | 54.2 | 59.3 | 50.5 | 40.0 | 20.6 | | | | | | |
| III | 535.9 | 58.8 | 69.8 | 59.7 | 74.5 | 41.3 | 20.6 | | | | | | |
| IV | 465.4 | 54.2 | 59.1 | 56.2 | 62.6 | 36.6 | 19.5 | | | | | | |

| | | | | | | | | | | | | | |
|---|---|---|---|---|---|---|---|---|---|---|---|---|---|
| **1985** | | | | | | | | | | | | | |
| I | 221.5 | 33.9 | 34.4 | 29.8 | 35.3 | 45.1 | 25.7 | 3.4 | 9.0 | −1.2 | 4.8 | 5.4 | 46.1 |
| II | 360.6 | 46.5 | 47.1 | 45.1 | 47.8 | 44.3 | 23.4 | | | | | | 68.9 |
| III | 247.2 | 36.5 | 17.7 | 32.9 | 29.2 | 47.9 | 25.8 | | 5.7 | −6.1 | 2.2 | 9.6 | 34.7 |
| IV | 28.7 | 6.5 | 1.0 | 8.5 | 5.2 | 48.1 | 24.4 | | | | | | |
| **1986** | | | | | | | | | | | | | |
| I | 7.4 | 1.8 | 0.0 | 1.7 | 9.0 | 55.5 | 30.2 | 1.9 | 2.6 | −0.4 | 2.5 | 0.5 | 27.2 |
| II | 29.6 | 6.7 | 0.1 | 5.9 | 7.4 | 52.1 | 28.3 | | 2.9 | 2.6 | 2.4 | −2.0 | 32.3 |
| III | 12.6 | 3.0 | −0.1 | 3.0 | 12.2 | 51.6 | 25.8 | | | | | | |
| IV | 30.6 | 6.9 | 0.0 | 8.1 | 5.2 | 49.5 | 24.8 | | 2.3 | −3.4 | 2.6 | 3.1 | 23.4 |
| **1987** | | | | | | | | | | | | | |
| I | 19.1 | 4.5 | | | | 52.2[c] | 27.4[c] | | | | | | |

Sources: (1) *Price Statistics Monthly*, various issues (Central Bureau of Statistics). (3) Bank of Israel, *Annual Report 1985*, table on p. 56 (Hebrew edition), and previous versions of the same table; *Foreign Currency Exchange Rates in Israel, 1948–1985* and *1986* (Jerusalem: Bank of Israel Foreign Department, Economic Unit); (5) *Recent Economic Developments*, nos. 38, 40, and 41 (Jerusalem: Bank of Israel Research Department), table 19. (6, 7) Quarterly data from *Recent Economic Developments*, nos. 40 and 41 (Jerusalem: Bank of Israel Research Department), table 13; yearly data for earlier years is obtained from table 19 of earlier issues of the same report; columns 7 and 8 are obtained by dividing those figures by nominal GNP figures from the Central Bureau of Statistics. *Monthly Bulletin of Statistics*, suppl. 5 (1985), p. 214. (8) *Monthly Bulletin of Statistics*, suppl. 1 (1987), tables on pp. 116 and 120 and earlier versions of the same tables; data used is from tables of current subsidies and capital grants to the business sector and tables for gross domestic product at market prices. (9–12) Bank of Israel, *Annual Report 1986*, p. 243 (in Hebrew). (13) Bank of Israel, *Annual Report 1986*, p. 249 (in Hebrew).

a. Unless stated otherwise, all rates of change are percentages per quarter. The rates of inflation are based on the CPI and its subdivision into controlled and free sectors.

b. Yearly average.

c. Based only on January and February 1987.

d. Including interest on domestic debt.

e. The sum of columns 10, 11, and 12 is equal to column 9. Small deviations occur at times because of rounding.

f. Net seigniorage is defined as expansion of high-powered money after adjustment for the following items: interest on high-powered money and on discount-window loans, fines on reserve deficiencies, and changes in the volume of discount-window loans.

g. The velocity of M1 is defined as total domestic uses of resources (excluding military imports) divided by the average yearly M1 balance.

Olivera-Tanzi effect, seems to be a common occurrence in high-inflation countries such as Argentina and Brazil. It implies that the simultaneous increase in inflation and in the budget deficit during 1984 reflected mostly a chain of causality from the inflationary acceleration to a loss of tax revenues to a larger budget deficit, rather than the more conventional causality running from the deficit to inflation.[5]

After the formation of the coalition government in 1984, the emphasis of policy shifted to slowing inflation through a series of agreements (package deals) among the government, the Histadrut,[6] and the association of private employers. The deals involved a mutually agreed partial freeze on wages, taxes, and the cost-of-living allowance. During and between the deals the government imposed direct import restrictions and continued to devalue the currency and increase the price of controlled goods (the relative price of controlled goods appears in figure 2.1). The deals were not effective in eradicating inflation from the system, and their performance progressively worsened. The basic problem was that the budget deficit was not decreased and monetary policy was highly accommodative. In addition, as stressed by Liviatan (1987), the government's continued tendency to devalue during the package deals, despite the wage freeze, raised Barro-Gordon-type dynamic inconsistency problems (Barro and Gordon 1983). These factors raised serious credibility issues and convinced policymakers that partial measures could not stabilize the rate of inflation. In this sense the package deals, despite their obvious drawbacks, paved the way for the comprehensive stabilization program of 1985.

More generally, the experience since the end of 1983 suggested that it is hard if not impossible to improve the balance of payments permanently without a substantial cut in the government's budget deficit. The little improvement achieved was reached at the cost of a large acceleration of inflation and its variability (see table 2.5), which was not deemed worth the bargain. This feeling was reinforced by the large loss in tax revenues during 1984, suggesting that large inflationary accelerations may produce results (such as a larger budgetary deficit) that would provide further fuel for future inflation.

There are three other background factors that contributed to disillusionment with the view that real stability can be maintained by indexation (with little or no regard for nominal stability). The first is the traditional shoe-leather costs of inflation, which are reflected in a large acceleration of monetary velocity (column 13 of table 2.1) and in a related expansion of the banking sector and the financial departments of business firms.[7] Second, during the high inflation years net seigniorage was usually less than 2% of GDP. As a matter of fact, most studies of the demand for money in Israel [recently summarized by Offenbacher (1985)] suggest that by the early 1980s the actual rate of inflation was higher than the rate that maximizes steady-state government revenue from the inflation tax. Thus collection of the inflation tax as a motive for (high-powered) monetary expansion lost some of its appeal as inflation accelerated further. Third, the spiral among the rate of exchange, wages, free prices, and the prices of controlled goods that developed in 1984 in reaction to policymakers' attempt to decrease real wages and wealth convinced the policymakers that it was preferable to achieve those aims by prior agreement than by non-coordinated price shocks because such shocks improve the balance of payments little at a tremendous inflationary cost. Prior commitments of this kind enabled policymakers to achieve the politically feasible cut in real wages without socially excessive inflation. This principle had been used in making the package deals but was implemented more efficiently as one component of a more comprehensive program during the 1985 stabilization. The high degree of unionization and centralization of wage negotiations facilitated reaching such prior agreement on restraint regarding the nominal variables under the parties' control.

Main Features of the Stabilization Program

In contrast to previous policy measures, which were designed to deal either with inflation or the balance of payments (usually at the expense of the other target), the stabilization program was designed to handle both problems simultaneously. Most important, the program involved a deep cut in the government's budgetary deficit and the imposition of a severe upper limit on the rate of growth of total bank credit. After an 18.8% devaluation of the shekel with respect to the dollar on July 1, 1985, and a substantial one-shot increase in the price of controlled goods, the rate of exchange was pegged at 1.5 shekels per dollar and free goods were allowed a one-time 17% adjustment on average and were then frozen for a period of three months. Wage indexation was suspended temporarily, and wages were frozen except for some preagreed adjustments that were to be spread over the next seven months. Over 50% of the decrease in government spending came from a cut in subsidies, which took the form of a large increase in the relative price of controlled goods (figure 2.1). This and other measures reduced the budget deficit from 12.1% of GDP in 1984 to 5.7% in the second half of 1985 to 2.6% in 1986 (column 9 of table 2.1).

The major monetary component of the program was a planned 10% real

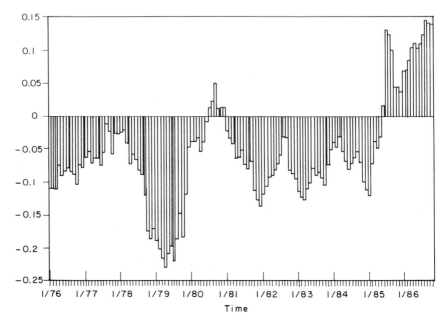

**Figure 2.1**
Relative price of controlled goods.

decrease in total bank credit in the first month and its nominal freezing thereafter. Because of a tremendous increase in real interest rates (see table 2.4), particularly on the nondirected portion of this credit, actual monetary policy was somewhat less restrictive than planned (column 5 of table 2.1). With the July 1, 1985, pegging of the shekel to the dollar, Israel effectively went back to a fixed exchange rate regime after more than ten years of a dirty float or crawling peg. But there was an understanding that, if wages increased too much, an adjustment of the rate would be considered. Wages were on a nominally precommitted path until February 1986. The price freeze was initially fairly comprehensive in coverage and was gradually lifted by freeing successive groups of goods from it or by giving permits to raise specific prices. An important input into the program's success was a $750 billion per annum increase in US government foreign aid.

The design of the program was shaped by the idiosyncrasies of Israeli institutions, such as the highly accommodative nature of the money supply and of credit, as well as by the lessons learned from failure of the package deals. A basic premise that influenced the program's design was that the program must stop inflation quickly without too large an increase in unemployment. Otherwise the political consensus necessary for implementing it would disintegrate, leading to loss of credibility and partial or total abandonment of the program. This is one of the reasons for basing the program not only on the traditional stabilizing instruments, such as fiscal and monetary contraction, but also on direct freezing of most prices, wages, and the exchange rate. On the other hand, the failure of the package deals prevented policymakers from following the politically easy but deceptive tack involving only a wage, price, and exchange rate freeze without the fundamental necessary contraction of fiscal and monetary policies. It was felt that the existing broad unity government and the recent increased awareness of the public to the costs of inflation presented a unique opportunity to deploy the political muscle necessary to eradicate inflation from the economy. This led to strong risk aversion on the part of the program's designers, who did not pass up any feasible opportunity to increase price stability by fortifying it with as many nominal anchors as possible.[8]

A more detailed discussion of the features of the stabilization package appears in an unpublished appendix that is available on request.

## 2.2 Experience to Date

Inflation and the Program's Credibility

The major achievement of the Israeli stabilization program was a swift and (so far) sustained decrease in the rate of inflation. From several hundred percent, inflation plummeted to less than 30% per year and has remained in this range ever since (columns 1 and 2 of table 2.1). This was achieved at the cost of only a modest increase in unemployment, which increased from 6.5% at the eve of the program to 7.5% in the first quarter of the program, coming back down somewhat later on (column 5 of table 2.2). A remarkable feature is the comparatively quick credibility commanded by the program. This can be seen from table 2.3, which displays data on inflationary expectations during the package deals as well as before and after the stabilization program.[9] After a big decrease between June and July 1985, inflationary expectations increased somewhat in August, probably reflecting the fear that the government would not be able to prevent the initial large policy-induced price shock from spreading. When this fear did not materialize, expectations started to decline sharply and steadily. For six months after the stabilization, expectations were higher than actual inflation, reflecting the fear that the program would break down. But as this fear did not materialize, the (negative) difference between actual and expected

**Table 2.2**
Quarterly trade balance at yearly rates, the real wage rate, unemployment, and real exchange rate

| Period | (1) Trade balance[a] | (2) Exports[a] | (3) Imports[a] | (4) Index of real wage per job | (5) Rate of unemployment (%) | Real exchange rate[d] | |
|---|---|---|---|---|---|---|---|
| | | | | | | (6) Against five-currency basket | (7) Against four-currency basket |
| **1983** | | | | | | | |
| I | −2907 | 5141 | 8048 | 132.2 | 4.4 | 91.2 | 81.4 |
| II | −3819 | 4642 | 8461 | 121.5 | 4.4 | 88.3 | 78.2 |
| III | −3980 | 3994 | 7974 | 128.3 | 4.2 | 89.6 | 76.8 |
| IV | −3216 | 5783 | 8999 | 109.3 | 4.9 | 95.4 | 81.4 |
| **1984** | | | | | | | |
| I | −2367 | 5899 | 8266 | 113.9 | 5.5 | 95.8 | 81.6 |
| II | −3045 | 5072 | 8117 | 124.8 | 5.8 | 95.2 | 80.8 |
| III | −3367 | 4960 | 8327 | 131.0 | 5.8 | 93.8 | 76.3 |
| IV | −1306 | 6544 | 7850 | 120.3 | 6.4 | 95.5 | 75.6 |
| **1985** | | | | | | | |
| I | −1496 | 6008 | 7504 | 124.7 | 5.9 | 102.2 | 78.2 |
| II | −2593 | 5711 | 8304 | 118.6 | 6.5 | 108.1 | 86.7 |
| III | −1963 | 5380 | 7343 | 101.3 | 7.5 | 114.6 | 97.0 |
| IV | −1709 | 7224 | 8933 | 100.2 | 6.7 | 108.9 | 97.1 |
| **1986** | | | | | | | |
| I | −1828 | 6856 | 8684 | 114.7 | 7.2 | 106.5 | 100.3 |
| II | −2595 | 6548 | 9143 | 120.0 | 7.9 | 101.4 | 99.1 |
| III | −2530 | 6794 | 9324 | 120.7 | 6.8 | 99.9 | 100.9 |
| IV | −2492 | 7458 | 9950 | 120.7[c] | 6.5 | 96.2 | 97.1 |
| **1987** | | | | | | | |
| I | −2955[b] | 6977[b] | 9932[b] | | | 100.5[e] | 106.1[e] |

Source: (1–3) *Recent Economic Developments*, nos. 39–41 (Jerusalem: Bank of Israel Research Department), table 5. (4) *Main Israeli Economic Indicators*, June 4, 1985, and February 8, 1987 (Jerusalem: Bank of Israel Research Department). The figures are quarterly averages of monthly indexes. (5) *Recent Economic Developments*, nos. 39 and 41 (Jerusalem: Bank of Israel Research Department), table 10. (6, 7) Calculations by Bank of Israel Research Department.

a. Seasonally adjusted in millions of US dollars.

b. Based on first two months of 1987.

c. Based on first two months of the quarter.

d. The real exchange rate indexes are based on the ratios of foreign to local wholesale prices, both in local currency, weighted by the shares of trade of the countries entering the index. The local wholesale price indexes exclude food prices that are controlled by the government.

e. Based on January 1987 only.

**Table 2.3**
Actual and expected[a] inflation before and after the stabilization program (%)

| | Inflation | | |
|---|---|---|---|
| | (1) | (2) | (3) = (1) − (2) |
| Month | Actual | Expected | Unexpected |
| **1984** | | | |
| January | 14.4 | 11.9 | 2.5 |
| February | 15.1 | 11.7 | 3.4 |
| March | 16.1 | 9.8 | 6.3 |
| April | 13.4 | 11.6 | 1.8 |
| May | 14.1 | 11.8 | 2.3 |
| June | 16.7 | 14.7 | 2.0 |
| July | 20.7 | 20.3 | 0.4 |
| August | 21.7 | 21.3 | 0.4 |
| September | 15.5 | 18.4 | −2.9 |
| October | 9.3 | 24.2 | −14.9 |
| November | 7.4 | 18.0 | −10.6 |
| December | 10.2 | 8.5 | 1.7 |
| **1985** | | | |
| January | 14.9 | 8.1 | 6.8 |
| February | 12.6 | 9.8 | 2.8 |
| March | 13.6 | 9.6 | 4.0 |
| April | 16.1 | 11.1 | 5.0 |
| May | 15.0 | 9.9 | 5.1 |
| June | 10.9 | 17.6 | −6.7 |
| July | 3.9 | 10.7 | −6.8 |
| August | 2.7 | 11.1 | −8.4 |
| September | 2.1 | 7.4 | −5.3 |
| October | 0.1 | 5.8 | −5.7 |
| November | 0.5 | 3.6 | −3.1 |
| December | 0.6 | 2.1 | −1.5 |
| **1986** | | | |
| January | 2.2 | 2.1 | 0.1 |
| February | 2.2 | 2.3 | −0.1 |
| March | 2.2 | 1.4 | 0.8 |
| April | 1.1 | 1.7 | −0.6 |
| May | 0.9 | 1.0 | −0.1 |
| June | 1.0 | 1.1 | −0.1 |
| July | 1.8 | 1.4 | 0.4 |
| August | 2.4 | 1.4 | 1.0 |
| September | 2.2 | 0.6 | 1.6 |
| October | 2.2 | 0.5 | 1.7 |

Source: Inflationary expectations up to March 1986 are from Yariv (1986), table 1. Later data are from Yariv (personal communication). Actual inflation is calculated from *Price Statistics Monthly*.

a. The expected rate of inflation is derived from the market prices of imperfectly indexed government bonds. The forecast horizon of the expectations is three months. Thus the 17.6% expected inflation corresponding to June 1985 is the average monthly inflation that was expected in June 1985 to occur between June 1985 and September 1985. The corresponding actual inflation of 10.9% is the actual rate of inflation over the same forecast horizon.

inflation decreased steadily, and by January 1986 there was no significant difference between actual and expected inflation (column 3 of table 2.3). Factors that contributed to quick establishment of credibility were:

1. The existence of a National Unity government and the high degree of personal involvement of the prime minister in bringing about an agreement between the major parties contributing to the program. The fact that the prime minister was from the same party as the majority in the Histadrut also helped.

2. The government's public resolve to cut the budget deficit and to limit seriously the expansion of short-term credit and the money supply.

3. Additional US foreign aid, which increased the public's confidence in the government's ability to peg the exchange rate and to withstand successfully possible speculative attacks against the currency.

4. The government's avoidance of the expected carryover of past expectations on its own future actions, leading rational observers of government to conclude that it will not accommodate and diffusing the associated problem of dynamic inconsistency.[10] The government achieved this by committing itself to freeze prices and the exchange rate for a limited period.

5. The speed with which the effects of the program affected the price level (the speed increased the public's confidence that a reversal of policy because of short political horizons was less likely).

The Balance of Payments, Net Debt, and the Real Exchange Rate

The program maintained the momentum of improvement in the trade balance for about nine months after its inception (column 1 of table 2.2). Because of this improvement but mainly because of the large increase in unilateral transfers, net foreign debt decreased slightly for the first time after over ten years of sustained increase. However, since mid-1986 the trade balance has been on a deteriorating path, which is no doubt related to the rebound in the real wage rate (column 4 of table 2.2). A similar pattern is displayed by the real exchange rate with respect to the five major currency blocks with which Israel trades. (For a precise definition of the real exchange rate, see note d of table 2.2.) The program initially reinforced the deterioration in Israel's real exchange rate, but from the fourth quarter of 1985 until the third quarter of 1986 the real exchange rate persistently improved (column 6 of table 2.2). The pattern is different, however, when the American dollar is excluded from the basket. In this case the real exchange rate deterioration not only lasted longer but actually continued through much of 1986 (column 7 of table 2.2). This difference is due to the depreciation of the dollar with respect to European currencies and the Japanese yen. This fortunate depreciation made it possible to use the exchange rate as a nominal anchor for a longer time.[11]

Consumption and Investment

During the first quarter of the program there was a decrease in all major components of domestic absorption. Private consumption (including, in particular, consumption of durables), government consumption, and investment all decreased in relation to GNP. Investment continued to decrease before picking up in early 1986; government consumption decreased to a lower plateau after picking up in the last quarter of 1985. Private consumption and in particular purchases of consumer durables have been on a sustained recovery path since the last quarter of 1985, actually returning at the end of 1986 to their 1982–83 levels as a fraction of GNP. The inevitable conclusion seems to be that the contractionary effects of the stabilization program on private consumption were highly temporary, probably because the public realized relatively quickly that there had been no serious decrease in permanent income.

Monetary Velocity and Net Seigniorage

Before the stabilization program velocity had been on an almost uninterrupted increasing course (column 13 of table 2.1). Part of this increase may be due to technical progress in the banking sector, but there is little doubt that the lion's share, particularly since 1976, is due to the acceleration of inflation. Following the 1985 stabilization the resource velocity of M1 went down for the first time in over fifteen years. However, it did not go down anywhere near the level it was at in the past at similar rates of inflation. This suggests that a substantial part of the upward adjustment of velocity to higher inflation involves long-run institutional and technical adaptations that remain in place even after inflation decreases to its former level.[12]

The increase in the demand for money underlying the decrease in velocity also produced a dramatic temporary increase in total seigniorage (column 12 of table 2.1). This phenomenon is familiar from other episodes of successful stabilization of hyperinflation (Sargent 1982; Dornbusch and Fischer 1986). In the Israeli case the increase in the demand for domestic money has been reinforced by the abolishment of foreign exchange checking (*Patam*) accounts at the inception of the program.

Real Interest Rates

Ex post real interest rates generally increased sharply after the stabilization (table 2.4). The average real interest rate on total short-term credit went up from −2% in the first half of 1985 to almost 34% immediately after the stabilization (column 1). Besides the policy-induced monetary contraction that obviously contributed to the rise in real rates, there are several additional factors. First is the increase in the demand for money discussed earlier. Second, because inflationary expectations did not adjust immediately by as much as the rate of inflation (column 2 of table 2.3), the ex post real rate turned out to be higher than the ex ante rate. Third, the short-run demand for credit is probably quite inelastic to unanticipated changes in the real rate, particularly when these changes materialize after the loan agreements have been signed and consummated. But this is only part of the story. Short-term credit is composed of several different types of credit, the most important of which are directed credit from the Bank of Israel and free credit. In addition, each of these types may be in either local or foreign currency. Because most of these credit types are limited by various institutional arrangements, their interest costs are generally different. This is the reason for the generally high variance of the real rate across types of credit (column 2 of table 2.4). Following stabilization this already high variance tripled. Particularly striking is both the general level and the poststabilization gigantic increase in the real rate on free short-term credit, which reached an incredible 168.3% in the second half of 1985 (column 3).[13]

Besides discriminating against borrowers whose major source of funds is the free credit market, segmentation of the loan market is also a drag on the conduct of monetary policy. By restricting the effects of policy to a narrow segment of the market, segmentation induces large fluctuations in rates, encouraging political opposition to contractionary monetary policies. Although monetary policy in Israel has normally played second fiddle to fiscal policy, its role is likely to become more important with the ongoing gradual liberalization of the capital market. Therefore removal of segmentation in the credit market and broadening of the scope and effectiveness of monetary policy are important structural changes that should be implemented in the future. Some rate unification in foreign short-terms loans is currently under way, but the overall credit market is still fragmented.

**Table 2.4**
Estimates of ex post real interest rates (% per year)

| Period | Short term | | | Long term | |
|---|---|---|---|---|---|
| | (1) Total short-term credit[a] | (2) Standard deviation[b] | (3) Free short-term credit | (4) Directed mortgages | (5) Credit to industry |
| 1978 | −11 | | 2 | −38 | |
| 1979 | −10 | | −11[c] | −32 | −26 |
| 1980 | 1 | | 19 | −18 | −6 |
| 1981 | 17 | 21.1 | 34 | −14 | −6 |
| 1982 | 4 | 15.2 | 5 | −10.9 | −2.6 |
| 1983 | 3.7 | 41.5 | −5.9 | −10.7 | −2.0 |
| 1984 | 25.5 | 41.6 | 67 | −10.3 | 0.0 |
| 1985 | 14.7 | 44.8 | 100.4 | −7.7 | 2.5 |
| 1986 | 6.0 | 16.5 | 30.4 | | |
| 1984 | | | | | |
| I | 15.0 | 19.3 | 34.0 | | |
| II | −5.8 | 22.5 | 35.5 | | |
| III | 39.6 | 35.0 | 79.8 | | |
| IV | 91.3 | 57.7 | 177.3 | | |
| 1985 | | | | | |
| First half | −2.0 | 26.8 | 49.7 | | |
| Second half | 33.9 | 62.2 | 168.3 | | |
| 1986 | | | | | |
| First half | 8.4 | 17.4 | 35.4 | | |
| Second half | 3.7 | 15.5 | 25.6 | | |

Source: Bank of Israel, *Annual Report 1985*, table on p. 227 and versions of the same table in the 1980, 1983, and 1984 reports. Later data is from Bank of Israel Research Department.
a. Weighted average of ex post before-tax real rates on the various types of credit constituting total short-term credit.
b. Standard deviation across the various types of credit.
c. During this period there were quantitative restrictions on free credit.

A possibly related phenomenon is the large spread between debitory and creditory banking rates. The spread, which was more than 9% on a monthly basis in the first two months after stabilization, was about 2.5% in November 1986. But even this seemingly modest number is rather high because it implies a yearly real differential of 34%. The high concentration of the Israeli banking industry is probably an additional important factor contributing to this large spread.[14]

In contrast to short-term rates, long-term subsidized rates to housing and industry were not seriously affected by the stabilization. They increased but substantially less than short-term rates (columns 4 and 5 of table 2.4).

Tax Revenues

The inflationary slowdown brought about by the stabilization package also improved the efficiency of tax collections, particularly of direct taxes from the self-employed and corporations. Total taxes as a fraction of GNP increased from 44.3% just before stabilization to 47.9% in the first quarter after stabilization and continued to increase further into the 50% range and above later (more details appear in columns 6 and 7 of table 2.1).

Gross Domestic Investment

Gross domestic capital formation as a fraction of GNP reached a peak in 1983. The stabilization program reinforced a steady decline in domestic capital formation that had started in early 1984. The bottom of 16.8% of GNP was reached in the second quarter after stabilization. Since then the rate of investment has been on a modest recovery path.

Inflation Variance and Relative Price Variability

Comparison of columns 1 and 2 of table 2.5 suggests that, generally, mean inflation and its variability are positively related, as they were in the previous decade (Cukierman and Leiderman 1985). Before the July 1985 stabilization inflation variability reached an all-time high of 5.6% after being only a little less than 4.8% in 1984. This dramatic increase in variability reflects the stop-go policies of government that intensified as the resolve to make fundamental changes crystallized during the latter part of 1984 and the first half of 1985. Following stabilization the variability of

**Table 2.5**
Inflation, sectoral inflation, inflation variance, and relative price variability[a] (yearly averages of monthly rates in percent)

| Period | (1) $\bar{\pi}$ | (2) $\sqrt{V(\pi)}$ | (3) $\sqrt{V(\pi^R)}$ | (4) $\bar{\pi}_F$ | (5) $\bar{\pi}_C$ |
|---|---|---|---|---|---|
| 1976[b] | 2.7 | 1.6 | 3.2 | 2.6 | 2.9 |
| 1977 | 2.9 | 2.6 | 3.5 | 2.8 | 3.2 |
| 1978 | 3.3 | 1.5 | 3.2 | 3.6 | 2.4 |
| 1979 | 6.3 | 2.1 | 5.1 | 6.0 | 7.0 |
| 1980 | 6.9 | 2.1 | 4.9 | 6.8 | 7.3 |
| 1981 | 5.8 | 2.0 | 5.0 | 6.2 | 4.9 |
| 1982 | 7.0 | 1.3 | 4.2 | 6.9 | 7.2 |
| 1983 | 8.9 | 4.3 | 5.1 | 8.8 | 9.1 |
| 1984 | 14.1 | 4.8 | 4.4 | 14.3 | 13.8 |
| 1985 (January–July) | 13.4 | 5.6 | 5.9 | 12.2 | 15.7 |
| 1985 (August–December) | 2.6 | 1.5 | 5.8 | 3.2 | 1.4 |
| 1986[c] | 1.0 | 1.3 | 3.3 | 0.6 | 1.6 |

Source: Calculations were made using raw data from *Price Statistics Monthly*, various issues.
a. $\bar{\pi}$ is the average monthly inflation during the year. $\sqrt{V(\pi)}$ is the standard deviation of monthly inflation over the year. $V(\pi^R)$ is a yearly average of the cross-sectional monthly variances of relative price changes. $\bar{\pi}_F$ is the average monthly inflation during the year in the free sector. $\bar{\pi}_C$ is the average monthly inflation during the year in the controlled sector. More precise definitions of the variables appear in Cukierman and Leiderman (1985).
b. Excluding January.
c. Excluding December.

inflation dropped immediately to levels similar to those experienced during the mid-1970s.

Relative price variability also generally increases with inflation (columns 1 and 3 of table 2.5). It reached a peak of 5.9% in the first seven months of 1985 and decreased only slightly after the stabilization, to 5.8%. But in 1986 relative price variability was back in the range it was in 1976, when yearly inflation was a little over 30%. The slow decrease in relative price variability following stabilization suggests that price controls were applied with a nonnegligible degree of flexibility. Despite the price freeze, substantial (by historical standards) changes in relative prices among major groups of goods were allowed. This may be one of the reasons for the small number of shortages observed after stabilization. Other possible reasons are discussed in section 2.3 (see in particular note 34). A factor that might have contributed to the slow decrease in relative price variability following stabilization is the large degree of asynchronization between the rate of growth of M1, which was very high—12.8% per month on average during the last five months of 1985—in comparison to average inflation of only 1.6% in the controlled sector of the economy. Theory suggests that asynchronization between those two nominal policy variables increases relative price variability (Cukierman and Leiderman 1984).

The Relative Price of Controlled Goods

As can be seen from figure 2.1, the stabilization reinforced a steady trend of increase in the relative price of controlled goods. This trend started during the first package deal at the end of 1984. Following stabilization there was some erosion in this relative price, but since the end of 1985 it has continued to increase and has remained overall at a high level by historical standards.

The Rate of Unemployment

The increase in unemployment following stabilization was relatively small (from 6.5% before stabilization to 7.5% in the first quarter after it) and short-lived. Details appear in column 5 of table 2.2. This is an additional symptom of the relatively high credibility commanded by the program.

## 2.3   Do Unorthodox Measures Improve the Efficiency of Stabilization?

The July 1985 Israeli stabilization package combined traditional anti inflationary measures, such as fiscal and monetary restraint, with unorthodox measures, such as pegging of the exchange rate and a temporary price freeze. Many well-bred economists would agree that, once the fundamental factors (excessive monetary growth and the associated budgetary deficit) have been straightened out, there is no further need to operate directly on the price level or on some of its components. Moreover, such actions are not only unnecessary but also harmful because they prevent the price system from performing its allocational function efficiently. On the other hand, it is somewhat hard to believe that a stabilization package based only on the fundamental components of the actual package would have brought Israeli inflation down so quickly, if at all.

A more likely scenario is that, because of high inflationary expectations at the inception of the program,[15] some wages and prices would have been adjusted upward. In the absence of any monetary accommodation, the increase in wages would have created an increase in unemployment. In addition, the increase in some free prices, by decreasing the relative price of subsidized goods, would have increased demand for these goods, forcing a higher subsidy budget on the government. Because Israeli policymakers are sensitive to unemployment, it is likely that the increase in unemployment would have triggered some monetary accommodation, thus validating at least part of the initially high inflationary expectations. A similar inflationary temptation would have been exerted by the larger real value of subsidies. In attempting to reduce the real budgetary spending on subsidies to its former level, the government would again increase the nominal price of subsidized goods, creating a further round of price increases and further validating the initially high inflationary expectations.[16]

The essential element of this counterfactual process is that high inflationary expectations at the inception of the program or a little before it induce policymakers to take actions that at least partly validate these expectations, thus justifying the policy's initial lack of credibility. The policymakers' actions then perpetuate the high inflationary expectations, which lead to a further round of the process and may even cause a total abandonment of stabilization. If, on the other hand, the price level is precommitted until inflationary expectations have declined, this process can be avoided altogether. Then, once the freeze is lifted, because expectations have already adjusted downward, the government has no incentive to accommodate or to increase the price of controlled goods, a fact the public is aware of. As a result, inflation stabilizes immediately at the lower level compatible with the lower budgetary deficit and slower monetary expansion. Essentially direct precommitment of the price level helps the (benevolent?) government to avoid the temptation to accommodate, so long as those temptations are the result of initially excessively high inflationary expectations.

In this section I derive a more precise example of the intuitive mechanism and identify circumstances under which a heterodox stabilization package involving both fiscal and monetary restraint and direct temporary fixing of the price level is preferable to a package featuring only orthodox measures. In Israel total direct fixing of the price level can be achieved by pegging the exchange rate, the price of controlled goods, and the price of nontradable goods. Credible pegging of the exchange rate precommits the price level of tradable goods to their internationally determined path but does not precommit the other two components. I assume, as a first approximation, that pegging of the exchange rate is sufficient to precommit credibly the entire price level.[17] This simplification is implemented formally by considering a one-good small open economy that takes international prices as given.

The example is based on a version of the Kydland-Prescott, Barro-Gordon dynamic inconsistency kind of monetary policy game in conjunction with staggered nominal wage contracts of the Fischer type.[18] In order to maintain the example within manageable proportions, I abstract from balance of payments and subsidization considerations and focus instead on the following three policy objectives:[19] (1) maintenance of unemployment at a target level that is lower than the natural rate, (2) derivation of some target revenues from the inflation tax, and (3) price stability. The policymakers are assumed to have a loss function that is a linear combination of the squared differences of unemployment, the inflation tax, and the rate of inflation from their respective targets. Unemployment in the economy decreases when the real wage rate falls. The real wage is lower (given the overhang of outstanding nominal contracts) when the current rate of inflation is higher. Because higher inflationary expectations at the time of contract negotiations mean higher nominal wages, so, for a given present inflation rate, higher past expectations will raise unemployment. But at a higher rate of unemployment policymakers have an incentive to increase inflation. Thus staggered nominal contracts and the increasing aversion of policymakers to unemployment create a positive link between recent past inflationary expectations and the degree of current monetary accommodation. This is true no matter what the size of the inflation tax that policymakers desire to extract from the process of money creation; the link is particularly clear when the target inflation tax falls.

Suppose now that the budgetary deficit is trimmed and that consequently the target inflation tax also goes down. This reduces the incentive of policymakers to inflate because of revenue considerations but does not immediately affect their incentive to inflate because of employment considerations. If recent inflationary expectations are high, the policymakers will continue to accommodate at a rate that is lower than the rate of accommodation before the budget cut but still higher than the rate they would have chosen had inflationary expectations been lower. Because labor unions are aware of these incentives, they expect inflation to come down somewhat, but not as much as they would have in the absence of the overhang of past expectations. Obviously the wage settlements made after the budgetary cut will incorporate these intermediate inflationary expectations, inducing policymakers to continue to accommodate at the intermediate rate. As a result, even if the inflationary process converges eventually to a long-run rate that is compatible with the diminished need for seigniorage, it may take awhile to get there.

Note that, because all goods are traded, there is a one-to-one relationship between the domestic price level and the rate of exchange. Hence the terms "inflation" and "devaluation" or "price level" and "rate of exchange" may be used interchangeably.

Consider, on the other hand, a credible temporary fixing of the exchange rate that is imposed concurrently with the decrease in the budget deficit and the target inflation tax. Because the fixing is credible, expectations come down immediately, eliminating the effect of the high prestabilization inflationary expectations on the poststabilization degree of accommodation. After awhile the fixing can be released without any increase in inflation because the link between the prestabilization high inflationary expectations and the poststabilization level of accommodation has been broken by the fixing. As a result, inflation is lower with a fixed exchange rate not only during the fixing but after it as well. Provided that the target inflation tax is reduced permanently, the long-run rate of inflation will eventually be the same with or without direct policy actions on the price level. But in the first case it will be lower on the transition path both during and after the fixing of the exchange rate. I now turn to a more detailed presentation of the economic and policymaking framework that underlies the preceding discussion.

The Labor Market and Unemployment

All of the labor force is unionized in three equally sized unions (labeled $a$, $b$, and $c$), each of which signs a three-period nominal wage contract every third period for the next three periods. Contracts are staggered so that in every period the first union is in the first period of its contract, the second union is in the second period of its contract, and the third union is in the last period of its contract. Each union aims at achieving some target average real wage over the contract period.[20] This real wage rate and the price levels expected by the union for the next three periods determine the nominal wage contract to be in effect during these periods.[21] Union $a$ signs its wage contract at the end of period $t - 3$ (knowing the price level of that period) on the basis of its price forecast for periods $t - 2$, $t - 1$ and $t$. More precisely it sets the nominal wage according to

$$W_{t-2}^a = \tfrac{1}{3}(_{t-3}p_{t-2}^* + {}_{t-3}p_{t-1}^* + {}_{t-3}p_t^* + v^a),$$  (2.1a)

where $W_{t-2}^a$ is the natural logarithm of the nominal wage rate and $_{t-3}p_t^*$ is the logarithm of the price level in period $t$ as forecasted by the union in period $t-3$.[22] $v^a$ is an index of the bargaining power or militancy of the union. The larger $v^a$ is, the higher the target real wage of the union. Similarly, the nominal wage rates agreed on by the other two unions in periods $t-2$ and $t-1$, respectively, are

$$W_{t-1}^b = \tfrac{1}{3}(_{t-2}p_{t-1}^* + _{t-2}p_t^* + _{t-2}p_{t+1}^* + v^b), \tag{2.1b}$$

$$W_t^c = \tfrac{1}{3}(_{t-1}p_t^* + _{t-1}p_{t+1}^* + _{t-1}p_{t+2}^* + v^c). \tag{2.1c}$$

The deviation of unemployment within each union from the natural rate of unemployment of the union is directly related to the real wage of the union:

$$U_t^a - U_n^a = 3\theta(W_{t-2}^a - p_t), \tag{2.2a}$$

$$U_t^b - U_n^b = 3\theta(W_{t-1}^b - p_t), \tag{2.2b}$$

$$U_t^c - U_n^c = 3\theta(W_t^c - p_t). \tag{2.2c}$$

Here $U_t^i$ and $U_n^i$ are the actual and the natural rates of unemployment within union $i$, $\theta$ is a positive parameter, and $p_t$ is the logarithm of the actual price level in period $t$. The deviation of total unemployment $u_t$ from the economy-wide natural rate $U_n$ is equal to the sum of the three terms in equations (2.2). By using this fact, substituting equations (2.1) into equations (2.2), and transforming price levels into actual or expected rates of inflation, we obtain

$$U_t - U_n = -\theta[6\pi_t + 3\pi_{t-1} + \pi_{t-2} - (\pi_{t-2}^* + 2\pi_{t-1}^* + 3\pi_t^*$$

$$+ 3\pi_{t+1}^* + _{t-1}\pi_{t+2}^* + v)], \tag{2.3}$$

where

$$\pi_t \equiv p_t - p_{t-1}, \qquad \pi_t^* \equiv _{t-1}p_t^* - p_{t-1},$$

$$_{t-1}\pi_{t+2}^* \equiv _{t-1}p_{t+2}^* - _{t-1}p_{t+1}^*, \qquad v \equiv v^a + v^b + v^c. \tag{2.4}$$

Equation (2.3) expresses the fact that, in general, the higher the actual inflation rates and the lower the expected inflation rates and the real wage rates demanded by unions, the lower the economy-wide rate of unemployment. The precise lag structures of actual and expected inflations in this equation reflect the structure of staggering and the relative size of the unions.

The Money Market, Aggregate Demand, and the Balance of Payments

The demand for money has the familiar form

$$(X_t^n)^\alpha e^{-\beta \pi_{t+1}^*} Y_t^{-\gamma},$$

where $X_t^n$ is the natural rate of output, $Y_t$ is a stochastic shock to money demand, $e$ is the base of the natural logarithm, and $\alpha$, $\beta$, and $\gamma$ are positive parameters.[23] Money market equilibrium implies

$$M_t/P_t = (X_t^n)^\alpha e^{-\beta \pi_{t+1}^*} Y_t^{-\gamma}, \tag{2.5}$$

where $M_t$ is nominal money balances and $P_t = e^{p_t}$. $P_t$ may also be written $P_t = q_t P^F$, where $P^F$ is the foreign price level that is taken as given and $q_t$ is the exchange rate. By normalizing $P^F$ to 1, we obtain $P_t = q_t$. Hence, given money demand, the equilibrium condition in equation (2.5) determines both the price level and the rate of exchange. Essentially, by choosing the money supply, policymakers determine the price level and the rate of exchange. By taking natural logarithms of equation (2.5), taking first differences of the resulting expression, and rearranging, we obtain

$$\pi_t = m_t - \alpha x_t^n + \beta(\pi_{t+1}^* - \pi_t^*) + \gamma y_t, \tag{2.6}$$

where

$$m_t \equiv \log M_t - \log M_{t-1},$$

$$x_t^n \equiv \log X_t^n - \log X_{t-1}^n,$$

$$y_t \equiv \log Y_t - \log Y_{t-1},$$

and $\pi_t$ is both the rate of inflation and the rate of depreciation of the currency. Equation (2.6) is a dynamic version of the money market equilibrium condition. It states that the rate of inflation increases when money growth is higher and increases as the rate of growth of natural output falls. The larger the increase in inflationary expectations between the current and the previous period and the larger the rate of decrease $y_t$ in the demand for real money balances between the current and the previous period because of exogenous shocks, the higher the rate of inflation. Such a decrease in the demand for domestic money, resulting from liberalization of restrictions on holdings of foreign exchange, was one of the causes for the acceleration of inflation in 1979. Because the main focus of the model is on the interaction between labor unions and policymakers, the description of demand and the balance of payments is sketchy. Excess demand takes the form of balance of payments deficits that are financed by unilateral transfers or increases in foreign indebtedness. Thus, when real wages rise, causing a decrease in employment and output, the resulting increase in excess demand is satisfied through an increase in the balance of payments deficit.

Policymakers' Objectives

The policymakers' loss function is

$$\frac{A}{2}\left(\ln \frac{T_{t-1}}{T_d}\right)^2 + \frac{B}{2}(U_t - KU_n)^2 + \frac{1}{2}\pi_t^2, \tag{2.7}$$

where $T_{t-1}$ and $T_d$ are, respectively, the actual and the desired inflation taxes as fractions of natural output; $A$ and $B$ are positive coefficients that reflect the costs to policymakers of being away from their preferred inflation tax and unemployment targets relative to being away from their preferred inflation target, which is 0. $K$ is a number between 0 and 1 that reflects the fact that the level of employment set by unions is lower than the level preferred by policymakers.[24] If we assume that, when policymakers increase the money supply between $t - 1$ and $t$ to buy goods, they buy those goods at period $t - 1$ prices, we obtain [using equation (2.5)]

$$T_{t-1} = \frac{M_t - M_{t-1}}{P_{t-1}X_{t-1}^n} = (e^{m_t} - 1)e^{-\beta\pi_t^*}(X_{t-1}^n)^{\alpha-1}Y_{t-1}^{-\gamma}. \tag{2.8}$$

I assume henceforth for expositional simplicity that $X_t^n = Y_t = 1$ for all $t$. As a consequence, equations (2.6) and (2.8) reduce to

$$\pi_t = m_t + \beta(\pi_{t+1}^* - \pi_t^*), \tag{2.6'}$$

$$T_{t-1} = (e^{m_t} - 1)e^{-\beta\pi_t^*}. \tag{2.8'}$$

By approximating $\ln(e^{m_t} - 1)$ linearly around some fixed positive value of $m$ (say, $\bar{m}$) and using equation (2.8'),[25] we obtain

$$\ln \frac{T_{t-1}}{T_d} = am_t - \beta\pi_t^* - (\ln T_d + a\bar{m}). \tag{2.9}$$

Using equations (2.3), (2.6'), and (2.9) in equation (2.7), the policymakers' objective can be reformulated as

$$\min_{m_t}\left[\frac{A}{2}(am_t - \beta\pi_t^* - \ln T_d - a\bar{m})^2 + \frac{B}{2}((1 - K)U_n - \theta\{6[m_t \right.$$
$$\left. + \beta(\pi_{t+1}^* - \pi_t^*)] + 3\pi_{t-1} + \pi_{t-2} - \pi^*\})^2 + \frac{1}{2}[m_t + \beta(\pi_{t+1}^* - \pi_t^*)]^2\right], \tag{2.10}$$

where

$$\pi^* = \pi^*_{t-2} + 2\pi^*_{t-1} + 3\pi^*_t + 3\pi^*_{t+1} + {}_{t-1}\pi^*_{t+2} + . v.$$

The policymakers take expectations as given and choose the rate of monetary growth $m_t$ so as to minimize their weighted losses resulting from deviations from their preferred targets for unemployment, inflation, and the inflation tax. From the necessary first-order condition for the minimization of these losses, we obtain

$$m_t = \frac{1}{D}\{G + 6\theta^2 B_{t-1}\pi^*_{t+2} + [18\theta^2 B - \beta(1 + 36\theta^2 B)]\pi^*_{t+1}$$

$$+ [18\theta^2 B(1 + 2\beta) + \beta(1 + aA)]\pi^*_t + 6\theta^2 B(\pi^*_{t-2} + 2\pi^*_{t-1}$$

$$- 3\pi_{t-1} - \pi_{t-2})\}, \quad (2.11)$$

where

$$D \equiv a^2 A + 36\theta^2 B + 1,$$

$$G \equiv aA \ln T_d + 6\theta(1 - K)BU_n + 6\theta^2 Bv + a^2 A\bar{m}.$$

Equation (2.11) is the accommodation rule followed by the policymakers. Note that they will choose to expand the money supply at a higher rate when the target inflation tax $T_d$ is higher, when the target rate of unemployment $KU_n$, is lower, when the real wages $v^i$ ($i = a, b, c$) demanded by unions are higher and when those past inflationary expectations that became embodied in labor contracts are higher.[26] This last element is crucial because it creates a positive relationship between current monetary expansion and past inflationary expectations. This relationship result from the policymakers' attempt to prevent large deviations of actual from desired unemployment in any given period. Substituting equation (2.11) into equation (2.6') and rearranging gives

$$\pi_t = \frac{1}{D}\{G + 6\theta^2 B_{t-1}\pi^*_{t+2} + (a^2\beta A + 18\theta^2 B)\pi^*_{t+1} + [a(1 - a)\beta A$$

$$+ 18\theta^2 B]\pi^*_t + 6\theta^2 B(2\pi^*_{t-1} + \pi^*_{t-2} - \pi_{t-2} - 3\pi_{t-1})\}. \quad (2.12)$$

Equation (2.12) describes the basic dynamic interaction between current inflation on the one hand and the rates of inflation currently expected for the future and previous inflationary expectations on the other hand. It embodies the structure of contracts in the economy and the accommodation rule of the policymakers.

Expectations, Steady State, and the Dynamics of Inflation

The unions' expectations are rational. Because they know the structure of the economy and the policymakers' decision rule, they use equation (2.12) in order to calculate $\pi_t^*$ as $\pi_t^* = E_{t-1}\pi_t$. In the presence of stochastic shocks (such as $y_t$), $\pi_t^*$ and $\pi_t$ will in general be different. However, because I have eliminated this uncertainty (by assuming $Y_t = 1$ for all $t$), $\pi_t^* = \pi_t$ and $_{t-1}\pi_{t+2}^* = \pi_{t+2}$ for all $t$.[27] Using those relations in equation (2.12) and rearranging, we obtain

$$\pi_{t+2} + d\pi_{t+1} - c\pi_t - \pi_{t-1} = \frac{-G}{6\theta^2 B} \quad \text{or}$$

$$\pi_t = \frac{G}{6\theta^2 Bc} - \frac{1}{c}\pi_{t-1} + \frac{d}{c}\pi_{t+1} + \frac{1}{c}\pi_{t+2}, \tag{2.13}$$

where

$$d \equiv \frac{1}{6\theta^2 B}(a^2\beta A + 18\theta^2 B), \tag{2.14a}$$

$$c \equiv \frac{1}{6\theta^2 B}\{a[a(1+\beta) - \beta]A + 18\theta^2 B + 1\}. \tag{2.14b}$$

The two forms of the difference equation in equation (2.13) are equivalent. The first one is useful for the mathematical solution, whereas the second one is easier to interpret in terms of the model's fundamentals. It states that, because of the structure of contracts and policymakers' objectives, current inflation depends on past and future inflationary expectations. In steady state $\pi_t = \pi$ for all $t$, given $G$. Substituting this condition into equation (2.13) and rearranging, we obtain

$$\pi = \frac{G}{6(c-d)\theta^2 B} = \frac{aA \ln T_d + 6\theta(1-K)BU_n + 6\theta^2 Bv + a^2 A\bar{m}}{1 + (a-\beta)aA}. \tag{2.15}$$

If $1 + (a - \beta)aA > 0$, an increase in either the target inflation tax $T_d$ or real wages $v^i$ ($i = a, b, c$) targeted by unions or a decrease in the target rate of unemployment $KU_n$ increases the steady-state rate of inflation. I assume that this is the case.[28] The positive effect of $T_d$ on $\pi$ reflects the fact that, if the policymakers have a higher target inflation tax, they choose a higher rate of monetary growth.[29] The negative effect of the unemployment target $KU_n$ on $\pi$ reflects the Kydland-Prescott, Barro-Gordon unsuccessful attempt of policymakers to push unemployment below the natural rate

(Kydland and Prescott 1977; Barro and Gordon 1983). The lower the target level of unemployment, the larger the steady-state inflation generated by this attempt. Similarly, the positive effect of the real wages demanded by unions on the rate of inflation reflects the unsuccessful attempt of policymakers to offset the negative effect of increases in these wages on the level of employment.

Comparison of Stabilization with and without Pegging of the Exchange Rate

*Orthodox Stabilization*
Suppose that until period 0 the budget deficit as a fraction of natural output is large; consequently the most preferred inflation tax as a fraction of natural output $(T_d)$ is also large. Starting from the end of period 0, policymakers unexpectedly stabilize by decreasing the budget deficit and therefore $T_d$. Suppose further that the decrease in the deficit and in $T_d$ is permanent and is implemented in a credible manner. Hence it is believed to be permanent. Let $\pi_H$ and $\pi_L$ be the steady-state rates of inflation [from equation (2.15)] corresponding to the values of $T_d$ before and after the budgetary cut, respectively. Because the cut takes effect at the end of period 0, $\pi_0$ is generated by the old regime, and $\pi_t$ for $t \geq 1$ is generated by the new regime. Furthermore, because the budgetary cut is a surprise, expectations formed before it about the poststabilization era are not necessarily fulfilled. Hence equation (2.12) [rather than equation (2.13)] describes the path of inflation during the first three periods following stabilization. The explicit form for the rates of inflation generated by this equation can be obtained by specializing it to the cases $t = 1, 2, 3$. For example,

$$\pi_3 = \frac{1}{D}\{G_L + 6\theta^2 B(\pi_1^* - \pi_1 + \pi_5 - \pi_2) + [a(1-a)\beta A + 18\theta^2 B]\pi_3$$

$$+ [a^2\beta A + 18\theta^2 B]\pi_4\}. \quad (2.16)$$

Note that $\pi_1^* \neq \pi_1$ because the expected inflation $\pi_1^*$ is formed in period 0 before the public becomes aware of the budget cut that takes place at the end of period 0. From the fourth period following the budget cut, equation (2.12) involves only expectations that are formed after stabilization. Hence expectations are fulfilled and the subsequent path of inflation is described by equation (2.13). This is a third-order difference equation whose general solution is

$$\pi_t = \pi_L + K_1\lambda_1^t + K_2\lambda_2^t + K_3\lambda_3^t, \quad (2.17)$$

where $K_i$, $i = 1, 2, 3$, are determined by the initial or end conditions of the system and $\lambda_i$, $i = 1, 2, 3$, are the roots of the polynomial

$$\lambda^3 + d\lambda^2 - c\lambda - 1 = 0. \tag{2.18}$$

It is shown in section A.1 of the appendix that at least one of the roots is larger than 1 in absolute value and at least one is smaller than 1 in absolute value. Thus, in general, the steady state in equation (2.15) is unstable because any shock that pushes the economy off the steady state starts a process of ever accelerating inflation or deflation. This rather unreasonable feature is shared by a whole class of models of money with perfect foresight and has been discussed before by Sargent and Wallace (1973). They eliminate the instability by imposing a transversality condition that prevents money and expectations from growing too fast.[30] This condition implies that, following the receipt of new information about the future course of money, the price level jumps discretely so as to put it on a stable path. In the context of the present model the analogous requirement is that the rate of inflation immediately following the budget cut jumps so as to equilibrate the money market following the news of stabilization and impose zero values on the coefficients $K_i$ of all the roots with absolute values that are larger than 1. Because at least one of the roots is larger than 1 in absolute value, this implies that the stable branch of the solution in equation (2.17) will involve only one or two roots. I focus, for simplicity, on the case in which the stable branch involves one root. Let $\lambda_2$ and $\lambda_3$ be the unstable roots and $\lambda_1$ the stable root. Stability requires that $K_2 = K_3 = 0$. This is achieved by suitably adjusting $\pi_1$ and $\pi_2$ subject to the constraint that they both lie along the new equilibrium path of inflation.[31] As a consequence, the path of inflation following the budget cut is characterized by

$$\pi_t = \pi_L + K_1 \lambda_1^t \qquad \text{for } t \geqslant 1, \tag{2.19}$$

which is stable because $|\lambda_1| < 1$. The constant $K_1$ is determined by the requirement that the rate of inflation in the third period following stabilization be equal to the right-hand side of equation (2.16) and that $\pi_t$ satisfy equation (2.19) for all $t \geqslant 1$, including in particular $t = 1$ and $t = 2$. The formal details of the solution are worked out in section A.2 of the appendix. The resulting solution for $K_1$ is

$$K_1 = \frac{6\theta^2 B(\pi_1^* - \pi_L)}{6\theta^2 B(\lambda_1 + \lambda_1^2 - \lambda_1^5) + (18\theta^2 B + a^2 \beta A)(1 - \lambda_1)\lambda_1^3 + [1 + aA(a - \beta)]\lambda_1^3}$$

$$\equiv k(\pi_1^* - \pi_L). \tag{2.20}$$

It is shown in section A.2 that $\lambda_1$ is positive. Because it is also smaller than 1 and because $1 + aA(a - \beta)$ is positive, the denominator of equation (2.20) is positive. Because the expectation $\pi_1^*$ had been formed before the budget cut became common knowledge, it is higher than the postcut steady-state inflation $\pi_L$. Hence the numerator is also positive, and thus $K_1$ is positive. Furthermore, the larger the cut in the budget deficit, the larger the difference $\pi_1^* - \pi_L$ and therefore the larger $K_1$.

Note that, although the rate of inflation "jumps" between period 0 and period 1, all $\pi_t - s$ for $t \geqslant 1$, including in particular $\pi_1$ and $\pi_2$, are part of the (new) stable equilibrium path because they all satisfy equation (2.19), which is the stable solution to the difference equation (2.13).[32]

*Heterodox Stabilization*
Consider now a stabilization program in which the same decrease in $T_d$ is accompanied by a direct credible precommitment for the rate of depreciation at $\pi_L$ in period 2.[33] Because now $\pi_2 = \pi_L$, equation (2.13) implies

$$\pi_3 = \frac{G_L}{6\theta^2 Bc} - \frac{1}{c}\pi_L + \frac{d}{c}\pi_4 + \frac{1}{c}\pi_5, \tag{2.13'}$$

where $G_L$ is the value of $G$ that corresponds to $\pi_L$ by means of equation (2.15). If expectations regarding future inflation also move to $\pi_L$, then $\pi_3 = \pi_L$ and the economy enters the new lower steady-state path in period 4. It is shown in section A.3 of the appendix that, if equation (2.19) is the solution for the path of inflation following a stabilization without exchange rate management, then a one-period intervention that sets $\pi_2 = \pi_L$ is sufficient to bring all future expected rates of inflation to $\pi_L$. Essentially the requirement of "no bubbles" or steady-state stability ensures (in the case of one stable root) that a one-period precommitment of the exchange rate causes both actual and expected inflation to jump to their steady-state values. This eliminates the problem of dynamic inconsistency resulting from past high inflationary expectations and the high-employment objective of the policymakers. The curve labeled $hh$ in figure 2.2 describes the path of inflation in this case. The difference between the paths of the rate of inflation with and without a freeze is given by [using equations (2.19) and (2.20)]

$$k(\pi_1^* - \pi_L)\lambda_1^t \qquad \text{for } t \geqslant 2. \tag{2.21}$$

Because $k > 0$, this is a positive difference that eventually disappears but that may be substantial for a while, particularly if the difference between $\pi_1^*$

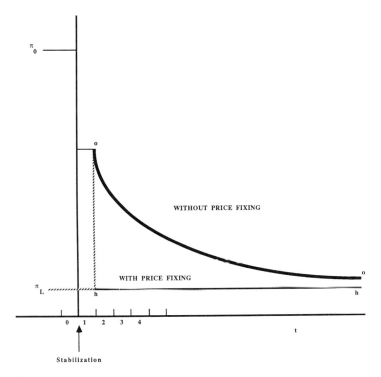

**Figure 2.2**
Path of inflation for orthodox and heterodox stabilizations. The curve *oo* is a continuous approximation of the exact curve that is a step function.

and $\pi_L$ is large, as it was in the case of the Israeli stabilization. (Further discussion of this point appears later.)

A further intuitive account of these results is as follows: A cut in $T_d$ reduces policymakers' incentive to inflate because of revenue considerations but does not eliminate their incentive to inflate in order to maintain high employment, particularly when prestabilization inflationary expectations are high. As a result, the overhang of these expectations continues to affect policymakers' actions after stabilization. Because unions understand this, they expect inflation to decrease slowly. They do not, therefore, cut the increase in their wage demands quickly, thus obligating the policymakers to respond with a nonnegligible degree of monetary accommodation even after stabilization. With a *temporary* credible precommitment of the price level by means of the exchange rate, expectations decline immediately because the precommitment is credible. As a result, policymakers' incentive to inflate because of employment considerations diminishes immediately. Unions are aware of this and tune down their wage demands accordingly. As a consequence, policymakers' incentives to inflate even after removal of the exchange rate precommitment are weaker. This result may explain why, despite the fixing of most major prices (including the exchange rate) during the Israeli stabilization, no substantial shortages developed (see also the discussion on relative price variability in section 2.2).[34]

The main conclusion of this section is that a suitably devised temporary direct intervention with the price level that comes after a budget cut allows the economy to reach the new lower steady-state rate of inflation more quickly.

Interpretation of the Model in Light of the Israeli Experience and Some Qualifications

The model presented is meant to illustrate the potential benefits of temporarily intervening to set the price level during stabilization in a framework that is not too dissimilar to the actual Israeli economy. However, because like all models it is an abstraction, further elaborations and qualifications are in order.

First, the model assumes that the price level can be totally precommitted by managing the exchange rate. This abstracts from the fact that even with a precommitted exchange rate other components of the price level, such as the price of nontradables and the price of controlled goods, can change. Tight control of the price level requires the precommitment of those prices as well. This is probably why a price freeze was imposed in addition to pegging the exchange rate during the Israeli stabilization. The model could be extended to incorporate a situation in which the exchange rate is only one of several factors determining the general price level. The novel element in this case is that full precommitment of the price level requires the use of several nominal anchors, as was done during the Israeli stabilization.[35] The result that such a temporary precommitment can speed the way to the lower steady-state inflation obviously still holds. Whether one or several anchors that operate directly on components of the price level are used depends on the risk aversion of unions and on whether there is a subset of anchors that can tightly precommit the price level. In general, the larger the number of anchors used, the higher the credibility of the precommitment to fix the path of the price level. This is probably why several direct anchors were used in the Israeli case. The cost of such a tighter precommitment is that less room is left for relative price adjustments during the period of price level fixing. Whether the benefit is worth the cost depends inter alia on the magnitude of the prestabilization inflation in comparison to the size of necessary relative price adjustments.

A related question is whether the price level should be precommitted through the money supply or through direct fixing of components of the price level, such as the exchange rate. In the absence of stochastic shocks the answer given by the model is that the two forms of precommitment are equivalent. However, once stochastic shocks (such as the money demand shock $y_t$) are acknowledged, direct precommitment of the price level, if feasible, is more credible because the relationship between the money supply and the price level is subject to noise.

Second, it should be stressed that the model supports *temporary* fixing of the price level rather than a long-term price freeze. Essentially the model interpreted broadly implies that fixing should be maintained for as long as inflationary expectations have not adjusted to the lower steady-state rate of inflation. Judging from the behavior of unexpected inflation from table 2.3, this point was reached somewhere at the beginning of 1986. On this view pegging of the exchange rate and the partial price freeze that were maintained later on did not contribute much to inflation stabilization.

Third, the precise dynamics of inflation in the model obviously depend on the postulated structure of contracts. But the result that a temporary precommitment of the price level following a budget cut speeds the way to the lower steady-state inflation transcends the particular structure presented here. The gains from price level or exchange rate fixing are an increasing function of the difference between prestabilization inflation and its poststabilization steady-state level. In the model presented, equation (2.21) suggests that the relevant variable is the difference between expected inflation just before stabilization, $\pi_1^*$, and the new steady-state inflation $\pi_L$. The numbers in table 2.3 give an idea of the order of magnitude involved. If we take $\pi_L$ to be 1.5% per month, this difference was 16.1% or 9.2% per month, depending on whether the last period before stabilization became common knowledge is taken to be June or July 1985. Even the lower number is quite substantial, suggesting that the direct setting of the price level initially contributed a lot to pacifying inflation.

Fourth, the model implies that an increase in the militancy or bargaining power of unions as measured by $v^i$, $i = a, b, c$, causes an increase in the equilibrium rate of inflation because of the government's attempt to maintain high employment. This is consistent with the positive correlation detected between the real wage and the rate of inflation in Israel (Helpman and Leiderman 1987).

Fifth, the model implies that, the lower the average level of real wages at the inception of stabilization, the smaller the government's temptation to inflate because of employment considerations. A low real wage rate diminishes the size of this temptation and therefore increases the program's credibility. On this view the large decrease in the average level of real wages at the program's inception (column 4 of table 2.2) was an important input into the program's success.

Sixth, if, as was the case in 1984, tax revenues decrease as the rate of inflation goes up, $T_d$ may not be independent of the rate of inflation. In terms of the model this implies that, by reducing the rate of inflation more, price or exchange rate fixing triggers a process that decreases the desired inflation tax. This induces a further contraction of nominal money growth and therefore enhances the credibility of the program.

Two final remarks regarding the appropriateness of the model for Israeli reality are in order. First, the model predicts that even with price fixing there is usually some increase in unemployment after stabilization. This is due to the surprise element, which increases the real wages of unions that concluded their wage contracts before stabilization became common knowledge. This implication is consistent with the observed movements in the rate of unemployment following stabilization (column 5 of table 2.2). Without the additional measures that decreased all real wages at the program's inception, unemployment would have been even higher. Second, the perfect foresight version of the model does not give a rationale for the eight months' precommitment of the path of nominal wages agreed on at the program's inception. However, in the presence of unforeseen shocks or in situations in which unions get real wages that are lower than desired, such a precommitment is needed to protect the government from unilateral hiking of wages after the exchange rate and other components of the price level have been precommitted.

## 2.4   Further Assessment of the Israeli Stabilization Program

The institutional structure of the Israeli economy makes it more likely that stabilization by orthodox means will succeed if accompanied by nonconventional measures. The relevant institutional features in this context are (1) practically total unionization of the labor force, (2) a high degree of openness of the economy, (3) a large proportion of labor force employed in the public sector (30% in 1985), (4) little control by the central bank of the money supply, and (5) a relatively large elasticity of the demand for money with respect to expected inflation, particularly at high rates of inflation.

Universal unionization, the large role of government as an employer, and the limited independence of the central bank create a situation in which stabilization becomes almost impossible without some agreement (a package deal) between the government and the Histadrut. Even if the government decides to engage unilaterally in contractionary policies, it is likely that wage demands will (at least for a while) continue unabated, pushing the government to accommodate. Hence no serious stabilization effort can be considered without some agreement between the government and the Histadrut. Paradoxically this centralization of power makes it easier to implement unorthodox measures, such as package deals, because the number of parties involved in negotiating them is limited. The high degree of openness of Israel facilitates such agreements because the government can, by precommitting the path of the exchange rate, exert a strong temporary influence on the domestic price level. However, this ability of the government and its ability to peg temporarily the prices of controlled goods are also liabilities because policymakers are encouraged to devise stabilization programs that are based only on such measures without (or with little) fiscal and monetary restraint. The failure of the 1984–85 package deals and the eventual failure of Aridor's policy at the end of 1983 suggest that such methods of stabilization are not viable in the long run and at times not even in the short run.

However, the success of the July 1985 stabilization and the dynamic inconsistency problems illustrated by the model presented here suggest that contractionary fiscal and monetary policies alone, unaided by package deals, are likely to take longer to deliver the same results. The lingering of inflation coupled with the increase in unemployment that would occur in such a case are undesirable features not only in their own right but also because they increase the danger that stabilization will be abandoned altogether. An essential feature of a viable stabilization package is that it deliver quick results.[36] Otherwise it is likely to be abandoned by policy-makers with short political horizons. The development of many instruments also raises the question of synchronization between them. By and large, synchronization and timing were in correct doses except perhaps for monetary policy, which might have been too restrictive initially.[37]

The Role of External Factors

Although good planning and a realistic assessment of policymakers' limitations (and of Israeli institutions) were important ingredients in the successful implementation of the 1985 stabilization, several fortunate external elements contributed to this success and its longevity as well. These were (1) the substantial two-year increase in US foreign aid; (2) the 1985–86 decrease in the price of oil, which alleviated the deficit in the balance of payments; (3) the depreciation of the US dollar in relation to European currencies, which maintained the competitiveness of Israeli exports in Europe (compare columns 6 and 7 of table 2.2) despite the pegging of the dollar rate of exchange for more than a year after July 1985 while wages and prices rose steadily from the last quarter of 1985; and (4) the decrease of the interest rate in international capital markets in 1985–86, which eased the burden of foreign debt service on the balance of payments. There is little doubt that in the absence of some or all of these developments it would have been necessary to adjust the exchange rate earlier, thus reducing its effectiveness as a nominal anchor.

Should the Exchange Rate Have Been Used As a Nominal Anchor?

There is an obvious conflict between using the exchange rate for stabilization purposes and using it as an instrument of balance of payments policy. How to use the exchange rate depends on the structure and the state of the economy and on the types of other policy instruments available. The high degree of openness, the high elasticity of money demand with respect to expected inflation, and the extensive system of indexation of the Israeli economy all favor the use of the exchange rate as a temporary instrument of stabilization.[38] The high degree of openness (including, in particular, the heavy dependence on imported raw materials) implies that a change in the exchange rate is swiftly incorporated into the local price level through costs, in contrast to fiscal and monetary changes that affect the price level with a longer lag. Because most of the national debt is indexed, the reduction in the public's wealth (and therefore the effect on aggregate demand and the balance of payments) that results from a devaluation is negligible. In addition, wage indexation transmits part of the increased price level to wages, further reducing the effectiveness of devaluation in correcting the balance of payments deficit and exacerbating inflation. There is some question as to whether or not this process leads to a permanently higher rate of inflation.[39] But there is little doubt that it reduces the effectiveness of the exchange rate as a potential equilibrator of the balance of payments and significantly increases the rate of inflation, at least temporarily. A large fraction of the government's budget is effectively indexed because government employee wages are indexed and many government procurement contracts are on a cost-plus basis. Hence an increase in inflation, even if temporary, creates an expansion in the nominal government budget.

The high elasticity of money demand with respect to expected inflation implies that a credible stabilization leads to a large increase in demand for real money balances, as evidenced by the large increase in seigniorage following stabilization (table 2.1). If the rate of exchange had been allowed to float and if strict money targets had been used, the increase in money demand would have put strong upward pressure on domestic real interest rates[10] and on the exchange rate, leading to a decrease in the competitiveness of exports and a fall in the level of employment. Even a central bank with as much independence as the Bundesbank and, a fortiori, the Bank of Israel would have found it difficult to implement monetary targets strictly under such circumstances. An obvious solution to this problem is to have flexible money targets that accommodate the increase in money demand resulting from stabilization but that otherwise adhere to some predetermined path. Such a modified monetary target requires precise knowledge of the elasticity of money demand and of the path for inflationary expectations during and after stabilization. Such a modified monetary anchor is difficult to implement because of the wide range of uncertainty regarding the change in money demand during stabilization. One of the advantages of an exchange rate anchor over a money anchor is that its implementation does not depend on the knowledge of the changes in money demand that are induced by the stabilization because the money supply adjusts automatically to fluctuations in money demand.

The obvious drawback of an exchange rate anchor is that it cannot be used for balance of payments adjustments. However, if other aggregate demand management instruments are used appropriately to restrain aggregate demand, the deficit in the balance of payments can be kept in line without frequent adjustments of the exchange rate. Another drawback of an exchange rate anchor is that, by ensuring relative nominal stability in the short run, it may weaken the resolve of policymakers to restrict demand by as much as necessary to maintain this exchange rate. Such a problem has been evident since early 1986 and is likely to worsen in 1987 as elections approach. Finally, an exchange rate anchor induces policymakers to encourage exports through various particular subsidization schemes that do not always reproduce the natural structure of comparative advantage for different exporters.

## 2.5   Concluding Comments

The Israeli stabilization effort managed to reduce inflation, almost instantaneously, from several hundred percent per annum to about 20% with only a minor decrease in economic activity. It also reduced temporarily domestic absorption and the real wage rate, contributing further to the balance of payments improvements that had started in late 1984. In terms of political will the major achievement was the large decrease in the government's budgetary deficit. But the program did not permanently decrease the deficit in the balance of payments, nor did it revive the stagnating growth rate of the Israeli economy.[41]

I would therefore be inclined to conclude that heterodox stabilization programs of the 1985 Israeli type can, under favorable external circumstances, stop inflation in its tracks almost immediately without significant unemployment and shortages. The speedy results and the small resource cost are due, in my opinion, to the combination of traditional aggregate demand contraction and an unorthodox temporary freeze of most major prices. The unorthodox component is needed in order to reduce dynamic inconsistency problems that would have slowed the process of disinflation otherwise. On the other hand, the failure of the package deals clearly demonstrates that unorthodox measures cannot do the job alone.

I believe that success on the inflation front is permanent in the sense that it is unlikely that inflation will penetrate the 50% range again within the next few years. Success in reducing the deficit in the balance of payments and in keeping domestic absorption down is likely to be substantially more temporary. There has been since early 1986 a persistent deteriorating trend in the balance of payments, and the recently approved 1987 budget is substantially more permissive than the 1986 budget. With elections coming up in 1988 and the recent cracks in the National Unity government, it is likely that this trend will intensify. This will create pressures on local prices, the balance of payments, and thus on net foreign debt. The prediction that success on the inflation front is likely to be more permanent than in the balance of payments area is based on two considerations: (1) the belief that policymakers will channel most of the excess demand pressures to imports, thus retarding their inflationary impact; (2) the fact that the same dynamic inconsistency problems (section 2.3) that slow down a process of disinflation also slow down the increase in inflation caused by increases in aggregate demand.

The Israeli experience with high inflation suggests that indexation is not a good substitute for nominal stability when the rate of inflation penetrates a certain threshold. Indexation certainly increases the "acceptable" rate of inflation and therefore postpones the enactment of serious stabilizing measures once high inflation develops. Paradoxically, in the final stages the existence of indexation actually speeded up the implementation of an overall stabilization package. The reason for this is that determined steps to improve the balance of payments and decrease the budgetary burden of subsidies could only be achieved, because of indexation, by raising inflation to levels at which small deviations from full indexation became important. But at those rates inflation became intolerable, precipitating serious corrective measures.

A built-in institutional arrangement that encourages policymakers to postpone the use of fundamental measures to control inflationary pressures are the subsidies to domestic production. Because of these subsidies, policymakers are constantly tempted to postpone the manifestation of inflationary pressures by not adjusting the prices of controlled goods. They thus temporarily avoid the need to take the more fundamental (but also more politically painful) demand-restricting steps. Corrective steps are finally taken but only after the expansion of aggregate demand has reached substantial proportions. This mechanism introduces more variability into the conduct of aggregate demand policy.

Now that inflation has been in the 20% range for more than a year and a half, the public and many policymakers take this relatively low level for granted and focus on other problems. As a consequence, a basic long-run policymaking weakness of the Israeli economy is likely to remain—an excessively permissive aggregate demand policy. In large part this is also due to increased foreign dependence, which, although not liked by anybody, is a source of strength for domestic politicians. A larger inflow of foreign capital, particularly if it is channeled through government, increases the politicians' power to distribute resources among their constituencies.[42] Given this tendency, the vascillations of policy between balance of payments equilibrium and low inflation that had characterized the pre-1985 stabilization are likely to continue in the future. But after the trauma of near hyperinflation their amplitude is hopefully going to be smaller.

## Appendix

### A.1 Investigation of the Roots of the Polynomial in Equation (2.18)

The following relations hold between the roots of the polynomial in equation (2.18) and its coefficients:

$$-d = \lambda_1 + \lambda_2 + \lambda_3, \tag{A.1a}$$

$$c = \lambda_1 \lambda_2 + \lambda_1 \lambda_3 + \lambda_2 \lambda_3, \tag{A.1b}$$

$$1 = \lambda_1 \lambda_2 \lambda_3. \tag{A.1c}$$

Because from equation (2.14a) $d > 3$, equation (A.1a) implies that not all three roots are equal to 1 in absolute value. Hence, by equation (A.1c) there are at least two distinct roots. Moreover, at least one root is larger than 1 in absolute value and at least one is smaller than 1 in absolute value. Because $d > 0$, equation (A.1a) implies that there is at least one root with a negative real part. Hence, if all roots are real, equation (A.1c) implies that two of the roots are negative and one is positive.

   An example of numerical values of the coefficients $d$ and $c$ that satisfy all those conditions and the condition $c > d > 3$ implied by equations (2.14) and note 28 are $c = 5.1835$, $d = 4.7323$. These coefficients imply $\lambda_1 = 0.1667$ and $\lambda_2 = \lambda_3 = -2.4495$. In this case the stable solution involves only the root $\lambda_1$, as assumed in equation (2.19a). It can be shown that, if two of the roots are complex conjugates and the third is real, the condition $d > 3$ implies that the two complex roots have absolute values that are greater than 1, whereas the real root is smaller than 1 in absolute value. Hence stable solutions cannot be cyclical in my example.

### A.2 Derivation of $K_1$ and Proof That $\lambda_1 > 0$

*Derivation of $K_1$*
Because equation (2.19) is the stable solution for the difference equation (2.13), all poststabilization rates of inflation and $\pi_3$ in particular have to

satisfy it. It follows from this consideration and from equation (2.16) that the right-hand side of equation (2.16) is equal to $\pi_L + K_1 \lambda_1^3$. Using equation (2.19) to express $\pi_1, \pi_2, \pi_3, \pi_4$, and $\pi_5$ in terms of $\pi_L$ and $\lambda_1$ and substituting into this equality, we obtain

$$\frac{1}{D}\{6(c-d)\theta^2 B\pi_L + 6\theta^2 B[\pi_1^* + K_1(\lambda_1^5 - \lambda_1^2 - \lambda_1) - \pi_L]$$

$$+ (a^2 \beta A + 18\theta^2 B)(\pi_L + K_1 \lambda_1^4) + [a(1-a)\beta A$$

$$+ 18\theta^2 B](\pi_L + K_1 \lambda_1^3)\} = \pi_L + K_1 \lambda_1^3. \quad \text{(A.2)}$$

This is a single equation with the single unknown $K_1$. Rearrangement and use of the identities in equation (2.14) yields equation (2.20) in the text.

*Proof That, If $|\lambda_1| < 1, |\lambda_2| > 1, |\lambda_3| > 1$, Then $\lambda_1 > 0$*
It is useful to prove separately the case in which all three roots are real and the case in which two of the roots are complex conjugates. By using equation (A.1c) in equation (A.1b), we get

$$c = \frac{1}{\lambda_1} + \frac{1}{\lambda_2} + \frac{1}{\lambda_3}. \quad \text{(A.3)}$$

Consider the case of three real roots first. Suppose that the stable root $\lambda_1$ is negative. Because (from section A.1) two of the roots are negative and one is positive, this implies that only one of either $1/\lambda_2$ or $1/\lambda_3$ is positive. Because $|\lambda_2| > 1$ and $|\lambda_3| > 1$, both $1/\lambda_2$ and $1/\lambda_3$ are smaller than 1 in absolute value. It follows that $c < 1$. But this contradicts the condition $c > d > 3$ [see equation (2.14)]. Hence $\lambda_1$ must be positive.

If two of the roots are complex and one is real, then given that there is only one stable root, it must be real because the two complex roots, being conjugates, have the same absolute value. Hence we need to look only at the case in which $\lambda_1$ is real and $\lambda_2$ and $\lambda_3$ are complex conjugates. Let $\lambda_2 \equiv \delta + \rho i$ and $\lambda_3 \equiv \delta - \rho i$, where $\delta$ and $\rho$ are real. Substituting into equation (A.1c) and rearranging, we obtain $\lambda_1 = 1/(\delta^2 + \rho^2)$, from which it follows that $\lambda_1 > 0$.

A.3   Proof That, If Equation (2.19) Is the Solution to Equation (2.13), a One-Period Freeze at $\pi_L$ Is Sufficient to Bring All Expectations about the Future to $\pi_L$

Let

$$\pi_t = h\pi_{t-1} + g_L \quad \text{(A.4)}$$

be the first-order difference equation of which equation (2.19) is a solution. The general solution of equation (A.4) in terms of the coefficients $h$ and $g_L$ is

$$\pi_t = \frac{g_L}{1-h} + rh^t, \tag{A.5}$$

where it follows by comparison of equation (A.5) with equation (2.19) that

$$h = \lambda_1, \tag{A.6a}$$

$$r = k(\pi_1^* - \pi_L), \tag{A.6b}$$

$$g_L = (1 - h)\pi_L. \tag{A.6c}$$

Equations (A.6) determine $h$, $r$, and $g_L$ uniquely in terms of $\lambda_1$, $k$, $\pi_1^*$, and $\pi_L$, establishing that equation (A.4) is the unique difference equation for which equation (2.19) is a solution. Note that in terms of equation (A.4) the steady-state inflation that corresponds to $g_L$ is determined by

$$\pi_I = h\pi_I + g_L. \tag{A.7}$$

Because equation (A.4) is the unique difference equation for which equation (2.19) is a solution, it can be used to determine the path of inflation. If $\pi_2$ is set as $\pi_L$ by a one-period freeze, this equation, in conjunction with equation (A.7), implies $\pi_2 = h\pi_L + g_L = \pi_L$. Hence, following the one-period freeze at $\pi_L$, $\pi_t = \pi_L$ for all $t \geqslant 1$. Because there is perfect foresight, this implies that, once the freeze is credibly imposed, all future inflationary expectations converge to $\pi_L$.

## Notes

I am particularly indebted to Elhanan Helpman and Nissan Liviatan for critical comments on an earlier version of the model in section 2.4. I also benefited from the detailed comments of Stanley Fischer, from useful discussions with Leo Leiderman and Zvi Eckstein, and from the cooperation of members of the Research Department of the Bank of Israel. The usual disclaimer applies. The Foerder Institute for Economic Research at Tel Aviv University provided partial financial support. Yossi Spiegel provided research assistance. Phyllis Avni, Stella Padeh, and Alberta Ragan efficiently typed several versions of the manuscript.

1. Related papers, some of which also discuss recent stabilization of high inflation in several Latin American countries are Bruno (1986), Blejer and Liviatan (1987), Dornbusch and Fischer (1986), Helpman and Leiderman (1987), and Liviatan (1986). Background papers that discuss the economic and institutional structure

within which the Israeli hyperinflation developed are Shiffer (1982, 1986), Cukierman (1985), and Bruno and Fischer (1986).

2. The prices of these goods, whose weight in the CPI is about 20%, are set by the government. Some of these goods are subsidized. As a consequence, when their price is adjusted by less than the rate of inflation in the rest of the economy, the real subsidy increases.

3. This is the thesis of Liviatan and Piterman (1986), who claim that periodic attempts to improve the balance of payments pushed the rate of inflation in Israel to higher levels. The developments during 1984 seem to conform to this pattern rather well, in the sense that inflation accelerated for longer than the initial impact lasted.

4. Hence firms can decrease their real tax burdens by simply shifting expenditures to the end of the tax year and receipts to its beginning. Sometimes this shift requires only changes in bookkeeping.

5. However, as pointed out by Drazen and Helpman (1986), the conventional direction of causality does not necessarily imply a positive relation between the deficit and inflation.

6. The Histadrut is a general labor union that serves as an umbrella organization for most more narrowly defined unions.

7. Marom (1986) estimates that the annual inflation-related expansion of the banking sector alone cost the economy more than 2% of GDP per year in the early 1980s.

8. This approach in developed in Bruno (1986). The notion that stabilization in Israel would have to be of the "cold turkey" type appears in Bruno (1981).

9. These expectations, which are derived from equilibrium market prices of imperfectly indexed bonds with short terms to maturity, are obtained in an interesting paper by Yariv (1986). I view them as the most meaningful (although not perfect) indicators of inflationary expectations available. On the one hand they are not subject to the criticism of not being based on actual actions that is leveled at survey-based expectations. On the other hand, they do not need to assume, as done by most empirical models of rational expectations, the precise economic model in which the public believes.

10. The details of this mechanism are illustrated in section 2.3.

11. Until August 1986 the shekel was pegged to the dollar and thereafter to a trade-weighted basket of five currencies.

12. The fact that velocity continued to increase between 1980 and 1981, despite a decrease in the rate of inflation, is consistent with this conclusion. A similar phenomenon has been detected for Israel and several Latin American countries by Piterman (1985) and Cukierman et al. (1985) for several EEC countries.

13. In 1986 this rate decreased markedly to the 25–35% range, which is still quite high in comparison to the marginal productivity of capital.

14. Cukierman and Hercowitz (1984) show that in the presence of a monopolistic banking industry the spread should increase with the rate of inflation. The fact that the spread decreased from an average monthly rate of 5.26% in 1984 to an average of 2.64% during the first eleven months of 1986 is consistent with the view that at least part of the large spread is due to limited competition in the banking industry. The debitory rate used for the calculation of the spread is the effective rate on overdrafts, and the creditory rate is the rate on marketable deposit certificates (*Tafas*).

15. That these expectations were initially quite high in comparison to actual inflation, despite the freeze and pegging the exchange rate, can be seen from columns 2 and 3 of table 2.3.

16. This process was strongly in evidence during 1984. See Bank of Israel (1984), pp. 54–56.

17. In view of the relatively large size of the tradable sector this may be a reasonable approximation. In any case the main argument does not depend on it, as explained later.

18. Kydland and Prescott (1977); Barro and Gordon (1983); Fischer (1977). Staggering is also a major component of Taylor's model (Taylor 1980). However, the contracts used here feature only forward-looking elements, whereas Taylor's model features both forward- and backward-looking elements in wage formation.

19. I believe that the basic point of the example is robust to the introduction of such considerations.

20. This real wage can be derived by postulating a union objective function. For brevity I do not present this additional layer of the model.

21. I abstract from wage indexation for simplicity. The main point of the example holds with partially indexed wage contracts, of the type prevailing in Israel, so long as indexation is not perfect.

22. By convention the contract nominal wage rate carries the time index of the first period for which it is in effect.

23. Note that an increase in $Y_t$ denotes a negative shock to money demand.

24. This conflict is an important element of recent literature on policy games. Examples are Canzoneri (1985), Rogoff (1985), Horn and Persson (1986), Tabellini (1985), and Alesina and Tabellini (1986). A popular survey of this literature appears in Cukierman (1986).

25. $a \equiv 1/(1 - e^{-\bar{m}})$ and it is positive for all $\bar{m} > 0$.

26. The effect of an increase in $\pi_{t+1}^*$ is ambiguous because of its conflicting effects on the attainment of the employment and the inflation targets.

27. This is just a statement of the obvious result that in the absence of stochastic shocks rational expectations reduce to perfect foresight.

28. Note that this implies that $c > d$.

29. This is true independently of whether policymakers operate in the elastic or inelastic range of money demand because they take inflationary expectations as given. See also Barro (1983).

30. Without such a requirement the steady-state paths of deterministic models of money and growth like that of Tobin (1965) and others are saddle-point paths, a fact that seriously undermines their usefulness.

31. This requirement also implies that $m_1$ and $m_2$ are adjusted so as to supply the money necessary to achieve $\pi_1$ and $\pi_2$ by means of equation (2.6′).

32. As in Sargent and Wallace (1973), this path is generally different from the path that would have been generated without a jump by using the initial conditions inherited from the prestabilization period. But, unlike in their model, prestabilization inflationary expectations affect the location of the new equilibrium path so long as it has not reached the steady state. The reason is that long-term overlapping contracts and policymakers' interest in maintaining high employment produce a higher-order difference equation than is the case in the Sargent and Wallace model. With sufficient staggering this creates an effect of the prestabilization expectations on poststabilization inflation even when the rate of inflation jumps in order to reach a stable path.

33. This implies that $m_2$ must be suitably precommitted [see equation (2.6′)] to avoid asynchronization problems between money and the exchange rate (or the price level) once the freeze is lifted.

34. An alternative explanation that is based on monopolistic competition appears in Helpman (1987). Both elements might have contributed to the absence of serious shortages. It is likely, however, that during the first few months following stabilization the mechanism discussed in the text was relatively more important than later, because of the huge difference between the prestabilization and the poststabilization steady-state rates of inflation.

35. Even that turned out not to be a foolproof commitment because the local currency was pegged to the dollar, which (luckily for the program's viability) depreciated in the poststabilization period.

36. This point is stressed by Bruno (1986) and was no doubt an important consideration in the program's conception.

37. This problem is to a large extent due to the segmentation of the credit market in Israel discussed in section 2.2.

38. This discussion partly draws on Fischer (1986), who discusses the factors affecting the relative desirability of money targets versus exchange rate targets as instruments of stabilization.

39. Liviatan and Piterman (1986) claim it did in some cases. Evidence to the contrary, based on vector autoregressions of monthly data between 1980 and 1985 appears in Leiderman and Razin (1986).

40. This is over and above the tremendous increase in real rates actually experienced with the exchange rate target (table 2.4).

41. However, it was not devised to achieve this goal.

42. Ben-Porath (1982, p. 332) puts it succinctly: "Foreign dependence is a source of domestic power" (translated from Hebrew).

# References

Alesina, A., and G. Tabellini. 1986. "Rules and discretion with non-coordinated monetary and fiscal policies."

Bank of Israel. 1984. *Annual Report.* Jerusalem: Bank of Israel.

Barro, R. J. 1983. "Inflationary finance under discretion and rules." *Canadian Journal of Economics* 16:1–16.

Barro, R. J., and D. B. Gordon. 1983. "Rules, discretion and reputation in a model of monetary policy." *Journal of Political Economy* 91:589–610.

Ben-Porath, Y. 1982. "The liberalization that did not materialize: Ideology and economic policy 77–81." *Economic Quarterly* 115:325–333. (In Hebrew.)

Blejer, M. I., and N. Liviatan. 1987. *Fighting Hyperinflation: Stabilization Strategies in Argentina and Israel, 1985–86.* IMF Working Paper. Washington, D.C.: International Monetary Fund.

Bruno, M. 1981. "A swift and determined blow." *Migvan* (February), 56:33–38. (In Hebrew.)

Bruno, M. 1986. "Sharp disinflation strategy: Israel 1985." *Economic Policy* 2:379–407.

Bruno, M., and S. Fischer. 1986. "The inflationary process: Shocks and accommodation," in *The Israeli Economy: Maturing through Crisis*, Y. Ben-Porath, ed. (Cambridge, Mass.: Harvard University Press), 347–371.

Canzoneri, M. B. 1985. "Monetary policy games and the role of private information." *American Economic Review* 75:1056–1070.

Cukierman, A. 1985. "Indexation and the political economy of the Israeli inflation." Paper presented at the 60th annual conference of the Western Economic Association, Anaheim, California.

Cukierman, A. 1986. "Central bank behavior and credibility: Some recent theoretical developments." *Federal Reserve Bank of St. Louis Review* (May), 68:5–17.

Cukierman, A., and Z. Hercowitz. 1984. "Inflation, the structure of financial inter-mediation and the real interest rate."

Cukierman, A., and L. Leiderman. 1984. "Price controls and the variability of relative prices." *Journal of Money Credit and Banking* (August), 16:271–284.

Cukierman, A., and L. Leiderman. 1985. "Relative price variability and inflation in the Israeli economy." *Bank of Israel Economic Review* (May), 59:47–64. (In Hebrew.)

Cukierman, A., K. Lennan, and F. Papadia. 1985. "Inflation induced redistributions via monetary assets in five European countries: 1974–1980." *Studies in Banking and Finance* (supplement to the *Journal of Banking and Finance*), 2:295–352.

Dornbusch, R., and S. Fischer. 1986. "Stopping hyperinflations past and present." *Weltwirtschaftliches Archiv* (April), 122:1–47.

Drazen, A., and E. Helpman. 1986. *Inflationary Consequences of Anticipated Macro-economic Policies. I, Taxes and Money Financing. II, Budget Cuts.* Tel Aviv: Foerder Institute for Economic Research, Tel Aviv University.

Fischer, S. 1977. "Long term contracts, rational expectations and the optimal money supply rule." *Journal of Political Economy* 85:191–205.

Fischer, S. 1986. "Exchange rates versus money targets in disinflation," in his *Indexing, Inflation and Economic Policy* (Cambridge, Mass.: MIT Press), 247–262.

Helpman, E. 1987. *Macroeconomic Effects of Price Controls: The Role of Market Structure.* Working Paper 3–87. Tel Aviv: Foerder Institute for Economic Research, Tel Aviv University.

Helpman, E., and L. Leiderman. 1987. "Stabilization in high inflation countries: Analytical foundations and recent experience." Paper presented at the April 1987 Carnegie-Rochester Conference on Public Policy.

Horn, H., and T. Persson. 1986. *Exchange Rate Policy, Wage Formation and Credibil-ity.* Working Paper 48. Rochester, N.Y.: Rochester Center for Economic Research.

Kydland, F. E., and E. C. Prescott. 1977. "Rules rather than discretion: The inconsis-tency of optimal plans." *Journal of Political Economy* 85:473–491.

Leiderman, L., and A. Razin. 1986. "Propagation of shocks in a high inflation economy: Israel, 1980–85."

Liviatan, N. 1986. *Inflation and Stabilization in Israel: Conceptual Issues and Interpreta-tion of Developments.* IMF Working Paper. Washington, D.C.: International Mone-tary Fund.

Liviatan, N. 1987. "The evolution of disinflationary policies in Israel (1980–1986)." *Economic Quarterly* 131:902–913. (In Hebrew.)

Liviatan, N., and S. Piterman. 1986. "Accelerating inflation and balance of pay-ments crises, Israel 1973–84," in *The Israeli Economy: Maturing through Crises,* Y. Ben-Porath, ed. (Cambridge, Mass.: Harvard University Press), 320–346.

Marom, A. 1986. *The Contribution of Inflation to the Size of the Banking Industry in Israel*. Discussion Paper 86.04. Jerusalem: Bank of Israel Research Department. (In Hebrew.)

Offenbacher, A. 1985. "Introduction: Empirical studies of money demand in Israel." *Bank of Israel Economic Review* 60 : 3–16. (In Hebrew.)

Piterman, S. 1985. "The irreversibility of the relationships between inflation and real money balances." *Bank of Israel Economic Review* 60 : 71–81. (In Hebrew.)

Rogoff, K. 1985. "The optimal degree of commitment to an intermediate monetary target." *Quarterly Journal of Economics* 100 : 1169–1191.

Sargent, T. J. 1982. "The ends of four big inflations," in *Inflation: Causes and Effects*, R. E. Hall, ed. (Chicago, Ill.: University of Chicago Press), 41–96.

Sargent, T. J., and N. Wallace. 1973. "The stability of models of money and growth with perfect foresight." *Econometrica* 41 : 1043–1048.

Shiffer, Z. F. 1982. "Money and inflation in Israel: The transition of an economy to high inflation." *Federal Reserve Bank of St. Louis Review* (August-September), 64 : 28–40.

Shiffer, Z. F. 1986. "Adjusting to high inflation: The Israeli experience" *Federal Reserve Bank of St. Louis Review* (May), 68 : 18–29.

Tabellini, G. 1985. "Centralized wage setting and monetary policy in a reputational equilibrium."

Taylor, J. B. 1980. "Aggregate dynamics and staggered contracts." *Journal of Political Economy* 88 : 1–23.

Tobin, J. 1965. "Money and economic growth." *Econometrica* 33 : 671–684.

Yariv, D. 1986. *Estimation of Inflationary Expectations in Israel and Analysis of Their Developments against the Background of Disinflationary Programs*. Discussion Paper 86.11. Jerusalem: Bank of Israel Research Department. (In Hebrew.)

# Comments on Part I

## Comment by Peter M. Garber

I consider the problem of inflation and disinflation in Israel from the point of view of the behavior of a wartime economy. Typically, when troops move toward the front, macroeconomists quickly abandon the field. We either ignore war by excising it from our data or treat it as nothing more than an unusual upsurge of government expenditure in a closed, peaceful economy. This has led to our ignoring two of the three most important macroeconomic disturbances by far of the century in forming our models and selecting our data.

Using peacetime jargon in our discussions perhaps does not greatly warp our perceptions of the recent history of most developed Western economies, but our lack of a serious modern analysis of wartime economies forces us to interpret the dynamics of Israel's economy with perhaps unsuitable language.

To illustrate the problems that may arise from this vacuum, I take as an example the US economy during World War II, usually considered the epitome of a fully mobilized war economy, at least in the United States. The United States spent an average of 40% of GNP on military activity in the four years of its participation in World War II, with a peak of 48% in 1944. In 1944 its military mobilized 12 million people out of a population of 140 million, or 8.5% of the population. Its war dead amounted to 0.18% of the population during the war. To implement its war strategy, the United States imposed central planning and administrative resource allocation, a large draft, serious capital controls, a strategic plan of economic and financial warfare, and a carefully tailored plan of war finance. We all consider this sort of environment to be too turbulent to apply our standard macroeconomic tools in a way that can integrate it with postwar data. Since World War II the United States has not spent more than 11% of

GNP on its military, except during the Korean War, when expenditures reached 15% of GNP.

In contrast, the Israeli economy has been involved in six discernible wars in forty years, plus several major skirmishes. Based on the historical record, it is nearly certain that Israel will fight another major war within eight years. It maintains a standing military of 140,000 and can mobilize 500,000 in 48 hours (4.2% and 15.2% of the population, respectively). These reserves are subject to up to forty days per year of military training, and full mobilization has occurred three times since 1956. From 1976 to 1982 Israel spent on average 27.5% of GNP on its military, not counting hidden expenditures on its nuclear weapons program and the true social costs of conscription. In the periodic major battles with various Arab coalitions, Israel has sometimes spent more than 100% of GNP in a few weeks. The average percentage of the population killed in these battles has been around 0.04% in the recent clashes. On an ongoing basis Israel receives aid of $2.5 to $3 billion from the United States, 15% of GDP. This is subject to periodic emergency supplements of the sort forthcoming at the time of the disinflation. Since 1985 this aid has consisted entirely of grants. The US government, holding slightly less than half the total, is the predominant creditor for the $22 billion of foreign debt, which approximately equals GDP. Because the grants from the US government are sufficient to finance the entire debt, however, the debt to the United States is only an accounting phenomenon so long as aid continues.

Most relevant for the present discussion, Israel conducted a major invasion and occupation of Lebanon from 1982 through 1985, a period coincident with its hyperinflation. The final withdrawal from Lebanon occurred in June 1985, the month before the disinflationary policy was implemented. This war cost $3.5 billion, 5.6% of GDP for three years. Unlike earlier wars, it yielded few benefits.

Simultaneously, Israel entered an agreement with the United States, making it a "strategic ally." The "Memorandum of Strategic Understanding," signed in November 1981, was not implemented until after the withdrawal from Lebanon. In return for locking in the stream of US aid, Israel gave the United States a contingent claim on Israeli military assets, including basing and warehousing rights, in times of crisis. In addition, the United States offered emergency aid to press for the reform of the economy. The granting of additional aid was contingent on a reduced level of government spending and on the introduction of an austerity program to curb inflation and the balance of payments deficit.

Oddly neither Cukierman nor Bruno and Piterman mention these events. Neither alludes to the Lebanon war, with its unreimbursed costs and faltering civilian morale, as a potential driving force for the inflation. Both mention the US emergency aid as a helpful, if tangential, aspect of the reform. Cukierman even claims: Although this additional aid is obviously not a component of the locally produced stabilization, it played an important role nevertheless. By increasing the public's confidence in the ability of the government to peg the exchange rate, it prevented speculation against the currency. Surely a promised reward of 7.5% of GDP over two years and an implicit threat to cut up to 15% of GDP per year would be a sufficient incentive for the competing Israeli coalitions to unite in at least a temporary reform in order to split up the new pie. To ensure the aid flow, it was vital to suspend the struggle over income shares; after all, the aid could be deposited temporarily in the Bank of Israel and split up in a renewed struggle for shares after the incentive program ended. Any credibility that the reform had must have flowed from the necessity and desirability of placating its only ally. The Israelis had been tricked before both on income policy package deals, and on fiscal and monetary reforms. The mere combination of the two programs should have promised no increased credibility without the intervention of the extrasovereign power.

The necessity of selling sovereignty to gain credibility is, after all, the standard method for consolidating a monetary reform. In the famous 1920s hyperinflations, reform was always accompanied by temporary loss of independence. The financial and economic affairs of Austria and Hungary, for example, were placed under the control of League of Nations commissions. Even Germany, which independently started its reform in 1923, secured its reform only after it received the Dawes loan, which required the appointment of Allied officers to the board of the Reichsbank.

How might analyzing Israel as a wartime economy change the description of events? As a point of departure, the primary motivation of a war government is success in the war game played with its adversaries, in this case a fluctuating coalition of Arab powers. Success could be defined as survival or, in a less radical conflict such as the Lebanon adventure, the reduction of future military expenditures through the acquisition of added security or possibly the de facto annexation of additional provinces to the Israeli economy. Thus Israel has incorporated a population exceeding 1 million (25% of the population of Israel proper) through its occupation of the West Bank and Gaza. Its failure to transfer Lebanon up to Beirut to friendlier hands was a costly failure. Because, unlike previous wars, this large investment would earn nothing, a reestimation of national wealth after the realization of this failure could set in motion a scramble for internal income redistribution and an associated inflation.

Whatever the objectives, the magnitude of military expenditure is an endogenous outcome of the game and sets finance requirements as a secondary problem. In addition, a country plays a game of no less import with its allies of the moment, who have their own objectives. An ally may find that it is in its interests to soften the impact on morale of a country's strategic military or political defeat by offering a set of incentives that force the choice of a stabilizing policy. It may set the proper ratio of carrot to stick by its choice of grants versus loans, making loans to permit it a future squeeze option. Thus, although the United States effectively finances the entire interest cost of the Israeli debt, it always retains the option of cutting subsidies and making the debt a serious operational constraint. Again, playing the game with a major ally would dominate any game played among internal coalitions contending for small shifts in the distribution of income. Thus I would consider the sort of standard peacetime macroeconomic game examined by Cukierman to be of secondary importance in characterizing these events.

Through its occupation of the West Bank and Gaza, Israel has taken control of a significant labor force relative to its own. Although the Arab work force adds 17% more workers to the de facto Israeli labor force, including those employed in Israel proper and those working in the occupied territories, only those working in Israel are included for labor force statistics and none are included in unemployment statistics. Although the limited rise in unemployment is used as an example of the success of heterodox reforms, the impact of the reform is difficult to gauge accurately without some data on the labor force and unemployment in the occupied territories. Arab laborers from the occupied territories, unrepresented in the Histadrut, would be unprotected in their jobs and would possibly be affected by employment fluctuations. Including employment data from the occupied territories would serve to provide a more complete picture of the impact of the policy changes.

### Comment by Nissan Liviatan

I begin my comments with a discussion of some of the issues raised by Bruno and Piterman. I then briefly turn to the model proposed by Cukierman. Finally, I discuss the relation between shock treatment and price controls.

Bruno and Piterman struggle with some difficult issues that arose in the course of the second year (which can also be considered the second stage) of the stabilizaton program in Israel. I comment on some of these issues.

A major problem is the apparent inconsistency between the severe fiscal contraction and the outburst of private consumption accompained by a rise in real wages and a real appreciation. These phenomena were typical of the much criticized attempts to reduce inflation by merely slowing down the rate of devaluation. However, why should these phenomena accompany a well-balanced stabilization program that is based on the elimination of the budget deficit?

Related questions that arise in this context are whether these developments are endogenous to the stabilization policy and whether they imply an unsustainable path.

The mechanism that brought about the rise in consumption and real wages is not quite clear. Bruno and Piterman point out some endogenous developments that tend to raise consumption, such as the rise in wealth associated with the increased sense of security that resulted from stabilization and from the increased confidence in government bonds. The rise in wages is also partly endogenous, being related to the reaction to the initial wage cut and to the rise in consumption demand. In addition, both consumption and wages were influenced by the easing of monetary policy in the second stage of stabilization.

It is not clear, however, whether these developments, which traditionally mark collapsing regimes, represent in fact an unsustainable course. The key consideration must be the balance of payments. The large current account surplus provides some reason for optimism. Even after deducting the special US aid and the increase in private transfers, there still remains some surplus. In addition, the foreign exchange reserves reached unprecedented records. Therefore one cannot rule out the possibility that the development of wages and consumption somehow reflect the improvement in the external position of the economy and thus are not the result of an overvalued currency.

Another important issue is the management of the nominal side of the economy in the second stage of stabilization and the explanation of the remaining two-digit inflation. If the budget deficit is eliminated, why should prices continue to rise at 1.5% per month?

The explanation of the creeping inflation provided by Bruno and Piterman is essentially based on the theory of a downward rigidity in prices. Under these conditions changes in relative prices entail an increase in the general price level. This raises the question of why the (downward) price rigidity is more pronounced in a poststabilization economy as compared with other normal economies. Is this another manifestation of inflationary inertia?

Bruno and Piterman point out a contributing factor to the difficulty of restraining the creeping inflation. This factor is associated with the political objection to the use of restrictive (antigrowth) monetary policy in the second stage of stabilization. However, one may ask again, Why should this difficulty be related to stabilization as such? Doesn't it reflect the inherent aversion to unemployment that was a contributing factor to inflation in the first place?

In any case, given the foregoing difficulties in restraining the creeping inflation, one must consider the appropriate exchange rate policy for this situation. It is clear that adjustments in the exchange rate are required, but these may lead to a nominal spiral involving the exchange rate, wages, and prices.

Bruno and Piterman's recommendation for dealing with this situation is to carry out periodic devaluations that are accompanied by "package deal agreements" with the trade unions in order to sterilize the cost-push effects of the cost-of-living allowance (COLA). An example of this type of policy is the January 1987 devaluation where the COLA was suspended. The remaining cost-push effect was sterilized by cutting the employer's contributions to national insurance (which is a form of a wage tax).

The policy of carrying out devaluations within the framework of a social agreement among the major economic factors (labor, employers, and government) is a basic innovation in the nominal sector. This policy represents a major departure from the prestabilization era, in which the government tried occasionally to erode the real wage by using the devaluation weapon while the trade unions raised nominal wages in anticipation of this policy (the theoretical model is discussed by Cukierman).

It must be pointed out, however, that the "package deal regime" raises difficulties of its own. In particular, in return for the COLA sterilization, labor required (relative) price stability even in the short run. The government could not deliver this price stability without imposing some degree of price control, which involves economic inefficiencies.

Is there any mechanism that will enable the gradual elimination of controls in the course of stabilization? It seems that at present one of the factors that makes the package deal regime attractive is the remaining high degree of indexation. Under these conditions the transmission of nominal shocks is still relatively easy, and therefore the need to contain inflationary outbursts by price controls is more acute. Continued price stability will bring about a gradual reduction in indexation, which will facilitate the dismantling of controls.

The policy game approach and the distinction between rules and discretion are relevant to the analysis of stabilization programs. Cukierman makes use of this approach to present important insights in the process of stabilization in Israel. Of special significance is his discussion of the credibility aspects of stabilization.

I confine myself to some aspects of the *theoretical* model that Cukierman constructs in order to show that disinflation with staggered wage contracts can be achieved quicker within the framework of a heterodox policy. Although the basic conclusion is plausible, the model raises some conceptual issues.

First, the model assumes that the *same* discretionary regime that characterized the inflationary era continues to exist after the stabilization. Thus the budget cut is carried out within the original framework of dynamic inconsistency. However, in Israel the budget cut was associated with a change of regime on the nominal side. For example, the fixed exchange rate commitment was used as a rule to overcome dynamic inconsistency problems. The budget cut and the change of regime should therefore be treated simultaneously in the analysis of stabilization dynamics.

In principle, one could use the Cukierman model to demonstrate that, even with no change in the original budget deficit, the level of inflation could be reduced considerably if the government could make a credible commitment to follow a low crawling peg. The developments in practice suggest, however, that this kind of credibility cannot be established without a severe budget cut. This suggests that the solution to the dynamic inconsistency problem and the elimination of the budget deficit are interrelated issues. This consideration should somehow be incorporated in the model.

## A Note on Shock Treatment and Excess Supplies

I wish to comment on an important feature of the policy of shock treatment based on (among other measures) price controls. This feature relates to the strategy of creating temporary conditions of general excess supply in the initial stage of stabilization. If this type of strategy is not followed, then the price freeze cannot be maintained without creating serious imbalances. In this respect there was a basic difference between Israel and Argentina on the one hand, and Brazil on the other.

In Israel and Argentina restrictive monetary and fiscal policies and a temporary cut in real wages (as a result of direct government pressure) were used to create conditions of excess supplies that could be maintained for some time because of downward rigidity of prices. This created a potential downward pressure on prices that counteracted the effect of the remaining inflationary inertia, which was expected to subside gradually.

In Brazil, on the other hand, the shock treatment was not supposed to create excess supplies. Not only were the monetary and fiscal measures mild, but also general excess demands were stimulated by an initial increase in real wages. Consequently the maintenance of the price freeze led to serious imbalances, as expected. Even if it is assumed, as was the case in Brazil, that the fundamentals are right, it is still necessary to create temporary excess supplies in order to counteract the inflationary inertia, which still prevails in the initial stage of stabilization.

### Comment by Elhanan Helpman

Among the three heterodox programs that have been implemented since mid-1985—in Argentina, Brazil, and Israel—the Israeli program has proved to be the most successful. For this reason it is likely to be used as an example for future stabilization efforts, making it important to draw the correct lessons from its implementation. Both Cukierman and Bruno and Piterman deal with the program and its results. However, Bruno and Piterman focus on the results, whereas Cukierman provides a new view of the government–trade union interaction. Because it is impossible to take up in this discussion a detailed evaluation of the program and its results, I concentrate my comments on two issues: (1) an interpretation of some major results and the lessons that can be drawn from them, relying on the Bruno and Piterman presentation; and (2) the suggestion by Cukierman to view a major difficulty of stabilization as resulting from a game between the government and labor unions and the role of price controls in resolving this difficulty.

### The Results

It is clear from the evidence that the new policy has succeeded in bringing down inflation from over 400% per year to about 20% and that it transformed the current account from a deficit to a surplus. This has been achieved without a major loss of output and employment. A massive reduction of the government deficit, bringing the budget close to balance, was a central component of the program that led to these outcomes. However, despite this budgetary policy and the maintaining of a fixed exchange rate, the rate of inflation did not decline to 0, and after a short time the balance of payments began to deteriorate. The first question, therefore, that requires an answer is, What brought about inflationary pressure and a deteriorating balance of payments in 1986 and at the beginning of 1987?

In answering this question, I tend to agree broadly with Bruno and Piterman's interpretation that rising real wages and private consumption were responsible. Rising consumption increased the demand for traded and nontraded goods alike, and it required a real appreciation of the shekel, which has materialized. However, given the fixed exchange rate policy, the real appreciation could not be attained through a decline in the nominal exchange rate and therefore had to be attained by means of an increase in the price of nontradables. Hence part of the inflation resulted from rising prices of nontradables, caused by rising private consumption.

Rising real wages have reinforced the real appreciation and the increase in prices of nontradables. Moreover, private consumption has increased, partly because of the real wage hike. Bruno and Piterman attribute a large part of the consumption increase to the wage increase, which is indeed justified (although they do not provide a good explanation for the increase in real wages, which is a major driving force in this episode). On the other hand, they seem to belittle the contribution of other factors that deserve more weight. These include the reduction of real interest rates, a significant rise in the availability of credit, restocking of durables in view of the lower stocks in 1984 and 1985 (when consumption declined), and speculation against real exchange rate developments. The last factor might have been especially important in the second half of 1986, when it became clear that the real exchange rate was too low and would require upward adjustment (a 10% devaluation took place in January 1987).

Finally, the initial exchange rate policy contributed somewhat to the resulting inflation. Initially the shekel was pegged to the US dollar. At that time the value of the US dollar was on the decline, thereby raising shekel prices of tradables whose prices were denominated in appreciating currencies (such as the deutsche mark). On the other hand, this policy generated some nominal depreciation of the shekel, thereby preventing an even deeper real appreciation. One may pose here an explicit question. Suppose that the shekel was pegged to a currency basket at that time, as it is today, instead of to the US dollar. Then the inflation rate would have been lower by perhaps 6–7% per annum. On the other hand, the real exchange rate would have been lower by about 3–4%. Is this outcome preferable to the actual one? The answer depends on the evaluation of the current situation and, in particular, of the balance of payments. The reason is that an additional real appreciation would have led to a further deterioration of the current account. Hence the alternative exchange rate policies embody a trade-off between lower inflation and a larger deficit in the balance of payments. My answer is that the choice was right, because Israel is now facing a balance of payments problem and the problem would have been more severe if the shekel had been pegged to a currency basket from the beginning.

The initial improvement in the balance of payments resulted from four sources: reduction in government spending, reduction in private spending, decline in oil and primary commodity prices, and special US aid. The special US aid has ended, oil prices have risen, private spending has been steadily increasing, and government spending is also expected to increase. Reliable estimates suggest that the current account deficit will be around $0.5 billion in 1987. In 1988 there are scheduled elections, which suggests that no contractionary policy should be expected in that year. If the deficit rises to $1 billion, it will not be sustainable for an extended period of time. These developments may force the abandonment of the fixed exchange rate policy, which has been a cornerstone of the program. So far the balance of payments problem has not manifested itself in severe pressure on the exchange rate (there is no significant black market premium on foreign exchange), because reserves have been large and there was a capital inflow that took advantage of the higher Israeli real interest rates and the economic stability. This capital inflow was a one-time portfolio adjustment that is unlikely to repeat itself (it stopped in the spring of 1987) but that may also be quickly reversed.

In order to avoid balance of payments difficulties, it is necessary to curb spending, unless growth resumes at suitable rates. Both seem unlikely in the near future unless the government takes explicit action to curb spending. Current wage negotiations in the public sector are of major importance for the future, both because the rise in real wages had a detrimental effect on the stabilization effort and because the results of these negotiations will provide an indication of the strength of the political will to achieve long-run economic stability.

As far as the exchange rate policy is concerned, there is more than one route that could have been taken with the inception of the program. However, in view of the difficulties in controlling monetary variables that have been experienced in the poststabilization era, one may conclude that the fixed exchange rate policy played a desirable role in this experiment (although some of the difficulties resulted undoubtedly from the exchange rate peg and the inability to control capital flows tightly). Naturally there are major dangers involved in pegging the exchange rate at the beginning of a stabilization program, when uncertainties and unexpected pressures may force the abandonment of the peg. However, in the Israeli case there were no shocks that significantly endangered this policy. To the contrary, the shocks proved to be rather favorable, such as the fall of the dollar and of oil prices. But it was not all good luck. The correct alignment of relative prices at the beginning of the program played an important role in preventing undesirable pressures.

The alignment of relative prices consisted of the adjustment of prices of subsidized products, a devaluation, a wage agreement, and price controls on many other products. Given the choice of the exchange rate and the nominal wage contract, it is hard to see the need for price controls (except for the case in which price controls are requested by labor unions in exchange for a concessional wage contract, as was the case in Israel, although it is not clear that this was the only possible bargain). Moreover, in the ensuing events it is impossible to identify visible benefits of the price controls. On the other hand, it is also not possible to identify significant damages, because there were no significant shortages of the type that developed in, say, Brazil. The central point is, however, that well-known damages of price controls would have materialized if the initial alignment of relative prices proved to diverge significantly from market-clearing values either because of miscalculations or as a result of unfavorable shocks. Clearly it makes no sense to pursue a policy that carries the risk of significant damages (including endangerment of the entire program) without prospects of beneficial effects. For these reasons price controls seem to be undesirable (as attested to by the experience of Argentina and Brazil). Israel's success is based on suitable fiscal restraint, a correct alignment of the nominal wage and the exchange rate at the beginning of the program (embodying a significant real wage reduction), an exchange rate peg, and helpful external shocks.

## Government-Union Interaction

It is clear that Cukierman disagrees with my assessment of price controls. He suggests that the existence of overlapping nominal wage contracts and a government objective function that includes unemployment, inflation, and the inflation tax provides a rationale for the use of price controls. (In the model with traded goods only, a fixed exchange rate is a substitute for price controls, but price controls are essential for the argument in the presence of nontraded goods. I therefore use price controls as the relevant policy tool.) It is assumed that as a result of this objective function the government cannot precommit itself to a monetary rule but can only choose the rate of money growth and thereby the rate of inflation for each period. A time-consistent solution is considered to be an equilibrium. In this equilibrium labor unions choose the contracted nominal wage rate for future periods on the basis of expected inflation, with the rate of inflation resulting from time-consistent government behavior.

This setup adds a new element of inflationary inertia to Taylor's overlapping contracts model, which stems from the endogenous monetary rule. The issue of interaction between the government and the labor unions is of major importance, and it might have a bearing on the problem at hand. One should therefore welcome attempts to advance our understanding of possible results of these interactions. However, the current analysis seems to suffer from a fundamental difficulty.

The new inertial component arises from the government's attempt to smooth out employment fluctuations. Thus, when the need for inflation tax revenue declines, the government's time-consistent strategy is not to bring down inflation immediately to its new long-run level. This results from the fact that past wage agreements were based on expectations of a higher price level, so that, if the government did reduce inflation sharply, the resulting unexpected high real wage rate would have generated a higher than desirable unemployment level. This is understood by labor unions that are signing new wage contracts, and they demand a nominal wage rate that is too high to reach the steady-state in the next period. The government accommodates these wage developments and pursues a monetary policy that brings about a further partial reduction in the rate of inflation. Thus the government's endogenous monetary rule, which is derived from its time-consistent strategy, generates a gradual reduction in the rate of inflation in the face of lower needs for the inflation tax. This is the source of the new inflationary inertia.

There do exist monetary rules that can bring down inflation much faster than the rule suggested by Cukierman. Why then doesn't the government use them? The answer is that they are not credible. The government cannot precommit itself to an arbitrary rule, because it is in its best interests to deviate in the short run from any such rule. Only the equilibrium rule has the property that it has no incentive to deviate from it. Cukierman shows that price controls bring down inflation much faster than the equilibrium monetary rule.

It might appear from this presentation, as is indeed argued by Cukierman, that for disinflation purposes price controls are more efficient than monetary policy. This conclusion is, however, not warranted. The reason is that the entire advantage of price controls stems from the fact that they constitute a suitably chosen rule that is *assumed* to be credible, whereas it is *assumed* that no monetary rule is credible unless it satisfies the time-consistency requirement. Hence it is not the advantages of monetary versus price rules that were considered but rather credible versus noncredible rules. This suggests that, although Cukierman identifies an interesting difficulty in disinflation policies, the advantage of his preferred policy tool in dealing with this problem is not derived but practically assumed. Nevertheless the discussion is interesting, and it brings out an issue that can and should be systematically analyzed.

A possible approach to a systematic analysis of this issue is as follows. One may specify a model in which there are various costs and benefits of using monetary and price rules. Then one may derive the time-consistent equilibrium for each rule separately. Having done this, one may calculate the value of the objective function in each one of these equilibria. A comparison of these values will reveal whether monetary policy or price controls are more efficient in resolving the difficulty.

### Reply to Helpman by A. Cukierman

Helpman agrees that, when the government dislikes unemployment, a stabilization that is based only on elimination of the budgetary deficit is subject to dynamic inconsistency problems that slow down convergence to the lower steady-state rate of inflation. However, he claims that this problem can be alleviated either by price fixing or by a suitably devised monetary rule. The advantage of price fixing, he claims, originates simply from the *assumption* that it is a credible precommitment, whereas a monetary rule is not.

I agree that, for price fixing (or, for that matter, a monetary rule) to work, it has to be believed. The important issue is which one of those two forms of precommitment is likely to be more credible. I believe that direct price fixing is likely to be a more credible form of precommitment than a monetary rule in the short run for the following reasons: First, the relation between money and prices is imperfect and particularly so in the short run. As a consequence, direct price fixing is likely to be more credible because it precommits more precisely the variable about which unions care—the price level. I tried to capture this uncertainty by introducing a stochastic shock $Y_t$ to money demand. This issue is actually discussed in section 2.3. Second, economists find it hard to agree on which of the many definitions of money is most closely related to the price level. Under those circumstances a union that is interested in the purchasing power of the nominal wage rate of its members will trust a direct precommitment of the price level more than a credible precommitment of a nominal stock whose precise relation with the price level is debated even among professional economists. Third, in Israel the government can change the price level, even when the path of money is precommitted, by changing the prices of controlled goods (the weight of those goods in the CPI is about 20%). Similarly, precommitment of money does not prevent the government from changing the price level within some range by altering the exchange rate. The upshot is that direct price fixing precommits the variable of interest to unions directly, whereas a monetary rule does not.

A monetary rule would seem important, however, in order to credibly maintain long-run price stability. It seems, therefore, that there is room for precommitment of money on a permanent basis as well as for temporary price level fixing of the type I discussed in chapter 2. During the Israeli stabilization both variables were actually partially precommitted.

Finally, it should be emphasized that "price fixing" should be understood as a general term for precommitting directly some or all of the components of the price level, which for Israel are the exchange rate, the prices of controlled goods, and other domestic prices. The price freeze that Helpman discusses refers only to the last component. Whether or not all those components should be precommitted when price fixing is used depends on several considerations, some of which are discussed at the end of section 2.3.

# II  Argentina

# 3 Stopping Hyperinflation: The Case of the Austral Plan in Argentina, 1985–87

Jose Luis Machinea and
Jose Maria Fanelli

## 3.1 Performance of the Economy in the Period before the Plan

In the years before the Austral Plan was initiated, instability and stagnation were the outstanding features of economic activity. Between 1975 and 1985 GDP rose at an annual average rate of approximately 0.5%; inflation amounted to 11% per month (average over a twelve-month period); the fiscal deficit never fell below 5% of GDP, and in some cases it even exceeded 15% of GDP; and the gross external debt increased by $42 billion (US dollars). These are examples of a discouraging performance of the economy, which may have been caused partly by structural distortions stemming from the development model that had been prevalent before 1975, the year in which the situation became critical.[1] But mostly, instability and stagnation resulted from the erroneous economic policies put into practice during the last decade and from the negative effect of stagnation within a context of profound imbalance.

Two factors are of crucial importance. On the one hand, the 1975 crisis produced a permanent change in the inflation rate, which, after the quasi-hyperinflation registered that year, practically never dropped below 100% per annum. On the other hand, the 1977–80 liberalization policies and the opening of the economy brought increased indebtedness because of massive capital flight (rather than excessive domestic expenditure).[2]

The instability and stagnation that characterized the 1975–85 decade took a turn for the worse in 1981. The collapse in 1980 of the two largest banks weakened the financial system. The policies implemented in previous years—particularly after 1978—crumbled, provoking a severe crisis in the external sector. Adjustment policies implemented in 1981 were partially successful in terms of the external accounts. A large and solid trade surplus was generated but failed to balance the current account because of the heavy burden imposed by the servicing of the external debt. Domestically the 1981 policy package led to a chaotic situation. Because the impact of these policies was still being felt when the Austral Plan was initiated, it is worth noting the policies' most outstanding features, which led to a kind of chaotic adjustment in an attempt to overcome the constraints set by the external sector.

The 1981–83 Adjustment Process

The adjustment process started in 1981 was characterized by both political and economic instability. In many instances the interaction of the two factors aggravated the disequilibrium of the economy.

In fact, the economic authorities' decision-making capacity was severely eroded by the political deficiencies of the government. Social groups affected by the stabilization measures managed to exert pressure to obtain public sector subsidization to compensate for private sector adjustment costs. Thus in 1981, as the private sector's external debt increased substantially because of the strong peso devaluation, the government was persuaded to convert a large part of foreign currency liabilities through a scheme of foreign exchange insurance subsidies. In 1982 domestic firms' liabilities—which constituted almost the whole of banks' investment portfolios—were also substantially reduced by the introduction of concessional terms that threw the burden of the cost on domestic savers and the Central Bank. This in turn led to an increase in the government's deficit. In 1983, as another result of their eroded power, the authorities fell to the pressures exerted by trade unions, and the recovery of real wages was not properly regulated. In 1982 wages were well below their historical or normal levels; the recovery was too sharp and chaotic, and it led to imbalances in the budget and to inflation.

Domestic imbalances worsened considerably as a result of these economic and political factors. The activity level dropped substantially, inflation accelerated, and relative prices fluctuated erratically. There was a heavy transfer of wealth between the private and the public sector and within the private sector itself. The financial system collapsed, and the economy was demonetized while budget deficit went out of control. The sharp decline in investment, which had long-term consequences on growth, was perhaps the main characteristic of this period. External debt negotiations did not reach any result, and arrears in payments started to accrue.

A brief analysis of some data illustrates the shocks that shattered the economy, beginning with the 1981 adjustment policy. This policy was aimed at correcting the peso appreciation that had been generating a strong disequilibrium in the external accounts since it began in 1978.

The adjustment process started with a drastic change in relative prices resulting from successive devaluations throughout the year. In 1981 the nominal exchange rate increased by 424%, leading to a considerable devaluation in real terms as inflation amounted to 131% during that year. In 1982 the value of the dollar increased by 364%, whereas domestic prices rose by 210%. Since then the real exchange rate has fluctuated around those levels (table 3.1).

To close the fiscal gap, which widened because of devaluations among other causes, the government resorted to real increases in public utility rates as a source of financing (although the government was not as consistent as with foreign exchange rates because there were times when public utility rates declined in real terms; see table 3.1). The attempt to change relative prices through devaluation and adjustment in public utility rates led to an acceleration in inflation, which rose from 100% in 1980 to over 200% in 1982 (table 3.2).

The mid-1983 wage push amid inflationary conditions led to an annual rate of inflation of 400%. As an illustration, it should be noted that during the last quarter of 1983 the nominal hourly wage in industry rose by almost 100% in nominal terms.

Real devaluations during 1981—83 succeeded in generating a strong trade surplus aimed at reducing the basic current account deficit because of the increased burden of interest payments (the increase in interest service stemmed not only from an increase in indebtedness but also from higher rates in international credit markets). This turned a trade deficit of $2.5 billion (US dollars) in 1980 to a surplus of $3.3 billion in 1983. As a result, the current account deficit was reduced by half over the same period (see table 3.3).

The trade surplus during those years is basically explained by a sharp reduction in imports. Exports increased significantly in physical terms but not in value because of the deterioration in the terms of trade. Domestically import reductions resulted from a sharp drop in the absorption level, particularly in investment. Total absorption as a percentage of GDP declined from 103% in 1980 to 95% in 1983, and investment expenditure fell from 23% to 14.8%. This weakness in real domestic demand led to a drop in activity levels. In 1982 output was 11% lower than in 1980. A recovery took place in 1983 as a result of increasing consumption, which was due to salary increases and negative real interest rates (table 3.4).

**Table 3.1**
Relative prices: Average of monthly data (1980 = 100)

| Period | Relative prices (agricultural/ nonagricultural) | Real exchanges rates[a] Dollar | Real exchanges rates[a] Basket of currencies | Public prices[b] Including taxes | Public prices[b] Excluding taxes | Terms of trade |
|---|---|---|---|---|---|---|
| **1980** | 100.0 | 100.0 | 100.0 | 100.0 | 100.0 | 100.0 |
| I | 101.8 | 108.9 | 108.1 | 94.7 | 95.9 | 104.5 |
| II | 103.1 | 103.7 | 103.1 | 97.1 | 99.0 | 91.8 |
| III | 104.2 | 97.7 | 99.2 | 100.3 | 102.4 | 91.1 |
| IV | 90.9 | 89.6 | 89.6 | 107.9 | 102.7 | 112.1 |
| **1981** | 88.8 | 121.2 | 112.1 | 114.3 | 104.3 | 106.7 |
| I | 82.2 | 91.0 | 88.8 | 114.7 | 105.1 | 121.8 |
| II | 83.2 | 118.7 | 110.8 | 108.8 | 98.8 | 107.4 |
| III | 91.5 | 132.7 | 118.3 | 110.1 | 100.6 | 100.6 |
| IV | 98.3 | 142.3 | 130.6 | 123.6 | 112.6 | 96.8 |
| **1982** | 104.2 | 208.4 | 181.5 | 98.8 | 85.7 | 89.1 |
| I | 94.6 | 168.6 | 152.9 | 114.0 | 101.8 | 102.3 |
| II | 99.0 | 191.9 | 171.0 | 102.9 | 86.8 | 85.0 |
| III | 113.5 | 220.7 | 188.3 | 87.2 | 74.0 | 86.6 |
| IV | 109.6 | 252.6 | 213.7 | 91.1 | 80.2 | 82.6 |
| **1983** | 109.3 | 246.4 | 202.3 | 111.8 | 103.9 | 86.7 |
| I | 105.8 | 252.7 | 216.5 | 100.5 | 90.1 | 88.2 |
| II | 102.9 | 257.3 | 212.8 | 112.9 | 104.0 | 83.8 |
| III | 117.1 | 239.5 | 192.3 | 121.9 | 114.5 | 85.7 |
| IV | 111.3 | 236.1 | 187.7 | 111.8 | 107.1 | 89.0 |
| **1984** | 106.6 | 229.4 | 174.5 | 128.3 | 104.5 | 93.4 |
| I | 110.9 | 243.5 | 192.5 | 119.0 | 108.5 | 94.0 |
| II | 110.2 | 217.5 | 170.7 | 121.0 | 102.2 | 100.1 |
| III | 103.2 | 214.3 | 159.7 | 138.5 | 104.0 | 93.8 |
| IV | 102.0 | 242.2 | 175.2 | 134.8 | 103.3 | 85.7 |
| **1985** | 79.3 | 267.4 | 193.3 | 139.4 | 120.2 | 81.2 |
| I | 86.5 | 254.2 | 177.2 | 130.5 | 107.8 | 84.0 |
| II | 65.8 | 258.1 | 182.3 | 132.7 | 117.2 | 78.5 |
| III | 76.5 | 282.3 | 204.7 | 149.8 | 130.1 | 77.9 |
| IV | 88.4 | 274.9 | 209.0 | 144.6 | 125.6 | 84.2 |
| **1986** | 103.7 | 252.8 | 216.2 | 137.5 | 118.2 | 72.5 |
| I | 92.4 | 263.6 | 215.5 | 138.5 | 120.2 | 71.4 |
| II | 97.0 | 253.9 | 214.6 | 139.7 | 119.5 | 68.1 |
| III | 109.6 | 246.3 | 214.7 | 138.1 | 117.6 | 70.5 |
| IV | 115.6 | 247.3 | 220.2 | 133.5 | 115.6 | 80.1 |
| **1987** | | | | | | |
| I | 103.2 | 254.5 | 235.9 | 133.7 | 115.8 | 65.3 |

Source: Banco Central de la República Argentina, Instituto Nacional de Estadística y Censos, and Sindicatura General de Empresas Públicas.
a. Exchange rate × USA CPI/0.5(CPI + IWPI), where IWPI is the industrial wholesale price index.
b. Price of goods and services produced by Public Enterprises, deflated by the average of the CPI and IWPI.

**Table 3.2**
Inflation rate (annual rate)

| Period | Consumer prices (%) | Wholesale prices (%) |
|---|---|---|
| **1980** | 87.6 | 57.5 |
| I | 103.8 | 61.8 |
| II | 98.9 | 90.3 |
| III | 63.4 | 41.1 |
| IV | 87.1 | 41.4 |
| **1981** | 131.3 | 180.2 |
| I | 80.0 | 62.7 |
| II | 159.2 | 330.6 |
| III | 164.1 | 204.8 |
| IV | 132.2 | 188.6 |
| **1982** | 209.7 | 311.3 |
| I | 131.9 | 151.0 |
| II | 80.1 | 219.9 |
| III | 493.6 | 881.3 |
| IV | 271.2 | 263.2 |
| **1983** | 433.7 | 411.3 |
| I | 352.6 | 327.6 |
| II | 276.5 | 230.9 |
| III | 555.6 | 616.8 |
| IV | 626.2 | 573.6 |
| **1984** | 688.0 | 625.9 |
| I | 527.9 | 446.2 |
| II | 616.1 | 655.8 |
| III | 1,079.9 | 852.5 |
| IV | 626.7 | 606.3 |
| **1985** | 385.4 | 363.9 |
| I | 1,230.9 | 1,003.5 |
| II | 1,898.8 | 3,532.6 |
| III | 55.3 | 4.8 |
| IV | 34.4 | 10.3 |
| **1986** | 81.9 | 57.9 |
| I | 44.5 | 9.0 |
| II | 68.3 | 49.8 |
| III | 140.6 | 127.0 |
| IV | 87.1 | 67.7 |
| **1987** | | |
| I | 136.0 | 117.3 |

Source: Instituto Nacional de Estadística y Censos.

**Table 3.3**
Balance of payments (millions of US dollars)

| Period | Exports | Imports | Trade balance | Interest payments | Other | Current account | Capital account | Change in net international reserves |
|---|---|---|---|---|---|---|---|---|
| 1980 | 8,021 | −10,540 | −2,519 | −2,175 | −74 | −4,768 | 2,275 | −2,493 |
| 1981 | 9,143 | −9,430 | −287 | −3,850 | −577 | −4,714 | 1,155 | −3,559 |
| 1982 | 7,624 | −5,337 | 2,287 | −4,926 | 281 | −2,358 | −3,808 | −6,166 |
| 1983 | 7,836 | −4,505 | 3,331 | −5,423 | −369 | −2,461 | −111 | −2,572 |
| 1984 | 8,107 | −4,584 | 3,523 | −5,537 | −377 | −2,391 | 647 | −1,744 |
| 1985 | 8,396 | −3,814 | 4,582 | −5,132 | −403 | −953 | 397 | −556 |
| 1986 | 6,849 | −4,700 | 2,149 | −4,291 | −679 | −2,821 | 746 | −2,075 |
| 1987 (first quarter) | 1,457 | −1,195 | 262 | −976 | −227 | −941 | 480 | −461 |

Source: Banco Central de la República Argentina.

**Table 3.4**
Gross domestic product (1980 = 100)

| Period | GDP | Consumption | Investment | Industrial production | Seasonally adjusted GDP | Seasonally adjusted Industrial production |
|---|---|---|---|---|---|---|
| **1980** | 100.0 | 100.0 | 100.0 | 100.0 | | |
| I | 95.8 | 97.4 | 89.7 | 89.4 | 98.8 | 101.1 |
| II | 97.5 | 95.6 | 94.3 | 102.2 | 97.8 | 99.5 |
| III | 101.4 | 99.7 | 104.1 | 106.2 | 101.5 | 101.3 |
| IV | 105.3 | 107.4 | 112.0 | 102.2 | 102.0 | 98.1 |
| **1981** | 93.2 | 95.6 | 76.6 | 84.0 | | |
| I | 94.9 | 106.6 | 73.8 | 84.5 | 97.9 | 94.3 |
| II | 95.8 | 97.0 | 78.5 | 88.7 | 95.2 | 86.0 |
| III | 89.8 | 87.4 | 71.4 | 81.1 | 90.5 | 77.3 |
| IV | 92.5 | 91.6 | 82.8 | 81.8 | 89.2 | 78.5 |
| **1982** | 89.0 | 85.9 | 61.5 | 80.0 | | |
| I | 88.2 | 100.8 | 51.9 | 73.3 | 90.4 | 81.2 |
| II | 86.1 | 80.7 | 58.0 | 76.6 | 87.0 | 74.9 |
| III | 87.5 | 82.1 | 65.4 | 83.8 | 88.4 | 80.5 |
| IV | 94.2 | 90.7 | 70.6 | 86.5 | 89.7 | 83.6 |
| **1983** | 91.5 | 89.0 | 54.9 | 88.7 | | |
| I | 88.8 | 89.1 | 41.5 | 78.3 | 90.7 | 87.2 |
| II | 89.6 | 85.6 | 55.3 | 90.1 | 90.7 | 88.1 |
| III | 91.2 | 86.4 | 63.7 | 94.7 | 92.9 | 91.0 |
| IV | 96.2 | 95.0 | 59.3 | 91.7 | 91.7 | 88.6 |
| **1984** | 93.8 | 94.3 | 49.1 | 92.3 | | |
| I | 90.7 | 92.4 | 34.7 | 80.5 | 92.6 | 89.7 |
| II | 93.4 | 90.5 | 52.1 | 97.0 | 94.0 | 94.6 |
| III | 92.3 | 94.1 | 46.4 | 97.7 | 94.6 | 94.2 |
| IV | 98.9 | 100.3 | 63.1 | 93.9 | 93.7 | 90.7 |
| **1985** | 89.6 | 88.3 | 39.3 | 82.6 | | |
| I | 89.5 | 91.3 | 40.9 | 77.5 | 91.4 | 85.6 |
| II | 88.9 | 82.6 | 42.0 | 84.1 | 89.0 | 82.1 |
| III | 84.2 | 81.7 | 32.1 | 79.1 | 86.6 | 76.5 |
| IV | 95.6 | 97.7 | 42.2 | 89.6 | 90.7 | 86.5 |
| **1986** | 94.3 | 95.6 | 46.2 | 93.2 | | |
| I | 90.2 | 92.2 | 42.8 | 81.7 | 92.8 | 90.4 |
| II | 94.3 | 93.9 | 40.8 | 92.9 | 94.2 | 90.7 |
| III | 93.6 | 95.2 | 42.5 | 100.2 | 95.7 | 97.1 |
| IV | 99.2 | 101.4 | 58.6 | 97.9 | 94.8 | 94.6 |
| **1987** | | | | | | |
| I | 92.6 | 94.9 | 45.4 | 83.4 | 94.9 | 92.5 |

Source: Banco Central de la República Argentina.

These imbalances contributed to a worsening of the fiscal and financial situation, and, as mentioned, political considerations led to the concession of subsidies to the private sector and to wealth redistribution within the sector itself.

On the financial side the severe adjustment produced a sharp increase in the interest rate, as a risk premium emerged between domestic and international rates.[3] This risk premium involved not only the likelihood of a devaluation but also a lack of solvency of the financial system, which had been deteriorating since 1980. Moreover, the existence of 100% state guarantees on deposits and a free interest rate in a context of reduced banking supervision also added to the high level of interest rates. Debt arrears started to accrue on loans made by banks, whereas bank liabilities dropped in real terms because money demand was falling as a consequence of inflation. In 1981 the financial fragility of banks and enterprises came to a climax. By 1982 generalized bankruptcies in firms and banks could be expected. To avoid it, private agents initially pressed the government to reschedule their long-term debts and, later, to reduce them through strongly negative interest rates. As a consequence, the demonetization process accelerated, and the average maturity for financial deposits was shortened.

The consequences of the adjustment process were not less disruptive in the fiscal sector. Government expenditure on external debt servicing increased sharply not only because of real devaluation but also because of the conversion of a large portion of private debt into public debt (table 3.5). In 1980 servicing of the external debt amounted to only 1.3% of operating expenditures, but in 1983 it had risen to 12%. The acceleration in inflation resulted in a decrease of real fiscal revenue through the "lag effect" (the Olivera-Tanzi effect).[4] The strong reduction in the activity level had the same effect. In addition, the fiscal deficit grew as a consequence of both public and private sector financial problems. Because of the lack of capital markets, there was an attempt to finance the deficit through enforced issue of bonds; this financing took the form of interest-bearing reserve requirements in the banking sector. The methods used to attempt a narrowing of the fiscal gap had a negative impact on public investment; this was the component of government expenditures that showed the largest reduction.

The Constitutional Government and Its First Economic Program

During its first year in office, the democratic government was not in a position to change the situation drastically. The new authorities were faced with two main issues: first, the need to look for an efficient and noncon-

**Table 3.5**
External debt (millions of US dollars)[a]

| Period | Public sector | Private sector | Total |
|--------|---------------|----------------|-------|
| 1975 | 4,021 | 3,854 | 7,875 |
| 1976 | 5,189 | 3,091 | 8,280 |
| 1977 | 6,044 | 3,635 | 9,679 |
| 1978 | 8,357 | 4,139 | 12,496 |
| 1979 | 9,960 | 9,074 | 19,034 |
| 1980 | 14,459 | 12,703 | 27,162 |
| 1981 | 20,024 | 15,647 | 35,671 |
| 1982 | 28,616 | 15,018 | 43,634 |
| 1983 | 31,709 | 13,360 | 45,069 |
| 1984[b] | 36,139 | 10,764 | 46,903 |
| 1985[b] | 39,868 | 8,444 | 48,312 |
| 1986[b] | 42,039 | 7,099 | 49,138 |

Source: Banco Central de la República Argentina.
a. Until 1978 the foreign public debt excluded terms shorter than 180 days.
b. For 1984 and 1985 and for January to September 1986 the stocks are estimates based on the debt flows involved in the balance of payments. Non-dollar-denominated obligations are calculated at the exchange rates of December 31, 1983.

flicting way to satisfy the demands of a population that had experienced a 15% decline in its per capita income over a five-year period; and, second, the need to reach an agreement with foreign creditors to cope with arrears that had been accruing since 1982 as well as to meet future maturities that were closing in.

Therefore an appropriate incomes policy and adequate negotiations on the external front were of utmost priority. The first issue was tackled by setting the rate of adjustment of prices and wages in an attempt to engineer a gradual slowdown of inflation. Nevertheless, shortly after these measures had been implemented, an increase in foodstuff prices (particularly beef) triggered inflation above anticipated levels. The attempt to index salaries on a monthly basis to preserve their purchasing power (as promised by the government during its electoral campaign) pushed the inflationary rates to a new higher monthly level.

The second issue was addressed through a negotiation strategy that sought new maturity agreements directly with creditor banks and the Paris Club rather than through the implementation of a new IMF standby agreement. By mid-year it was evident from the upward trend in inflation and the reluctance of commercial banks and industrial countries to negotiate without a prior agreement with the IMF that this strategy would not be successful.

Toward the end of 1984 an agreement was reached with the IMF, and implementation of the policy contained in the memorandum of understanding was started in the last quarter. However, this would be a short-lived plan. The strong monetary contraction together with the attempt to increase public utility rates and to devalue the peso currency in real terms did not lead to a significant slowdown in inflation and caused a sharp drop in economic activity. Furthermore, amid the pressures exerted by wage demands and an acceleration in inflation, the government could not attain the targets in nominal terms for the fiscal deficit. In January 1985 the agreement became null because the IMF did not approve the fiscal goals. This put an end to the first stage of the democratic government's economic policy. It was evident that gradualist policies, like the ones that followed at the beginning of 1984, could not endure strong changes in relative prices (for example, an increase in the price of beef) and that demand policies (such as a sharp reduction in money supply) would lead to significant imbalances if applied within an environment of high inflation.[5]

## 3.2   Some Hypotheses on the Behavior of the Economy

Bearing in mind the behavior pattern of the economy, we can formulate some hypotheses to explain the situation that led to the design and implementation of the Austral Plan.

The Issue of Domestic Transfer

Increased external indebtedness and its servicing raised the issue of seeking resources to meet these obligations. The transfer of resources abroad has external and domestic dimensions. The external aspect refers to the generation of a sufficient trade surplus and/or how to obtain the necessary external financing.

The domestic issue is more complex and introduces highly disturbing elements of the economic behavior. It can be briefly described as follows: After the adjustment process, most of the external indebtedness was of a public nature (table 3.5). Therefore the responsibility for its servicing fell mainly on the government. Furthermore, the trade surplus used to meet those interest payments was in the hands of the private sector. Because of the lack of access to foreign capital markets, the government had to "purchase" the surplus to meet obligations. To raise the necessary funds, the public sector had to reduce operating expenditures or increase the tax burden. Both measures tend to depress economic activity. If neither of these measures was implemented, ceteris paribus, the fiscal deficit would increase and would have to be financed either by issuing currency or by placement of debt. The first option is inflationary (in fact, the deficit is being financed through an inflation tax), and the second one has disruptive effects on financial sector behavior (because it entails a sharp increase in interest rates and in the system's fragility). The 1981–84 adjustment can be interpreted as a combination of all these measures, which in fact implied an acceleration of inflation, increases in the inflation tax and in interest rates, a drop in the activity level (particularly in investment), and negotiations with international organizations to try to overcome the credit constraints imposed by creditor banks.[6]

Financial Fragility and Dollarization of the Economy

As mentioned, disequilibrium during the 1981–83 period resulted in an acceleration of the inflation rate, and therefore the demand for domestic financial assets declined. Thus a demonetization of the economy took place, and maturities for contracts denominated in domestic currency became shorter. Denationalization of domestic financial savings, as economic agents substituted external assets for domestic assets in an attempt to maintain the real worth of their financial wealth, was the counterpart of "vanishing" money and effacing long-term capital markets. In other words, a "dollarization" of the economy took place. At the same time, the decline in the demand for domestic financial assets spurred a strong fall in available credit that negatively affected the enterpreneurial sector while the financial system became more fragile because of the shortening of deposit maturity.[7]

Inflation and Expectations

The price system under rapid inflation not only clears the market for goods but also redistributes income and wealth. Any error in price expectations can lead to an ex post imbalance in income flows and to significant changes in agents' wealth. For that reason a constant information flow is crucial to the agents. In such a dynamic scenario, characterized by disequilibrium and high inflation, there is a constant change of the "environment" (fresh "news"), and any "delay" in receiving information may cause heavy capital and revenue losses.

The price increase in the previous "period" is a quick reference source that permits forecasting of future inflation. In a context of disequilibrium the inflation rate of the previous period (here, a "period" may be one month or even less) can be a more reliable source for forecasting the next period's than any analysis of the public deficit or the money supply, although these variables may explain "long-term" inflation. Indexation to past inflation appears to be an efficient way to minimize eventual capital or revenue losses, and therefore inflation incorporates a strong element of inertia.[8]

However, during shock periods, characterized by sharp increases in inflation rates, it may be more appropriate "to look ahead" instead of "backward." A clear example is the large increase in wages that took place in June 1975 as a result of a devaluation in excess of 100%.

## Uncertainty and Duration of Contracts

The inertial features of the inflationary phenomenon are embodied in the surge of indexed contracts in both the real sphere (wage agreements, agreements with state companies' suppliers) and the financial sphere (indexed deposits). In an environment of high inflation, the main goal is to allow for prolonged contractual agreements that will minimize risks of capital and revenue loss. The basic rationale is to avoid the costs of a permanent recontracting process between interested parties.[9]

Nevertheless, recontracting costs diminish relative to eventual losses when the inflation rate is erratic or when there is a large change in relative prices, precluding a clear perception of each sector's situation by considering only average inflation. This is precisely what happens when a shock accelerates inflation (empirical evidence shows that an acceleration in inflation leads to changes in relative prices). In an uncertain context in which incentives to increase recontracting exist, contract durations shorten. This leads to an inverse relation between uncertainty and duration of contracts. In Argentina wage contracts had a three- or four-month duration before 1981, shortening to one month in the period before the Austral Plan was initiated. In the financial sector most deposits had a maturity of less than thirty days.

## Investment Decline As a Typical Feature of the Adjustment Process

Investment was severely affected during the crisis as a result of all the structural features described (table 3.4). When public sector expenditures increased because of the rise in external debt service payments, the government attempted to reduce public expenditures, especially investment expenditure. In Argentina public and private investment are complementary. Private investment dropped as a result of the reduction in public investment. In addition, deceleration effects resulting from the drop in GDP operated in the same direction. Moreover, fluctuations in relative prices (particularly with regard to exchange rates and salaries) allowed for a highly uncertain estimate of future benefits, from both the cost and benefit sides. Finally, financial distortions contributed to a decline in expenditures on capital investment. The domestic aspect of the transfer issue, which resulted from the lack of fiscal revenues, led the government to design policies to promote the increase in the demand for financial assets in order to absorb the "monetization" of the trade surplus. In other words, financial investment was promoted to the detriment of physical investment. In addition, the dollarization of the economy facilitated the interaction between domestic and international interest rates. As uncertainty mounted, the domestic interest rate increased because of the rising risk premium. Besides, international interest rates showed an upward trend during the chaotic period. These two factors led to an increase in the opportunity cost of investment, and productive projects were dropped.

## 3.3 The Austral Plan

Previous Considerations

The monthly average rate of inflation during 1984 was 18.8%; it increased to 24.1% in the first quarter of 1985. In April it was decided to implement a heterodox shock program. This program entailed actions in both aggregate demand (basically monetary and fiscal policy) and direct control of prices and wages. The situation in the external sector had to be solved at the beginning of the shock in view of the balance of payments position resulting from the high external debt and its implications for expectations. Finally, it was impossible to consider a program aimed at a significant reduction in inflation if there was also a concurrent realignment of some basic relative prices. Therefore relative prices had to be adjusted before the program could start. Before analyzing the June 14 program in detail, it is appropriate to comment on the three topics just mentioned.

Let us begin with the last one, that is, the adjustment of relative prices. The attempt to realign certain key relative prices within the context of a strong reduction in demand usually deepens recession without achieving a decline in inflation rates. This is true at least during the first few months, and it has been proved by experience in Argentina and Latin America as well as in most IMF programs. This fact, together with the decision to freeze most of the prices during the inflation stabilization, implied that any realignment in relative prices had to take place before the program could be implemented.

Therefore, beginning in April and until June 12, 1985, four steps were taken:

1. Controls on industrial prices were made more flexible. In many cases these controls were removed.

2. Public utility rates were increased in order to increase fiscal revenue. (They were increased by an average monthly rate of 37% from April to June compared with an increase of 28% in consumer prices.)

3. In order to improve the balance of payments position and to reduce the expectation of a devaluation after the freeze, the peso was devalued in real terms against the dollar from April to June. The monthly rate of devaluation was 34%. On the other hand, the increase in the exchange rate was compensated for by an increase in export taxes (approximately 10%; figure 3.1). In other words, the devaluation in real terms also had a fiscal goal (revenue increases represented approximately 1% of GDP). The negative

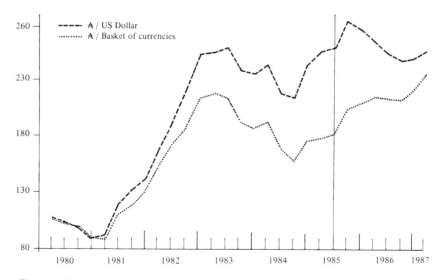

**Figure 3.1**
Real exchange rates. Average of monthly data (1980 = 100). Exchange rate × USA CPI/0.5 (CPI + IWPI).

fiscal effect of devaluation, as a consequence of the high external public debt, was more than offset by this measure.

4. Steps were taken to increase beef prices, which had been lagging behind historical real levels.

Realignment of relative prices led to an acceleration in the rate of inflation. This took place despite a rather tight monetary policy and a substantial fall in aggregate demand. Real wages decreased because of inflationary acceleration within the context of an indexed economy and also because in April the government decided to index wages by 90% of past inflation. This measure was applied in a private sector facing a drop in demand and a decrease in working hours.

In regard to the external sector, the government believed that, before the program could be implemented, it was necessary to reach certain agreements that would allow for adequate external financing and give credibility to the exchange rate policy. It should be remembered that Argentina had an external debt aproximately five times higher than its exports and that no possibility of balancing the current account could be foreseen. Furthermore, arrears amounted to $3.3 billion (US dollars).

To this end, a standby agreement, was negotiated with the IMF. This agreement proposed a strong fiscal adjustment and secured financing for the balance of payments disequilibrium. The agreement reached with the IMF one week before the policy was implemented did not mention a strategy of "generalized shock."

Finally, we review the arguments that led to a heterodox shock in order to show the difference from shocks applied in, for example, European hyperinflations of the past. An extrapolation of that type of experience was not fully applicable in the Argentine case: In Argentina there was neither total dollarization nor continuous indexation; there was contractual inertia, although for short periods. Agreements were in force for at least one month. Also, Argentina had experienced ten years of erratic inflation, but in the 1975−84 period the monthly average had been 11%. From 1945 to 1974 the average monthly inflation had amounted to 2.1% per month. These inflation rates were addressed by stabilization programs that failed in most cases or did not achieve a permanent reduction in inflation rates.

On the other hand, it is not clear that the mere enunciation of a fiscal and monetary shock causes changes in expectations capable of breaking the inflationary inertia. For this to happen, the shock must be credible. Furthermore, the attitude of economic agents depends on the economic model each one has in mind as well as on the expected reactions from other economic agents.[10] However, "a global price realignment based on expectations that the Government will stabilize the aggregate demand requires a synchronized halt of overall price increases. It is not clear whether all agents will coordinate actions so that this may occur" (Heymann 1985, p. 154).

In all probability some prices will continue on an upward trend,[11] and a recession, the duration of which would depend on expectations, would set in. A recession would have two effects. First, there would be expectations that the stabilization effort could hardly last in the context of a decrease in employment and in real wages. A drop in employment opportunities and in real wages would be considered unfair and would bring about strong social and political reactions that would, in turn, nourish inflation expectations. In Argentina this is of decisive importance because the population has experienced a sharp decline in per capita income during the last few years and also felt the impact of marked decreases in real wages during the military government. Second, the strong hold of Argentine trade unions in a nonauthoritarian context must be borne in mind. Furthermore, most of these trade unions were politically opposed to the government in office.

For all these reasons a demand shock without a price and wage freeze was out of the question.

The Measures

The Austral Plan was structured as a consistent and coordinated effort on all fronts where imbalances were most evident. Thus the shock policy was oriented toward an immediate change in price expectations, in the amount and the mechanisms for financing the fiscal deficit, and in external equilibrium. The purpose was to introduce changes in the exogenous data constraining agents' behavior and to shorten as much as possible the adaptation period of their behavior to the new environment. This would reduce adjustment costs resulting from decision-making errors caused by lack of understanding of the new rules of the game. In other words, the goal was not only a new equilibrium but also minimizing the cost and length of the dynamic adjustment to the new situation.

In order to deal with agents' expectations functions while eliminating the inertial component of inflation, the government decreed a general wage and price freeze. Specifically all prices, except those in flexible price markets, were frozen at the levels prevailing two days before the launching of the Austral Plan. The exchange rate was pegged to the US dollar (0.8 austral = 1 dollar), and wages were adjusted for the last time according to a proportion of the preceding month's inflation (this represented a 22% nominal increase).

The feasibility of these measures was eased by the reduction in contract length. As all settlements were short term, a marked disalignment in relative prices was not expected to take place during the freeze. (Moreover, as it has already been mentioned, their correction had been promoted in former months.) On the other hand, the freeze did not affect those markets in which prices are instantaneously adjusted by changes in supply and demand. In these markets, in which indexed contracts do not exist, it was expected that a downward movement in inflation rates would be achieved through the control of aggregate demand.

On the fiscal and financial side the government implemented measures consistent with the wage and price policy. A sharp reduction in the deficit in fiscal accounts was envisaged. This deficit amounted to 12% of GDP during the first half of 1985 and was anticipated to decline to 2.5% in the second half. Such a reduction would primarily stem from a significant rise in public sector revenue, which would derive from the increase in public utility rates (which had been increased in real terms before the freeze), an increase in the tax burden on foreign trade, a rescheduling of direct taxes (new legislation was sent to Congress for approval), and the revenue increase caused by the converse of the "fiscal lag" as inflation fell. Moreover, these measures were strengthened with the implementation of a forced savings mechanism for income for wealthy taxpayers. Public expenditures of the central government were also to be cut (although it was agreed that massive layoffs would be avoided and that reductions in social benefits would not be made). Likewise, the government expected a decline in operating losses of the Central Bank in view of the sharp drop in nominal interest rates.

The most important action in the financial sector was the implementation of a monetary reform. A new currency, the austral, was introduced to replace the Argentine peso. One austral would be equivalent to one thousand Argentine pesos. As of the date of implementation, the austral would be revalued daily against the peso. Contracts in Argentine pesos with maturity dates after June 14 were depreciated (according to a conversion table) against the austral by an amount equivalent to the inflation rate prevalent before the plan. This measure was designed to avoid a wealth redistribution that would favor creditors over debtors because of the drop in the inflation rate, as existing contracts incorporated the expected inflation rate. The regulated interest rate was reduced from 28% to 4% per month.

On the other hand, the government agreed to stop issuing money to finance the fiscal deficit. The fiscal deficit would be entirely financed with external credit. The purpose of that commitment was to control the sources of money creation to have consistency between income and monetary policies. Furthermore, this measure was an attempt to affect expectations, giving credibility to the program's feasibility.

Once the plan was implemented, a new agreement was signed with the IMF, and an agreement was reached with creditor banks concerning the 1984—85 Financial Plan that would provide the necessary external financing.

### 3.4    The Evolution of the Economy during the Austral Plan

The Austral Plan has now been in force for almost two years. During that time new events caused by the plan itself have arisen in the Argentine economy. However, an integral part of its existing behavioral structure has remained in action. The stabilization plan has harvested achievements and failures. We divide the analysis into two sections in order to follow an orderly scheme. We first analyze the results of the shock policy and cover the nine-month period after the program was launched, that is, until the freeze was abandoned (June 1985—March 1986). Second, we cover the rest of the period, that is, April 1986—May 1987.

The Effects of the Shock

Once the program had been implemented, a series of credibility tests had to be passed within a short time. First, had the freeze succeeded as a coordination instrument for private expectations in the process of eliminating the inertial component of inflation, the pace of price increases should have fallen sharply without shortages. Second, given the considerable decline in interest rates, had the public not believed in the program, there would have been a mass withdrawal of deposits from the banking system. In view of the behavior of portfolio selection during the period of chaotic adjustment, if this had happened, it would have been reflected in the demand for external assets. Therefore a third credibility test resulted from the exchange rate gap, that is, the difference between the official foreign exchange rate and the one recorded in the black market.

The program passed these tests successfully. When banks reopened (a bank holiday was decreed when the plan was announced), deposits were massively renewed and the conversion table from pesos to australs was applied without any difficulty (ad hoc agreements between individuals developed without any major problems arising). There were some conflicts over public sector contracts but they were solved within a reasonable time. In the foreign market portfolio response was satisfactory. The exchange rate gap was nil for several days.

Although some representatives of the workers and the firms opposed the plan, the population in general massively supported the price freeze. This was crucial for the program's success. The population expressed its support by means of spontaneous price controls. The lengthening of the "searching" period for purchases acted in the same direction. Until then the search period was short, because the continuous price increase made the cost of search excessively high.

With some exceptions the period of strict implementation of the measures lasted nine months, until March 1986. The goals formulated in the plan were satisfactorily met. For the first time since the 1980–81 crisis, a deep and substantial change was introduced in the dynamics of the Argentine economy. The most relevant aspects are discussed in what follows.

The freeze effects on inflation were quickly noticed. Measured by the wholesale price index, inflation fell from 42.3% in June 1985 to $-0.9\%$ in July. In terms of consumer prices, inflation dropped from 30.5% to 6.2% over the same period (the difference between both indexes was mainly due to statistical carry-over in consumer prices). During the nine-month freeze the average monthly rate of inflation in wholesale prices was below 1%, whereas it reached 3% for consumer prices. In the nine months preceding the plan those values amounted to 7% and 25%, respectively (see table 3.6 and figure 3.2). These results were achieved without governmental strict price controls and without any product shortages.

The figures given confirm in principle the hypothesis that the inertial component of inflation was successfully eliminated. However, the same is not true in connection with the structural features. During the period under analysis, relative prices fluctuated significantly, and, because prices still could not be reduced, these fluctuations implied positive inflation. In other words, the premise that a realignment of relative prices implies an increase in the general price level continued to be valid.

The most important changes took place in the foodstuffs sector, that is, in markets with flexible prices. There were also significant increases in the price of services. These contributed to a systematically higher inflation rate for consumer prices than for wholesale prices because foodstuffs and services have a higher weight in the consumer basket. A comparison of the growth rate in the different components of the aggregate wholesale price

**Table 3.6**
Selected variables: Monthly changes in %

| Period | Consumer prices | Wholesale prices | Wages[a] | Public utility rates | Exchange rates | Monetary aggregates[b] |
|---|---|---|---|---|---|---|
| **1985** | | | | | | |
| January | 25.1 | 21.1 | 20.4 | 19.3 | 25.0 | 20.4 |
| February | 20.7 | 17.8 | 15.4 | 15.5 | 20.6 | 19.7 |
| March | 26.5 | 27.7 | 21.4 | 25.6 | 26.4 | 18.9 |
| April | 29.5 | 31.5 | 24.9 | 26.1 | 29.4 | 19.2 |
| May | 25.1 | 31.2 | 31.7 | 40.0 | 32.4 | 21.5 |
| June | 30.5 | 42.3 | 28.7 | 48.7 | 40.3 | 36.3 |
| July | 6.2 | −0.9 | −2.8 | 6.9 | 8.7 | 28.2 |
| August | 3.1 | 1.5 | 0.0 | 0.0 | 0.0 | 9.2 |
| September | 2.0 | 0.6 | 1.0 | 0.0 | 0.0 | 8.5 |
| October | 1.9 | 0.7 | 1.9 | 0.0 | 0.0 | 8.5 |
| November | 2.4 | 0.7 | 1.9 | 0.0 | 0.0 | 7.7 |
| December | 3.2 | 1.0 | 5.5 | 0.0 | 0.0 | 8.2 |
| **1986** | | | | | | |
| January | 3.0 | 0.0 | 5.2 | 0.0 | 0.0 | 6.7 |
| February | 1.7 | 0.8 | 1.7 | 0.0 | 0.0 | 5.1 |
| March | 4.6 | 1.4 | 0.8 | 0.4 | 0.0 | 5.7 |
| April | 4.7 | 3.0 | 6.5 | 6.4 | 3.3 | 5.3 |
| May | 4.0 | 2.7 | 5.3 | 3.9 | 2.6 | 7.0 |
| June | 4.5 | 4.6 | 5.0 | 4.0 | 2.8 | 6.3 |
| July | 6.8 | 5.1 | 6.8 | 7.0 | 3.4 | 6.5 |
| August | 8.8 | 9.4 | 9.0 | 6.0 | 6.8 | 5.5 |
| September | 7.2 | 6.8 | 1.8 | 4.0 | 8.8 | 3.7 |
| October | 6.1 | 5.3 | 11.0 | 4.0 | 4.1 | 6.5 |
| November | 5.3 | 4.9 | 4.7 | 5.0 | 5.2 | 8.7 |
| December | 4.7 | 3.0 | 2.5 | 5.8 | 5.4 | 7.4 |
| **1987** | | | | | | |
| January | 7.6 | 5.3 | 7.8 | 6.5 | 6.5 | 5.6 |
| February | 6.5 | 6.9 | 3.6 | 6.9 | 7.5 | 5.0 |
| March | 8.2 | 7.9 | 2.2 | 7.0 | 11.0 | 4.7 |
| April | 3.4 | 1.9 | 8.5 | 0.0 | 0.0 | 4.3 |
| May | 4.2 | 4.9 | 3.9 | 4.0 | 3.2 | 6.1 |

Source: Instituto Nacional de Estadística y Censos, Sindicatura General de Empresas Públicas, and Banco Central de la República Argentina.
a. Industrial sector. Normal hourly wage.
b. Refers to M4. The increase during the last quarter of 1986 is overestimated because during that period nonregistered financial operations were incorporated into the institutional financial system.

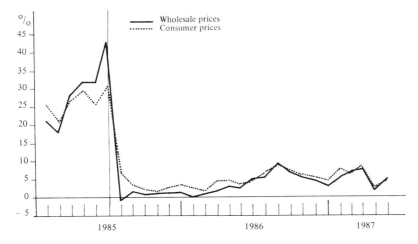

**Figure 3.2**
Rate of inflation, monthly changes.

index shows the evident inflationary effect of the increase in foodstuffs prices. In June 1985 the agricultural/nonagricultural price ratio was 0.61; in March 1986 the ratio was 0.93, which represents a 52% increase. Two factors seem to have been mainly responsible for this effect. When the policy was implemented, the relative value of foodstuffs was well below customary levels. Moreover, the decline in the inflation rate eliminated the devastating effects of inflation on the purchasing power of workers because of the temporal gap between wage payment and spending. Likewise, the overall income of workers tended to improve (see table 3.7). Besides that, after the first few months of the plan economic activity showed signs of reactivation, which permitted wage drift and an increase in working hours.[12] Therefore both substitution and income effects contributed to an increase in the real demand for foodstuffs. In the short term the supply of these products is inelastic, and consequently prices were adjusted upward.

Changes in the financial and monetary environment were no less significant. The sharp drop in price increases provoked a change in the demand for money. Because of a reduction in the cost of holding liquid assets, the demand for those assets increased substantially. The ratio between M1 and GDP more than doubled during the nine months under review. It rose from 3.3% in the second quarter of 1985 to 8.1% in the first quarter of 1986. The ratio M4/GDP rose by 72% over the same period (table 3.8). By effectively

**Table 3.7**
Real wages and purchasing power for the industrial sector, normal hourly wage
(1982 = 100)

| Period | Real wages[a] | Purchasing power[b] |
|---|---|---|
| **1980** | 118.9 | |
| I | 117.4 | |
| II | 116.3 | |
| III | 118.2 | |
| IV | 123.8 | |
| **1981** | 113.1 | |
| I | 121.0 | |
| II | 112.1 | |
| III | 107.2 | |
| IV | 112.1 | |
| **1982** | 100.0 | 100.0 |
| I | 102.3 | 107.7 |
| II | 96.2 | 100.3 |
| III | 94.9 | 90.5 |
| IV | 106.6 | 101.5 |
| **1983** | 124.1 | 117.7 |
| I | 107.7 | 106.4 |
| II | 119.2 | 113.0 |
| III | 130.1 | 121.2 |
| IV | 139.3 | 130.2 |
| **1984** | 157.7 | 147.5 |
| I | 149.6 | 143.1 |
| II | 158.3 | 146.5 |
| III | 159.5 | 146.9 |
| IV | 163.3 | 153.4 |
| **1985** | 138.4 | 136.2 |
| I | 151.4 | 142.5 |
| II | 144.2 | 128.6 |
| III | 129.9 | 139.6 |
| IV | 128.2 | 134.0 |
| **1986** | 130.6 | 134.7 |
| I | 131.0 | 137.5 |
| II | 131.1 | 134.6 |
| III | 130.1 | 133.3 |
| IV | 130.0 | 133.2 |
| **1987** | | |
| I | 123.5 | 127.8 |

Source: Instituto Nacional de Estadística y Censos and Banco Central de la República Argentina.
a. Real wages are estimated as follows: $SR_t = W_t/P_t$, where $SR_t$ is real wages in month $t$, $W_t$ is nominal wages in month $t$, and $P_t$ is consumer price index for month $t$.
b. Purchasing power is estimated as follows: $PA_t = (0.75\,W_{t-1} + 0.25\,W_t)/P_t$, where $PA_t$ is purchasing power for the month, $W_{t-1}$ is nominal wages in month $t - 1$, $W_t$ is nominal wages in month $t$, and $P_t$ is the index of consumer prices for month $t$.

**Table 3.8**
Monetary aggregates (% of GDP)

| Period | M1[a] | M1 Private | M4[b] | M5[c] |
|---|---|---|---|---|
| **1980** | 10.5 | 7.5 | 31.3 | 33.0 |
| I | 10.1 | 7.4 | 31.7 | 33.2 |
| II | 10.3 | 7.4 | 30.8 | 32.5 |
| III | 10.6 | 7.5 | 31.3 | 32.8 |
| IV | 10.8 | 7.7 | 31.5 | 33.3 |
| **1981** | 8.4 | 6.2 | 30.3 | 33.0 |
| I | 10.9 | 8.1 | 35.1 | 37.7 |
| II | 8.1 | 5.8 | 30.0 | 32.6 |
| III | 7.5 | 5.6 | 28.4 | 31.5 |
| IV | 7.2 | 5.4 | 27.5 | 30.3 |
| **1982** | 6.3 | 4.8 | 21.4 | 23.6 |
| I | 6.6 | 4.9 | 27.2 | 29.6 |
| II | 7.2 | 5.5 | 26.7 | 29.2 |
| III | 6.1 | 4.7 | 17.7 | 19.6 |
| IV | 5.4 | 4.1 | 14.0 | 16.1 |
| **1983** | 4.9 | 3.8 | 14.7 | 14.7 |
| I | 5.0 | 3.8 | 15.6 | 15.6 |
| II | 5.1 | 3.8 | 15.8 | 15.8 |
| III | 4.9 | 3.8 | 14.4 | 14.4 |
| IV | 4.7 | 3.6 | 12.9 | 12.9 |
| **1984** | 4.7 | 3.7 | 14.5 | 14.5 |
| I | 5.1 | 4.0 | 15.9 | 15.9 |
| II | 4.9 | 3.7 | 14.1 | 14.1 |
| III | 4.6 | 3.6 | 14.6 | 14.6 |
| IV | 4.1 | 3.3 | 13.5 | 13.5 |
| **1985** | 5.0 | 3.5 | 14.1 | 14.4 |
| I | 3.7 | 2.8 | 14.6 | 14.7 |
| II | 3.3 | 2.4 | 11.3 | 11.7 |
| III | 5.7 | 4.0 | 14.8 | 15.2 |
| IV | 7.1 | 4.7 | 15.7 | 15.8 |
| **1986** | 8.1 | 5.6 | 19.7 | 19.9 |
| I | 8.1 | 5.5 | 19.4 | 19.5 |
| II | 8.3 | 5.7 | 19.7 | 19.9 |
| III | 8.2 | 5.6 | 20.0 | 20.2 |
| IV | 7.7 | 5.4 | 19.8 | 19.9 |
| **1987** | | | | |
| I | 7.1 | 5.0 | 21.1 | 21.3 |

Source: Banco Central de la República Argentina.
a. Currency plus current account deposits. Seasonally adjusted.
b. M1 plus time deposit.
c. M4 plus government and Central Bank bonds.

and immediately reducing inflation, the Austral Plan reversed the demonetization of the economy.

The government honored strictly its commitment not to issue any new
money to finance public expenditure. The increase in high-powered money
can be wholly explained by the external sector, rediscounting grants to
financial institutions, and interest payments on reserve requirements.

The expansion in the monetary base originated in the external sector
and was significant in the period right after the implementation of the
program because of large inflows of foreign capital. Later, this source of
money creation was offset by measures taken to eliminate the imbalances
caused by these capital movements. The minimum deposit maturity for
foreign financial capital was increased from 180 to 360 days, and the term
for export prefinancing was shortened from 180 to 90 days.

Other monetary base creation factors reflected both policy targets and
endogenous mechanisms of money generation (endogeneity caused by the
prolonged disorganization of the financial system). The monetary regulation account reflects, in part, the Central Bank's deficit that arose from its
efforts to conciliate terms and rates as the only real financial intermediary
in a quite weakened monetary system. In turn, rediscounts increased
because credit policies were targeted at selected activities (exports) and
because of distortions in financial institutions (mismatching between indexed deposit and credit terms).

Real interest rates during this period were highly positive because nominal rates, although in a sharp downward trend, did not drop as fast as
inflation rates (see table 3.9 and figure 3.3). The impact on the financing
conditions of enterprises was mitigated by the subsidization of their interest rates through special credit lines based mainly on Central Bank rediscounts.[13] Furthermore, the drop in nominal interest rates in fact lengthened
debt maturities, and, finally, the remonetization of the economy resulted in
an increase in credit availability. The increase in sales during the months
following the implementation of the plan and the two elements just mentioned above, contributed to a sounder liquidity position of firms.

On the fiscal front the objectives of the program were satisfactorily met.
The fiscal deficit (cash basis) declined abruptly from a quarterly average of
11.9% of GDP during the semester preceding the plan to 3.2% of GDP in
the three subsequent quarters. When the fiscal deficit of the Central Bank is
excluded, these figures are 7.2% and 1.9%, respectively (see table 3.10).

This improvement in fiscal accounts basically originated in an increase in
revenue because public expenditures remained more or less constant (tables
3.10 and 3.11). First, income in real terms increased mainly because of the

**Table 3.9**
Monthly interest rates (%)

| | Regulated market | | | | Nonregulated market | | | |
|---|---|---|---|---|---|---|---|---|
| | Lending rate | | Deposit rate | | Lending rate[b] | | Deposit rate | |
| Period | Nominal | Real[a] | Nominal | Real[a] | Nominal | Real[a] | Nominal | Real[a] |
| **1985** | | | | | | | | |
| January | 19.5 | 0.2 | 17.5 | −1.4 | 24.9 | 4.7 | 24.6 | 4.4 |
| February | 20.0 | −5.5 | 17.9 | −7.1 | 22.3 | −3.7 | 22.4 | −3.6 |
| March | 22.0 | −6.5 | 19.9 | −8.0 | 25.5 | −3.8 | 24.9 | −4.2 |
| April | 26.0 | −1.6 | 24.0 | −3.2 | 28.8 | 0.5 | 28.0 | −0.0 |
| May | 32.0 | −3.2 | 30.0 | −4.6 | 40.4 | 3.0 | 32.4 | −2.9 |
| June | 17.9 | (c) | 16.0 | (c) | 26.7 | (c) | 20.2 | (c) |
| July | 5.0 | 2.6 | 3.5 | 1.2 | 7.6 | 5.3 | 5.9 | 3.5 |
| August | 5.0 | 3.6 | 3.5 | 2.1 | 8.6 | 7.2 | 6.3 | 4.9 |
| September | 5.0 | 3.6 | 3.5 | 2.1 | 6.2 | 4.8 | 5.7 | 4.2 |
| October | 4.5 | 2.8 | 3.5 | 1.9 | 5.3 | 3.7 | 4.6 | 2.9 |
| November | 4.5 | 2.3 | 3.1 | 1.0 | 5.5 | 3.3 | 5.0 | 2.8 |
| December | 4.5 | 2.9 | 3.1 | 1.5 | 5.9 | 4.4 | 5.2 | 3.6 |
| **1986** | | | | | | | | |
| January | 4.5 | 3.2 | 3.1 | 1.8 | 5.6 | 4.4 | 5.2 | 3.9 |
| February | 4.5 | 1.4 | 3.1 | 0.0 | 5.5 | 2.4 | 5.2 | 2.1 |
| March | 4.5 | 0.6 | 3.1 | −0.7 | 4.4 | 0.5 | 4.9 | 1.0 |
| April | 4.5 | 1.0 | 3.1 | −0.2 | 4.6 | 1.2 | 4.3 | 0.8 |
| May | 4.5 | −0.0 | 3.1 | −1.3 | 4.5 | −0.0 | 4.2 | −0.3 |
| June | 4.7 | −1.1 | 3.1 | −2.6 | 4.4 | −1.4 | 4.3 | −1.5 |
| July | 5.0 | −3.7 | 3.3 | −5.2 | 5.1 | −3.6 | 4.6 | −4.1 |
| August | 6.6 | −0.3 | 3.5 | −3.2 | 6.5 | −0.4 | 6.2 | −0.7 |
| September | 6.0 | 0.3 | 5.1 | −0.5 | 7.3 | 1.6 | 7.0 | 1.2 |
| October | 6.5 | 1.3 | 4.5 | −0.5 | 8.1 | 2.9 | 7.7 | 2.4 |
| November | 7.0 | 3.0 | 5.0 | 1.0 | 8.2 | 4.2 | 7.8 | 3.7 |
| December | 7.0 | 0.5 | 5.5 | −0.8 | 9.3 | 2.7 | 8.2 | 1.6 |
| **1987** | | | | | | | | |
| January | 7.0 | 0.2 | 5.5 | −1.1 | 9.0 | 2.2 | 8.1 | 1.3 |
| February | 6.8 | −1.1 | 5.8 | −2.4 | 8.7 | 0.7 | 7.4 | −0.5 |
| March | 4.0 | 1.3 | 3.0 | 0.3 | 4.4 | 1.7 | 4.0 | 1.3 |
| April | 5.2 | 0.6 | 4.2 | −0.3 | 8.2 | 3.5 | 7.4 | 2.7 |
| May | 5.7 | −1.5 | 4.7 | −2.5 | 8.2 | 0.8 | 7.9 | 0.5 |

Source: Banco Central de la República Argentina and Cronista Comercial.
a. Deflated by the arithmetic average of wholesale and consumer price indexes of the subsequent month.
b. Prime rate.
c. The real rate computation for June 1985 is worthless because of the Austral Plan implementation on June 14, 1985.

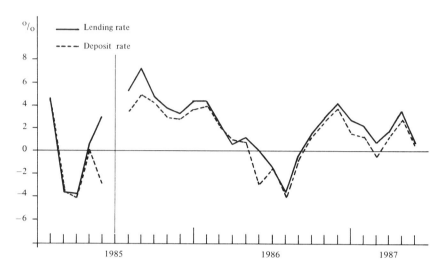

**Figure 3.3**
Real interest rates (monthly averages) deflated by the arithmetic average of wholesale and consumer price indexes of the subsequent month.

Olivera-Tanzi effect as inflation declined. Before the plan treasury losses on this account amounted to approximately 2.5% of GDP. After the plan they dropped to 0.5% of GDP. Second, revenue increased as a result of heavier taxes on foreign trade and fuel. Third, tax evasion controls were improved and, as we have already mentioned, a forced savings system was implemented.[14]

To conclude the analysis of the shock effects, we should mention that the downward trend in inflation, the deficit reduction, and the remonetization of the economy had a beneficial impact on the activity level. In fact, after a short period a significant upswing in effective demand was evident during the first quarter of the plan's implementation. Nevertheless the increased dynamism in sales did not have an immediate impact on production levels. Commercial firms, having to face highly positive real interest rates, chose to reduce stocks—onerous to maintain—in order to keep up with increasing sales. In the third quarter of 1985 this was reflected in a drop in the level of stocks in a number of industrial activities (see table 3.12). Later, production was expanded significantly to meet the sustained real demand and the need to replenish stocks. In the last quarter of 1985 overall seasonally adjusted GDP increased over 4% and industrial product rose by 13%. This reactivation of production was maintained during 1986, leading to an increase in GDP of 5.7%. It should be pointed out that during

**Table 3.10**
Expenditures, revenues, and deficit of the public sector: Cash basis (% of GDP)

| Period | Nonfinancial public sector | | | (4) Central Bank deficit | (5)=(3)+(4) Total deficit |
| | (1) Expenditures[a] | (2) Revenues[b] | (3)=(1)−(2) Deficit[c] | | |
| --- | --- | --- | --- | --- | --- |
| **1983** | 34.7 | 23.6 | 11.1 | 1.1 | 12.2 |
| I | 35.4 | 28.3 | 7.1 | 0.3 | 7.4 |
| II | 37.7 | 30.5 | 7.2 | 1.4 | 8.6 |
| III | 34.3 | 25.1 | 9.2 | 0.5 | 9.7 |
| IV | 33.9 | 19.9 | 14.3 | 1.4 | 15.7 |
| **1984** | 31.2 | 22.9 | 8.3 | 2.7 | 11.0 |
| I | 32.3 | 22.8 | 9.5 | 5.6 | 15.1 |
| II | 33.4 | 23.1 | 10.3 | 6.0 | 16.3 |
| III | 29.2 | 22.9 | 6.3 | 3.1 | 9.4 |
| IV | 31.5 | 22.9 | 8.6 | 2.3 | 10.9 |
| **1985** | 31.0 | 27.5 | 3.5 | 2.4 | 5.9 |
| I | 29.5 | 22.0 | 7.5 | 4.4 | 11.9 |
| II | 28.9 | 22.0 | 6.9 | 5.0 | 11.9 |
| III | 30.4 | 28.6 | 1.8 | 1.2 | 3.0 |
| IV | 33.1 | 31.8 | 1.3 | 0.9 | 2.2 |
| **1986** | 28.6 | 25.9 | 2.7 | 1.6 | 4.3 |
| I | 30.2 | 27.8 | 2.4 | 1.8 | 4.2 |
| II | 28.7 | 27.8 | 0.9 | 1.3 | 2.2 |
| III | 28.1 | 27.3 | 0.8 | 1.3 | 2.1 |
| IV | 27.9 | 22.5 | 5.4 | 2.2 | 7.6 |
| **1983** | | | | | |
| I[d] | 26.1 | 22.7 | 3.4 | 1.9 | 5.3 |

Source: Banco Central de la República Argentina and Secretaría de Hacienda
a. Includes national and provincial governments, social security system, and current account deficits of public enterprises.
b. Excludes current revenue of public enterprises.
c. Secretary of Treasury estimation.
d. Preliminary.

**Table 3.11**
Expenditures, revenues, and deficit of the nonfinancial public sector: Budget basis
(% of GDP)

| Period | Expenditures[a] | Revenues[b] | Deficit |
|--------|-----------------|-------------|---------|
| 1980   | 43.9            | 36.4        | 7.5     |
| 1981   | 49.1            | 35.8        | 13.3    |
| 1982   | 48.2            | 33.1        | 15.1    |
| 1983   | 51.6            | 34.8        | 16.8    |
| 1984   | 46.2            | 33.4        | 12.8    |
| 1985   | 47.4            | 41.5        | 5.9     |
| 1986[c] | 43.4           | 39.8        | 3.6     |

Source: Secretaría de Hacienda, Dirección Nacional de Programación Presupuestaria.
a. Includes expenditures of national and provincial governments, social security system, and public enterprises.
b. Includes revenues of national and provincial governments, social security system, and public enterprises.
c. Final budget.

1986 the stabilization plan succeeded in reverting one of the main characteristics of the period of chaotic adjustment: the fall in capital goods expenditure. Fixed gross investment increased by 11.1%, and the process was led by purchases of productive equipment (16.7%) (figure 3.4).

This increase in demand was mainly due to two factors. First, although the traditional measure of real wage showed a decline during the first few months of the plan, a more accurate estimation showed a different result. Wages are paid either at the end of the month or, in the case of industrial workers, at the end of every two weeks. But they are spent during the following month or two weeks. Consequently a drop in the inflation rate produces an automatic rise in purchasing power. When this correction is introduced, the purchasing power of wages showed an increase in July 1985 (see table 3.7 and figure 3.5). Another way of analyzing this effect is to say that the elimination of the inflation tax redistributes income in favor of workers. This rise in purchasing power generated an increase in demand. Second, the reduction in nominal interest rates favored the purchase of durable goods in installments because the amount of the first installment was substantially reduced.

Despite the increase in real demand, it should be borne in mind that the reactivation process took place toward the end of the third quarter of 1985. The low levels of GDP during the first half of the year initiated a sharp drop in imports and an increase in industrial exports as commercial firms

**Table 3.12**
Stocks of finished goods

| Period | January (1980 = 100) |
| --- | --- |
| **1985** | |
| January | 115 |
| February | 113 |
| March | 103 |
| April | 104 |
| May | 109 |
| June | 124 |
| July | 119 |
| August | 108 |
| September | 102 |
| October | 107 |
| November | 105 |
| December | 99 |
| **1986** | |
| January | 97 |
| February | 98 |
| March | 100 |
| April | 99 |
| May | 101 |
| June | 94 |
| July | 102 |
| August | 102 |
| September | 99 |
| October | 103 |
| November | 105 |
| December | 105 |
| **1987** | |
| January | 100 |
| February | 99 |
| March | 100 |
| April | 99 |
| May | 98 |

Source: Associación Cristiana de Dirigentes de Empresa.

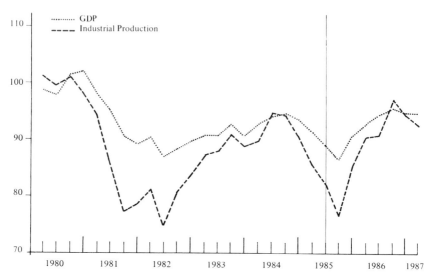

**Figure 3.4**
Gross domestic product and industrial production, seasonally adjusted (1980 = 100).

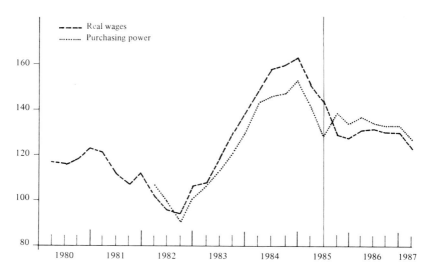

**Figure 3.5**
Real wages and purchasing power in the industrial sector, normal hourly wage (1982 = 100).

attempted to place stocks abroad that had not been sold in the domestic market. This led to a record trade surplus of $4.5 billion (US dollars) in 1985. The current account deficit was the lowest since 1980 (see table 3.3), and there was some increase in foreign reserves, which improved the country's negotiating position.[15]

Flexibility and Management of Imbalances

The main goal of the shock program designed in June 1985 was to eradicate the threat of hyperinflation. This threat was seen in soaring prices, a constant demonetization of the economy, and a public sector plagued by an increasing deficit. The plan succeeded in achieving this target. Inflation declined sharply, the economy was remonetized, and fiscal accounts were significantly closer to balance. An important political limitation not only from a factual point of view but also as an expressed goal of the governing team was to avoid both unemployment and a drop in workers' real income. The program took this limitation into consideration. Activity levels recovered, and the purchasing power of wages was preserved.

The basic triumph of the shock program was to achieve those goals quickly in the context of a highly imbalanced economy. Once the short-term goals had been achieved, it was necessary to focus on structural restrictions: an oligopolistic economy characterized by a closed internal market and a lack of competitiveness, an inefficient public sector, a regressive tax structure, the external debt maturities profile, an inefficient and weak financial system, the volatility of supply and the inefficiency of the distribution network in the foodstuffs sector. The plan was the necessary condition for work to start on these issues. These structural issues are not short-term problems, nor can they be addressed by stabilization policy. Therefore they are not analyzed here.

The postshock period that began in March 1986 contained several elements that weakened the stabilization: the remaining structural imbalances and new external shocks. These problems appeared in the acceleration of inflation and difficulties in the management of monetary, fiscal, and incomes policies. In a context of increased stability created by the shock program, the government attempted to manage these imbalances through policy packages that would gradually change the rules of the game established in June 1985. The rest of this chapter is devoted to the analysis of these issues.

As we have already seen, significant changes in relative prices were evident from June 1985 to March 1986. In turn, a positive rate of inflation was registered because the shock program succeeded in eliminating the inflationary inertia but failed to destroy the core of inflation.[16]

At the beginning of the second quarter of 1986 the economic authorities were faced with a dilemma. The longer the freeze was maintained, the higher the accrued imbalance in relative prices and the higher the potential risk of inflation in the succeeding period due to the structural characteristics of the economy. On the other hand, had the freeze been extended, the economic agents might "forget" past inflationary experiences, and therefore a return to defensive indexing measures could be averted in the post-freeze period. (Frenkel and Fanelli 1987, p. 30)

Toward March–April 1986 the measures implemented in June 1985 were modified to defuse pressures that had become evident during the freeze. A price control system was adopted wherein realignments would be concomitant with changes of costs. Likewise, exchange rate variations would be set in terms of a crawling peg to maintain the exchange rate value in real terms. Public utility rates would shift in accordance with preannounced increases, and nominal wages could be adjusted within a preset band. An upward trend in the inflation curve was anticipated as a consequene of the lifting of the freeze. Inflation increased in the postfreeze quarter, reaching a level of slightly over 4% on a monthly average. However, inflation did not remain stable at that level. An upward surge was registered toward July, and the average of consumer and wholesale price indexes reached a monthly value of 7.6% in the following quarter.

The fiscal deficit cannot be blamed for the increase in the inflation rate. During the second and third quarters of 1986 it averaged 3% of GDP (including the fiscal deficit of the Central Bank). Renewed inflation was mainly caused by wage push in June and July and a passive monetary policy from April onward. Nominal interest rates lagged behind inflation, and in some months real rates turned negative (see table 3.9).[17] Unexpectedly, the gap between the official and black market exchange rates declined from April to July and became almost nil in July. From then on it surged (see table 3.13 and figure 3.6).

There was a sustained level of activity, and the recovery period initiated by the program remained on firm ground. In the second and third quarters of 1986 seasonally adjusted real GDP increased by over 2% on a quarterly average. If the goals of the program were to be maintained, this strong reactivation in a context of passive monetary policy and acceleration of inflation could not be maintained.

In order to turn around the negative aspects of the situation, a new set of anti-inflationary measures was announced in September. It was announced

**Table 3.13**
Exchange rate (australs per dollar)

| Period | (1) Official market | (2) Black market | (2) − (1)/(1) (%) |
|---|---|---|---|
| **1985** | | | |
| January | 0.201 | 0.240 | 19.4 |
| February | 0.242 | 0.317 | 31.0 |
| March | 0.306 | 0.403 | 31.7 |
| April | 0.396 | 0.527 | 33.1 |
| May | 0.525 | 0.619 | 17.9 |
| June | 0.737 | 0.798 | 8.3 |
| July | 0.801 | 0.943 | 17.7 |
| August | 0.801 | 0.952 | 18.9 |
| September | 0.801 | 0.940 | 17.4 |
| October | 0.801 | 0.925 | 15.5 |
| November | 0.801 | 0.898 | 12.1 |
| December | 0.801 | 0.855 | 6.7 |
| **1986** | | | |
| January | 0.801 | 0.899 | 12.2 |
| February | 0.801 | 0.861 | 7.5 |
| March | 0.801 | 0.909 | 13.5 |
| April | 0.828 | 0.922 | 11.4 |
| May | 0.850 | 0.900 | 5.9 |
| June | 0.874 | 0.895 | 2.4 |
| July | 0.904 | 0.915 | 1.2 |
| August | 0.965 | 1.086 | 12.5 |
| September | 1.050 | 1.222 | 16.4 |
| October | 1.094 | 1.198 | 9.5 |
| November | 1.151 | 1.350 | 17.3 |
| December | 1.213 | 1.565 | 29.0 |
| **1987** | | | |
| January | 1.293 | 1.714 | 32.6 |
| February | 1.383 | 1.712 | 23.8 |
| March | 1.541 | 1.880 | 22.0 |
| April | 1.541 | 2.039 | 32.3 |
| May | 1.599 | 2.067 | 29.3 |

Source: Banco Central de la República Argentina and Fundación de Investigaciones Económicas Latinoamericanas.

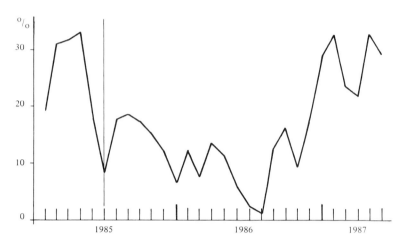

**Figure 3.6**
Black market premium for dollars (%).

that public utility rates and the exchange rate would increase by 3% per month in order to meet the inflation target. The monetary policy was made more strict in order to meet those goals. The measures resulted in a downward inflationary curve, an increase in real interest rates that turned strongly positive, and a slowdown in the economic activity level.

From October to December 1986 a sustained decline in inflation was observed, and it settled down to a monthly average of slightly over 5%. The contraction of the activity level, which fell by over 1% in the last quarter, was mainly caused by a tougher monetary policy. It contributed to lower inflation. Besides that and contrary to the pattern observed during the period of implementation of the program, the relative prices of foodstuffs lost ground.

Nevertheless, the inflation rate crept up again in January–March 1987, and it reached a level similar to that registered in the third quarter of 1986, that is, above 7% per month. A new set of measures was designed to face this situation. In February some prices that were lagging were realigned and a new price freeze was implemented. Public utility rates, the exchange rate, and wages were also frozen. Interest rates were significantly lowered, and the government announced that Central Bank rediscounts would be curtailed.

The new freeze did not show results until April, when consumer price inflation and wholesale price inflation reached 3.5% and 1%, respectively. In March inflation was high because of the lagged effect of adjustments before the freeze on wages, public utility rates, and the exchange rate. In May the rate of inflation was 4.2%.

Finally, it is worth noting that the Argentine economy was subject to a large-scale external shock during the period of implementation of the Austral Plan. During 1985 and 1986 the terms of trade deteriorated by almost 22% (see table 3.1). This shock, basically a result of a fall in prices of agricultural products, added a distorting factor during the implementation of the program.

The first unfavorable consequence was a significant decline—$2 billion (US dollars)—in the 1986 trade surplus as compared to 1985. This resulted in a $2.5 billion current account deficit, a level similar to that registered in the period before the plan. The expansion of imports generated by the reactivation of the economy and the increase in investment expenditure also contributed to this situation. The negative effects of the behavior of the external sector were offset by progress in negotiations with commercial banks and the Paris Club, which allowed a rescheduling of maturities to much longer periods.

The shock in the terms of trade was also felt in the fiscal accounts. Export duties were drastically reduced in order to minimize the effects of the drop in international prices on the revenues of domestic exporters. Because the expenditure level remained the same, the drop in fiscal revenue widened the budget gap during the last quarter of 1986 and the first quarter of 1987. The end of the forced savings mechanism, a scheme of limited duration that had been implemented when the plan went into effect, also affected the fiscal situation.

To summarize, during the postfreeze period, some of the achievements that had been attained earlier were eroded, whereas others were preserved.

With regard to the variables that showed deterioration during early 1986, reference should be made, first, to the upward trend in inflation. During the nine postshock months, consumer price inflation amounted to a monthly average of 3.1%[18] (wholesale price inflation was 0.9%); in the subsequent stage those averages were 5.8% and 5.1%, respectively. This acceleration was basically activated by the structural components of inflation that were triggered by the significant increment in the relative prices of foodstuffs and by a push in nominal wages in mid-1986. Furthermore, in this context of inflationary pressure, the control on aggregate demand was relaxed because of the loss of control, first, over the money supply and, later, over the size of the fiscal deficit. It is important to bear in mind that the external shock resulting from the distortion in the terms of trade and the struggle for income distribution was heavily felt in the fiscal sector. The distortion in the terms of trade deteriorated fiscal revenue, and the income distribution problem made it difficult to control the budgets of the central government, the provinces, and public enterprises. The money supply, on the other hand, became endogenous from April to August 1986 because of the pressure from different sectors to improve their financial positions in the context of a weak financial structure.

Although there had been obvious imbalances, the stabilization shock induced by the program in its first stage has been strong enough to resist the pounding of successive disturbing elements. Although inflation showed an upward trend, the 1986 rate was the lowest level registered in the last twelve years. Activity levels and investment grew at rates that had not been observed for years; relative prices fluctuated within a narrower margin than before; and the fiscal deficit was the lowest in many years. The negotiated debt rescheduling has been the most advantageous since the 1980–81 crisis. In short, the capacity of the authorities to administer the shocks has improved significantly.

Therefore the Argentine economy is in a better position to face the structural changes necessary to set the foundations for long-term stabilization. A permanent reduction in the fiscal deficit is without question the main element in this stabilization process.

**Summary**

There is no doubt that the heterodox shock treatment was successful in controlling the high rate of inflation. A sharp decline in the inflation rate, without shortages and with a narrow gap between the dollar value in the black and official markets, was evident in the twelve months following the implementation of the Austral Plan, particularly in the nine months of the freeze.

The abrupt fall in the inflation rate almost eliminated the inflation tax. Its replacement with explicit taxes produced a change in income distribution in favor of workers. This effect mainly explains the demand increase from almost the beginning of the program.

The period 1985–86 was one of significant remonetization of the economy. It is difficult to assess whether or not the expansion of the money supply that accompanied this remonetization was excessive. Nevertheless, the evolution of real interest rates[19] (with the exception of the second quarter of 1986) and of the dollar exchange rate in the black market are clear signals that money creation was not excessive during that period.

Interest rates showed a downward trend during June 1985–June 1986. The fiscal deficit remained more or less constant during these twelve months; therefore that decline can be explained by the increase in credit supply[20] and/or the increased probability that inflation would not accelerate sharply and, especially, by the confidence that exchange rates would not fluctuate significantly.

Nominal variables had to be realigned as of April 1986. This was due to the strong increase in the relative price of food evident in the second half of 1985 and to the "indexing culture," which stemmed from many years of inflation and manifested itself in new wage settlements during the last quarter of 1985.

The increase in inflation that started in mid-1986 is mainly explained by a wage push in the context of a passive monetary policy. Undoubtedly the strong increment in demand that has been evident since the implementation of the new economic policy facilitated the wage push.

The behavior of inflation after implementation of the Austral Plan can be basically explained by previous Argentine experience. Considerable progress has been made in reducing the inflation rate and uncertainty. Nevertheless, it is evident that there has been a return to certain practices: contract indexing; an excessive fiscal deficit, considering that the monthly inflation rate is 2–3%; and uncertainty resulting from the struggle for income distribution, the fiscal deficit, and the external debt negotiation. As regards this last issue, negotiations with several actors—the IMF, the World Bank, the Creditor Banks' Committee, Creditor Banks, and the Paris Club—add uncertainty, especially because only short-term arrangements have been made. This uncertainty compounds the well-known consequences that external debt has on the economies of debtor countries.

The fiscal deficit was reasonable until the third quarter of 1986. From then on it increased substantially. The reason, besides the fall in international prices of agricultural goods, which accelerated the reduction of export taxes, is that temporary taxes that were raised at the beginning of the program were not replaced by more permanent budgetary measures, especially in the tax scheme.

The higher interest rates registered since October 1986 are related to a more restrictive monetary policy, but they can also be explained by mounting uncertainty and a larger fiscal deficit since the last quarter of 1986. Despite high real interest rates, this mounting uncertainty has been reflected since August 1986 in a widening of the gap between the dollar exchange rate in the black and official markets.

## Concluding Remarks

The inflation rate can be significantly reduced without large costs in employment, real wages, and economic activity level by means of a shock strategy combining orthodox measures (monetary and fiscal) and heterodox measures (price and wage freeze).

It is difficult to believe that an "orthodox shock" may significantly change expectations so as to reduce inflation rates quickly without high social and economic costs when dealing with economies characterized by many years of high inflation and where different stabilization measures have been attempted. Therefore a heterodox shock seems to be the only solution to high inflation rates in those countries with complex social and political structures.

Sudden fluctuations in the inflation rate induce heavy income and wealth transfers from preexisting contracts. The conversion scheme employed in Argentina shows that, in the context of a shock treatment, those transfers can be avoided.

Many years of high inflation rates shorten the contract period, increasing the synchronization of relative prices in near-hyperinflation periods. This fact facilitates the application of a heterodox shock policy because relative prices are aligned most of the time.[21]

At the moment of implementation of a shock policy, a prolonged history of high inflation is beneficial but represents a handicap in the postshock period. Defensive mechanisms against inflation, especially indexation clauses in contracts, have been an integral part of the behavior of economic agents for many years. A few months of low inflation rates cannot drastically change this behavior. In this context the permanence of short-term contracts, particularly in the financial system, together with indexation mechanisms, mainly in wages, contribute to the fragility of the stabilization effort. The Argentine experience clearly shows that fluctuations in relative prices that increase the rate of inflation almost immediately induce an increment in nominal wages, thus hampering the stabilization process.

The burden of the external debt on the fiscal sector is almost unmanageable. The task of generating revenues of 5% of GDP, besides closing the operational gap that in Argentina oscillated between 3% and 7% of GDP during the 1970s, seems almost impossible except for short periods of time. Therefore a permanent solution to the fiscal situation is closely tied to a permanent solution to the external debt problem.

# Notes

1. For an analysis of the period before 1975, see Mallon and Sourrouille (1975).

2. For an analysis of the period 1978–81, see Canitrot (1981), Feldman and Sommer (1983), and Machinea (1983). For an estimation and analysis of capital outflows, see Fanelli and Frenkel (1985b).

3. See Frenkel (1983).

4. See Olivera (1972) and Tanzi (1977). For a quantification of this effect in the Argentine case, see Domper and Streb (1986).

5. Fanelli and Frenkel (1985a) analyze several agreements with the IMF and especially the one signed in 1984.

6. Frenkel et al. (1986) analyzed in a formal model the "domestic transfer problem" with special reference to the 1981–83 period.

7. Dreizen (1985) developed a model of financial fragility for economies with a high rate of inflation in which the shortening of deposit maturity is tackled.

8. See Frenkel (1985) and Figuereido (1985).

9. See Okun (1981) for the cost associated with a recontracting process.

10. See Di Tata (1983) and Phelps (1983).

11. It is not clear why private sector wages would not increase in the first month as a consequence of their indexation to consumer price. It is difficult to believe that a practice followed for almost ten years may be changed by the mere announcement of a new fiscal and monetary policy.

12. The increase in working hours that took place during 1985–86 was the counterpart of the entrepreneurial reluctance to increase the number of workers. This behavior may have reflected skepticism that the higher level of economic activity would be preserved.

13. It should be noted that free interest rates accounted for only 45% of total credit in the financial system at that time. Other credits were indexed by prices and the exchange rate or at regulated rates. The regulated rates were substantially lower in real terms (see table 3.9). Therefore the average lending interest rate for business firms was substantially lower than the free rate.

14. The fiscal deficit of the Central Bank declined mainly as a consequence of a drop in nominal interest rates.

15. The realignment in international reserves despite the current account deficit was due to external financing, resulting from the agreement with the IMF, and the higher trade surplus.

16. Nominal wages began to increase in the private sector in October 1985, mainly as a response to price increases.

17. At the same time and mainly as a consequence of increasing demand, the relative price of foodstuffs rose once more. The price of agricultural goods in the wholesale index increased 33.4% relative to domestic nonagricultural goods.

18. If July is not considered, the average monthly rate was 2.7%.

19. We are assessing ex post rates, but it is difficult to believe that there was a constant divergence between estimated and registered inflation rates.

20. See Dornbusch (1987).

21. We refer to "aligned" rather than "equilibrium" prices because, in economies with monthly inflation rates of 20−30% (that is, economies with significant imbalances), it is difficult to define what must be understood as equilibrium prices.

## References

Arida, P., and A. Lara-Resende. 1985. "Inertial inflation and monetary reform: Brazil," in *Inflation and Indexation: Argentina, Brazil and Israel*, J. Williamson, ed. (Washington, D.C.: Institute for International Economics), 27−45.

Blejer, M. I., and N. Liviatan. 1987. "Fighting hyperinflation: Stabilization strategies in Argentina and Israel." International Monetary Fund. Mimeo.

Canitrot, A. 1981. "Theory and practice of liberalism: Anti-inflation policy and open economy in Argentina." *Desarrollo Económico* 82:131−189. (In Spanish.)

Di Tata, J. C. 1983. "Expectations of others' expectations and the transitional non-neutrality of fully believed systematic monetary policy," in *Individual Forecasting and Aggregate Behavior: Rational Expectations Considered*, R. Frydman and E. Phelps, eds. (Cambridge: Cambridge University Press), 47−68.

Domper, J., and J. Streb. 1986. "Influence of price stabilization on collection of taxes." Banco Central de la Republica Argentina (BCRA). Mimeo. (In Spanish.)

Dornbusch, R. 1985. "External debt, budget deficits and disequilibrium exchange rates," in *International Debt and the Developing Countries*, G. Smith and J. Cuddington, eds. (Washington D.C.: World Bank), 213−235.

Dornbusch, R. 1987. "Restrictive fiscal policy and easy money: The key to Argentinian stabilization." *Estudios* (January-March), 10(41):21−38. (In Spanish.)

Dornbusch, R., and S. Fischer. 1986. "Stopping hyperinflation: Past and present." *Weltwirtschaftliches Archiv* (April), 122:1−47.

Dreizen, J. 1985. *Financial Fragility and Inflation.* Buenos Aires: Centro de Estudios de Estado y Sociedad. (CEDES). (In Spanish.)

Fanelli, J. M., and R. Frenkel. 1985a. "Argentina and the Fund in the last decade," in *El FMI y la crisis latinoamericana*, Sistema Económico Latinoamerica, ed. (Mexico City: Siglo XXI). (In Spanish.)

Fanelli, J. M., and R. Frenkel. 1985b. "The foreign debt in Argentina: A case of forced indebtedness." *Política, Economía y Sociedad* 1:43–65. (In Spanish.)

Feldman, E., and J. Sommer. 1983. *Financial Crisis and Foreign Debt*. Centro de Economía Transnacional (CET). (In Spanish.)

Figueiredo, J., et al. 1985. *Employment and Wages in Latin America*. Rio de Janeiro: Programa de Estudios Conjuntos sobre Integración Económica Latinoamerica (ECIEL). (In Spanish.)

Frenkel, R. 1979. *Price Determination under High Inflation*. Buenos Aires: Estudios CEDES. (In Spanish.)

Frenkel, R. 1983. "The financial market, exchange expectations, and movement of capital." *El Trimestre Económico* 200:2041–2076. (In Spanish.)

Frenkel, R., and J. M. Fanelli. 1987. "The Austral Plan: A year and a half later." CEDES. Mimeo. (In Spanish.)

Frenkel, R., J. M. Fanelli, and C. Winograd. "Stabilization and adjustment programmes and policies in Argentina." CEDES. Mimeo.

Gerchunoff, P., and C. Bozalla. 1987. "The possibilities and limits of a heterodox stabilization program: The case of Argentina." Instituto Torcuato di Tella.

Helpman, E., and L. Leiderman. 1987. "Stabilization in high inflation countries: Analytical foundations and recent experience." Paper presented at the Carnegie-Rochester Conference. Mimeo.

Heymann, D. 1985. *Three Experiments in Inflation and Stabilization Policies*. Comisión Económica para America Latina. (In Spanish.)

Machinea, J. 1983. "The use of the exchange rate as an anti-inflation instrument in a stabilization-liberalization attempt: The southern cone experience." Ph.D. dissertation, University of Minnesota.

Mallon, R., and J. Sourrouille. 1975. *Economic Policy in a Conflicting Society: The Case of Argentina*. Buenos Aires: Amorrortu. (In Spanish.)

Minsky, H. 1975. *John Maynard Keynes*. New York: Columbia University Press.

Okun, A. 1981. *Prices and Quantities: A Macroeconomic Analysis*. Washington, D.C.: Brookings Institution.

Olivera, J. H. G. 1972. "Inflation and fiscal balance." *Revista de Ciencias Económicas* 6/7:85–109. (In Spanish.)

Phelps, E. 1983. "The trouble with rational expectations and the problem of inflation stabilization," in *Individual Forecasting and Aggregate Outcomes: "Rational*

*Expectations Examined*, R. Frydman and E. Phelps, eds. (Cambridge: Cambridge University Press), 31–45.

Sargent, T. 1982. "The ends of big inflations," in *Inflation: Causes and Effects*, R. Hall, ed. (Chicago: University of Chicago Press), 41–96.

Tanzi, V. 1977. "Inflation, the balance in tax collection, and the real value of tax revenue." *Ensayos Económicos* 2:5–23. (In Spanish.)

Tobin, J. 1980. *Asset Accumulation and Economic Activity*. Oxford: Basil Blackwell.

# 4

## Inflation Stabilization or Hyperinflation Avoidance? The Case of the Austral Plan in Argentina: 1985–87

Alfredo J. Canavese and
Guido Di Tella

In June 1985 the Argentine government launched an economic program, the so-called Austral Plan, to stop the steady growth in the rate of inflation, which had increased from 10–15% per month in the second semester of 1982 to 20–30% per month in the early part of 1985, reaching 30% in the first two weeks of June. Such a level of inflation had been reached twice in the last ten years: in June–August 1975 and in March–April 1976.

Our purpose here is to analyze the main features of the stabilization program set against the broader background of Argentina's inflationary experience and to follow the events since the plan's implementation almost two years ago.[1]

The main hypothesis is that the Austral Plan must be understood as a program to avoid hyperinflation and not as an attempt to remove inflation, particularly that of structural origin.

Argentina has experienced a long history of inflation, the origins of which can be traced back to World War II and the immediate postwar years. Up to 1946–48 price increases were positively correlated with high levels of economic activity, low rates of unemployment, and expansionary monetary policies. From 1949 onward the link between these three factors and inflation weakened (Diaz Alejandro 1970). In 1949, 1952, 1956, 1959, 1962, 1975, 1976, and 1978 and since 1982, recessions and accelerations in the inflation rate have been positively correlated as a result of the increased importance of problems that may be called structural.

This has been the consequence of the interplay of several factors. The first factor is the increased importance of an import-substituting kind of industry, in itself a fixed price sector, established as part of a set of policies with a strong anti-export bias. This has reduced the importance of trade, enhanced the oligopolistic behavior of industry, and made the supply curve more inelastic and the economy price sensitive to demand shocks. The second factor is that the economy has been increasingly subject to an

external constraint aggravated in recent years by the servicing of a mounting debt, something that has forced repeated devaluations to change relative prices; this has been achieved only temporarily and at the cost of
triggering inflation. The third factor is the increasing conflict over shares of
income between sectors and within sectors, again giving rise to temporary
changes in relative prices, always at the cost of substantial rises in the price
level. No wonder the oscillation of relative prices has increased so much
and has been so intimately associated with increasing inflation (Di Tella
1979). A fourth factor is that the increasing inflation has, in turn, given rise
to de facto or legal indexation, which has allowed the economy to function
even under conditions of high and continuous rises in prices, at the cost
of creating an inertial mechanism that has made inflation even more intractable. Finally, fiscal and monetary policies have also been affected, for
they have been endogenously determined by the inflationary process. The
fiscal deficit has been affected by the inflationary erosion of tax collections,
the so-called Olivera-Tanzi effect, so that, the higher the inflation rate, the
higher the deficit. Recently devaluations or increases in the nominal rate of
interest have increased the cash cost of servicing the foreign and local debt,
affecting the fiscal deficit as well. Moreover, high nominal local rates have
also increased the payments made by the Central Bank to private banks to
compensate for the required high reserves, giving rise to the so-called
quasi-fiscal deficit.[2]

It is not that monetary policies have been determined solely endogenously but that monetary policy must be judged by taking into account that
a good part of the policy is determined by the inflationary process in itself.

Summing up, supply inelasticities, relative price oscillations, the generalization of indexation, and the endogenous character of part of the fiscal
deficit and monetary behavior have contributed to create a most intractable
inflationary process.

Recurrently governments have tried to control inflation through the
distortion of some crucial price that affects wages and profits, such as public services' prices, interest rates, and exchange rates and have succeeded
temporarily. But, when the distorted market is brought back to equilibrium,
inflation picks up again, giving rise to inflation cycles, distinct from those
affecting income and so characteristic of Argentina's inflationary experience (Di Tella 1986).

But this is not the whole story, especially not for Argentina. Inflation
reduced the demand for money and consequently reduced the base for the
inflation tax. Beyond a certain point more inflation means less, not more,
inflation tax. If at that point conventional and inflationary taxes are not

enough to finance the deficit, the system starts on the path to hyperinflation, precisely the situation Argentina was approaching toward the beginning of 1985. There is a rate of inflation that constitutes a hyperinflation threshold (Canavese 1985). It depends positively on the degree of monetization of the economy and negatively on the weight of the government deficit on GNP and on the responsiveness of the demand for money to the inflation rate.

## 4.1 The Austral Plan: Initial Conditions and Measures

From mid-1982 on, the monthly rate of inflation climbed to the two-digit level, showing an accelerating trend up to the first half of 1985. The previous high peaks of inflation of June–August 1975 and March–April 1976 had taken place with the M1/GNP ratio more than three times the June 1985 figure. Those peaks receded after a short while, at most two to three months. The much lower value of the demand for money in June 1985 for rates of inflation of the same magnitude as those ruling during 1975 and 1976 suggests that a downward shift in the demand for money had taken place. Either the demand for real balances at zero inflation had dropped or the responsiveness of money demand to inflation had increased or both. These changes may be seen as the outcome of the events that took place during 1981–82.

Expectations of "bail outs" were fulfilled in 1982 when the domestic financial system was nearing insolvency, partly because of the high real rates of interest prevailing at the time and the taking up of some private external debts by the state. The inflow of external funds not only stopped but reversed, and Argentina began a "net" repayment of its external debt. This repayment required a trade surplus, which was accomplished through a real depreciation of the exchange rate, which in turn required larger government expenditure to procure the needed trade surplus. Moreover, during 1984 the new constitutional government tried to raise real wages by increasing nominal wages beyond inflation, fulfilling electoral promises that ignored the increases of real wages in 1983. This also affected wages of public employees and consequently added to government expenditure. But what was even more crucial was that the value of the hyperinflation threshold was reduced.

The situation had become impossible, and by mid-1985 a belief that the economy was quickly approaching hyperinflation became generalized. A new way to fight inflation was mandatory.

It can now be seen that a preparatory stage for stabilization had already started at the beginning of the year, for the first three months quite reluctantly and from March onward quite deliberately. Real wages were reduced purposely, and the real price of energy was increased (for fiscal purposes), although no other major attempt to redress relative prices, particularly the real exchange rate, was tried. It was feared that in such a loose situation redress of relative prices could become the sort of shock that would move the economy into hyperinflation. This pre–Austral Plan set of measures is usually ignored but should be considered an integral part of the program.

The Austral Plan was launched on June 14, 1985. The plan was built on three main pillars: reduction of the fiscal deficit, introduction of a new currency, and a temporary price and wage freeze.

The reduction of the fiscal deficit, including that of the Central Bank, was reckoned on a cash basis. The deficit was reduced from a level of 12.8% of GNP, reached in 1984, to 2.5% of GNP during the second semester of 1985. This drastic reduction was achieved by increases in the real prices of public services; higher taxes applied on international trade, particularly exports; improved collection of direct taxes and a compulsory "loan" given to the treasury by taxpayers in proportion to the taxes paid on income and wealth in 1984; an increase in the real value of taxes collected, a result of the elimination of the Olivera-Tanzi effect; and a reduction in the Central Bank deficit resulting from the fall in nominal interest rates.

The residual deficit was to be entirely financed by external credit. During the first two weeks of June the Central Bank gave the treasury some important loans to let the plan start with a buffer, but a formal commitment was made that, as of June 14, no new money was to be issued to finance the treasury.

The introductions of a new currency (the *austral*) and of deindexation (*desagio*) were aimed at different effects. The new currency was supposed to give psychological support to the idea that an important change in monetary and fiscal policy was actually taking place. The deindexation was directed at dealing with the problems of inertial inflation and unexpected capital gains. This was achieved by enforcing a downward adjustment of all forward contracts signed before June 14 and to be fulfilled after that date. Contracts were adjusted downward by a daily rate equivalent to approximately 30% per month—the inflation rate the economy was suffering and expecting before June 14. The deindexation meant no real loss or gain, provided that future inflation was equal to the new expected one, in this case, 0.[3]

The temporary price and wage freeze included the exchange rate (previously devalued) and public services prices (previously increased). Prices were frozen at the levels they were at on June 12, but for goods having wide seasonal changes in supply (meat, fruits, vegetables) only maximum "markups" were fixed. Maximum prices were published for a basket of mass consumer goods. Wages were increased by 23% before the freeze to compensate for the loss they suffered during the first fourteen days of June. The exchange rate parity was set at 0.80 austral to 1.0 US dollar but not fixed against any other basket of currencies. Interest rates on deposits and loans were reduced from 28% and 30% per month, respectively, to 4% and 6% per month, respectively.

The measures undertaken to reduce the deficit and the pegging of the exchange rate are typical of major stabilization efforts to stop hyperinflation (Sargent 1982).

Introducing a new currency and deindexation and freezing wages and prices are unorthodox measures. They were directed at dealing with the problem of inertial inflation and at bringing down expectations in the hope that they would contribute to disinflation and avoid recession. The deindexation ensured convergence to the new rate of inflation, hopefully 0. The freeze, in turn, was supposed to avoid the transitory recession that would be needed if expectations were not rational and if some prices were sticky downward.

The adjustment of some key prices made a few days before the launching of the program was supposed to avoid a gross distortion of relative prices[4] and to continue the trend that had begun in the preparatory stage of the program (from January to June 1985). Although these relative price changes tried to cope with the so-called conversion problem (Arida and Lara-Resende 1985), they went only part way, as the repercussions of these changes in the prices of other related goods and services were not allowed to crystallize, creating serious tensions that appeared later, particularly during the unfreezing.

Almost two years after the launching of the Austral Plan we can distinguish four stages. The first one lasted ten months, from June 1985 until March 1986, and was characterized by a price freeze and fiscal austerity. The second stage, from April to September 1986, was characterized by an attempt to administer prices in an easy money environment, resulting in a reindexing of the economy and an acceleration of inflation. In the third stage, from October 1986 to February 1987, a restrictive monetary policy to curb the renewed inflationary process was tried, despite the increased fiscal deficit. And finally, in the fourth stage, from February on, a new price and wage freeze and an announcement of a devaluation path until July 1987 were made. A synthesis of the four periods can be seen in table 4.1.

**Table 4.1**
A synthetic overview of the four stages of the Austral Plan (monthly rates of change and trends)

| Period | Indicator | Target | Actual |
|--------|-----------|--------|--------|
| **Stage 1** | | | |
| June 1985–March 1986 | Price index | 0 | 1.7 |
| | Exchange rate | 0 | 0 |
| | Fiscal deficit | cut | cuts achieved |
| | Real interest rate | low positive | much higher than target |
| **Stage 2** | | | |
| April 1986–September 1986 | Price index | 2 | 5.3 |
| | Exchange rate | 2 | 4.2 |
| | Fiscal deficit | constant | constant |
| | Real interest rate | low positive | as target |
| **Stage 3** | | | |
| October 1986–February 1987 | Price index | 3 | 5.6 |
| | Exchange rate | 3 | 6.1 |
| | Fiscal deficit | constant | increase |
| | Real interest rate | positive | higher than target |
| **Stage 4** | | | |
| March 1987–July 1987 (?) | Price index | 0 | 7.0 |
| | Exchange rate | 1 | 6.0 |
| | Fiscal Deficit | cut | increase |
| | Real interest rate | positive | higher than target |

## 4.2 The First Stage: Fiscal Austerity, Monetary Prudence, and Deindexation of the Economy

The initial package brought down the rate of inflation quite dramatically: from 30.5% in June 1985 for consumer prices to 6% in July, including the statistical carryover, and to 3% in August (42%, −0.9%, and 1.5%, respectively, for wholesale prices). There had been previous price and wage freezes with similar spectacular initial effects (such as the one enforced from June to December 1973), but what was new this time was that the freeze was accompanied by the ingenious deindexation scheme, a serious effort to reduce the fiscal deficit, and a formal commitment not to finance the deficit internally.

All this produced a sharp change in expectations: The freeze was believed, and the black market rate of exchange went down to the new official parity. But what was to become a serious problem was that the price vector that was frozen was the one that happened to prevail on June 14, when, as is typical in any highly inflationary economy, relative prices were oscillating. Only by chance would relative prices have been in line with their long-term equilibrium values. The same freeze that was responsible for the initial spectacular success of the program built into the system and perpetuated disequilibrium situations in myriad markets.

Some crucial prices had been realigned before the freeze, and that improved matters. But their effects on costs had not been taken into account by the rest of the economy, and this made things worse. Moreover, despite the freeze, prices continued to rise by 1–3% per month, which "solved" some disequilibria at the cost of reinforcing others. Pressures stemming from the inevitable need to realign prices troubled the Austral Plan and made the unfreezing essential. But at the same time the end of the freeze had a troubling effect on inflation, as it became apparent in the following year.

The fiscal deficit, which in 1984 had almost reached 13% of GNP, dropped to 7% of GNP in the first half of 1985 (it had already been reduced as a result of the measures taken in preparation for the Austral Plan) and to 2% of GNP in the second half. It stayed at that level during the first half of 1986, better even than the target. This is particularly noteworthy because of the negative impact of servicing the external debt, taken up by the government before 1983, which, even though only partially honored, has required 3% of GNP every year. The reduction of the fiscal deficit took place despite the limited decrease in government expenditure, from 36% to 34% of GNP.

The increase in fiscal revenue was the key variable, rising from 23% to 28% of GNP. Almost four percentage points of this increase were the consequence of the automatic increase in tax collection in real terms, as taxes were no longer eroded by inflation.

The performance of the central government was much better than that of the provinces and public enterprises. The Central Bank reduced its deficit because of the lowering of the nominal rate of interest paid to compensate banks for their high reserve requirements. Money issued to finance the treasury, which had reached a peak of 15% of GNP in 1983, was reduced to 6% of GNP in 1984 and to 2.3% of GNP in 1985, dropping to zero for the second semester of that year.

But the sudden stabilization brought about an immediate increase in the demand for money, driving up interest rates to extremely high levels, a process encouraged by the government as an additional "safety" measure.

The fiscal deficit as a source of monetary expansion was replaced by five other sources: (1) an inflow of Argentine capital from abroad that initially tried to take advantage of the interest differential (a process the government tried to check), (2) a trade surplus of more than $2 billion from July to December, (3) the refinancing of more than half of the interest payments on the foreign debt, (4) a reduction in bank reserve requirements, and (5) Central Bank rediscounting of commercial bank paper. Money (M1) increased from a minimum of 3.5% of GNP before June to about 7.3% by February 1986, the highest level reached since the launching of the program.

The government faced one of the typical stabilization dilemmas. It had to issue money in substantial amounts and in a way that would not affect the credibility of the program in order to drive down the real rate of interest to the level of the marginal productivity of capital. The government had initially fixed the regulated passive rate of interest at about 4% per month (and 6% active), whereas the free market moved along with higher values, three more percentage points per month. These high rates had contradictory effects. On the one hand they ensured that interest-bearing deposits in the financial system would be maintained (and increased) and that the black market dollar would not move too far away from the official quotation, but on the other hand it made these equilibria suspect, as they were the result of a basic disequilibrium in the money market.[5] Again, it could be suspected that the market was being distorted to bring other markets under apparent control. The novelty was that this time the money market was the one to be distorted. People tended to believe that the high rates would go down, compromising the precarious situation obtained, or would be followed by price increases, making the interest rates not so high in real terms. Ex post, however, they ended up exceeding a real rate of more than 3.5% per month. The ex ante real rate of interest was not as high as the ex post one because inflationary expectations, as detected by opinion polls during this period, were systematically higher than actual rates. But the longer this situation lasted, the more the belief in future bailouts increased, even if the small indebtness of the private sector, a consequence of the previous bailouts of 1982–83, made this more a potential than an immediate problem.

Another important and benefical effect of the sudden stabilization was the increase in certainty and the consequent perceived reduction in costs, something that had a significant impact on the reactivation of the economy. Consumers and producers now "knew" their future, or so they thought, and began to have favorable expectations, immediately noticeable in consumption rather than in investment. In fact, during the last quarter of 1985, consumption, which had dropped sharply during the second quarter, went up, even if fixed investment did not react until the second and third quarters of 1986, when real interest rates became negative.

Stabilization also affected the real values of all future prices, even of those contracted for only a few days. The deindexation tried to cope with the longer-term contracts, whereas the Olivera-Tanzi effect was counted on to increase tax collection. But there were similar effects on all sorts of near-cash payments, even when "near" meant only a week or so—not a trivial issue when inflation runs at 1% a day.

An unintended effect of this kind affected real wages, which had been going down in preparation for the Austral Plan since the beginning of the year, and an adjustment was made for the first fourteen days of June. But because wages are paid either every two weeks or at the end of the month and are spent in the following interval, stabilization brings about an automatic rise in purchasing power even if wages remain unchanged in nominal terms. The real purchasing power is not accurately measured if nominal wages are deflated by the price index of the period in which they are earned because they should be deflated by the price index of the period in which they are spent. Purchasing power, or accurately measured real wages, increases when inflation decreases.

Real wages measured either in the "old" or "new" way had declined in the first semester of 1985. The old measure suggests that they continued to go down from July on, but measured in the new way, they began to rise, even if they did not reach the 1984 level. For white-collar workers, paid monthly, the effect was much larger than for blue-collar workers, paid every two weeks.

Despite the high real interest rates, a reactivation of the economy began to take place during the last quarter of 1985, and it was accentuated in 1986. This is particularly so if the comparison is made against the low level reached in the third quarter of 1985, the third consecutive quarter of decline. This was the consequence of the stimulating effect of the reduction in the degree of uncertainty on consumers' behavior—which only later affected investment—coupled with the reversal in the downward movement in the purchasing power of wages.

When the second half of 1985 is compared with the first half, the lower uncertainty and higher real wages entailed a moderate demand pull, affecting first consumer goods and then durables and then, in 1986, investment.

Idle capacity in the industrial sector declined from 32% during the second quarter of 1985 to 23% during the second quarter of 1986. Employment did not go up because firms preferred to increase overtime to avoid hiring new workers and the risk of dismissals if reactivation proved to be only temporary. Near full employment capacity constraints appeared much earlier than expected, forcing a rise in the prices of food and of some services well above the average registered by the index of consumer prices in the period July 1985–March 1986.

Wholesale prices, which had changed little from July 1985 to March 1986 and lagged behind consumer prices, began to rise as well. The gap had been due to the fact that at the wholesale level prices included some financing that had not been adjusted as other forward contracts had been. As a consequence, these prices actually went up in real terms, at the time of the freeze, becoming higher than the prices actually paid. The relative movement of the two indexes suggests that by March 1986 the cushion created in June 1985 had disappeared and that from then on both kinds of prices were bound to rise together.

All the while the reaccommodation of relative prices was pushing up prices with increasing force. Still the prices of public services were frozen and the exchange rate pegged, both lagging behind the general rise in prices. This forced a reallocation of expenditures in favor of nondurables, foreshadowing an upward push in prices when readjusted.

## 4.3 The Second Stage: The End of the Freeze, Easy Money, and Reindexation

There were more signs that the end of the freeze was about to come. Nominal wage increases granted by the private sector beyond the official guidelines became quite generalized. The real exchange rate, which by June had reached the level it had in December 1982—a level many think implied some sort of long-run equilibrium—had become overvalued by more than 20% by March 1986, particularly vis-à-vis the dollar, whereas the external trade balance for the first quarter of 1986, which was partly affected by the fall in export prices, appeared much worse compared to the figures for the first quarter of previous years. The external trade surplus and the improved fiscal behavior were in danger. Some sort of unfreezing was mandatory and began to be expected.

The formal end of the first stage took place on April 4, 1986, when the finance minister announced the end of stabilization as a target: The key prices of the economy would be changed as often as needed to "avoid the erosion of the real wage, the appearance of disequilibria in public finances and the loss of competitiveness of Argentina's exports" (Sourrouille 1986b). A new era of "controlled rates of inflation" had begun.

This second stage implied the end of the original philosophy of the Austral Plan. The new phase readopted indexation mechanisms: fortnightly devaluations and quarterly wage adjustments allowing the reinstallation of inertial inflation. Moreover, the government attempted a readjustment of relative prices, which is good for efficiency and bad for inflation.

The reindexation of key prices coincided with an easy monetary policy, accelerating inflation. The average of consumer and wholesale price indexes rose by 4% per month during the second quarter of 1986 and by 7% per month during the third quarter of 1986.

The government replaced the freeze with administered prices for the larger enterprises and granted a rise of 8.5% for wages for the second quarter of 1986. In April there was a small devaluation (3.75%), and higher prices for public services were fixed. It was announced that, from then on, exchange rates and public services prices were to follow the inflation path: The economy was indexed again, although price adjustment was to be at longer intervals. Unions and entrepreneurs were invited to discuss the way to include previous wage increases in the new quarterly guidelines to prepare the grounds for collective bargaining during 1987.

The money supply had been increasing faster than prices since June 1985, but demand for real balances also grew, reaching a peak of 7–7.5% of GNP in the first quarter of 1986, only to start a slow but steady decline. Even so, the money supply kept growing around 5% per month after April 1986. The commitment not to finance fiscal deficits by printing money was held, but some public enterprises failed to collect enough revenues to pay interest on their external debts, forcing the Central Bank to take care of those external payments using reserves without a corresponding absorption of money, a covert way to bypass the original commitment. More-over, the Central Bank rediscounted paper of official financial institutions, which were financing debts of the provinces, even if it was quite unlikely that they would be repaid. These are two corrections needed for the series of fiscal deficits and with good reason, even if there is some discrepancy as to the correct figures (Cavallo and Peña 1986).

The easy money policies coupled with indexation drove down the active real interest rates, which became negative by the end of the period. Wages in the private sector grew beyond the guidelines because, after the initial rise, they were indexed by consumer prices. On top of this, the govern-ment granted substantial wage increases to some specific unions, about 30% to be spread from September to December 1986. The oligopolistic structure of industrial markets allowed enterprises to pass on the higher costs to prices, maintaining the historical markups. The government tried to avoid lags in public services prices, and only the exchange rate and agricultural prices fell behind moderately. Prices of services and of food kept pace and maintained their earlier relative improvement. In this envi-ronment the inertial component became significant. Consumer prices reached a peak of almost 9% in August 1986, a remarkable acceleration, accompanied that same month by a 30% rise of the black market exchange rate.

This was a period in which indexation was being generalized without a nominal anchor, accelerating the inflationary process but reducing relative price oscillation. It is clear that during the first stage the realignment of relative prices accounted for the bulk of the change in the price index, whereas in this second stage indexation explains the change to a larger extent.

### 4.4   The Third Stage: The Monetary Crunch

A monetary crunch was inevitable. It lasted from October 1986 to Feb-ruary 1987. The change in monetary policy and the increase in the fiscal deficit characterize this third phase.

The behavior of prices during July and August had revealed that gener-alized indexation and easy money were an explosive combination, shaping a system without any nominal anchor. The government tried to bring down inflation by introducing some friction into the indexation mecha-nisms while increasing control over monetary expansion. In September 1986 guidelines for the growth of prices and the exchange rate were announced, and at the same time wages rose, as had been agreed for the fourth quarter of 1986. Because the inflation target was about 3–4% per month, the growth of the money supply was made compatible with such a rise in prices. Active real interest rates began to go up steadily from 0% in September to a peak of almost 5% per month in December. Goods and services were grouped in three sets with different guidelines for each set: (1) For wage goods (excluding vegetables, fruits, and meat) maximum prices were to be changed only every forty-five days; (2) industrial goods prices had to follow guidelines set every month; (3) for non-state-supplied services, seasonal foodstuffs, and agricultural goods, no guidelines were set and prices were left free. Prices in sets 1 and 2 were imperfectly indexed and were to move below the inflation rate, whereas prices in set 3 were to be controlled by the reduction of demand brought about by the restrictive monetary policy. The exchange rate was perfectly indexed while public services prices were "overindexed" to help public enterprises and the treasury solve the fiscal problem. The price of labor was to be predetermined in nominal terms assuming a by then "low" 3–4% monthly rate of inflation, a rate that was actually exceeded, depressing real wages. M1 as a percentage of GNP continued to decrease, even if slowly, and the real rate of interest that had been low since April began to rise steadily. The fiscal deficit shot up, nearing 9% of GDP by the last quarter of 1986, much more than the promised target.

The reason why interest rates rose can now be attributed to the attempt to control with monetary devices an economy that was out of equilibrium, a strategy that, in turn, gave rise to perverse expectations as the new rates could not be believed to last for long and were taken again as evidence of the basic disequilibrium of the economy.

A situation that had been seen in the past was repeated: A strong disequilibrium in one market (in this case the money market) was induced to bring other markets under control. A situation not so different from the one prevailing at the end of 1980 when all markets were in *apparent* equilibrium with the exception of the foreign sector, in which a grossly overvalued peso ran parallel to a grossly unbalanced trade balance. The cyclical behavior of Argentina's inflation appeared again. Price rises are checked by the distortion of the price of a particular market, whose imbalance foreshadows the precariousness of the situation and its eventual reversal leads to a concomitant increase in the rate of inflation.

Industrial activity declined in December 1986 to the August 1985 level at the beginning of the Austral Plan. This fall in activity entailed a reduction in tax collections, contributing to the increase in the fiscal deficit. The commitment made in June 1985 was held, and no money was issued to finance the deficit, but use was made of some sterilized deposits that the public sector held in official banks. This was equivalent to an increase of the money supply and meant an abandonment of the attempt to check price rises through monetary policy. Inflation was rekindled in January and February 1987, when the monthly rates were about 7% per month, signaling the failure of this short-lived phase.

### 4.5   The Fourth Stage: A Desperate Freeze

On February 27, 1987, the government introduced, in despair, a new wage and price freeze and a modest crawling peg to be in force until May and June. Frozen prices did not enjoy the buffer they had when the Austral Plan was launched, no deindexation on contracts was tried, and expectations were not at all reassuring, as they had been in June 1985. Moreover, an attempt to drive down interest rates was abandoned a few days later when contradictory signals on the future wage policy appeared as a new pro-union labor minister joined the cabinet.

The events taking place in this last phase dramatically emphasize the dilemma governments always confront when they try to defeat inflation without undertaking structural reforms: Either a social consensus or a monetary crunch is unavoidable, precisely the situation in May and June 1987.

Looking back over the whole of the Austral Plan, it has to be admitted that, contrary to what happened in other hyperinflationary stabilization programs, in this one the existence of a sizable foreign debt equal to about 70% of GNP imposed a significant additional burden on the economy and on the program. The need to create an external surplus and to collect internally the necessary funds to service the debt—even after strenuous negotiations it requires nearly half of the value of exports and more than 3% of GNP— created serious difficulties for an already strained situation. The necessary fiscal surplus meant even more taxes, even lower wages, and even lower investment and gave rise throughout to doubts about the possibility of maintaining the fiscal deficit within bounds. But the transfer of the surplus to foreign creditors posed an additional problem and required a further adjustment of relative prices necessary to create a substantial trade surplus, something that forced a more depreciated exchange rate, pushed the economy nearer to hyperinflation, and compounded the lowering of wages. It is fair to say that the repayment of the debt is the single most important reason for the relative failure of the plan.[6]

It is unavoidable to point out the similarity between economic and social effects that the burden of the debt and war reparations have on, especially, the balance of payments, relative prices, government expenditure, levels of activity, growth, and social cohesion (Llach 1987). The big European hyperinflations were successfully stabilized once the reparations problem was solved and external aid provided (Dornbusch and Fischer 1986, table 20), and some of the new hyperinflations, such as Israel's, have also been helped crucially by external support.

The story should not end without a comment on the presumed costless character of hyperinflationary stabilizations. In Argentina, whether the temporary initial stabilization was achieved with or without costs in terms of foregone national income and employment is still an open question. Industrial activity during the third quarter of 1985 was near the post-1974 minimum reached during the second quarter of 1982, at the time of the Malvinas War, but climbed steadily to reach a level near the historical maximum in the third quarter of 1986.

It is clear that post–June 1985 costs were negligible, but it cannot be denied that during the first semester of 1985 some key preparatory economic policies were implemented so that the costs of the plan could not be accurately reckoned if measured against the level of economic activity at the moment of the plan's formal implementation. The choice of a "right" base period for a valid comparison is crucial. The last quarter of 1984 was "too good," but the third quarter of 1985, which is the one generally used, was the worst since 1982. If the average activity of 1984 is taken as a base, it can be seen that the economy suffered significant losses during the whole of 1985: 5% of GNP and 4% in wages. Both losses were canceled in 1986 when GNP and wages went back to 1984 levels.

But the costs appear to be smaller than those expected from more orthodox policies based only on fiscal and monetary restraint. Argentina is a closed economy with oligopolistic industries and strong unions: A fall in demand gives rise to quantity reductions rather than price cuts; price elasticities are low, as are speeds of adjustment in the real sector. Moreover, experience has taught economic agents that monetary restraint is always abandoned when governments face sharp recessions and firms reach high levels of indebtness. A dramatic recession would have been needed to tame inflationary pressures just through monetary measures. Orthodox programs are more suitable for dealing with inflationary problems either in simple underdeveloped economies without an oligopolistic industrial structure in which wages can be easily reduced or in developed complex and open economies in which oligopolies face foreign competition.

## 4.6   Conclusions

We can now reflect on two of the main issues made clearer by experience with the Austral Plan. The first one is linked to the oscillation of relative prices and the so-called conversion problem. The second is the difference between long-standing inflations and hyperinflations, and the stabilization strategies best suited to cope with them.

The oscillation of relative prices, defined as the ratio between the standard deviation of the rates of change of the components of the wholesale price index and the rate of change of the index itself, is characteristic of Argentina's inflation (Di Tella 1979). This fact is connected with the kind of structural distortions induced by the development of an import-substituting, small, anti-export, strongly oligopolistic industrial sector and an equally oligopsonistic labor movement. Under such conditions growth induces imports and higher demand for food, reduces agricultural exports, and inevitably brings about balance of payments crises followed by recurrent devaluations, which are required to change relative prices. This reduces the level of activity, drives down wages, and shifts resources out of industry and into primary production, obtaining a new external equilibrium. This new solution is strongly resisted and gives rise to strong inter- and even intrasectoral fights between oligopolistic contenders to go back to some previous fair level of relative prices, reversing the original change brought about by devaluation. This alternating process gives Argentina's inflation its oscillatory character (figure 4.1).

Moreover, at times, inflation has been forced down by suppressing the rise of some key price: exchange rates, interest rates, wages, profits, prices of public services. When a specific market is thrown out of equilibrium, a short-term benefical effect on inflation is felt. However, this lowering of the inflation rate is the temporary consequence of the distortion of the long-run equilibrium price vector, something that ensures that it will be short-lived, for the basic disequilibrium has to be redressed eventually.

The Austral Plan froze the relative price set prevailing on a particular day: June 14, 1985. But as sectoral prices had been departing from their mean values, the price freeze inevitably caught them off their historical average. This, in turn, gave rise to the so-called conversion problem. As Arida and Lara-Resende have said:

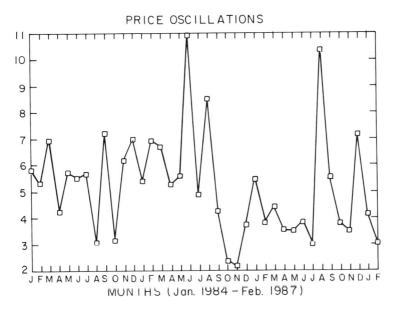

PRICE OSCILLATIONS

**Figure 4.1**
The oscillation of relative prices (defined in text).

To freeze nominal prices by legislative fiat would inevitably freeze disequilibrium relative prices. If the announced freeze is too short, it would fail to suppress the inflation drive inherited from the past; if too long, the inconsistency of relative prices as well as any shocks to supply and demand would have to be absorbed by rationing. The lifting of the freeze would probably be followed by strong pressures to restore previous relativities, which would revive inflation. (Arida and Lara-Resende 1985, p. 31)

It is some sort of average historical price vector that has allowed markets to clear and not that of any particular moment. If everyone accepted average historical values, everyone would be approximately equally well off. But this can only be imposed by the state through an incomes policy or a social pact. The Austral Plan adjusted some particular prices—wages for the first fourteen days of June; the rate of exchange, which was devalued by 15%; and public prices, which were raised by 20%—while freezing all other prices at the values prevailing before the implementation of the plan, certainly off their average relative values. Not surprisingly the pressure for three major relative price readjustments created serious upward pressure on prices. The first readjustment stems from the fact that prices were frozen when oscillation was high, giving rise to a strong pressure to go back to the historical sectoral average values through a relative price change. The second relative price readjustment is, in turn, due to the initial attempt to increase the real price of public services and the rate of exchange while not allowing spillover into other prices. This spillover will sooner or later have to take place. Finally, a third relative price readjustment is required by the structurally better situation resulting from stabilization, such as lower costs and increased productivity, which could be observed right after the implementation of the program.

In an ideal world prices should have been frozen not at the June 14 values but at the values reached after these three adjustments. The conversion problem is inherent to any stabilization program, and, if not tackled, as in the austral case, a permanent pressure to redress relative prices gives rise to an upward pressure on the general price level, forcing an unduly restrictive monetary policy.

The second main issue made more clear by the Austral Plan has to do with the fact that, as already mentioned, the Argentine economy from 1982 on and particularly in the earlier part of 1985 was leaving behind "traditional" inflation and entering a hyperinflationary period. It is possible to say that before 1982 inflation depended on the change in relative prices induced by demand or supply shocks in flexible price markets (something that may be called "structural factors"), on past inflation (a result linked to propagation mechanisms and indexation devices now called "inertial forces"), on the rate of devaluation (connected to the external constraint on growth that a highly indebted and closed economy confronts), and on the state of aggregate demand (including fiscal and monetary behavior that is partially determined endogenously).

In such a state of affairs, once inflation starts, it may continue even without any demand or supply shock, only because of past inflation, the so-called memory of the system. Only extreme monetary policies that can overcome the effects of the endogenously determined part can put an end to the process, but at a high cost. To put it another way, only disproportionately small dampening effects on prices may be expected, even from tight monetary policies. Before 1982 there was no reason to think that runaway inflation would take hold. The situation can become dangerous if inflation reduces the amount of real money held by the public to the point where the inflation tax is not enough to cope with a fiscal deficit, which tends to increase because of the erosion of tax collections induced by that same inflation.

It can be shown that there is an inflation rate that plays the role of a threshold beyond which the economy runs away into hyperinflation

(Canavese 1985). The threshold is the rate of inflation beyond which the inflation tax is not enough to support the fiscal deficit. The value of the threshold depends positively on the degree of monetization of the economy and negatively on the fiscal deficit to GNP ratio and on the responsiveness of the demand for money to inflation. At the threshold rate inflation is in a steady state, even if unstable. There is another steady state at a lower, stable rate at which a rise in inflation increases the inflation tax collected by more than that foregone in legal taxes (because of fiscal lags). An inflation shock important enough to push the inflation rate beyond the high steady-state rate throws the economy into hyperinflation.

During the second quarter of 1985 the receipts from the inflation tax collected by the government were about 5.2% of GNP (Frenkel and Fanelli 1986), and the loss in (legal) tax collection due to the Olivera-Tanzi effect reached a peak of 3.9% of GNP (Domper and Streb 1986). The economy was about to reach the high steady-state rate of inflation. In such a situation any correction of relative prices, in a world of sticky nominal prices, without a sharp reduction of government expenditures would have thrown the economy into hyperinflation. Because a relative price adjustment was badly needed, a shock treatment that included a price freeze, aimed at bringing the economy back to the stable region of inflation rates, was inevitable. The unorthodox shock was essential, but the impossibility of freezing equilibrium relative prices implied that creeping inflation was to remain present even without indexation, during the unfreezing. This could only have been avoided by removing the structural causes of inflation, a task beyond the capabilities of the unorthodox shock.

We can sum up by saying that the Austral Plan was a consistent set of policy measures devised to stop hyperinflation with a small and quickly regained cost in terms of foregone output. The plan successfully attacked the inertial behavior of prices but failed to get rid of structural pressures. Hyperinflation was avoided but inflation was not defeated. Structural changes to render the economy more competitive, reallocate government expenditure, increase monetization, and induce larger and more diversified exports to loosen the external constraint on growth are still necessary if inflation is to be defeated.

# Appendix: Statistical Tables

**Table 4A.1**
Aggregate production and spending (seasonally adjusted)ᵃ in australs (at 1970 prices)

| Period | GDP at market prices | Imports, goods, and services | Total consumption | Gross domestic product | | Exports, goods, and services | GDP, manufacturing, at factor prices |
|---|---|---|---|---|---|---|---|
| | | | | Total | Fixed | | |
| **1980** | 11,297.0 | 2,053.0 | 9,390.7 | 2,682.3 | 2,571.5 | 1,297.0 | 2,463.4 |
| I | 11,122.5 | 1,984.5 | 9,037.6 | 2,854.5 | 2,587.6 | 1,330.7 | 2,425.3 |
| II | 10,959.9 | 1,828.0 | 9,046.2 | 2,596.5 | 2,372.8 | 1,142.8 | 2,454.6 |
| III | 11,499.5 | 2,023.8 | 9,539.4 | 2,614.1 | 2,605.3 | 1,335.2 | 2,549.6 |
| IV | 11,606.1 | 2,375.8 | 9,939.4 | 2,664.0 | 2,720.1 | 1,379.1 | 2,423.9 |
| **1981** | 10,539.1 | 1,873.1 | 8,988.4 | 2,068.2 | 2,132.2 | 1,351.1 | 2,077.4 |
| I | 11,017.2 | 2,347.1 | 9,888.5 | 2,347.1 | 2,387.9 | 1,150.7 | 2,291.4 |
| II | 10,762.1 | 2,094.4 | 9,176.1 | 2,162.1 | 2,152.2 | 1,457.7 | 2,131.6 |
| III | 10,183.2 | 1,619.7 | 8,406.9 | 1,793.9 | 2,073.3 | 1,587.7 | 1,946.3 |
| IV | 10,193.7 | 1,431.0 | 8,482.0 | 1,969.6 | 1,915.5 | 1,208.4 | 1,940.2 |
| **1982** | 10,054.5 | 1,077.0 | 8,074.0 | 1,643.5 | 1,544.6 | 1,409.6 | 1,972.9 |
| I | 10,238.2 | 1,231.0 | 8,367.2 | 1,651.5 | 1,717.2 | 1,403.2 | 1,989.5 |
| II | 9,678.2 | 1,054.2 | 7,639.0 | 1,598.4 | 1,531.6 | 1,443.4 | 1,839.7 |
| III | 9,922.0 | 985.3 | 7,895.7 | 1,643.5 | 1,512.7 | 1,357.7 | 2,009.9 |
| IV | 10,379.7 | 1,037.4 | 8,394.1 | 1,680.7 | 1,416.8 | 1,434.1 | 2,052.3 |
| **1983** | 10,331.6 | 1,026.9 | 8,368.4 | 1,463.7 | 1,459.2 | 1,522.1 | 2,184.2 |
| I | 10,310.5 | 962.6 | 8,269.9 | 1,320.8 | 1,402.3 | 1,587.4 | 2,123.5 |
| II | 10,065.2 | 1,067.5 | 8,097.3 | 1,523.8 | 1,537.5 | 1,460.7 | 2,165.6 |
| III | 10,342.2 | 1,084.5 | 8,310.9 | 1,599.7 | 1,545.7 | 1,511.3 | 2,272.1 |
| IV | 10,608.5 | 992.8 | 8,795.3 | 1,410.5 | 1,351.3 | 1,529.0 | 2,175.4 |

| | | | | | | | |
|---|---|---|---|---|---|---|---|
| **1984** | 10,599.4 | 1,088.9 | 3,869.1 | 1,302.2 | 1,327.4 | 1,506.1 | 2,271.7 |
| I | 10,532.5 | 962.2 | 3,572.9 | 1,104.3 | 1,300.7 | 1,682.3 | 2,185.1 |
| II | 10,497.1 | 1,089.9 | 3,568.8 | 1,436.3 | 1,379.6 | 1,525.8 | 2,329.1 |
| III | 10,471.9 | 1,172.4 | 9,052.5 | 1,165.5 | 1,364.7 | 1,467.6 | 2,344.4 |
| IV | 10,895.9 | 1,131.1 | 9,282.1 | 1,502.5 | 1,264.5 | 1,348.5 | 2,228.1 |
| **1985** | 10,118.3 | 946.7 | 8,291.8 | 1,084.1 | 1,195.0 | 1,686.6 | 2,036.8 |
| I | 10,396.7 | 1,071.9 | 8,474.4 | 1,299.7 | 1,223.5 | 1,592.3 | 2,102.3 |
| II | 9,988.7 | 930.4 | 7,821.9 | 1,151.0 | 1,174.1 | 1,844.6 | 2,020.8 |
| III | 9,545.5 | 901.5 | 7,856.2 | 822.0 | 1,229.5 | 1,794.9 | 1,898.2 |
| IV | 10,542.4 | 882.8 | 6,014.8 | 1,063.5 | 1,153.0 | 1,514.7 | 2,125.8 |
| **1986** | 10,692.4 | 1,119.5 | 6,024.7 | 1,268.1 | 1,322.3 | 1,515.5 | 2,293.4 |
| I | 10,475.7 | 1,028.8 | 8,552.8 | 1,377.2 | 1,167.4 | 1,475.9 | 2,215.7 |
| II | 10,596.1 | 1,118.5 | 8,935.5 | 1,114.1 | 1,286.9 | 1,593.7 | 2,231.3 |
| III | 10,658.6 | 1,197.8 | 9,119.8 | 1,153.6 | 1,521.2 | 1,620.3 | 2,484.0 |
| IV | 11,039.0 | 1,132.7 | 9,490.5 | 1,427.3 | 1,313.5 | 1,372.1 | 2,322.4 |
| **1987** | | | | | | | |
| I | 10,758.5 | 1,182.1 | 8,809.4 | 1,462.6 | 1,340.2 | 1,571.8 | 2,262.2 |

Source: CEPAL, Buenos Aires Office, based on data from the Central Bank of the Argentine Republic.

a. By the method of moving averages. Seasonally adjusted series do not necessarily satisfy the national accounts identities. Annual figures are averages of quarterly seasonally adjusted data.

**Table 4A.2**
Inflation, exchange rates, wages, and money (monthly growth rates) (%)

| Period | CPI | WPI | Exchange rates[a] | | "Normal" hourly wages in manufacturing[c] | "Normal" wages per worker in manufacturing[d] | Prices of public enterprises | M1[e] | M2[f] |
| | | | Official[b] | Parallel | | | | | |
|---|---|---|---|---|---|---|---|---|---|
| **1984** | | | | | | | | | |
| January | 12.5 | 11.4 | 17.0 | 24.8 | 21.0 | 12.9 | 18.8 | 23.8 | 24.5 |
| February | 17.0 | 15.9 | 11.6 | 31.7 | 15.1 | −0.9 | 12.1 | 22.4 | 17.5 |
| March | 20.3 | 18.4 | 11.1 | 23.5 | 13.3 | 50.6 | 13.6 | 20.2 | 14.2 |
| April | 18.5 | 19.7 | 13.7 | 9.1 | 32.4 | 30.6 | 20.4 | 16.5 | 13.9 |
| May | 17.1 | 18.8 | 16.4 | 18.8 | 14.7 | 21.4 | 24.9 | 12.2 | 14.9 |
| June | 17.9 | 16.6 | 16.6 | 6.7 | 19.7 | 18.5 | 23.8 | 14.3 | 18.4 |
| July | 18.3 | 15.5 | 18.0 | 9.1 | 21.9 | 18.2 | 30.7 | 15.1 | 25.1 |
| August | 22.8 | 21.9 | 21.8 | 30.0 | 17.4 | 22.4 | 23.8 | 13.8 | 17.8 |
| September | 27.5 | 24.7 | 21.9 | 15.3 | 29.1 | 19.0 | 16.6 | 13.7 | 16.7 |
| October | 19.3 | 15.4 | 25.0 | 7.9 | 22.1 | 34.4 | 15.6 | 14.4 | 16.5 |
| November | 15.0 | 14.7 | 27.9 | 36.6 | 16.1 | 14.6 | 18.0 | 17.5 | 20.0 |
| December | 19.7 | 23.2 | 20.6 | 8.3 | 20.0 | 1.5 | 25.8 | 19.4 | 22.7 |
| **1985** | | | | | | | | | |
| January | 25.1 | 21.2 | 24.1 | 32.8 | 20.4 | 6.6 | 19.3 | 17.2 | 21.8 |
| February | 20.7 | 17.8 | 20.9 | 32.2 | 15.4 | 1.9 | 15.6 | 19.6 | 19.1 |
| March | 26.5 | 27.7 | 26.9 | 27.0 | 21.4 | 66.0 | 25.6 | 19.8 | 18.6 |
| April | 29.5 | 31.5 | 28.5 | 30.9 | 24.9 | 30.2 | 26.1 | 18.8 | 14.0 |
| May | 25.1 | 31.2 | 31.9 | 17.4 | 31.7 | 31.1 | 39.9 | 17.7 | 31.6 |
| June | 30.5 | 42.3 | 41.8 | 28.8 | 28.7 | 14.4 | 48.5 | 34.4 | 28.3 |
| July | 6.2 | −0.9 | 8.8 | 18.2 | −2.7 | 2.7 | 7.2 | 38.7 | 15.6 |
| August | 3.1 | 1.5 | 0.0 | 1.0 | 0.3 | 3.1 | 0.0 | 17.8 | 5.0 |
| September | 2.0 | 0.6 | 0.0 | −2.6 | 1.3 | 4.9 | 0.0 | 9.2 | 4.3 |
| October | 1.9 | 0.7 | 0.0 | −1.6 | 1.1 | 7.8 | 0.0 | 11.1 | 6.2 |
| November | 2.4 | 0.7 | 0.0 | −2.3 | 2.3 | −2.5 | 0.0 | 7.0 | 3.9 |
| December | 3.2 | 1.0 | 0.0 | −5.4 | 4.6 | 0.0 | 0.0 | 7.5 | 6.9 |

**1986**

| | | | | | | | | | |
|---|---|---|---|---|---|---|---|---|---|
| January | 3.0 | 0.0 | 0.0 | 5.4 | 5.4 | -3.8 | 0.0 | 9.2 | 8.4 |
| February | 1.7 | 0.8 | 0.0 | -4.1 | 2.1 | -14.8 | 0.0 | 6.1 | 5.1 |
| March | 4.6 | 1.4 | 0.0 | 5.6 | 0.0 | 28.9 | 0.2 | 4.4 | 4.5 |
| April | 4.7 | 3.0 | 3.4 | 1.1 | 7.2 | 20.1 | 6.5 | 3.9 | 4.7 |
| May | 4.0 | 2.7 | 2.5 | -2.3 | 5.6 | 8.0 | 3.1 | 3.3 | 6.0 |
| June | 4.5 | 4.6 | 2.9 | -0.7 | 4.2 | -15.3[g] | 4.0 | 4.5 | 6.2 |
| July | 6.8 | 5.1 | 3.3 | 2.2 | 7.4 | 31.0[g] | 7.0 | 3.2 | 6.5 |
| August | 8.8 | 9.4 | 6.9 | 19.2 | 9.0 | 11.6 | 5.9 | 4.8 | 5.2 |
| September | 7.2 | 6.8 | 8.8 | 12.4 | 1.8 | 0.7 | 4.0 | 3.2 | 4.7 |
| October | 6.1 | 5.3 | 4.2 | -1.8 | 11.0 | 12.5 | 4.2 | 5.4 | 7.5 |
| November | 5.3 | 4.9 | 5.3 | 12.2 | 4.7 | -2.4 | 5.0 | 6.6 | 9.8 |
| December | 4.7 | 3.0 | 5.3 | 16.2 | 2.5 | -2.1 | 5.8 | 8.8[h] | 10.1 |

**1987**

| | | | | | | | | | |
|---|---|---|---|---|---|---|---|---|---|
| January | 7.6 | 5.3 | 6.2 | 9.2 | 7.8 | -6.6 | 6.4 | 7.5[h] | 10.1 |
| February | 6.5 | 6.9 | 7.8 | 0.7 | 3.6 | -11.3 | 6.9 | 6.4[h] | 4.7 |
| March | 8.2 | 7.8 | 10.9 | 8.9 | 2.2 | 43.9 | 7.0 | | |
| April | 3.4 | 1.9[h] | 0.0 | 8.2 | 8.5 | 7.6 | 0.0 | | |
| May | 4.2 | 4.9[h] | 3.1 | 1.7 | 5.0[h] | | | | |
| June | 8.0 | 6.7[h] | 7.2 | 0.3 | 6.0[h] | | | | |

Source: CEPAL, Buenos Aires Office, based on data from INDEC (National Statistical Office), the Central Bank of the Argentine Republic and SIGEP.

a. Monthly averages.

b. During periods with double official exchange markets (June–December 1981 and July–November 1982) this is the commercial rate.

c. Unit value of "normal" wages per hour. "Normal" wages are defined as the sum of basic wages (including overtime) and bonuses (excluding legal half-year and end-year bonuses). The series is not seasonally adjusted.

d. Unit value of "normal" wages per worker. This variable has a highly seasonal behavior, especially because of the effect of summer vacations), which has not been corrected in the series shown in the table.

e. Currency outside banks and demand deposits (except government deposits), monthly averages, seasonally adjusted.

f. M1 + domestic currency savings and time deposits in commercial banks (excluding government deposits), including interest or indexation on those deposits.

g. Influenced by strikes.

h. Provisional figures.

**Table 4A.3**
Borrowing requirements of the consolidated public sector (percentage of GDP)[a]

| Component | 1980 | 1981 | 1982 | 1983 | 1984 | 1985 | 1986 |
|---|---|---|---|---|---|---|---|
| **Expenditures** | 35.3 | 38.9 | 38.5 | 40.4 | 35.6 | 33.8 | 31.7 |
| **Receipts** | 27.8 | 25.5 | 23.4 | 23.6 | 22.8 | 27.9 | 28.1 |
| Taxes | 23.3 | 20.4 | 18.7 | 18.7 | 18.1 | 22.0 | 22.9 |
| Other | 4.5 | 5.1 | 5.0 | 5.0 | 4.7 | 5.9 | 5.2 |
| **Borrowing requirements** | 7.5 | 13.4 | 15.1 | 16.8 | 12.8 | 5.9 | 3.6 |
| Internal and external credit | 3.4 | 8.3 | 6.4 | −1.5 | −1.0 | 0.6 | 2.9 |
| Money emission | 3.5 | 5.0 | 4.8 | 15.4 | 5.8 | 2.3 | − |
| Other | 0.6 | 0.1 | 3.9 | 2.9 | 8.0 | 3.0 | 0.7 |

Source: National Budget Law, 1987.
a. The consolidated public sector includes the national administration, provincial governments, Buenos Aires city government, and the social security system.

**Table 4A.4**
Liquidity coefficients (percentage of GDP)

| Month | M1[a] | M2[b] |
|---|---|---|
| **1984** | | |
| January | 5.4 | 12.5 |
| February | 5.6 | 13.4 |
| March | 5.4 | 12.6 |
| April | 5.2 | 11.4 |
| May | 5.0 | 10.9 |
| June | 5.0 | 10.5 |
| July | 5.2 | 10.8 |
| August | 4.8 | 10.2 |
| September | 4.2 | 9.1 |
| October | 3.6 | 8.2 |
| November | 3.5 | 8.1 |
| December | 4.1 | 8.7 |

**Table 4A.4** (continued)

| Month | M1[a] | M2[b] |
|---|---|---|
| **1985** | | |
| January | 4.2 | 9.3 |
| February | 3.9 | 9.2 |
| March | 3.6 | 8.6 |
| April | 3.4 | 7.8 |
| May | 3.1 | 7.6 |
| June | 3.6 | 8.1 |
| July | 5.4 | 10.7 |
| August | 5.6 | 10.9 |
| September | 5.6 | 10.5 |
| October | 5.6 | 10.1 |
| November | 5.9 | 10.3 |
| December | 6.5 | 11.1 |
| **1986** | | |
| January | 7.3 | 12.3 |
| February | 7.3 | 12.6 |
| March | 7.0 | 12.4 |
| April | 6.7 | 12.1 |
| May | 6.9 | 12.3 |
| June | 7.0 | 12.5 |
| July | 7.3 | 12.8 |
| August | 6.8 | 12.3 |
| September | 6.4 | 11.6 |
| October | 5.9 | 10.8 |
| November | 5.9 | 10.6 |
| December | 6.5 | 11.3 |
| **1987** | | |
| January | 6.5 | 11.5 |
| February | 6.4 | 11.3 |
| March | 6.2 | 11.0 |
| April | 6.2 | 10.8 |

Source: Carta Económica.

a. M1 is the currency outside banks plus demand deposits (except those held by the government and state agencies).

b. M2 is M1 plus term deposits in commercial banks, including interest and indexation adjustments accrued but not settled on those deposits.

**Table 4A.5**
Purchasing power of wages (indexes, 1983 = 100)

| Period | "Normal" hourly wages[a] deflated by CPI in: | | | | Monthly "normal" wages per worker[a] deflated by CPI in: | | | |
|---|---|---|---|---|---|---|---|---|
| | Month of earnings[b] | 2/3 month of earning, 1/3 following month[c] | Average, month of earning, following month[d] | Following month[e] | Month of earnings[b] | 2/3 month of earning, 1/3 following month[c] | Average, month of earning, following month[d] | Following month[e] |
| **1980** | 99.0 | 103.7 | 102.1 | 108.1 | 98.5 | 103.2 | 101.7 | 107.7 |
| **1981** | 93.0 | 96.2 | 95.2 | 99.1 | 88.4 | 91.5 | 90.5 | 94.3 |
| **1982** | 80.6 | 82.4 | 81.8 | 84.1 | 79.2 | 81.0 | 80.4 | 82.6 |
| **1983** | 100.0 | 100.0 | 100.0 | 100.0 | 100.0 | 100.0 | 100.0 | 100.0 |
| **1984** | 127.1 | 124.2 | 125.1 | 121.8 | 128.1 | 125.3 | 126.2 | 123.0 |
| **1985** | 111.6 | 112.6 | 112.2 | 114.1 | 106.0 | 107.3 | 106.9 | 109.0 |
| **1984** | | | | | | | | |
| January | 124.3 | 123.1 | 123.5 | 122.0 | 112.3 | 111.3 | 111.6 | 110.3 |
| February | 122.3 | 119.3 | 120.3 | 116.8 | 95.1 | 92.8 | 93.5 | 90.9 |
| March | 115.2 | 113.3 | 113.9 | 111.6 | 119.1 | 117.2 | 117.8 | 115.5 |
| April | 128.7 | 127.4 | 127.8 | 126.2 | 131.3 | 130.0 | 130.4 | 128.9 |
| May | 126.1 | 124.3 | 124.9 | 122.8 | 136.1 | 134.3 | 134.9 | 132.7 |
| June | 128.0 | 126.0 | 126.6 | 124.3 | 136.8 | 134.7 | 135.4 | 133.0 |
| July | 131.9 | 127.2 | 128.6 | 123.3 | 136.7 | 131.9 | 133.4 | 128.0 |
| August | 126.1 | 119.1 | 121.2 | 113.5 | 136.2 | 128.7 | 131.0 | 122.7 |
| September | 127.7 | 125.0 | 125.9 | 122.9 | 127.0 | 124.5 | 125.3 | 122.4 |
| October | 130.6 | 130.6 | 130.6 | 130.5 | 143.0 | 143.1 | 143.1 | 143.0 |
| November | 132.0 | 129.1 | 130.0 | 126.6 | 142.5 | 139.5 | 140.5 | 136.9 |
| December | 132.3 | 126.3 | 128.1 | 121.4 | 120.9 | 115.4 | 117.1 | 111.1 |

| | | | | | | | | |
|---|---|---|---|---|---|---|---|---|
| **1985** | | | | | | | | |
| January | 127.3 | 124.0 | 125.1 | 121.2 | 103.0 | 100.3 | 101.2 | 98.1 |
| February | 121.8 | 115.6 | 117.5 | 110.6 | 87.0 | 82.6 | 83.9 | 79.0 |
| March | 116.9 | 109.5 | 111.8 | 103.7 | 114.1 | 106.9 | 109.1 | 101.3 |
| April | 112.8 | 107.7 | 109.3 | 103.6 | 114.8 | 109.6 | 111.2 | 105.5 |
| May | 118.8 | 110.7 | 113.2 | 104.5 | 120.8 | 112.2 | 114.6 | 105.9 |
| June | 117.1 | 122.0 | 120.4 | 126.6 | 105.4 | 109.9 | 108.5 | 114.1 |
| July | 107.2 | 113.4 | 111.3 | 119.4 | 102.0 | 108.0 | 106.0 | 113.7 |
| August | 104.0 | 110.6 | 108.4 | 117.1 | 102.0 | 108.5 | 106.4 | 114.9 |
| September | 102.9 | 109.5 | 107.3 | 115.9 | 104.9 | 111.7 | 109.5 | 118.3 |
| October | 102.9 | 109.2 | 107.1 | 115.4 | 110.9 | 117.9 | 115.6 | 124.6 |
| November | 102.4 | 108.3 | 106.3 | 114.0 | 105.7 | 111.8 | 109.8 | 117.7 |
| December | 104.7 | 110.8 | 108.8 | 116.7 | 102.4 | 108.5 | 106.5 | 114.3 |
| **1986** | | | | | | | | |
| January | 106.9 | 113.9 | 111.6 | 120.7 | 95.6 | 102.0 | 99.9 | 108.1 |
| February | 106.9 | 112.2 | 110.5 | 117.3 | 80.1 | 84.2 | 82.9 | 88.0 |
| March | 103.0 | 108.1 | 106.4 | 112.9 | 98.7 | 103.6 | 102.0 | 108.3 |
| April | 104.7 | 110.2 | 108.4 | 115.5 | 113.2 | 119.3 | 117.3 | 125.1 |
| May | 105.9 | 111.3 | 109.5 | 116.4 | 117.5 | 123.5 | 121.5 | 129.2 |
| June | 106.4 | 110.6 | 109.3 | 114.5 | 95.2f | 99.0f | 97.7f | 102.5f |
| July | 106.5 | 108.6 | 109.6 | 112.4 | 116.7 | 119.1 | 120.2 | 123.4 |
| August | 106.7 | 109.4 | 110.6 | 114.3 | 119.7 | 122.8 | 124.2 | 128.4 |
| September | 101.3 | 104.2 | 105.6 | 109.7 | 112.4 | 115.8 | 117.3 | 121.9 |
| October | 106.0 | 109.3 | 110.9 | 115.6 | 119.3 | 123.1 | 125.0 | 130.3 |
| November | 105.4 | 108.9 | 110.5 | 115.5 | 110.6 | 114.4 | 116.1 | 121.4 |
| December | 103.1 | 105.6 | 106.7 | 110.1 | 103.4 | 105.9 | 107.1 | 110.5 |

**Table 4A.5** (continued)

| Period | "Normal" hourly wages[a] deflated by CPI in: | | | | Monthly "normal" wages per worker[a] deflated by CPI in: | | | |
|---|---|---|---|---|---|---|---|---|
| | Month of earnings[b] | 2/3 month of earning, 1/3 following month[c] | Average, month of earning, following month[d] | Following month[e] | Month of earnings[b] | 2/3 month of earning, 1/3 following month[c] | Average, month of earning, following month[d] | Following month[e] |
| **1987** | | | | | | | | |
| January | 103.3 | 106.1 | 107.5 | 111.4 | 89.8 | 92.3 | 93.5 | 97.0 |
| February | 100.5 | 102.7 | 103.7 | 106.6 | 74.8 | 76.4 | 77.2 | 79.5 |
| March | 94.9 | 98.5 | 100.3 | 105.4 | 99.5 | 103.3 | 105.2 | 110.6 |
| April | 99.6 | 103.1 | 104.8 | 109.8 | 103.6 | 107.3 | 109.1 | 114.3 |
| May[g] | 100.5 | 102.7 | 103.8 | 106.9 | | | | |

Source: CEPAL, Buenos Aires office, based on data from INDEC (National Statistical Office).

a. "Normal" wages are defined as the sum of basic wages (including overtime) and bonuses (excluding the legal half-year and end-of-year bonuses). The nominal indexes for each month measure wages accrued during that month. The series have considerable seasonal movements (due, in particular, to the effect of summer vacations) that have not been corrected in the data shown in the table.

b. Corresponds to the case where the wages accrued during a month were paid at mid-month and spent at the same moment.

c. Represents the case of fortnightly payments (at mid-month and at the end of the month) and spending somewhat concentrated immediately after payment dates.

d. Corresponds to the case of monthly payments (at the end of the month) and instantaneous spending, or to that of fortnightly payments at mid-month and the end of the month and a uniform spending rate between payment dates.

e. Corresponds to the case of monthly payments (at the end of the month) and a uniform spending rate.

f. Data affected by a fall in the number of hours worked, caused by strikes.

g. Provisional.

**Table 4A.6**
Employment and unemployment (indexes, 1970 = 100)

| Period | Employment in manufacturing[a] | Unemployment rate[b,c] (%) | Open underemployment rate[b,d] (%) |
|---|---|---|---|
| **1980** | 88.2 | 2.6 | 5.2 |
| I | 93.6 | | |
| II | 90.1 | 2.6 | 4.5 |
| III | 85.0 | | |
| IV | 83.9 | 2.5 | 5.8 |
| **1981** | 77.1 | 4.8 | 5.5 |
| I | 81.9 | | |
| II | 77.7 | 4.2 | 5.0 |
| III | 74.9 | | |
| IV | 74.0 | 5.3 | 6.0 |
| **1982** | 73.0 | 5.3 | 6.6 |
| I | 76.2 | | |
| II | 72.0 | 6.0 | 6.7 |
| III | 71.0 | | |
| IV | 72.9 | 4.6 | 6.4 |
| **1983** | 75.4 | 4.7 | 5.8 |
| I | 76.7 | | |
| II | 75.7 | 5.5 | 5.9 |
| III | 73.7 | | |
| IV | 75.6 | 3.9 | 5.6 |
| **1984** | 77.6 | 4.6 | 5.5 |
| I | 77.9 | | |
| II | 77.1 | 4.7 | 5.4 |
| III | 76.8 | | |
| IV | 78.4 | 4.5 | 5.6 |
| **1985** | 74.8 | 6.1 | 6.9 |
| I | 81.9 | | |
| II | 74.6 | 6.3 | 6.6 |
| III | 70.7 | | |
| IV | 71.9 | 5.9 | 7.2 |
| **1986** | 71.7 | 5.0 | 3.7 |
| I | 74.8 | | |
| II | 69.8 | 4.8[e] | 6.2 |
| III | 69.9 | | |
| IV | 72.1 | 5.2 | 7.3 |
| **1987** | | | |
| I | 74.0 | | |

Source: INDEC (National Statistical Office).
a. Index of blue-collar employment in large manufacturing establishments.
b. Unemployment and underemployment figures are gathered twice a year, in April and October.
c. Unemployed as a percentage of the economically active population in a group of large and medium-sized urban areas.
d. Proportion of the employed population who worked less than 35 hours in the week of the survey and would want to work more hours, in a group of large and medium-sized urban areas.
e. Greater Buenos Aires.

**Table 4A.7**
Balance of payments (millions of US dollars)

| Period | Current account | | | | Capital Account[a] | | | Change in foreign reserves[c] |
|---|---|---|---|---|---|---|---|---|
| | Total | Balance of trade | Real services | Financial services | Total | Public[b] | Private | |
| **1980** | −4767.8 | −2519.2 | −740.1 | −1531.4 | 2409.5 | 2815.0 | −405.5 | −2796.1 |
| I | −767.3 | −223.2 | −419.4 | −125.3 | 1188.8 | 663.8 | 525.0 | 187.3 |
| II | −988.7 | −361.3 | −150.2 | −490.6 | −751.0 | 613.3 | −1364.3 | −1477.0 |
| III | −1145.0 | −746.6 | −11.0 | −394.0 | 1508.5 | 302.0 | 1206.5 | 301.5 |
| IV | −1866.8 | −1188.1 | −159.5 | −521.5 | 463.2 | 1235.9 | −772.7 | −1807.9 |
| **1981** | −4714.0 | −287.0 | −704.9 | −3699.7 | 1410.1 | 4454.2 | −3044.1 | −3806.5 |
| I | −2091.7 | −624.1 | −699.9 | −756.0 | −779.7 | 2476.6 | −3256.3 | −2985.3 |
| II | −913.0 | 226.0 | −77.5 | −1056.5 | 1032.6 | 1099.2 | −66.6 | 30.0 |
| III | −220.0 | 524.7 | 71.0 | −807.2 | 211.0 | 322.2 | −111.2 | −82.5 |
| IV | −1489.3 | −413.6 | 1.5 | −1080.0 | 946.2 | 556.2 | 390.0 | −768.7 |
| **1982** | −2357.7 | 2286.8 | 42.5 | −4718.5 | 2211.5 | 3957.8 | −1746.3 | −651.1 |
| I | −304.0 | 686.6 | −71.5 | −922.5 | 477.7 | 76.6 | 401.1 | 168.3 |
| II | −302.6 | 1012.8 | −23.7 | −1304.8 | 534.9 | 2539.1 | −2004.2 | −127.4 |
| III | −618.0 | 407.4 | 101.1 | −1131.5 | 664.4 | 293.1 | 371.3 | 5.8 |
| IV | −1133.1 | 180.0 | 36.6 | −1359.7 | 534.5 | 1049.0 | −514.5 | −697.8 |
| **1983** | −2461.0 | 3331.1 | −399.5 | −5408.0 | 1783.2 | 3447.6 | −1664.5 | 243.7 |
| I | −602.0 | 956.7 | −129.9 | −1434.2 | 1442.2 | 1246.1 | 196.0 | 834.0 |
| II | −483.9 | 921.9 | −68.9 | −1337.6 | 528.5 | 731.1 | −202.6 | 14.9 |
| III | −789.1 | 792.5 | −120.6 | −1464.4 | −22.8 | 481.2 | −504.0 | −867.0 |
| IV | −586.0 | 660.0 | −80.1 | −1171.8 | −164.7 | 989.2 | −1153.9 | 261.8 |

| | | | | | | | | |
|---|---|---|---|---|---|---|---|---|
| **1984** | −2390.9 | 3523.0 | −204.7 | −5712.0 | 2759.7 | 4441.1 | −1681.4 | 264.8 |
| I | −197.0 | 1294.0 | −143.3 | −1351.4 | 951.6 | 1826.3 | −874.7 | 672.6 |
| II | −137.5 | 1350.0 | −38.4 | −1448.2 | 455.8 | 796.5 | −340.7 | 297.8 |
| III | −749.6 | 755.0 | −32.6 | −1471.6 | 255.5 | 882.0 | −626.5 | −488.3 |
| IV | −1306.8 | 124.0 | 9.6 | −1440.8 | 1096.8 | 936.3 | 160.5 | −217.3 |
| **1985** | −952.8 | 4582.0 | −231.1 | −5303.8 | 3212.2 | 3519.4 | −307.2 | 2493.1 |
| I | −779.8 | 826.0 | −162.5 | −1441.1 | 557.7 | 447.4 | 110.3 | −288.3 |
| II | 186.9 | 1643.0 | −29.0 | −1428.5 | 843.9 | 347.1 | 496.8 | 821.6 |
| III | 109.9 | 1331.0 | 0.2 | −1221.6 | 1138.6 | 755.0 | 383.6 | 1436.6 |
| IV | −469.8 | 782.0 | −39.8 | −1212.6 | 672.0 | 1969.9 | −1297.9 | 523.2 |
| **1986**[d] | −2770.0 | 2130.0 | −500.0 | −4400.0 | 2070.0 | – | – | −700.0 |
| I | −810.7 | 591.9 | −256.6 | −1146.0 | 375.7 | 208.0 | 167.7 | −435.0 |
| II | −271.3 | 813.9 | −48.0 | −1037.2 | 1941.6 | 1441.5 | 500.1 | 1441.3 |

Source: Central Bank of the Argentine Republic.

a. Includes noncompensatory and compensatory capital movements.

b. Includes the national government, local governments, and public enterprises.

c. Differs from the sum of the current and capital accounts balances by the amount of the items "errors and omissions," "unilateral transfers," and "other international payments."

d. Estimated figures.

**Table 4A.8**
Contributions to the growth of base money (%)[a]

| Period | Base money | Foreign sector (net) | Domestic credit Total | Credits to the government Total (net) | Monetary regulation account[b] | Other credits Total (net) | Foreign currency financing (net)[c] | Other financing (net)[d] | Credits to financial institutions (net) | Other accounts (net) |
|---|---|---|---|---|---|---|---|---|---|---|
| **1984** | | | | | | | | | | |
| January | 14.6 | 6.6 | 8.0 | 23.0 | 15.9 | 7.1 | | 7.1 | −4.4 | −10.6 |
| February | 16.2 | 1.9 | 14.3 | −0.8 | −6.3 | 5.5 | | 5.5 | 3.6 | 11.5 |
| March | 16.6 | 2.4 | 14.2 | 12.5 | 7.0 | 5.5 | | 5.5 | 4.6 | −2.9 |
| April | 14.9 | 4.7 | 10.2 | 10.5 | 7.1 | 3.4 | | 3.4 | 2.8 | −3.1 |
| May | 8.4 | 2.6 | 5.8 | 9.8 | 5.7 | 4.1 | | 4.1 | 4.5 | −8.5 |
| June | 18.1 | 3.1 | 15.0 | 10.5 | 4.2 | 6.3 | | 6.3 | 8.0 | −3.5 |
| July | 11.6 | 0.9 | 10.7 | 12.1 | 6.4 | 5.7 | | 5.7 | 8.6 | −10.0 |
| August | 10.0 | −4.1 | 14.1 | 11.8 | 6.5 | 5.3 | | 5.3 | 4.1 | −1.8 |
| September | 17.2 | 2.2 | 15.0 | 11.8 | 8.1 | 3.7 | | 3.7 | 6.6 | −3.4 |
| October | 18.1 | 5.1 | 13.0 | 10.3 | 7.1 | 3.2 | | 3.2 | 60.5 | −57.8 |
| November | 9.8 | −3.6 | 13.4 | 12.9 | 6.7 | 6.2 | | 6.2 | 4.7 | −4.2 |
| December | 25.7 | −13.5 | 39.2 | 16.3 | 10.1 | 6.2 | | 6.2 | 24.1 | −1.2 |
| **1985** | | | | | | | | | | |
| January | 13.0 | 4.2 | 8.8 | 14.6 | 10.4 | 4.2 | | 4.2 | 6.8 | −12.6 |
| February | 9.1 | −4.8 | 13.9 | 23.3 | 12.2 | 11.1 | | 11.1 | 5.7 | −15.1 |
| March | 12.5 | −2.0 | 14.5 | 21.3 | 15.4 | 5.9 | | 5.9 | −5.7 | −1.1 |
| April | −9.8 | 6.9 | −16.7 | 26.2 | 13.9 | 12.3 | | 12.3 | 34.4 | −77.3 |
| May | −1.2 | 18.4 | −19.6 | 41.7 | 28.9 | 12.8 | | 12.8 | 3.2 | −64.5 |
| June | 89.7 | −4.0 | 93.7 | 64.3 | 19.9 | 44.4 | 21.5 | 22.9 | 50.5 | −21.1 |
| July | 21.0 | 17.2 | 3.8 | 4.6 | 1.3 | 3.3 | 2.9 | 0.4 | 19.2 | −20.0 |

|  | | | | | | | | | | |
|---|---|---|---|---|---|---|---|---|---|---|
| August | 14.1 | 10.3 | 3.8 | 4.5 | 4.5 | 0.0 | 0.0 | 0.0 | 24.5 | −25.2 |
| September | 4.8 | 0.1 | 4.7 | 3.4 | 3.5 | −0.1 | −0.2 | 0.1 | 10.5 | −9.2 |
| October | 11.2 | 6.4 | 4.8 | 5.0 | 3.2 | 1.8 | 0.8 | 1.0 | 7.9 | −8.1 |
| November | 11.0 | 4.9 | 6.1 | 3.2 | 3.0 | 0.2 | 0.2 | 0.0 | 0.1 | 2.8 |
| December | 16.3 | −49.8 | 66.1 | 62.5 | 0.7 | 61.8 | 61.6 | 0.2 | 9.5 | −5.9 |
| **1986** | | | | | | | | | | |
| January | −3.3 | 4.7 | −8.0 | 3.1 | 2.4 | 0.7 | 0.9 | −0.2 | 1.1 | −12.2 |
| February | −8.9 | −0.2 | −8.7 | 6.3 | 2.5 | 3.8 | 3.9 | −0.1 | 7.1 | −22.1 |
| March | 13.5 | −5.4 | 18.9 | 11.5 | 3.4 | 8.1 | 8.1 | 0.0 | 3.2 | 4.2 |
| April | 1.7 | 5.4 | −3.7 | 6.1 | 3.2 | 2.9 | 3.0 | −0.1 | 4.3 | −14.1 |
| May | 3.7 | 4.0 | −0.3 | 7.0 | 3.5 | 3.5 | 3.6 | −0.1 | 3.8 | −11.1 |
| June | 7.2 | −1.7 | 8.9 | 8.0 | 3.5 | 4.5 | 4.9 | −0.4 | −0.2 | 1.1 |
| July | 5.3 | 1.4 | 3.9 | 10.3 | 3.7 | 6.5 | 6.5 | 0.1 | 3.3 | −9.7 |
| August | 7.4 | 1.2 | 6.2 | 6.0 | 5.0 | 1.0 | 1.1 | −0.1 | 0.2 | 0.0 |
| September | −4.6 | −0.4 | −4.2 | 3.4 | 5.1 | −1.7 | −1.8 | 0.1 | 3.9 | −11.5 |
| October | −4.5 | −1.4 | −3.1 | 7.8 | 5.8 | 2.0 | 2.0 | 0.0 | 12.4 | −23.3 |
| November | 7.4 | −6.3 | 13.7 | 16.0 | 8.2 | 7.3 | 7.9 | −0.1 | 8.7 | −11.0 |
| December | 7.8 | −5.5 | 13.3 | 13.1 | 7.7 | 5.4 | 5.9 | −0.5 | 14.6 | −14.4 |
| **1987** | | | | | | | | | | |
| January | 6.0 | −0.5 | 6.5 | 11.3 | 7.6 | 3.7 | 3.2 | 0.5 | 3.8 | −8.6 |
| February | −5.7 | −3.8 | −1.9 | 13.7 | 6.8 | 6.9 | 7.3 | −0.4 | 7.1 | −22.7 |
| March | 3.6 | 0.2 | 3.4 | 7.9 | 5.6 | 2.5 | 5.1 | −2.8 | 8.0 | −12.5 |
| April | 2.8 | −6.9 | 9.7 | 11.3 | 6.7 | 4.0 | 5.6 | −1.0 | 11.7 | −13.3 |
| May | 10.2 | 3.0 | 7.2 | 13.6 | 8.8 | 4.8 | 3.4 | 1.4 | 6.1 | −12.5 |

Source: CEPAL, Buenos Aires Office, based on data from the Central Bank of the Argentine Republic.

a. All variables are defined as $[X(t − 1) − X(t − 1)]/B(t − 1)$, where $X(t)$ is the stock of X at the end of period $t$ and $B(t − 1)$ is the stock of base money at the end of period $t − 1$.

b. Measures the accumulated net interest on bank reserves and rediscounts.

c. Credits, net of deposits. This account, created in June 1985, includes foreign loans taken by the Central Bank and transferred to the national government. In the monetary statistics these loans are debited in the "foreign sector" account.

d. Includes advances to the government, government bonds held by the Central Bank, and the value of credits to the government, net of deposits of public agencies at the Central Bank.

**Table 4A.9**
Foreign debt (millions of US dollars)[a]

| End of year | Total | Public | Private |
|---|---|---|---|
| 1975 | 7.9 | 4.0 | 3.9 |
| 1976 | 8.3 | 5.2 | 3.1 |
| 1977 | 9.7 | 6.0 | 3.7 |
| 1978 | 12.5 | 8.4 | 4.1 |
| 1979 | 19.0 | 10.0 | 9.0 |
| 1980 | 27.2 | 14.5 | 12.7 |
| 1981 | 35.7 | 20.0 | 15.6 |
| 1982 | 43.6 | 28.6 | 15.0 |
| 1983 | 45.1 | 31.7 | 13.4 |
| 1984 | 46.9 | 36.1 | 10.8 |
| 1985[b] | 48.3 | 39.9 | 8.4 |
| 1986[b] | 50.0 | | |

Source: Central Bank of the Argentine Republic.
a. Including arrears.
b. Estimated figures.

**Table 4A.10**
Interest rates (30 days, monthly equivalent, %)

| | Nominal | | | | Real | | | |
|---|---|---|---|---|---|---|---|---|
| | Active | | Passive | | Active | | Passive | |
| Period | Con-trolled | Free | Con-trolled | Free | Con-trolled | Free | Con-trolled | Free |
| **1984** | | | | | | | | |
| January | 12.5 | 12.8 | 11.5 | 12.9 | 1.3 | 1.6 | −0.9 | 0.3 |
| February | 11.0 | 12.8 | 10.0 | 12.5 | −1.8 | −0.2 | −6.0 | −3.8 |
| March | 11.0 | 13.5 | 10.0 | 13.4 | −6.1 | −4.0 | −8.5 | −5.7 |
| April | 14.0 | 19.3 | 13.0 | 17.5 | −3.9 | 0.6 | −4.6 | −0.8 |
| May | 14.0 | 17.4 | 13.0 | 20.8 | −2.7 | 0.2 | −3.5 | 3.2 |
| June | 14.0 | 18.2 | 13.0 | 20.3 | −4.3 | −0.8 | 4.2 | 2.0 |
| July | 17.0 | 19.4 | 15.5 | 19.3 | −2.4 | −0.4 | −2.4 | 0.9 |
| August | 17.0 | 18.4 | 15.5 | 18.5 | −4.7 | −3.6 | −6.0 | −3.5 |
| September | 17.0 | 21.1 | 15.5 | 22.1 | −6.5 | −3.2 | −9.4 | −4.3 |
| October | 19.0 | 25.9 | 17.0 | 24.2 | 1.5 | 7.4 | −1.9 | 4.1 |
| November | 19.0 | 22.1 | 17.0 | 20.0 | 3.2 | 5.9 | 1.8 | 4.4 |
| December | 19.0 | 33.2 | 17.0 | 30.9 | −1.9 | 9.8 | −2.2 | 9.4 |

**Table 4A.10** (continued)

| | Nominal | | | | Real | | | |
|---|---|---|---|---|---|---|---|---|
| | Active | | Passive | | Active | | Passive | |
| Period | Con-trolled | Free | Con-trolled | Free | Con-trolled | Free | Con-trolled | Free |
| **1985** | | | | | | | | |
| January | 20.0 | 25.1 | 18.0 | 24.9 | −1.2 | 3.0 | −5.7 | −0.2 |
| February | 20.0 | 22.8 | 18.0 | 20.9 | 0.3 | 2.6 | −2.2 | 0.2 |
| March | 22.0 | 25.5 | 20.0 | 23.5 | −5.0 | −2.3 | −5.1 | −2.4 |
| April | 28.0 | 35.6 | 26.0 | 27.4 | −1.7 | 4.1 | −2.7 | −1.6 |
| May | 32.0 | 42.1 | 30.0 | 31.1 | 2.3 | 10.1 | 3.9 | 4.8 |
| June 1−14 | 30.0 | 40.7 | 28.0 | 28.9 | | | | |
| June 15−30 | 6.0 | 9.1 | 4.0 | 6.9 | | | | |
| July | 5.0 | 7.2 | 3.5 | 5.2 | 2.7 | 4.8 | −2.5 | −0.9 |
| August | 5.0 | 8.7 | 3.5 | 5.7 | 2.7 | 6.3 | 0.4 | 2.6 |
| September | 5.0 | 6.2 | 3.5 | 5.3 | 3.5 | 4.7 | 1.5 | 3.2 |
| October | 4.5 | 5.3 | 3.1 | 4.3 | 3.1 | 3.9 | 1.1 | 2.3 |
| November | 4.5 | 5.5 | 3.1 | 4.4 | 2.8 | 3.8 | 0.7 | 2.0 |
| December | 4.5 | 5.7 | 3.1 | 4.4 | 2.6 | 3.8 | −0.1 | 1.2 |
| **1986** | | | | | | | | |
| January | 4.5 | 5.7 | 3.1 | 4.4 | 2.6 | 3.8 | 0.1 | 1.3 |
| February | 4.5 | 5.6 | 3.1 | 4.5 | 2.6 | 3.7 | 1.4 | 2.8 |
| March | 4.5 | 4.3 | 3.1 | 4.9 | 1.9 | 1.7 | −1.5 | 0.2 |
| April | 4.5 | 4.5 | 3.1 | 4.4 | −0.4 | −0.4 | −1.6 | −0.3 |
| May | 4.5 | 4.6 | 3.1 | 4.4 | −0.2 | −0.1 | −0.9 | 0.3 |
| June | 4.7 | 4.5 | 3.3 | 4.3 | 0.3 | 0.5 | 1.2 | 0.3 |
| July | 5.0 | 5.1 | 3.5 | 4.6 | −1.1 | −1.0 | −3.1 | −2.0 |
| August | 6.6 | 6.6 | 5.5 | 6.5 | −1.5 | −1.4 | −3.0 | −2.1 |
| September | 6.0 | 7.4 | 4.5 | 6.9 | −0.6 | 0.7 | −2.6 | −0.3 |
| October | 6.5 | 8.2 | 5.0 | 7.9 | 0.3 | 1.9 | −1.0 | 1.7 |
| November | 7.0 | 8.3 | 5.5 | 7.7 | 1.8 | 3.1 | 0.2 | 2.3 |
| December | 7.0 | 9.3 | 5.5 | 8.3 | 2.6 | 4.8 | 0.7 | 3.4 |
| **1987** | | | | | | | | |
| January | 7.0 | 9.0 | 5.5 | 8.3 | 0.0 | 1.9 | −1.9 | 0.7 |
| February | 7.0 | 8.7 | 6.0 | 7.5 | 0.5 | 2.1 | −0.5 | 0.9 |
| March | 4.0 | 4.3 | 3.0 | 4.0 | −3.3 | −3.1 | −4.8 | −3.9 |
| April | 5.5 | 8.3 | 4.5 | 7.0 | 2.7 | 5.5 | 1.3 | 3.7 |

Source: Carta Económica.

## Notes

1. Antecedents for the discussion may be found in Di Tella (forthcoming) and Canavese and Petrecolla (forthcoming).

2. The Central Bank deficit is usually known as "quasi-fiscal deficit" and has two main sources: the payment of interest on mandatory reserve requirements of financial institutions and the rediscounting of financial institutions' paper at interest rates below the market rates paid by the Central Bank (Pieckarz 1984). The payment of interest on mandatory reserve requirements is unavoidable in a system with high reserve requirements if the banking activity is not to work at a loss.

3. For further details on deindexation, see Heymann (1986).

4. Some of these changes, such as the increase in import and export tariffs, were made for fiscal purposes.

5. Actually this problem was to become crucial from the third stage onward. It is interesting to point out that those firms that demand credit can be divided into two different subsets: firms in which investment and working capital are usually financed out of profits and firms in which financing comes mainly from the use of credit. For those in the first subset the interest rate is only an opportunity cost that determines the amount of credit demanded or supplied, but those in the second subset quickly become highly indebted with high real rates and they must decide whether to continue getting more indebted or to go bankrupt. This second subset has an interest-inelastic demand for credit because expectations of "bailouts" are strong. If there are many firms in the second subset, reductions in the money supply induce disproportionately large increases in interest rates.

6. Moreover, the risk of partial default influenced the value of Argentine government paper in international and domestic markets. Quotations well under par imply a high real rate of interest, which sets a high ceiling for real internal rates. Annual renegotiations of principal and service payments create high uncertainty on the durability of economic policies because they are revised in each renegotiation. Both factors further discouraged investment.

## References

Arida, P., and A. Lara-Resende. 1985. "Inertial inflation and monetary reform: Brazil," in *Inflation and Indexation: Argentina, Brazil and Israel*, J. Williamson, ed. (Washington D.C.: Institute for International Economics), 27–45.

Baer, W., and I. Kerstenetzky, eds. 1964. *Inflation and Growth in Latin America*. New Haven, Conn.: Yale University Press.

Berlinski, J., and D. Schydlowsky. 1977. "Incentives for industrialization in Argentina." Washington, D.C.: International Bank for Reconstruction and Development.

Bruno, M., and S. Fischer. 1985. "Expectations and the high inflation trap." MIT and Falk Institute.

Cagan, P. 1956. "The monetary dynamics of hyperinflation," in *Studies in the Quantity Theory of Money*, M. Friedman, ed. (Chicago, Ill.: University of Chicago Press), 25–117.

Canavese, A. J. 1982. "The structuralist explanation in the theory of inflation." *World Development* 10(7):523–530.

Canavese, A. J. 1985. *Inflationary Tax, Fiscal Balance, and Hyperinflation*. Working Paper 127. Buenos Aires: Instituto Torcuato di Tella. (In Spanish.)

Canavese, A. J., and A. Petrecolla. Forthcoming. "The Austral Plan: A structuralist view," in *The Austral Plan*, G. Di Tella and A. Canavese, eds. (Buenos Aires). (In Spanish.)

Cardoso, F. 1986. "Inflation and seigniorage." Medford, Mass.: Fletcher School of Law and Diplomacy.

Cavallo, D., and A. Peña. 1986. "The fiscal deficit and the causes of inflation." *Novedades Económicas* (December), 9(72):10–15. (In Spanish.)

Cukierman, A. 1984. *Inflation, Stagflation, Relative Prices and Imperfect Information*. Cambridge: Cambridge University Press.

De Pablo, J. C. 1976. "A model of passive money of various samples." *Económica* 22(2/3):161–172.

Diaz Alejandro, C. F. 1970. *Studies in the Economic History of the Argentine Republic*. New Haven, Conn.: Yale University Press.

Di Tella, G. 1979. "Price oscillation, oligopolistic behaviour and inflation: The Argentine case." *World Development*, 1043–1052.

Di Tella, G. 1986. "The last inflationary cycle in Argentina: 1979–1985," in *The Debt Crisis in Latin America*, R. Thorp and L. Whitehead, eds. (Bogotá: Siglo XXI), 147–184. (In Spanish.)

Di Tella, G. Forthcoming. "The second stage of the Austral Plan" in *The Austral Plan*, G. Di Tella and A. Canavese, eds. (Buenos Aires).

Domper, J., and J. Streb. 1986. "Influence of price stabilization on collection of taxes." Mimeo. (In Spanish.)

Dornbusch, R. 1985. "External debt, budget deficits and disequilibrium exchange rates," in *International Debt and the Developing Countries*, G. Smith and J. Cuddington, eds. (Washington, D.C.: World Bank), 213–235.

Dornbusch, R. 1987. "Restrictive fiscal policy and easy money: The key to stabilization in Argentina." *Estudios* 10(41):21–38. (In Spanish.)

Dornbusch, R., and S. Fischer. 1986. "Stopping hyperinflation: Past and present." *Weltwirtschaftliches Archiv* 122 : 1–47.

Frenkel, R., and J. M. Fanelli. 1986. "On the chaotic adjustment to the Austral Plan." Buenos Aires: Centro de Estudios de Estado y la Sociedad. (In Spanish.)

Gerchunoff, P. 1987. *Possibilities and Limits of a Heterodox Stabilization Program: The Case of Argentina.* Working Paper 143. Buenos Aires: Instituto Torcuato Di Tella. (In Spanish.)

Heymann, D. 1986. *Three Experiments on Inflation and Stabilization Policies.* Discussion Paper 18. Buenos Aires: Comisión Económica para America Latina. (In Spanish.)

Llach, J. J. Forthcoming. "The institutional and international characteristic of hyper-stabilizations," in *The Austral Plan,* G. di Tella and A. Canavese, eds. (Buenos Aires). (In Spanish.)

Olivera, J. H. G. 1964. "On structural inflation and Latin American structuralism." *Oxford Economic Papers,* n.s., 16(3):321–332.

Olivera, J. H. G. 1967. "Money, prices and fiscal lags: A note on the dynamics of inflation." *Banca Nazionale del Lavoro Quarterly Review* 20:258–267.

Olivera, J. H. G. 1970. "On passive money." *Journal of Political Economy* 78:805–814.

Pieckarz, J. A. 1984. "Compensation of small real reserves: The importance of monetary regulation, the preliminary results of the Central Bank, and the transformation of the Argentine financial system." Buenos Aires: Instituto Torcuato Di Tella. (In Spanish.)

Sargent, T. 1982. "The ends of four big inflations," in *Inflation: Causes and Effects,* R. Hall, ed. (Chicago, Ill.: University of Chicago Press), 41–96.

Tanzi, V. 1977. "Inflation, lags in collection and the real value of tax revenue." *IMF Staff Papers* 24:154–167.

# Comments on Part II

## Comment by Daniel Heymann

Although it has been two years since the announcement of the Austral Plan, I am impressed by how high the Argentine inflation still is in comparison to other countries and by how much it has been reduced with respect to its level before the plan was implemented. Both the success of the program in dealing with an extremely rapid inflation and the evident difficulties in achieving a definite stabilization are subjects that deserve analysis. Canavese and Di Tella and Machinea and Fanelli present two informative perspectives of the program and its effects. Although they write from quite different angles, they avoid giving a one-sided interpretation of the plan.

My comments concentrate on three issues raised by the Argentine experience: the design of policies to attack high inflation, the groping for a sustainable inflationary path after attaining a transitory stabilization, and the management of the dynamics of nominal variables in an economy that remains unstable even when the imminent threat of runaway inflation has been dissipated.

As pointed out by both Canavese and Di Tella and Machinea and Fanelli, the Argentine big inflation was of a particular nature: On the one hand, it was so high as to suggest a comparison with actual hyperinflations (and to pose the question, raised by Canavese and Di Tella, of whether the process that governed prices was not actually explosive). On the other hand, some inertial mechanisms were still at work; that is, there still remained a sizable (although shrinking) volume of nominal contracts, and most prices were still set in the domestic currency, without direct reference to an "auction" price, such as the parallel exchange rate. Those conditions did not seem conducive to the usual remedies for either moderate inflations or proper hyperinflations.

In order to produce a rapid drop in the inflation rate, the Austral Plan combined aggregate demand instruments with a comprehensive price and wage freeze and a mechanism to adapt contracts to the sudden shift in the price trend. These aspects of the program were interdependent. A sharp reduction in the fiscal deficit was, of course, necessary to make a freeze feasible; in turn, the freeze was expected to increase tax revenues through the fiscal lag effect. The currency reform was meant to adjust outstanding contracts to a discrete change in the inflation rate in order to avoid large wealth redistributions. This could not be done without a definite indication that inflation would in fact fall: A currency reform of the kind applied in Argentina needs the support of a price freeze.

Machinea and Fanelli mention several arguments for the use of incomes policies in the Austral Plan. In discussions of these measures the main question has usually been whether prices would automatically converge to the "equilibrium" inflation rate, given a credible fiscal policy. When pricing is not completely "dollarized" or based on a similar standard, this is quite doubtful: A program that relies simply on the announcement effect puts a heavy burden on the cognitive and decision skills of price makers, who have to act in the dark with respect to other agents' possible reactions and to the government's response in the event of a price overshooting. (If markets were really that effective in finding the "optimal" response to shifts in the environment, the costs of inflation would be rather small and stabilization would lose much of its purpose.) A freeze, by contrast, short-cuts the transition by setting a low reference price growth; needless to say, this makes sense only if aggregate demand behaves accordingly.

There is no doubt that price controls have many problems. Canavese and Di Tella refer to the fact that the freeze starts from a given set of relative prices; if nominal prices are somewhat inflexible downward, the necessary relative price movements would result in a "residual" inflation. The authors make a useful classification of the potential sources or relative price disequilibrium at the time of a freeze: (1) Individual prices oscillate relative to one another and are "caught" at a particular instant in the course of their adjustment; (2) prices, set by the government, such as the exchange rate and public sector prices, may be set either too low for budget or external balance or too high, in the sense that their current nominal values are not consistent with all other prices staying constant; and (3) equilibrium relative prices after stabilization may not be the same as under high infla-tion. None of these sources is caused specifically by the use of incomes policies. Any stabilization program, no matter what its features, begins at a certain date with a certain initial set of relative prices. A residual inflation through relative price shifts is possible with or without a freeze; one could in principle fear that a freeze would prevent the equilibrating price movements and thus cause disturbances in supplies (which were not observed in Argentina) but not fault it for creating an initial relative price maladjustment. On the other hand, it seems that the standard for a comparison should not be the hypothetical equilibrium price vector but rather the prices that would prevail under alternative policies; it is probable that a sudden policy shift of any kind would imply relative price movements during a transition period.

In any case, it is clear that the initial set of relative prices is of great significance. The Austral Plan started with high values of the real exchange rate and public sector prices and low real prices for certain primary goods. These relative prices proved not to be sustainable. The resulting inflation was propagated by the still active indexation mechanisms, and that defined a sort of floor for the inflation rate, given the public's expectations of an acceleration following the freeze and the perception that the authorities were not likely to interrupt the then incipient real recovery.

Still, this is only part of the story. A heterodox shock manages disinflation by acting simultaneously on several fronts. One of its advantages is that it does not rest on a narrowly defined mechanism to decelerate prices. Its policies try to influence aggregate demand, expectations, and prices at the same time. In exchange, at some moment the freeze has to be lifted, and that raises the problem of how to do it smoothly. This has been shown to be possible. But, in addition, it is difficult to conceive of a heterodox shock that would not start with a zero inflation rate as a short-run objective. A freeze is a relatively simple and easy-to-understand measure (so that it has a good chance of being to a certain extent self enforcing), whereas policies aimed at a less extreme target may be much more complicated to manage. This poses a dilemma: The low inflation implicit in the initial stage of the shock (to make the transition easier) is not necessarily sustainable over a long period.

Even though they highlight different matters, Canavese and Di Tella and Machinea and Fanelli agree that inflationary tendencies remained strong in Argentina. After a long period of nominal and real instability, "normal" relative prices were not easy to guess, which increased the chance of inconsistencies in price and wage setting. The fiscal deficit, although it dropped significantly, was reduced in part through transitory means, and many groups continued to express large demands for government assistance, either directly through the budget or through financial instruments. More generally, there was no clear-cut answer to the question of how to find a set of noninflationary fiscal policies in an economy with a chronic budget imbalance that has to bear in addition the burden of the foreign debt. All this made the stabilization fragile and caused uncertainty regarding the "permanent" inflation rate.

Once inflation has been brought down from high levels, one can think of three alternatives. In the first, the government commits its policies to a low inflation target and is successful. In the second, it does likewise but fails. The third course is to adopt a flexible approach, in which policies try to limit the inflation rate to moderate values but without strong commitments about the paths of policy instruments. Obviously the first option is the best, but the second is possibly the worst possible case because the break-down of a policy that tries unsuccessfully to keep inflation much below a longer-run feasible level might cause a large disruption. The problem, then, is to determine to what extent the uncertainty about the inflationary pressures can be removed and to incorporate them into the policy design; the trade-off is between lacking clear signals over more than a short horizon (which automatically reduces the benefits to the drop in the infla-tion rate) and making a wrong judgment of the prospects of a definite stabilization that can eventually be costly.

The Argentine authorities chose to apply relatively flexible policies. According to Canavese and Di Tella, the policies that started in April 1986, of frequent devaluations and price-wage guidelines instead of a freeze, represented a crucial change in the economic program. Machinea and Fanelli, by contrast, consider those measures as a natural transition from the first stage. Which view you take probably depends on your judgment about the chance of reaching low inflation: If, as seems plausible, this prob-ability was not high, then the option of avoiding a bet with unfavorable odds would seem reasonable.

The decision to validate a definitely nonzero price drift implied that policies would have to grope for a long-run inflation rate and that the guidelines that could be offered would necessarily be quite diffuse. The inflation rate was kept on average much lower than in the recent past, which helped to simplify economic decisions. Still, in 1986 and early 1987, inflation remained high and volatile, with several accelerations that caused the authorities to vary their incomes and monetary policies. Managing an inflationary process such as the one in Argentina is far from easy. The dynamics of prices are not well understood, beyond the fact that the public has developed strong inflationary habits and that the propagation of up-ward shifts can be quite rapid. In addition, there are intertemporal trade-offs: An attempt to reduce the fiscal deficit by increasing real public sector prices, for example, would start by raising the inflation rate. In other words, there do not seem to be simple recipes to handle the distributive conflict, avoid large swings in relative prices, and keep inflation at tolerable levels.

The recent worsening of the country's terms of trade has tightened the external constraint and complicated fiscal policies. With these restrictions, the performance of the Argentine economy since mid-1985 does not compare badly with the past record. But the current state of the economy presents many serious and urgent problems, and there seem to be clear limits to the ability of short-run policies to deal with them.

Canavese and Di Tella conclude that the Austral Plan was effective in stopping high inflation but that the stabilization was only partial. Machinea and Fanelli stress improvements in the macroeconomy but also note a return to old inflationary patterns, remarking that a solid stabilization would require structural reforms. Clearly inflation has deep roots in Argentina; one particularly important element is the weakness of the fiscal system and the lack of a social consensus about the longer-run features of government spending and its financing. More generally, distributive and more narrowly instrumental debates remain intense, and international conditions pose additional difficulties. In contrast, there seems to be a more or less widespread recognition of the high costs of price instability and of the insufficiency of day-to-day policy management. The way in which this tension is solved will probably have much influence on the future course of the economy.

### Comment by Juan Carlos de Pablo

The Austral Plan is three years old. The following remarks, with due apologies to Machinea and Fanelli and Di Tella and Canavese, refer more to the subject than to their informative and interesting discussions.

1. Table 1 presents the key figures of the Austral Plan, namely, those referring to the semester before the launching of the plan and those corresponding to its first two years. Three alternative "readings" of the numbers are presented: the official reading, contrasting the previous situation with the average of the two Austral Plan years (showing a remarkable improvement); the critics' reading, ignoring the previous situation (showing a continuous deterioration from the initial success); and the correct reading, integrating both approaches, showing the initial success and the subsequent deterioration of indicators.

Compared with Argentina's history of anti-inflationary programs (a rich one, with plans started in 1952, 1959, 1962, 1967, 1973, 1976, 1979, and 1982), the results of the Austral Plan are impressive indeed, not only because of the fantastic decline in the rate of inflation, without rationing, but also because of the absence of costs in terms of a decline in GDP, employment, or real wages (on the contrary, in Argentina, the Austral Plan

**Table 1**
The Austral Plan: Alternative presentations of the data

| Period | Inflation (monthly, %) | | Treasury | | Money (monthly increase, %) | | National accounts (seasonally adjusted, 2nd quarter 1985 = 100) | | | | Purchasing power of real wages, manufacturing (June 1985 = 100) |
| --- | --- | --- | --- | --- | --- | --- | --- | --- | --- | --- | --- |
| | Consumer | Wholesale | Real expenditures (March 1987 = 100) | Revenue/expenditures (%) | M1, nominal | M4, nominal | GDP Total, real | Manufacturing, real | Real consumption | Fixed investment, real | |
| **Official reading** | | | | | | | | | | | |
| January–June 1985 | 26.2 | 28.6 | 102.3 | 50.2 | 23.4 | 22.7 | 102.3 | 102.5 | 102.6 | 105.7 | 105.7 |
| July 1985–June 1987 | 4.9 | 3.5 | 106.0 | 87.5 | 7.4 | 7.4 | 105.2 | 109.3 | 114.8 | 112.7 | 104.5 |
| **Critics' reading** | | | | | | | | | | | |
| July–December 1985 | 3.1 | 0.5 | 98.6 | 103.2 | 15.0 | 11.3 | 100.1 | 99.1 | 110.9 | 105.9 | 100.4 |
| January–December 1986 | 5.1 | 3.9 | 111.6 | 83.2 | 5.1 | 6.4 | 106.9 | 113.5 | 117.2 | 115.5 | 106.5 |
| January–March 1987 | 7.4 | 6.7 | 98.2 | 80.1 | 2.8 | 5.1 | 108.3 | 112.9 | 113.3 | 115.3 | 102.7 |
| June 1987 | 8.0 | 6.7 | | | 6.0 | 7.9 | | | | | 107.7 |
| **Correct Reading** | | | | | | | | | | | |
| January–June 1985 | 26.2 | 28.6 | 102.3 | 50.2 | 23.4 | 22.7 | 102.3 | 102.5 | 104.5 | 102.6 | 105.7 |
| July–December 1985 | 3.1 | 0.5 | 98.6 | 103.2 | 15.0 | 11.3 | 100.1 | 99.1 | 110.9 | 105.9 | 100.5 |
| January–December 1986 | 5.1 | 3.9 | 111.6 | 83.2 | 5.1 | 6.4 | 106.9 | 113.5 | 117.2 | 115.5 | 106.5 |
| January–March 1987 | 7.4 | 6.7 | 98.2 | 80.1 | 2.8 | 5.1 | 108.3 | 112.9 | 113.3 | 115.3 | 102.7 |
| June 1987 | 8.0 | 6.7 | | | 6.0 | 7.9 | | | | | 107.7 |

Sources: INDEC, Secretaria de Hacienda, Banco Centrale, and Carta Economica.

improved output, unemployment, and the purchasing power of wages).

2. The comparison of measures and results adopted in Israel, Brazil, and Argentina shows quite clearly the importance for success of the orthodox component of the programs implemented. In Israel the rate of inflation was kept low (whereas in Argentina it rose but did not return to the previous level and in Brazil it doubled in the twelve months after the implementation of the plan); yet in the three cases key nominal variables were frozen, whereas fiscal measures were strongest in Israel, rather mild in Argentina, and nonexistent in Brazil. The lesson is remarkably neat: Those who, for whatever reason, forget the orthodox component of the program eventually pay the consequences.

3. Table 2 evaluates the Austral Plan, pointing out its main advantages and disadvantages. In this connection I think it is important to differentiate between *endogenous* and *exogenous* factors, and it is also important to do it fairly. Most of the issues included in table 2 are clear enough, but the inclusion of President Alfonsin in 1986 and 1987 on the "minus" side of the evaluation deserves an explanation. I want to stress presidential decisions that have nothing to do with the Austral Plan but with, say, "pure politics" (such as the attempt to change the "who is who in the labor movement" or the attempt to barter a constitutional reform for introducing Peronist labor legislation eliminated by the military regime), decisions that introduce important "noise" in the decision making and in the performance of the economy.

4. So far, the Austral Plan has had five stages: (1) the initial one, beginning in June 1985; (2) a flexibility stage, after April 1986; (3) "monetarism," from September 1986; (4) new freezing, starting in March 1986; and (5) "living with inflation in a politicized setting," since May 1986. Is this the result of the dynamics of this type of program or the consequence of exogenous shocks? The second stage was expected from the beginning; the third one, when interpreted as the orthodox complement, also could be expected. The fourth cannot be reconciled with the logic of Austral Plan, and the fifth is clearly exogenous.

5. Finally, a word on inflation and changes in relative prices, an important issue for Di Tella and Canavese and in general in the structuralist approach to inflation. Table 3 presents regressions indicating that the direct relationship between rate and variability of inflation is mild at best, at least in the case of consumer prices. This is the case whether variability is measured incorrectly, by the standard deviation of the sectoral rate of inflation, or correctly, by this same standard deviation divided by one plus the rate of inflation (see figures 1 and 2).

**Table 2**
Evaluation of the Austral Plan

| Type of effect | Against | In favor |
| --- | --- | --- |
| Endogenous | 1. Distortions in relative prices, resulting from, in practice, controlled and uncontrolled prices. Potentially dangerous; almost nonexistent when compared with previous experiences in Argentina.<br><br>2. Lack of orthodox component of the plan, given the initial success of the initial freeze. Most important difficulty; being recognized even by the authorities. | 1. Alfonsin, 1985. Courage for implementing a program of this type.<br><br>2. Political success. Given the social demand for "doing anything," the government that tries this becomes an instant hero.<br><br>3. Reactivation, increase in purchasing power of wages. The feeling that chaos is over increases all economic activity; wage earners are particularly better off because they are the most important payers of inflation tax.<br><br>4. Scale of conversion. Fundamental tool for avoiding injustice in the presence of contracts based on old inflationary expectations, with maturity after the start of the program. |
| Exogenous | 1. Alfonsin, 1986. To get rid of trade union leader Ubaldini, Alfonsin gave rival trade union leader Miguel substantially greater wage increases.<br><br>2. Alfonsin, 1987. In addition to repeating the 1986 wage episode, Alfonsin put another trade union leader as labor minister, politicizing short- and long-run economic policy (wage policy and bringing back Peronist labor legislation). | None |

**Table 3**
Results of OLS regressions

| Dependent variable | Period | Regression coefficient ($t$-statistic) | | $R^2$ | $F$ |
| | | Intercept | Rate of inflation | | |
| --- | --- | --- | --- | --- | --- |
| Standard deviation | March 1974–May 1987 | 1.998 (6.5) | 0.176 (7.1) | 0.24 | 49.7 |
| | | 2.063 (5.68)[a] | 0.167 (5.8) | 0.27 | 28.4 |
| | | 0 | 0.308 (19.1) | 0.03 | |
| | | 0[a] | 0.289 (13.1) | 0.13 | |
| Standard deviation/ (1 + inflation) | March 1974–May 1987 | 2.196 (8.0) | 0.117 (5.3) | 0.15 | 27.6 |
| | | 2.280 (7.0)[a] | 0.108 (4.3) | 0.17 | 16.4 |
| | | 0 | 0.263 (17.4) | 0.20 | |
| | | 0[a] | 0.235 (10.8) | 0.06 | |
| Standard deviation | July 1985–May 1987 | 2.158 (2.2) | 0.16 (0.8) | 0.03 | 0.7 |
| | | 2.057 (2.2)[a] | 0.18 (1.0) | 0.04 | 0.4 |
| Standard deviation/ (1 + inflation) | July 1985–May 1987 | 2.213 (2.3) | 0.119 (0.7) | 0.12 | 0.4 |
| | | 2.110 (2.4)[a] | 0.141 (0.9) | 0.03 | 0.3 |

a. Corrected for autocorrelation using Cochrane-Orcutt method. "Inflation" in independent variable refers to monthly percentage change in consumer price level divided by 100.

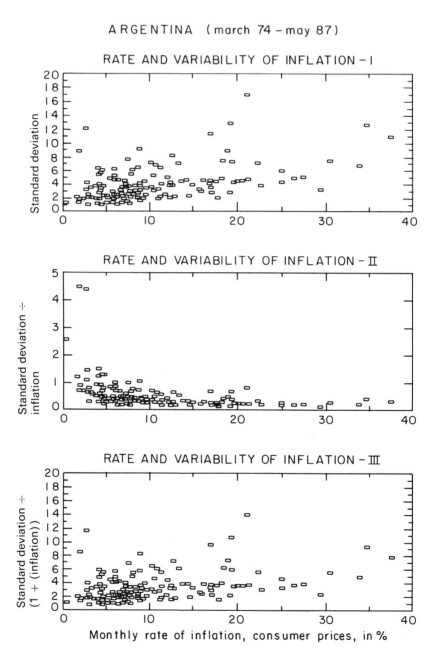

**Figure 1**

Variability of inflation in Argentina, March 1974 to May 1987.

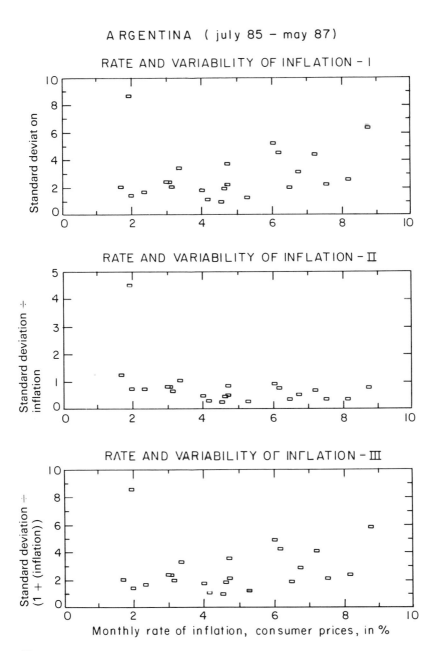

**Figure 2**
Variability of inflation in Argentina, July 1985 to May 1987.

### Comment by Carlos Alfredo Rodriguez

Canavese and Di Tella indicate that one of the main mistakes of the Austral Plan was to freeze not the "historical price vector" but the one prevailing on a given day. I would like to start my comments referring to this point.

First, the equilibrium relative price vector of an economy is a dynamic concept, more related to future events than to past averages. Without price controls it is likely that today's price vector is more nearly market clearing than the historical average, however constructed. Because relative prices and wages were manipulated in the few months and days before the beginning of the Austral Plan, it is likely that the price vector chosen on June 14 may not have been the market-clearing one. But the plan did not fail because of that. It failed because it froze some prices and kept pumping liquid assets into the economy at rates that exceeded the demand for them. This induced a dynamic distortion similar to the one in the period 1980–81; the set of prices became divided into two: controlled prices and free prices.

In the 1980–81 experience the prices supporting the burden of the anti-inflation plan were those of products facing foreign competition, traded goods. In 1985 and thereafter the controlled prices were mainly those of the industrial sector at the wholesale level. In both experiences the industrial sector fell under the controlled category. Free prices in both cases were

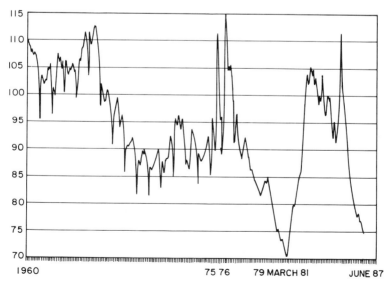

**Figure 1**
Ratio of controlled to uncontrolled prices (average 1956/1975 = 100).

those of the services sector, for which the CPI is a good indicator. Controlled prices are best captured by the industrial component of the WPI. Figure 1 shows the historical evolution of the ratio of controlled to free prices. We can see that there are two historical low levels for this variable: one in the second quarter of 1981, when the policy of the Tablita was abandoned, and one right now, with the Austral Plan still in effect. That ratio has fallen each and every quarter since the Austral Plan begun, and the accumulated fall from the second quarter of 1985 to the second quarter of 1987 is 27%. This price lag may be an important source of repressed inflation.

There is some evidence that repressed inflation is present in Argentina. Every time the government loosens price controls, inflation immediately picks up. True, there are no significant shortages, but there is also no investment and there is widespread overpricing by retailers that makes one doubt the real wage gains being claimed by the authors of the plan. There were also no shortages during the worst moments of the exchange rate lag. Apparently firms are willing to sell at some loss, if they expect the price control to be temporary, in order to maintain their market share.

I agree with Canavese and Di Tella that the Austral Plan may have chosen the initially wrong relative price vector but, worse than that, it allowed the distortion to grow, taking the relative price of controlled products to their second lowest historical level, at least in the last fifteen years.

Let us now go to the facts. What was the Austral Plan? It was (1) a price, wage, and exchange rate freeze; (2) a promise of no issuing of money to finance the treasury; and (3) a promise of fiscal restraint. Of those three points only the freeze was fulfilled, although partially. The freeze was supposed to be temporary. As soon as it was lifted, inflation came back, so it was imposed again. It was again lifted and reimposed for a second time in 1987 and lifted again in May 1987. Inflation is, of course, picking up again.

Point 2 was not achieved. There are many ways to give money to the government without directly borrowing from the Central Bank: Give rediscounts to provincial banks so they do not go to the Central Bank; do the same for government enterprises; and issue all types of short-term debts with any imaginable type of indexation clause (BONOR, BONIN, BARRA, BAGON, DENOR, TIDOL, VAVIS, TCD, etc.). Finally, instead of the treasury getting australs from the Central Bank, it may borrow dollars, as is being done. Of course, the Central Bank had to print australs to buy those dollars.

It is of no surprise that in the period from December 1985 to December 1986 total austral liabilities of the Central Bank grew by 70.5% and that average inflation (averaging the CPI and the WPI) was 69.85%. The growth in the actual monetary base was kept relatively low at the expense of new borrowing (at positive real rates) by the Central Bank. This aggravates the problem of the quasi-fiscal deficit, to which I turn later. Nonetheless, the monetary base has grown by 180% from June 1985 to February 1987.

With respect to point 3, we might say that there has been some improvement in the deficit figures. Most of it, however, has been due to temporary factors or tax collection increases resulting exclusively from the price freeze (the Olivera-Tanzi effect plus lower nominal interest rates). On this point I agree with Canavese and Di Tella, but I would go even further.

Let me analyze in detail each of the tax measures implemented under the Austral Plan that are mentioned by Canavese and Di Tella.

1. The real price of public services was increased. This increase was the result of the price freeze. The government cannot charge as much as it wants for its public services. Only by freezing prices in the private sector can it maintain any arbitrary relative price. As soon as the price freeze is lifted, firms raise prices to recover normal profits. If it were so easy, governments would have solved the deficit problem long ago. But everybody knows that relative public sector prices can only be raised so far before other prices react.

2. Export taxes were raised. This temporary measure was imposed at a time of declining terms of trade and the need for an increased trade surplus. In 1987 the trade surplus will reach a mere $1.2 billion, with $4.5 billion due in interest. This policy contradicted the export growth objective of the administration and resulted in two years of consecutive important deteriorations in the trade surplus.

3. A temporary measure of forced saving was voted by Congress. It was to be applied only once.

4. There was increased collection of general taxes. This measure was also price freeze induced, thanks to the Olivera-Tanzi effect. As soon as the freeze was lifted, taxes fell and inflation rose.

5. Last, there was a reduction in the quasi-fiscal deficit because of lower interest rates. This was another price-freeze-induced measure. As soon as the freeze was lifted, if inflation rose, interest rates also rose.

Of these five measures of fiscal improvement, two are temporary and three depend on the existence of the price freeze. Suppose that we try the following reasoning: There will be no more inflation when there is no more deficit. This will be believed if it is shown that the deficit has been effectively reduced in a sustainable way. However, the causality seems to be the opposite: The deficit is reduced because there is no more inflation. A new line must be added: There is no more inflation because of the price freeze. It therefore turns out that there is no more inflation or deficit thanks to the price freeze. But the freeze was the only element of the plan expected to be temporary! No wonder that, every time the freeze was lifted, inflation started again, each time with more strength as repressed inflation kept building.

Canavese and Di Tella think of the Austral Plan as a plan to avoid hyperinflation and repeatedly refer to the inflationary threshold being surpassed by mid-1985. The topic is not new to me. In April 1984, with R. Fernandez, I published an article in *La Nacion* defining the inflationary threshold as that inflation rate for which seigniorage revenue is maximized. Any attempt to raise more revenue than that maximum would end in hyperinflation. At that time we forecast (based on an estimation of the demand for money) that the inflation rate associated with the hyperinflationary threshold was 30.8% and that the maximum inflation tax collection would be 8.3% of GDP. It came as no surprise that the government more than one year later announced a plan to stop the hyperinflation precisely in the month that CPI inflation reached 30.5% (June 1985). It is also the case that the fiscal deficit, which was 7.78% of GDP in the first quarter of 1985, jumped to 11.91% in the second quarter, exceeding the threshold Fernandez and I had announced!

**Structural Pressures**

Canavese and Di Tella refer to the need for an incomes policy in order to eliminate the pressures that result in more inflation. I agree with them, but who will apply the incomes policy to the government, which is the one sector that wants a larger share of the pie than it can have?

My approach suggests that inflation has little to do with sectoral pushes for higher incomes coming from the private sector. Argentina has had periods of high inflation and periods of low inflation. Thirty million people cannot be altogether cyclothymic and periodically modify the level of their desired relative income shares. I do observe, however, that government deficits have changed and that they are extremely well correlated with variations in inflation.

The following regression shows the effect of the fiscal deficit (consolidated nonfinancial public sector, computed according to IMF methodology) as a percent of GNP on the inflation rate measured by the CPI.

$$\text{INFL} = -78.6 + 20.06 \cdot d(-1) + 12.43 \cdot d(-2) + 4.79 \cdot d(-3),$$
$$\phantom{\text{INFL} = } (-1.9) \quad (4.45) \qquad\qquad (7.16) \qquad\qquad (1.04)$$

INFL = annual percentage increase in CPI.

$d$ = deficit/GNP.

Sample period: 1965–1986.

Adjusted $R^2$ = 0.717.

D.W. = 1.89.

$t$-statistics in parentheses.

$F(22)$ = 27.67.

All data is shown in table 1.

The coefficients of $d$ were estimated with PDL(2, 1, 0).

Canavese and Di Tella elaborate the theory that the same deficits now give more inflation than before because the demand for money has shifted down. This would add another structural explanation to inflation, or at least to its oscillations. They present as evidence the fact that the demand for money was lower in June 1985 than in 1975 and 1976, when there were rates of inflation of similar magnitude. I have tried to check the presumption of some structural change having taken place in the process generating inflation after 1985 by adding a dummy variable to the regression. The dummy takes the value of 1 in 1985 and 1986 and 0 previously. The results presented in what follows indicate that the dummy is not significantly different from 0. This provides some evidence rejecting the hypothesis of a demand for money shift having taken place in 1985–86.

$$\text{INFL} = -75.5 + 22.21 \cdot \text{DUMMY} + 20.3 \cdot d(-1) + 12.15 \cdot d(-2)$$
$$(-1.7) \quad (0.2) \quad\quad\quad (4.2) \quad\quad\quad (5.4)$$
$$+ 3.99 \cdot d(-3).$$
$$(0.6)$$

Adjusted $R^2$ = 0.70.

D.W. = 1.88.

$F(22)$ = 17.5.

The $d$ coefficients were estimated with PDL(2, 1, 0).

The Quasi-Fiscal Deficit

In Argentina the Central Bank pays interest on much of its liabilities. That interest is paid by issuing more liabilities. Those liabilities are in part

**Table 1**
Data used in the regression analysis

| Year | Inflation rate | Deficit/Y |
|------|----------------|-----------|
| 1961 | 13.70000 | 3.301856 |
| 1962 | 26.20933 | 6.250251 |
| 1963 | 25.99303 | 5.618874 |
| 1964 | 22.06858 | 5.088582 |
| 1965 | 28.59084 | 2.997197 |
| 1966 | 31.88865 | 3.802603 |
| 1967 | 29.22790 | 1.150297 |
| 1968 | 16.20839 | 1.323478 |
| 1969 | 7.578730 | 0.977847 |
| 1970 | 13.57698 | 1.024823 |
| 1971 | 34.72627 | 3.559996 |
| 1972 | 58.46753 | 4.297491 |
| 1973 | 60.29461 | 6.416453 |
| 1974 | 24.21716 | 6.710452 |
| 1975 | 182.2123 | 14.36775 |
| 1976 | 444.0069 | 9.433837 |
| 1977 | 176.0554 | 3.037379 |
| 1978 | 175.5077 | 3.555305 |
| 1979 | 159.5107 | 3.201828 |
| 1980 | 100.6851 | 7.509616 |
| 1981 | 104.5568 | 13.29814 |
| 1982 | 164.7769 | 15.07453 |
| 1983 | 343.8091 | 16.81265 |
| 1984 | 626.7219 | 12.78924 |
| 1985 | 672.1400 | 6.011602 |
| 1986 | 90.42999 | 6.203742 |

$Y = $ GNP.

extremely short term, and the rest are payable on demand to the commercial banks only under certain conditions, such as an important fall in deposits. This kind of nondisposable commercial bank assets (loaned to the government) is a new invention that has practically eliminated all types of Commercial Bank credit to the private sector other than the renewal of existing loans. The issuance of Central Bank liabilities to pay interest on the existing liabilities is the source of the quasi-fiscal deficit. It makes those liabilities rise with the interest rate plus whatever the normal deficit imposes. Because much of the liabilities of the Central Bank are liquid, the quasi-fiscal deficit is blamed as the primary source of monetary creation and therefore of inflation.

It is true that the quasi-fiscal deficit is a source of money creation but it is *not* the original force causing inflation. It just multiplies the inflation rate that would be generated by the normal fiscal deficit. I now provide a brief explanation of this fact.

Consider for simplicity that all Central Bank liabilities are the money supply ($M$). Suppose that a fraction $a$ of those liabilities earns interest at the rate $i = \pi + R$, where $\pi$ stands for inflation and $R$ for the real interest rate. The Central Bank also prints money to finance the "normal" treasury deficit ($D$). The rate of expansion of the money supply is therefore

$$(1/M)dM/dt = a(\pi + R) + D/M. \tag{1}$$

Dividing and multiplying the last term of equation (1) by GNP and using $d = D/\text{GNP}$ and $V = \text{GNP}/M$, we obtain

$$(1/M)(dM/dt) = a(\pi + R) + Vd. \tag{2}$$

I finally assume that the money market is in steady-state equilibrium (no changes in $\pi$ expected or actual) so that $(1/M)(dM/dt) = \pi$ and obtain the basic equation determining the rate of inflation:

$$\pi = (aR + Vd)/(1 - a). \tag{3}$$

The term $aR$ is really government spending and should be part of the "normal" treasury deficit $d$. We can see that, if there is no "normal" deficit, there is no inflation. However, if $d > 0$, inflation would be $Vd$ multiplied by the term $1/(1 - a) > 1$, the multiplier effect of the quasi-fiscal deficit. What has been done since the Austral Plan is to increase the fraction of interest-earning liabilities of the Central Bank, that is, increasing the value of $a$. In the short run this reduces liquidity, and the black market dollar rate falls and interest rates rise. But this lasts only for a few days, after which the dollar recovers but interest rates do not fall as inflation rises. As my formulas indicate, the long-run effect of increasing $a$ is to raise the rate of inflation. Trying to raise the demand for money by paying interest on money and financing this by printing more money is a silly game. One ends up with more inflation and the same amount of real money. In the short run, however, some merits can be claimed, and then, when the quasi-fiscal deficit shows up, one can blame it on the distant past.

The Austral Plan did not attack the quasi-fiscal deficit; it increased its size. By trying to enforce the promise of not issuing conventional money, the plan forced the Central Bank to pay positive real interest on money substitutes that also count for the generation of inflation.

Printing money to pay interest on money is not the way to cut inflation. The analysis indicates that the only way to reduce inflation is to reduce the "normal" treasury deficit to 0 and then, just in case, to turn it into surplus for a while. This would enable redemption of the outstanding Central Bank short-term debt so that the quasi-fiscal deficit does not act again as a multiplier at the first burst of inflation.

## Comment by Sylvia Piterman

I found Machinea and Fanelli's and Canavese and Di Tella's discussions of the Austral Plan informative and interesting. My comments cover three main subjects: First, I try to offer a different view of the inflationary process in Argentina, based on the analysis of the Israeli experience. Second, I add some remarks about the connection between the debt problem and the outcomes of the Austral Plan. And finally, I discuss the authors' conclusions that the Austral Plan only avoided hyperinflation and lacked the elements to deal more seriously with the inflationary process in Argentina.

### Inflation and Balance of Payments Crises

Canavese and Di Tella analyze the roots of the Argentine inflationary process. They connect it to the following phenomena: (1) supply inelasticities, which made the economy very price sensitive to demand shocks; (2) relative price oscillations caused by devaluations and the fight for income; (3) the generalization of indexation; and (4) the endogenous character of the fiscal and monetary policy.

These four factors cannot explain the level of inflation (as, for example, the revenue from money printing) but can characterize the dynamics of inflation. In this connection we can ask whether there is some main mechanism explaining the big accelerations of inflation and why the same mechanism was not capable of bringing inflation back to its former level.

If we look at the data presented by Canavese and Di Tella and Machinea and Fanelli, we can see that the main accelerations of inflation were in the mid-1970s and in the early 1980s. Inflation accelerated at nearly the same time in Brazil and Israel, suggesting that there was probably a common factor influencing all these economies, namely, the oil crisis in the mid-1970s and the debt crisis in the early 1980s.

It seems, therefore, that the main factor behind the big accelerations of inflation during the 1970s and 1980s that accounts for some of those factors analyzed by Canavese and Di Tella are balance of payments crises and the remedy that was devised to solve them: price shocks (big devaluations and an attempt to increase the relative price of public services and subsidized commodities).

The question is, Why didn't inflation return to its former level once the balance of payments was under control and the crisis was over? It seems that the answer lies in the failure of orthodox programs dealing with inflation in the framework of political constraints, generalized indexation, and endogenous fiscal and monetary policy. Even if orthodox programs are based on restrictive fiscal and monetary policies and they are successful in stabilizing the balance of payments, they may still accommodate a high rate of inflation.

The experience of Argentina seems to show, however, that heterodox programs are not successful in decreasing inflation. Nevertheless, as explained later, heterodox programs such as the Austral Plan are much more effective in decreasing inflation than orthodox programs. The problem is that the external situation of the economy during the implementation of the Austral Plan was delicate and undermined the success of the plan. This brings me to the next point.

## Stabilization under the Threat of Renewed Crisis

So long as the balance of payments is in a state of crisis, the most that can be done is to avoid hyperinflation. Moreover, even if the balance of payments is under control before the implementation of a stabilization program, the stabilization itself has a built-in mechanism that leads to some worsening of the balance of payments. As Machinea and Fanelli and Canavese and Di Tella mention and as Bruno and I also noted for Israel, the stabilization itself brings an increase in real wages and a boom in demand. These tend to destabilize, as they lead to price increases, real appreciation, and a growing import surplus. Therefore they might bring the economy again to a crisis, especially if the balance of payments situation is still fragile.

Because the authorities were aware of this situation (given the experience of the late 1970s and the early 1980s), they tended to be careful with respect to movements in the real exchange rate and the balance of payments. This was probably the case in Argentina. The heavy burden of debt that led to a relatively weak external position can explain what happened, namely, the fact that the authorities turned at a relatively early stage to nominal devaluations and other price shocks in order to achieve more fiscal restraint, erosion of real wages, and correction of the real exchange rate path. This policy obviously led to renewed inflation but avoided the loss of control over the situation, as had occurred several times during Argentine economic history and recently in Brazil.

Canavese and Di Tella point out that the debt problem was the main factor behind the relative failure of the plan. Machinea and Fanelli also concluded that the fiscal situation cannot be improved permanently without a substantial improvement in the external debt situation. Nevertheless, it seems to me that the debt problem was not emphasized enough as a central factor explaining developments and the policy options adopted by the authorities.

## Has the Austral Plan Actually Failed?

If we look at the original goals of the Austral Plan, it obviously failed. But I would like to make two comments on this subject. First, Machinea and Fanelli argue that the plan achieved control over the high rate of inflation, or, as Canavese and Di Tella emphasize, the Austral Plan was successful in avoiding hyperinflation. However, in my opinion, this is an understatement. The rate of inflation in 1986 and even in 1987 is still not higher than it was 1977–82, before the last acceleration. This dramatic decrease in inflation was achieved with a higher real exchange rate and much less real appreciation of the currency than the smaller decrease in inflation in the late 1970s. The Austral Plan was therefore successful not only in avoiding hyperinflation but also in decreasing inflation from high levels much more efficiently than former policies.

Second, the aspiration of those who implemented the Austral Plan, as in the cases of Israel and Brazil, was to achieve a once and for all decrease of inflation to low levels. It was too ambitious. How can it be possible to decrease inflation permanently from more than 20% per month to 2–3% per month in one step? How is it possible to synchronize nominal variables and relative prices in one step after they have been oscillating at enormous rates?

The problem is that much more attention was paid to what had to be done at the implementation of the program than what had to be done when there were deviations from sustainable paths. The question arises, therefore, of whether the options actually adopted by the authorities were adequate as a continuation of the Austral Plan.

As Canavese and Di Tella state, the Austral Plan was actually abandoned in April 1986, with the beginning of frequent devaluations and the reindexation of the economy. A better option perhaps would have been to implement a new program similar to the original Austral Plan. Moreover, similar programs can be implemented several times. Namely, when the path of the economy becomes undesirable, the authorities can perform a nominal and real adjustment immediately followed by a stable exchange rate and a renewed price and wage freeze (a policy that was actually implemented in Argentina in March 1987 and to some extent in Israel in January 1987). The stability of the exchange rate can be made conditional on the path of real wages. This can enhance credibility as the authorities avoid a general feeling that they are cheating when they perform some nominal adjustment. But it may have, of course, contradictory influences on the unions. (On the one hand, it may enhance wage pressures because of expectations that inflation will not be reduced through higher unemployment, but, on the other hand, it can restrain wage pressures because the authorities make it clear that nominal wage increases can lead to higher inflation but not to higher real wages.)

If the fiscal and monetary policies are restrictive enough, the needed price shock can be smaller than the preceding one. The oscillations of relative prices can therefore decrease over time and, with them, the danger of catching entire sectors far from equilibrium.

It seems that, taking into consideration the actual balance of payments situation of Argentina, I agree with Machinea and Fanelli and Canavese and Di Tella that it is impossible to erase inflation completely. However, it dose not mean that the inflation rate has to be stabilized at 5−7% a month. An inflation rate of 1−2% per month with a fixed exchange rate adjusted from time to time is perhaps also suitable to deal with the pressures arising from structural problems and the need for austerity, especially now after a much more favorable agreement has been achieved with respect to the debt problem.

# III

Brazil

# 5

# The Cruzado First Attempt: The Brazilian Stabilization Program of February 1986

## Eduardo M. Modiano

During the first half of the 1980s economic policy in Brazil was mainly geared toward fighting rampant inflation. The first doubling of the rate of inflation occurred at the end of 1979, when it jumped from 50% to 100% per year. The conjunction of the second oil shock with a domestic policy of setting "realistic prices" and simultaneously increasing the frequency of wage adjustments from twelve to six months contributed to increase inflation. The second doubling occurred in 1983, when inflation reached 200% per year. The acceleration of inflation in this case can be primarily attributed to the cruzeiro maxidevaluation of February 1983. By early 1986 another doubling of the inflation rate was imminent as agricultural prices rose to reflect the drought that affected Brazilian harvests. At this moment the Cruzado Plan was launched.

The orthodox stabilization policies adopted from 1981 to 1984 had little effect on the trajectory of inflation. Inflation seemed to resist the deflationary forces of recession and unemployment. During this period several theoretical and empirical studies attempted to show that the Brazilian inflation had special properties and followed unique dynamics. The predominance of inflation inertia, caused by widespread indexation, over aggregate demand and supply conditions was demonstrated by Lopes and Lara-Resende (1981), Lopes (1982), and Modiano (1983, 1985b) among others. Research efforts were then concentrated on alternative ways to eliminate inertial inflation.

By the second half of 1984 Arida and Lara-Resende (1985) presented the indexed currency, or Larida, proposal. They suggested the introduction of a new currency that would circulate simultaneously with the cruzeiro. The new currency would have a fixed parity with the Obrigações Reajustáveis do Tesouro Nacional (ORTN), whose nominal value in cruzeiros was monetarily corrected monthly on the basis of past inflation. Conversion to the new currency would be voluntary, but, according to the authors, public acceptance would be guaranteed by its stability and credibility. Simonsen (1984) and Modiano and Carneiro (1984) questioned that stability, showing that, if inflation in cruzeiros accelerated during the conversion period, the new currency would lose some of its value, damaging its credibility. The risk of reindexation under the new currency was also shown to be present.

Approximately at the same time, Lopes (1984a) proposed the so-called heterodox shock to curb Brazilian inflation. His original suggestion was a wage and price freeze at levels consistent with the status quo of the distribution of income and widespread deindexation of the economy. Later he incorporated the idea of a simultaneous monetary reform, introducing the cruzado. The rules for conversion from cruzeiros to cruzados were further developed by Modiano (1985a).

In section 5.1 I present the basic diagnosis of the Brazilian inflationary process that inspired the Cruzado Plan. I use a simple analytical model to illustrate the plan's theoretical foundations. In section 5.2 I discuss the inflationary tensions that led to the announcement of the Cruzado Plan at the end of the first year of the Brazilian New Republic. In section 5.3 I describe the plan in greater detail, pointing out some of its risk factors, such as the magnitude of the wage bonus, the wage sliding scale, the neglected price adjustments, and the lack of monetary and fiscal targets. I analyze in section 5.4 the mismanagement of economic policy, which led one year later to cruzado inflation rates that exceeded cruzeiro inflation rates. Finally, I conclude with a discussion of the current prospects for Brazilian inflation and the alternative of a second attempt.

## 5.1   The Inertia and Conflict Inflation Model[1]

The Cruzado Plan favored the interpretation that Brazilian inflation was mainly inertial. Inflation inertia resulted from the indexation mechanisms for nominal correction of prices, wages, the exchange rate, and financial assets that tended to perpetuate past inflation. In the absence of shocks the inflation rate tended to remain as it was. This perception of the inflationary process is perfectly compatible with the model of income distribution conflict that characterizes structuralist macroeconomics, as recently formalized by Bacha (1982) and Taylor (1983). Movements of the inflation rate, as opposed to movements of the price level, would result from an ex ante inconsistency in the distribution of income.[2]

The inflationary process that originates from an income distribution conflict can be explained with a simple model of an economy with an

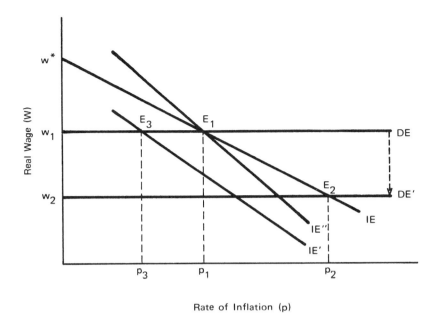

**Figure 5.1**
Inflationary and income distribution equilibria.

aggregate production function and only two inputs: labor and imported intermediary products. Then the price frontier of the economy establishes an inverse relation between the real wage $w$ and the real exchange rate $e$, given by

$$w = f(e), \qquad f_e < 0. \tag{5.1}$$

The income distribution equilibrium implied by equation (5.1) is represented graphically by curve $DE$ in figure 5.1. Notice in equation (5.1) that a real devaluation (an increase in $e$) results in a decline in real wages (a decrease in $w$). In figure 5.1 a real devaluation is represented by a downward movement of $DE$ to $DE'$.

An inverse relation between the real wage and the rate of inflation $p$ completes the model. Denoting by $h$ the rule for adjustments of the nominal wage and by $w^*$ the peak real wage, we can show that

$$w = g(p, w^*, h), \qquad g_p < 0, \ g_w^* > 0. \tag{5.2}$$

The inflationary equilibrium determined by equation (5.2) is represented in figure 5.1 by curve $IE$. The intercept on the vertical axis $w^*$ indicates the real wage that would prevail in the short run if inflation stopped abruptly after a nominal adjustment. In figure 5.1 a decline in the peak real wage would displace *IE* downward to *IE'*. A decrease in the frequency of nominal wage adjustments would rotate *IE* clockwise to *IE"*.

Equations (5.1) and (5.2) determine simultaneously the equilibrium real wage and rate of inflation of the economy. This general equilibrium is represented in figure 5.1 by $E_1$, at the intersection of curves *DE* and *IE*. According to this stylized interpretation of the Brazilian inflationary process, the economy's real wage depends solely on the pattern of income distribution, which might be rigid in the short run. Changes in indexation rules or in peak real wages would affect only the rate of inflation without altering the real wage. In the absence of shocks the rate of inflation would remain constant because of indexation; it is an inertial process. A supply shock, such as a real devaluation, would cause, as *DE* moves downward to *DE'* in figure 5.1, both a permanent decline in real wages and a permanent rise in the inflation rate.

The inverse relation between the real wage and the rate of inflation in equation (5.2) can be easily derived for the case of fixed-periodicity adjustments, which dominated the Brazilian economy until the Cruzado Plan was launched. Figure 5.2 illustrates the dynamics of real wages (and to a certain extent any relative price for which nominal values are corrected by past inflation at fixed intervals of time). The peak real wage is restored at the

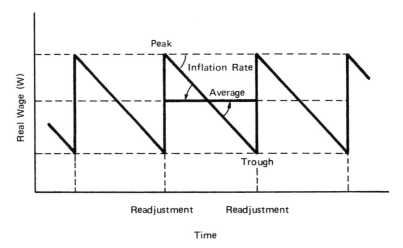

**Figure 5.2**
The dynamics of real wages.

moment the nominal wage is adjusted. Although the nominal wage is kept constant, the real wage declines because of the continuous inflationary process, and a trough is reached exactly before another adjustment is due. Note in figure 5.2 that, because the real wage oscillates, a more stable measure of purchasing power is given by the average real wage. Hence equations (5.1) and (5.2) should be reinterpreted in terms of the real wage averaged over an interval of time equal to (or a multiple of) the fixed interval between successive and adjustments.

Denoting the fixed interval between nominal wage adjustments in months by $h$ and the monthly rate of inflation by $p$, we obtain

$$w = \frac{(1 + p)^{h+1} - 1}{(h + 1)p(1 + p)^h} w^*. \tag{5.3}$$

For the specific case of wage adjustments every six months, as it prevailed in the Brazilian economy until February 28, 1986, it suffices to make $h = 6$.[3] With expression (5.3) the inverse relation between $w$ and $p$ postulated in the inflationary equilibrium represented by equation (5.2) can be easily proved.

Figure 5.2 illustrates one major technical difficulty involved in the design of a stabilization program for the Brazilian economy: the lack of synchronism in wage adjustments. If the inflationary process was terminated abruptly, workers with the same average real wage could be left with different real wages because they were caught at different stages of the same "inflationary slide." Major redistributions of income could result. The same observation applies to all other sources of income that were corrected in nominal terms after fixed intervals but that were not synchronized, such as rents, profits, and the exchange rate.

The Cruzado Plan was designed to overcome these difficulties. Its technical foundations can also be explained with the aid of figures 5.1 and 5.2. Notice in figure 5.2 that a decline in the peak real wage, which leaves the average real wage unchanged, corresponds to a counterclockwise rotation of the "slide" around the mean. Because the angle of the slide is the rate of inflation, a reduction of the peak real wage implies a decline in the rate of inflation. In the limit the slide turns horizontal, and the inertial component of inflation vanishes without affecting the income distribution equilibrium determined in figure 5.1. In figure 5.1 the process of disinflation corresponds to a downward movement of IE until the peak real wage coincides with the equilibrium (average) real wage. Hence it becomes clear that the main ingredients for price stabilization are the equality of actual and average relative prices and the suppression of indexation mechanisms that link current to past inflation. The monetary reform and the wage and price freeze only reinforce such a stability.

## 5.2    From Inflation to the Cruzado[4]

The Brazilian New Republic took office in March 1985, after twenty-one years of military rule. Although the necessity of a social pact to reconcile real wage claims with disinflation had been emphasized strongly during the electoral campaign, an orthodox economic policy was announced by the new government. Besides facilitating negotiations with the International Monetary Fund (IMF), the cut in public expenditures and the slowdown of monetary expansion were presented as the government's initial contribution to a social pact, which never materialized.

Because restrictive fiscal and monetary policies could take some time to produce a decline in inflation rates, which by that time had reached 12% per month, a price freeze was established for the month of April. Also, in order to dampen the acceleration of inflation, the formulas for computing monetary correction and exchange rate devaluation were modified, extending the "memory" of past inflation from one to three months. A scheme of daily minidevaluations, preset every month, was introduced.

Immediately after the announcement of the new economic policy, inflation dropped significantly, from 12.7% in March to 7.2% in April. However, this result could be almost entirely explained by the suspension of price adjustments for two groups of products: steel and fuel. Private prices, which were not under strict control, did not seem to follow the freeze. At any rate, the government decided to extend the duration of the price freeze. Because costs increased in real terms during these months and because the existing lags in the formulas for wage, exchange rate, and monetary correction passed along past higher inflation rates, the price freeze was put under great pressure.

In June the government announced the first increases for a few publicly and privately controlled prices. In order to avoid an inflationary rebound, minor adjustments were conceded in the first round. An increase in the frequency of later adjustments was to compensate for the losses in profit margins incurred during the freeze. Inflation jumped from 7.8% in June to 8.9% in July.

The adjustment of prices had just begun when the economy suffered a major agricultural supply shock with wholesale food prices rising 19.0% in August. The General Price Index (IGP-DI) increased 14.0% in the same month, signaling the failure of the anti-inflationary package of March and the end of the first phase of the New Republic economic policy.

The new finance minister announced a more modest inflation target to be pursued: stabilization at the rate of 10% per month. The indexation rules were once more altered in order to avoid the propagation of the August inflation rate. The memory of past inflation in the formulas for monetary and exchange rate correction was reduced from three months to one month. Important publicly and privately controlled prices would be corrected on a monthly basis and hence at smaller percentages to minimize the impact on the general price index. This suggested that the stabilization of the inflation rate would be obtained at the expense of an increase in the degree of indexation of the economy. Interest rates, which skyrocketed during April–July, would decline as a result of a less restrictive monetary policy.

The new indexation rules suggested that the economy was on the route of the "indexed currency" proposal, as price, exchange rate, and financial asset nominal adjustments became increasingly linked to monthly variations of the ORTN. However, there was not a clear and widely acceptable rule for the indexation of nominal wages, which remained guided at least officially by the six-month adjustments established in 1979. The perspective of returning to inflation rates of 10–12% per month, after the failure of the price freeze, gave a new impulse to the demand for more frequent nominal wage adjustments.

The proposals for a new wage policy included adjustments every three months, adjustments every month according to the variation of the ORTN, and a sliding scale of 30%. While the public discussions proceeded, the government allowed free negotiation of bonuses, advances, and alternative indexation schemes so long as these were not passed along to prices. The price control agencies would not consider for the purpose of cost computation any wage increase that was not in strict accordance with the official rule of six-month cost-of-living adjustments. Real wages increased substantially during this period.

If on the one hand the "fine-tuning" of price adjustments maintained inflation at 9% per month during September and October, on the other hand it did not allow any compensation for the losses incurred mainly by public prices during the freeze of April–July. Repressed inflation combined with a major supply shock originating from the drought that reduced the food harvest raised the general price index by 15% in November. Deindexation then proceeded along an alternative line: The price index that officially measured inflation was changed from the general price index to the ample consumer price index (IPCA), which showed an inflation rate of only 11.1% in November.

The IPCA also became the universal index for capital and labor incomes, which used to be corrected using the IGP-DI and the INPC (restricted consumer price index), respectively. Although this move was announced as one step toward social justice, the frequency of nominal wage adjustments was maintained at six months. The main advantage of the IPCA over the other index was its slower response to supply shocks, so it would help to dampen the expected increase in inflation. This gain had to be balanced against the fact that consumer prices were less subject to controls than wholesale prices, which comprised 60% of the IGP-DI.

At this point, as a new acceleration of inflation seemed inevitable, the application of a heterodox shock or the negotiation of a social pact was already the order of the day. The main discussion, motivated by the usual association between recession and orthodox. stabilization programs, concerned the eventual contractionary effects on economic activity. In fact, the fear of a recession based on the experiences of Argentina and Israel seemed to be the major obstacle to overcome.

Inflation, as measured by the new index, reached 13.4% in December and 16.2% in January. The agricultural supply shock finally showed up at the consumer level, as the price of foodstuffs increased approximately 17% per month during December and January. At the wholesale level food prices increased 26% in January. There was little doubt that, with the widespread indexation of the Brazilian economy, the annual inflation rate would move quickly to a new plateau of 400% to 500% per year. The government would not be able to keep wage adjustments at six-month intervals, which could result in another cost push that would drive the economy into hyperinflation. Also, the jump in monthly rates frustrated the exchange rate policy, as the preset daily minidevaluations could not keep pace with inflation. A program of gradual recovery of the real price of public services had to be abandoned because the nominal adjustments in December and January ended up falling behind the monthly rates of inflation.

The failure of gradualism in producing the stability of monthly inflation rates ended the second phase of the New Republic economic policy. Rampant inflation threatened not only the economic ministries but also the political coalition that supported the government. The legitimacy of the indirect voting process that elected Tancredo Neves and of the presidential succession after his death was once again at stake. Even the president's political party seemed on the verge of a major rupture. Not many options were left, and, on February 28, 1986, President José Sarney decreed a new stabilization program: the Cruzado Plan.

The preconditions for the plan were considered most appropriate: Industrial output had grown 9.2% during the twelve months before February; the trade balance had accumulated $12.8 billion (US dollars) during the previous twelve months; the public sector deficit was believed to be roughly balanced for 1986 as a result of the fiscal package of December 1985; the price of oil, which accounted for 45% of Brazilian imports, was declining in world markets; and the dollar was depreciating against European currencies and the Japanese yen.

## 5.3   The Cruzado Plan

The Brazilian stabilization program of February 28, 1986, promoted a monetary reform that established the cruzado (Cz$) as the basic unit of national currency. The rate of conversion was fixed at 1,000 cruzeiros per cruzado. As explained in section 5.1, the lack of synchronism in wage and price adjustments required the design of specific rules for conversion, if major redistributions of income and wealth were to be avoided. These rules aimed at producing a "neutral shock" that would restore under the cruzado the same patterns of income and wealth distribution as recently under the cruzeiro.

Several reasons concurred for the shock to be not as neutral as purported in its original form. For example, the stabilization program was launched when inflation was in fact accelerating and hence before a new inertial inflation and a new income and wealth distribution were settled. Also, as will be ascertained from the discussion that follows, the neutrality was impaired by political commitments and technical difficulties.

The Conversion of Wages

Wages were converted into cruzados on the basis of the average purchasing power of the past six months. Even though quarterly adjustments had become widespread during the second half of 1985, the official wage policy of 1979 still determined adjustments every six months. The wage conversion formula computed the average real wage between September 1985 and February 1986, valued at the prices of the end of February. It modified equation (5.3) to consider the actual, as opposed to the uniform, monthly inflation rate.

The rule for conversion, established by Decree Law 2283 of February 28, 1986, can be expressed analytically as

$$W(\text{Cz\$}) = \tfrac{1}{6} \sum_{t=0}^{5} W_{T-t}(\text{Cr\$}) \prod_{j=0}^{t} (1 + p_{T+1-j}), \tag{5.4}$$

where $W(\text{Cz\$})$ is the wage in cruzados, $W(\text{Cr\$})$ is the monthly wage in thousands of cruzeiros, and $p$ is the monthly rate of inflation. Time period $T$ refers to February 1986, $T - 1$ to January 1986, $T - 2$ to December 1985, and so forth. The last term on the right-hand side of equation (5.4) is the product of the "present-value factors" to the end of February 1986. The rate of inflation for March 1986, time perod $T + 1$ in equation (5.4), was set to 0.

An underlying hypothesis for equation (5.4) was that wages were normally paid on the last day of the month, even if they were set at the beginning of the month. The erosion of the real wage that occurred during the thirty days of the month was not compensated for.[5] Besides, all wages were assumed to be spent when they were received, on the last day of the month. Weekly or fortnightly advances as well as alternative paydays were disregarded.

One advantage of the conversion procedure adopted by the Cruzado Plan over the utilization of preset conversion factors that would have been applied to February nominal wages according to the month of the last wage adjustment, as earlier suggested by Modiano (1985a), stemmed from encompassing bonuses, advances, quarterly adjustments, and other benefits freely negotiated between September 1985 and February 1986.

Another advantage of the adopted conversion procedure for wage earners resulted from the conversion's "backward-looking" direction. Wages were converted into cruzados on the basis of the average purchasing power of the past six months. The rise in monthly inflation rates from 12.8%, which corresponded to the average between September 1985 and February 1986, to 14.6%, which corresponded to the average between December 1985 and February 1986, would result, according to equation (5.3), in a decline of 3.9% in the six-month average real wage. This means that, had inflation rates remained at 14.6% per month with wage adjustments occurring every six months after March 1986, the average purchasing power for the following six months would fall by 3.9%. Hence a "forward-looking" conversion procedure would set wages in cruzados at levels 3.9% lower than the backward-looking conversion.

Wage Bonus and Cost-of-Living Adjustments

A bonus of 8.0% was conceded to all wage earners, irrespective of prior gains obtained through labor negotiations from September 1985 to February 1986, when inflation accelerated.[6] The minimum wage, which used to be adjusted in November and May, was raised to Cz$804,000 from Cr$600,000 in February 1986. With respect to the average purchasing power of the past six months, the new minimum wage implied a bonus of 16.1%. If the average purchasing power of the following six months is taken as a reference, the bonuses amounted to 12.2% for all wage earners and 20.6% for the minimum wage.

There was no economic rationale for the magnitude of the wage bonus. This resulted from a political decision to promote a redistribution of income toward wage earners, favoring still further the lower classes.[7] The New Republic, installed in March 1985, was committed to restoring real wages to pre-1983 levels. The recession and the wage deindexation of 1983, in the aftermath of the foreign debt crisis, had reduced the real wage by approximately 20%.

Wages were not frozen with the Cruzado Plan. Instead, the annual wage negotiation dates that had prevailed until November 1979 were restored. Hence the asynchronism in wage adjustments that complicated the launching of any stabilization program for the Brazilian economy was not eliminated. The only difference is that the interval between successive wage negotiations has been extended, from six months to twelve months. At first, wages were supposed to be freely negotiated on a yearly basis with no automatic compensation for past inflation. However, a second version of the decree law established an automatic cost-of-living adjustment at the negotiation dates, equivalent to 60% of the variation of consumer prices accumulated from either March 1, 1986, or the previous negotiation date, whichever came last.[8]

The Sliding Scale for Wages

A sliding scale for wage adjustments had been a constant demand in labor negotiations during 1985. The political party that came into power in March 1985 had endorsed such a claim before its electoral success. The government then felt that acceptance by the working class of the wage conversion scheme would be enhanced if a sliding scale for protection of real wages was introduced with the stabilization program. Hence the Cruzado Plan established, over and above the annual automatic partial compensations, that wages would be automatically adjusted whenever the inflation rate reached the trigger of 20% per year. The trigger counter was set initially at 0% on March 1, 1986, and would be reset either at the annual negotiation dates or each time the trigger was reached.

Given the instability associated with wage adjustments without a fixed periodicity, it was thought that the trigger of 20% would indicate an annual inflation rate that was tolerable without further monetary or fiscal restraint. For the sliding scale to remain inoperative and wage adjustments to be limited to the annual negotiation dates, inflation rates had to be kept below 1.67% per month, which is equivalent to 20.0% in eleven months and 22.0% in one year.

It can be shown with equation (5.3) that with an inflation rate of 1.67% per month equality between the real wage after the plan (averaged over twelve months) and the real wage before the plan (averaged over six months) would be obtained if the cruzado wages were set 9.4% above the average purchasing power of the cruzeiro wages from September 1985 through February 1986.[9] This theoretical bonus, which would guarantee no losses in real wages in the worst case, was of the same magnitude as the politically determined bonus of 8%.

An expression for the average real wage $w$ in terms of the peak real wage $w^*$ with a sliding scale coupled to annual wage negotiations can be obtained as an extension of equation (5.3). If we denote by $p$ the uniform monthly inflation rate, we can show that

$$w = \left\{ \frac{hn}{12} \left[ \frac{(1+p)^{h+1} - 1}{(h+1)p(1+p)^h} \right] + \frac{12 - hn}{12} \left[ \frac{(1+p)^{13-hn} - 1}{(13 - hn)p(1+p)^{12-hn}} \right] \right\} w^*,$$

$$(5.5)$$

where $h$ is the number of months between two successive wage adjustments and $n$ is the number of times automatic wage adjustments are triggered within a year. Clearly $n$ must be the integer that results from the division of 12 by $h$. Consistency with the trigger mechanism further requires that $(1+p)^{h-1} \leqslant 1.2$ and $(1+p)^h \geqslant 1.2$.

The instability of the rate of inflation with the sliding scale is illustrated in table 5.1. It uses equation (5.5) to show different combinations of $p$ and $h$ (and hence $n$) that result in the same decline in the average real wage with respect to the peak that would prevail under the zero-inflation hypothesis.[10] Note that the average real wage would decline by the same percentage of the official wage bonus of 8% under alternative inflation rates that run from 1.4% to 3.9% per month. In the best case the sliding scale would not be

**Table 5.1**
Alternative inflation rates consistent with an 8% decline in real wages

| Monthly inflation rate (%) | Annual inflation rate (%) | Number of months until next wage adjustment | Number of times sliding scale is triggered | Number of months until next negotiation date |
| --- | --- | --- | --- | --- |
| 1.4 | 18.4 | 12 | 0 | 12 |
| 1.7 | 22.3 | 11 | 1 | 1 |
| 2.0 | 26.7 | 10 | 1 | 2 |
| 2.3 | 31.4 | 9 | 1 | 3 |
| 2.6 | 35.9 | 8 | 1 | 4 |
| 2.8 | 39.3 | 7 | 1 | 5 |
| 3.9 | 57.7 | 5 | 2 | 2 |

triggered and wage adjustments would be limited to annual negotiations. In the worst case automatic wage adjustments would be triggered twice within the year, at the end of the fifth and tenth months.

Table 5.2 shows the inflation rates that are consistent with the same adjustment of the average real wage under alternative indexation schemes. Besides the sliding scale introduced by the Cruzado Plan, two fixed-periodicity regimes are considered: adjustments every twelve months that coincide with the annual negotiation dates and adjustments every six months, which were in force before the Cruzado Plan.[11] For the sliding scale the smallest rates of inflation were selected.

Notice that, up to an 8% decline in average real wages, the sliding scale would not be triggered and the rate of inflation would be the same as under the policy of adjustments every twelve months: 1.4% per month or 18.4% per year. Six-month adjustments would imply a higher rate of inflation: 2.9% per month or 40.4% per year. If real wages have to decline by more than 10%, the rates of inflation under the three regimes become markedly different. A rate of inflation of 1.8% per month, or 24% per year, under annual adjustments is consistent with 5.6% per month, or 91.4% per year, under the sliding scale. In the latter case adjustments would be triggered every four months. The distance between inflation rates under the alternative regimes becomes larger, the larger the required decline in real wages. Real wages would fall by 16% with inflation rates of either 3.1% per month under the fixed periodicity of twelve months or 47.1% per month under the 20% sliding scale.[12]

The importance of setting prices "right" at the onset of a stabilization program, which at the same time introduces a sliding scale for protection of

**Table 5.2**
Consistent inflation rates (%)

| Real wage adjustments (%) | 12-Month adjustments | | 6-Month adjustments | | 20% Sliding scale | |
|---|---|---|---|---|---|---|
| | Monthly | Yearly | Monthly | Yearly | Monthly | Yearly[a] |
| 0 | 0.0 | 0.0 | 0.0 | 0.0 | 0.0 | 0.0 (12) |
| −2 | 0.3 | 4.2 | 0.7 | 8.5 | 0.3 | 4.2 (12) |
| −4 | 0.7 | 8.6 | 1.4 | 17.9 | 0.7 | 8.6 (12) |
| −6 | 1.1 | 13.4 | 2.1 | 28.5 | 1.1 | 13.4 (12) |
| −8 | 1.4 | 18.4 | 2.9 | 40.4 | 1.4 | 18.4 (12) |
| −10 | 1.8 | 24.0 | 3.7 | 53.9 | 5.6 | 91.4 (4) |
| −12 | 2.2 | 30.0 | 4.5 | 69.4 | 9.3 | 189.1 (3) |
| −14 | 2.6 | 36.6 | 5.3 | 86.9 | 17.3 | 575.8 (2) |
| −16 | 3.1 | 43.6 | 6.2 | 106.8 | 47.1 | 10130.4 (1) |

a. The values in parentheses indicate the number of months between successive wage adjustments.

real wages, becomes clear. Should large price corrections be needed afterward, the inflation rate may grow exponentially as wage readjustments become frequently triggered. The numerical example in table 5.2 shows that in the presence of a 20% sliding scale the need to raise prices by as much as 16% above wages could move the economy from stabilization to the beginning of hyperinflation.

The Conversion of Prices and the Exchange Rate

Prices should have been converted into cruzados following basically the same rule that applied to wages. Relative prices under the cruzeiro, with respect to either a composite cost index or the wholesale price index, should have been averaged out over a predetermined period of time. In the example carried out by Modiano (1985a), in which the inflationary process was purely inertial, average relative prices were computed considering a time interval equal to the fixed periodicity of adjustments. In practice, however, major technical difficulties were involved.

As discussed in section 5.2, from April to July 1985 a partial price freeze was adopted by the Brazilian authorities. In order to avoid a major inflationary rebound, the new economic administration, installed in September 1985, did not promote major price realignments when the freeze was lifted. The losses incurred with the freeze were to be compensated for gradually. For public sector prices the situation was even more critical, as these had already been frequently used during the early 1980s as part of the anti-inflationary policy.

Under the prevailing conditions it seemed clear that some "right" prices could be well above the averages computed for one, two, or even six months. As pointed by Modiano (1985a), disregarding such lags could create a potential inflation for the new currency. The technical difficulties involved in determining the right levels were not overcome, and prices, except for industrial electricity, which was raised by 20%, were frozen at the consumer levels prevailing on February 27, 1986. A technically fragile price freeze was to become the fundamental element of the stabilization program.

Rough estimates of the maximum price lags with respect to the averages, disregarding the generalized pressures on the price index resulting from past repressed inflation, can be obtained with the help of equation (5.3). By using the actual average inflation rates for the interval between successive adjustments, one obtains that price lags could run from at most 6.7% for monthly adjustments to as much as 45.1% for six-month adjustments. The six-month adjustments were limited by February 1986 to a few public tariffs. It was thought that in the absence of generalized demand pressures relative price distortions could be corrected during the plan without much inflationary impact by matching some price increases with other price decreases.

The Cruzado Plan also modified the consumer price index (IPCA) that had been adopted in November 1985 as the official measure of inflation. Its structure, which measured the prices of a consumption basket for workers with income up to thirty times the minimum wage, was not altered, but the price basis was displaced to February 28, 1986. The new index was named the "consumer price index" (IPC).

The rationale for such a move was to avoid what has been called the "Alfonsin effect." Lopes (1986) has shown that, with prices measured by daily or weekly averages, the IPCA would register an increase in the first month after the plan even if prices remained stable all along. Approximately half of the February 1986 inflation rate, which amounted to 14.4%, would show up in the index for March. This effect was first observed one month after the Argentine Austral Plan was launched. For the Cruzado Plan such a statistical effect was considered unbearable, as it could inappropriately trigger the wage sliding scale.

A second advantage of the displacement of the price basis of the IPCA (now, IPC) was that it opened the way for major price adjustments before the freeze, with no harm to the zero-inflation target set for March 1986. However, because of the technical difficulties and the political costs involved in backdating price increases of early March to February 28, this opportunity was bypassed.

As mentioned in section 5.2, starting in March 1985 the exchange rate was adjusted on a daily basis. After September the daily minidevaluations were preset to equal the inflation rate of the past month. Under an inflation rate that ran at less than 0.5% per day, it was reasonable to assume that peak and average real exchange rates coincided. Hence the exchange rate was converted to cruzados at the level prevailing on February 27, with 1,000 cruzeiros per cruzado.

The comfortable external position of the Brazilian economy and the depreciation of the US dollar, to which the cruzeiro was pegged, against European currencies and the Japanese yen in late 1985 and early 1986 seemed to eliminate the need for a maxidevaluation before the plan. However, as flexibility was desired, the exchange rate was not frozen but fixed for an unlimited time. It was thought that this semantic difference would not associate an eventual devaluation with a rupture for the price freeze.

### The Conversion of Rents

Before the Cruzado Plan residential rents were adjusted based on 80% of past inflation every six or twelve months. The conversion to cruzados could use the same procedure adopted for wages. However, as with partial indexation, real rents tended to decline, and a forward-looking rule was enforced. Average-to-peak ratios were computed for both six- and twelve-month adjustments based on an inflation rate of 14.6% per month, which corresponded to 0.45% per day for 30.4 days.

The general formula for computation of the average-to-peak ratio $r$ was

$$r = \frac{1.146^h - 1}{h(0.146)(1.146)^{h-1}}, \qquad h = 6 \text{ or } 12,$$

which resulted in $r = 0.7307$ for $h = 6$ and $r = 0.5266$ for $h = 12$. Before applying the average-to-peak ratios, residential rents were nominally updated to February 28, 1986. This procedure assumed that all residential rents were paid on the last day of the month.

Commercial rents did not have such well-defined periodicities for adjustments. Corrections were based on the variation of the ORTN, which was updated every first day of the month based on the rate of inflation of the previous month. By February 1986 most commercial rent contracts were updated every three months. However, monthly as well as yearly adjustment contracts also existed.

The procedure for converting commercial rents into cruzados followed the same scheme adopted for wages. The government announced multiplicative coefficients, which were to be applied to the nominal rents of February 1986 according to the periodicity of adjustments and the month of the last adjustment and which reproduced the average real rents over an interval equal to the period between adjustments.

The Conversion of Future Contracts

Basically two types of contracts for future payments in cruzeiros existed in the Brazilian economy before the Cruzado Plan. The difference resided in whether interest rates were preset or postset. Contracts with postset rates did not impose major problems for conversion into cruzados: With the suppression of nominal correction the percentages contracted over and above nominal correction would become the nominal interest rates in cruzados. This has been the case for all contracts that lasted less than one year; with the Cruzado Plan indexation was forbidden within such a time span. The only exception was for savings deposits, which remained indexed. An "insurance against inflation," to be credited quarterly, substituted for the monthly monetary correction that prevailed before the plan.

Preset contracts imposed a major difficulty, as inflation accelerated from December 1985 to February 1986. In contrast to the Argentine case, there existed in the Brazilian economy preset contracts that had been signed up to one year before the plan. Clearly contracts signed in the near past had already taken into account the rise in inflation rates, whereas older contracts still projected inflation rates of 10% per month. Hence the elimination of the inflationary expectations embedded in such contracts, in the style of the austral *tablita*, involved a greater degree of arbitrariness.

The Cruzado Plan preset the future inflation of the cruzeiro at 0.45% per day, which corresponded to the daily average of the inflation rate between December 1985 and February 1986. Based on this inflation rate, a table for daily conversion of future cruzeiros into cruzados was established for the following twelve months. Certainly the conversion table would promote a major redistribution of income between debtors and creditors. However, this would be no different from the redistribution of income that would result if the cruzeiro inflation rate had stabilized at 0.45% per day.

Monetary and Fiscal Policies

The Cruzado Plan did not indicate any rules or targets for monetary and fiscal policy to complement the stabilization program. This did not mean, however, that demand policies were considered unimportant for successful stabilization. On the contrary, as pointed out by Modiano (1986), the general belief was that aggregate demand policies, although impotent to deal with inflation rates of 200–400% per year fed back by widespread indexation, would regain vitality under one- or two-digit annual inflation rates.

Flexibility to control aggregate demand was desired to counteract any abrupt changes in economic activity during the plan. However, monetary and fiscal policies were left to the discretion of the economic authorities. As mentioned earlier, the 20% sliding scale imposed an annual inflation limit that could be tolerated without further restraint because the triggering of wage adjustments would increase the risk of a widespread reindexation of the economy. The major difficulty would stem from the proper assessment of potential inflation once the price freeze was lifted.

According to Arida and Lara-Resende (1985), the decline in inflation would provoke an increase in the demand for real money balances. The implicit objective of monetary policy during the first months of the plan was to accommodate such a spurt in money demand, as this movement was viewed as noninflationary. It would be the consequence of a portfolio shift toward the stable new currency. The difficulty here was to evaluate when the process of natural remonetization ended and further monetary expansion was deemed inflationary. Interest rates would signal excessive or insufficient remonetization.

Monitoring interest rates during the first months of the plan would prove to be a difficult task, however, as several restrictions applied. Higher interest rates could negatively affect investment programs that were badly needed; the rate of investment in the Brazilian economy had declined from 22.5% of GDP in 1980 to 16.3% of GDP in 1985. Also higher interest rates would increase the burden of the domestic public debt, which amounted to approximately 21.3% of GDP in December 1985. On the other hand, lower interest rates could stimulate speculation in inventories and foreign currency, threatening stabilization.

Concerning fiscal policy, the government announced in December 1985 a fiscal package that would eliminate the public sector borrowing requirement (operational concept) projected for 1986. The income tax refunds due in 1986 were divided into four annual installments to reduce current cash pressures. The tax structure on capital incomes was changed to include taxes on nominal gains, which would be considerably reduced with abrupt disinflation. At this time the Cruzado Plan was under discussion, but there was no clear sign that it would in fact be launched. Six-month income statements, which would only increase government revenue during the second half of 1986, were required from large enterprises. In addition, measures were taken to reduce the fiscal lag, the inflationary erosion of governmet revenues. On the other hand, withholding taxes on labor incomes were reduced, increasing net wages in 1986 but decreasing that volume of tax refunds in 1987.

It was clear that some of the benefits of the December 1985 fiscal package, such as the taxation of nominal capital gains, would not survive the Cruzado Plan. Others, such as the shorter fiscal lags, would reduce the benefits normally associated with the process of disinflation. Also the fiscal package of December 1985 could not take into account the loss of the inflation tax that would follow price stabilization after February 28, 1986.

## 5.4    From the Cruzado Plan to Inflation[13]

In this section I review the results of the Cruzado Plan between March 1986 and May 1987. The analysis of these fifteen months is divided into three periods. During the first period, from March to June 1986, disinflation was actually achieved but the first problems of the stabilization program became visible. The second period, from July to October 1986, is characterized by the total immobility of the government in the face of worsening product shortages and deteriorating external accounts. The third period, from November 1986 to May 1987, confirms the failure of the Cruzado Plan, with the return to high inflation rates.[14]

From the Cruzado Plan to Disinflation: March 1986–June 1986

The Cruzado Plan was enthusiastically received by the population. Even though it was implemented through a decree law, the plan obtained ample support as, after twenty-one years of military rule, it satisfied Brazilian society's desire for greater participation in deciding the destiny of the country. The president's request for the population to police the price freeze was understood as a civic duty, and the technically fragile price freeze, discussed earlier, immediately became the fundamental element of the stabilization program. The government's excessive commitment to the freeze planted the seeds of the difficulties that the Cruzado Plan would face in the near future.

The main challenge faced by the government during the first month was to convince the labor unions that the complicated average-plus-bonus wage conversion formula did not imply any losses in purchasing power. The government actually succeeded because a March protest movement, organized by the most important labor union, did not gather more than a few participants. Government efforts were also concentrated on convincing the population that the plan would not lead to recession and unemployment and that the deflation projected for March, as a result of the elimination of the financial costs embedded in term sales prices, did not mean the beginning of a great depression.

Inflation, as measured by the new consumer price index, in fact declined in the first months of the Cruzado Plan. From March to June the maximum monthly inflation rate was 1.4%, reached in May. For some government officials these results confirmed the proposition that a substantial reduction in inflation rates could be obtained without a major recession and that the way was paved to deal with the fundamental sources of inflationary pressure. For others, however, these results gave the false impression that all inflationary pressures could be knocked down with strong will and faith.

The decomposition of the monthly rates of inflation for this period revealed the first symptoms of excess demand in the economy. The prices of clothing and used cars, which were hard to control and accounted for approximately 15% of the IPC, were increasing at the rates of 4–5% per month. The distortion of relative prices between strictly frozen prices and uncontrollable prices that had started in early March only intensified during the extended freeze.

A consumption boom was triggered by the redistribution of income favoring wage earners, the voluntary dissavings caused by monetary illusion, the decline in withholding of personal income taxes, the reduction of interest rates, the repressed consumption during the previous recession years, and the freezing of some prices at low levels. Some government officials maintained that this movement was a consumption bubble that would vanish after the renewal of consumer durables stocks. Consumer purchases had picked up in March, but industrial production was practically paralyzed while interindustry prices were negotiated. In April, however, the rate of growth of industrial production surpassed the February peak of 9.2%.

The first shortages appeared during this initial period, but they would not represent a generalized problem until the second period. Between

March and June shortages were observed in the milk, meat, and automobile markets. The milk shortage was typical of an administered frozen price lagging behind costs. The government decided to subsidize milk producers; this would become a more general practice in the following period. The meat shortage had a different origin; it resulted from a seasonal decline in supply and speculation. In this case the government opted for massive imports, but these proved late and insufficient. The meat crisis lasted the entire freeze and constituted a major battleground for the government. The failure to enforce the freeze, even under the threat of cattle seizure, eroded public confidence. Automobile prices were frozen at relatively low levels because they had not been compensated for the losses incurred during the partial freeze of 1985. As a result, queues grew in the new car market, raising the prices of used cars above that of the new models.

Besides these sectoral problems other indicators suggested that generalized excess demand could be building up. The increase in money supply during the first months seemed to exceed the natural rise in money demand that followed abrupt disinflation. It was argued that the decline in the opportunity costs of holding money should have provoked a portfolio shift from indexed assets to paper currency and demand deposits with no net effect on the broader monetary aggregates. However, the rate of growth of the broader monetary aggregate M4 reached 21.1% between the end of February and the end of June.

The liquidity slack from excessive monetization reflected itself in terms of ex post real interest rates during this period. As a consequence, stock prices increased 50%, the premium on the dollar parallel market jumped from 26% to 50%, and the prices of real assets increased significantly. Although maintaining low nominal interest rates in March could be viewed as contributing to reinforce the expectations of zero inflation, later efforts by the Central Bank to restrain monetary policy and raise interest rates faced strong political opposition and hence did not succeed.

During the March–June period there was also a growing awareness that the public sector budget at the onset of the stabilization program was far from balanced. This situation would only grow worse during the Cruzado Plan as a result of the increase in expenditures on the government wage bill, direct and indirect subsidies, tax exemptions, and transfers to state enterprises and state and local authorities. The government started to recognize that the deficit could reach 2.5% of GDP, as opposed to the 0.5% projected after the fiscal package of December 1985. The lack of trustworthy and regular information on the public deficit raised suspicions that the actual number was even higher than 2.5%. The expected increase in government real revenues resulting from the elimination of the inflationary erosion of tax receipts was not materializing in due proportion and in due time. By the time government revenue started to increase, reflecting also the rise in economic activity, it was more than matched by an increase in expenditures to support the price freeze and win the November elections for state governments and the constituent congress.

The magnitude of the economic overheating in June can be further illustrated by a few figures. Consumer purchases increased 22.8% in the first six months of 1986 with respect to the same period in the previous year. The production of consumer durables increased 33.2% during the previous twelve months. The open unemployment rate declined from 4.4% in March to 3.8%, and real wages increased approximately 12% from the end of February.

At the end of this period economic policy had apparently only two options: either lift the price freeze or slow down output growth by means of a severe and quick cut in aggregate demand. The first option could break the implicit pact between the government and the Brazilian society and would face the wage trigger trap. The political costs were deemed unbearable. The second option, which basically involved an increase in direct taxes, could be viewed as contractionary and would face the "growth at any cost" trap. The political costs were also deemed unbearable. The Cruzadinho was the government solution to this impasse.

From Disinflation to Cruzado II: July 1986–October 1986

On July 24, the government announced the Cruzadinho, a timid fiscal package designed to dampen consumption. It involved basically a compulsory savings scheme: the creation of new indirect taxes on purchases of gasoline and automobiles that would be refunded after three years. It also introduced nonrefundable taxes on the purchases of foreign exchange for travel and international airplane tickets. The proceeds of the new taxes would finance the Plano de Metas, a program of public and private investments that contemplated a GDP growth rate of 7% per year launched at the same time. The observation that these tax receipts fell short of the Plano de Metas financial needs and that the sources of the residual funds were not announced gave the impression that the Cruzadinho was merely an emergency act to finance a deteriorating public deficit.

The credibility of the program was also harmed by the decision of the government to purge the increases in automobile and gasoline prices from the consumer price index. The main objective of the purge was to avoid fueling the wage trigger counter. After long discussions the government decided to publish both indexes (purged and nonpurged) but determined that the purged index should be considered for indexation purposes. The implied rupture with the price freeze led to the feeling that a general lift of the freeze was nearby. To the speculative inventory accumulation, the government responded with only a mildly more restrictive monetary policy—raising interest rates. From July to October real interest rates, deflated by the official rates of inflation, turned slightly positive.

From August to November 15, all government efforts were concentrated on winning the elections, which immobilized economic policy. As expected the Cruzadinho fell short of restraining consumption. On the contrary the expectation of an imminent price liberalization gave a new impulse to consumer purchases. Industrial output growth peaked at the annual rate of 12.2% in September, with several sectors operating at virtually full capacity. There were severe shortages of raw materials and intermediate products.

Official inflation during this period remained at low rates, displaying only a slightly ascending trend. The pattern of sectoral rates was not different from the one observed immediately after the plan. For the sectors in which the freeze could not be enforced, for example, clothing, household items, and transportation (used cars), the rate of price increase was approximately double that of the official inflation rate. It is noteworthy also that the reported or collected prices were less related* to the prices actually practiced in the market because overprices and new brands had become common expedients to circumvent the freeze. The discrepancy between official and actual inflation during this period raises doubts about the utilization of official price indexes to deflate wages, the exchange rate, and interest rates. By the end of October shortages were increasingly frequent and queues had become part of the daily routine.

Until August the trade surplus did not reflect the excess demand in domestic markets, with export revenues fairly stable and the increase in nonoil import expenditure accommodated by the decline in oil prices. This situation changed in September and more drastically in October, as export revenue fell from $2.1 billion to $1.3 billion (US dollars). Two basic reasons led to this move: the profitability of domestic sales with disguised overpricing in contrast to foreign sales with a fixed exchange rate, and the speculation over a cruzado maxidevaluation, as signaled by the premium on the dollar parallel market, which reached 90% in October.

Finally, still in October, the government devalued the cruzado by a modest 1.8% and announced a policy of eventual minidevaluations based on an exchange rate–wage indicator. Because the indicator suggested that the exchange rate was overvalued by at least 10% with respect to the end of February, the expectation of a new and larger devaluation further stimulated the postponement of exports and the acceleration of imports. And because only a few weeks were left until the November 15 elections, the government did not respond to the continuous loss of foreign exchange reserves.

## From Cruzado II to Inflation: November 1986–May 1987

One week after the government party had won the elections, Cruzado II was announced. Given the political costs associated with increases in direct taxes and cuts in public expenditures, the government decided again to raise indirect taxes. For this reason consumer prices for automobiles increased by 80%, cigarettes by up to 120%, and beverages by 100%. Public sector prices were also adjusted: gasoline by 60%, electricity and telephone by 35%, and postal tariffs by 80%. Cruzado II was in fact a fiscal package with little regard for either price stabilization or demand price elasticities. It aimed to increase government revenue by 4% of GDP at the cost of a violent inflationary shock. Inflationary expectations were further fueled by the announcement that the adjustment was not complete: Steel and milk prices would be increased later on. The government expected that all remaining prices would respect the freeze still in force.

Cruzado II also determined that the price increases for automobiles, cigarettes, and beverages should be purged from the consumer price index. This purge would reduce the official rate of inflation by approximately ten percentage points between November and December, and its main objective was to delay the first triggering of the wage sliding scale. The purge immediately became a political issue, as newly elected governors and deputies opposed it. It was clear also that, with the labor market still overheated, such a purge would not be easily accepted. A few weeks later the government backed off and reinstituted the restricted consumer price index (INPC) as the index. The wage sliding scale would be triggered for the first time in December, with a new proviso: Trigger adjustments would be limited to 20% with the residual carried over to the next trigger.

The government proclaimed that Cruzado II represented a definite end to indexation. At the same time it reinstituted the daily minidevaluations of the cruzado and linked all financial contracts to the returns on the Letras do Banco Central (LBC), which, in order to avoid an outflow of funds into the dollar parallel market, soon became overindexed, geared not to the lower past inflation rates but to the higher future expected inflation rates. One week later, as nominal interest rates on preset sixty days CDs reached 200% per year, the government allowed the banks to reissue CDs with postset rates. As one would expect, given the magnitude of the inflationary shock promoted by Cruzado II, indexation was returning in full force, even though it was officially termed a short interlude. Inflation, measured by the new official index, the INPC, increased from 3.3% in November to 7.3% in December 1986.

During December the government neither started administering the lift of the price freeze nor discarded the possibility of imposing another freeze. Although at that point the chances of success for a second freeze were minimal, the return of the wage-price spiral to the proportions reached in mid-1987 could have been avoided. Because Cruzado II provided an escape valve for all the inflationary pressure that had been built up during the extended freeze, the overpricing that had become a general disguised practice started to be disclosed and revealed by the price collection agencies in January 1987. Under the threat of an inflationary explosion the government initiated discussions with representatives of the entrepreneurs and wage earners, aiming at signing a social pact. But the lack of tradition in negotiations of such pacts did not allow for a rapid reconciliation of the conflicting objectives. The failure of the social pact became evident in late January.

The inflation rate in January reached 16.8%, which meant that the first trigger wage adjustment, which would benefit approximately 50% of the working class and would be paid by the end of January, accounted for little more than the loss of purchasing power that occurred during that same month. The extent of real wage protection conceded by the sliding scale was at stake. Although the government still discussed whether it should undertake a gradual lifting of the price freeze or determine another freeze, considerable pressure for liberalization was being exerted by the industrial sector.

The government acquiesced in early February, retaining control over only a restricted set of prices. With the abrupt lifting of price controls, inflation in February was expected to reach the rate of 20%. The government interest rate and exchange rate policies sanctioned these expectations, arguing that a more restrictive monetary policy would postpone the threat of hyperinflation posed by the February rate. At the end of the month it was verified that the rate of inflation for February was 13.9%, which meant that the government achieved a significantly positive real interest rate and promoted a mididevaluation of the cruzado.

On February 27, as the Cruzado Plan reached its first anniversary, with a monthly inflation rate projected at 20% the reindexation of the economy, initiated in November, was completed with the reintroduction of monthly nominal corrections. The fixed periodicities for adjustments of the old cruzeiro contracts were all renewed except for labor contracts, which with the sliding scale gained a flexible periodicity. Consequently the economy became more heavily indexed than on the last days of the cruzeiro, which meant that the high rates of inflation of January and February would continue to increase, but at a much faster pace.

Because the figures for the monthly trade balances were not showing signs of recovery, the government decided in late February to suspend interest payments on the foreign debt to private banks for an unlimited time. The official objectives of this "technical moratorium" were to stop the loss of foreign exchange reserves and to start a new stage of debt negotiations. A third unofficial objective of the moratorium was to regain popular support; government credibility was being considerably harmed by the failure of the Cruzado Plan. None of the objectives were attained in the short run. The demands of foreign bankers and the lack of support in the major political party for a deal with the IMF were major obstacles to resuming negotiations. As the obstacles were never overcome, the impasse for negotiations continued.

At the same time the sales statistics suggested that Brazil was on the verge of a strong slowdown of economic activity. Although the replenishment of inventories approximately sustained the level of industrial production during the first quarter of 1987, consumer purchases fell significantly as a result of the decline in real wages, the rise in interest rates, and the increase in uncertainty.

The economic activity slowdown also had supply-side origins. Limits were imposed on imports of essential raw materials and intermediate products because of the scarcity of foreign exchange, and domestic markets were disorganized by the abrupt lifting of price controls with no guidelines regarding either future cost adjustments or a new freeze. The diagnosis that demand restraints prevailed led the government to take some expansionary measures in March: The maximum time span for consumer credit was extended from four months to nine months; withholding taxes on labor income were reduced; and the time allowed for paying 1986 personal income taxes was extended to eight months with no monetary correction.

In mid-March the February inflation was known, and in April the government reinitiated the process of realigning public tariffs and administered prices, which was interrupted in March because of the threat posed by the expectation that February inflation would reach 20%. Further inflationary pressure was added by a wave of rumors that a new freeze was going to be announced in late April. Consequently the rate of inflation jumped from 14.4% in March to 21.0% in April, producing for the first time a simultaneous trigger adjustment for all wage earners at the end of May. In the meantime the finance minister, who had become popular in the wake of the Cruzado Plan, left office because the inflationary bubble (the idea that inflation would vanish once the process of price realignment was complete) never actually burst, and the foreign debt renegotiations, intended to reunite the forces of the Brazilian society, came to a new deadlock.

The new finance minister, in office since late April, started by announcing that the GDP growth rate for 1987 should be limited to 3.5%, which collided with the 7% growth aspiration of the ruling political party and his predecessor. The new minister seemed ready to accept negotiations with the IMF, if deemed necessary, but faced severe opposition within the party. The mididevaluation of 7.5% of the cruzado, announced on May 1, was seen as one more step toward a more orthodox economic policy, which is rejected by the party. A sympathizer of the heterodox shock, the minister could not contain the constant wave of rumors of an imminent price freeze.[15]

The rate of inflation for May is projected to be above 21%, and the risk of hyperinflation is again present. The real money stock is still considerably higher than the levels observed under the cruzeiro. The budget deficit for 1987 is already officially projected at 7.0% of GDP, most probably underestimating the inflationary erosion of tax receipts and the expenditures and subsidies granted by the federal government to the public and private sectors to avoid bankruptcies resulting from the decline in economic activity, rampant inflation, and high interest rates. The feared wage sliding scale, with the November upper limit of 20%, is now perceived by the government as a powerful instrument for the stabilization of inflation rates around 20% per month.

## 5.5   Current Prospects and Conclusions

My purpose here has been to review the conceptual framework and the conjunctural environment of the Brazilian Cruzado Plan of February 28, 1986. Success or failure of a stabilization program depends not only on a technically sound basis but also on the proper evaluation of the economic conditions at the time of the plan's announcement, the compromise between theory and practice in the plan's formulation, and the scope and ability of economic policy to fine tune policy during the plan's implementation. The analysis of the results of the Cruzado Plan shows that proper and mistaken assessments and decisions have occurred in all three instances.

Concerning the economy's prior conditions, it has to be recognized that part of the demand pressure that the Cruzado Plan faced after a few months was built up before the plan's announcement. Also, the heterodox shock, designed to deal with inertial inflation, was launched when inflation was moving to a new plateau and the inherent distributive conflicts were being resolved.

In its formulation the Cruzado Plan compromised with a fair income redistribution program that could, however, put at risk the stabilization target. In addition, relative prices were frozen at levels that were not consistent with a longer-term equilibrium, and indexation was not fully abolished. On the contrary the introduction of the sliding scale for wage adjustments represented a high-risk factor, as reindexation could not be avoided once wage adjustments started to be triggered without a fixed periodicity. It was thought, however, that errors in the assessment of the economy's prior conditions and in the plan's formulation could be corrected during the plan. But the same political constraints that helped to launch it on February 28, 1986, remained active, restricting the action of economic policy.

The political fear of a recession dominated the first months, even though the plan was proving to be highly expansionary. Corrective action to counteract the consumption boom was delayed for electoral purposes. For this reason the technically fragile price freeze was extended for nine months, and no significant fiscal or monetary restraint was undertaken. Once the elections were won by the government party, Cruzado II was announced. However, by that time significant inflationary pressure had built up, the economy was nearing full capacity, and the excess domestic demand had spilled over to the foreign sector. The late and mistaken Cruzado II, based on major increases in indirect taxes, represented by itself a major inflationary shock and was closely followed by an abrupt lifting of all price controls. Reindexation could not be avoided as monthly inflation rates quickly approached and surpassed the cruzeiro threshold of 15%, which had triggered the Cruzado Plan.

At present, with inflation skyrocketing to 20% per month, the discussions concerning disinflation in Brazil are back to the issues of late 1984, when the first proposals to deal with inertial inflation were presented. The alternative of a pure orthodox shock should be discarded, for the Argentine and Israeli stabilization programs and also the Cruzado Plan in its first months have shown, according to Dornbusch and Simonsen (1987) and Ocampo (1987), that the proper combination of incomes policy with demand policies can produce a significant decline in inflation rates with small output costs. By the same token it is widely recognized that fiscal and monetary austerity should complement any heterodox treatment if this is to result in something more than just a temporary inflation relief.

On the possible heterodox options to deindex the economy and to dampen or to eliminate the new inertial component of inflation, discussions are centered once again on variants of a heterodox shock, the Larida proposal, and heterodox gradualism. The heterodox shock and the Larida proposal face at present the same type of difficulty: There is no sound basis for freezing prices in cruzados or for establishing the proper conversion rules from cruzados into indexed currency because relative prices still seem to be far from a stable equilibrium. Under these conditions a price and wage freeze, the main ingredients of a heterodox shock, would have to be limited and brief and hence would not command public support. Also, as relative prices move toward equilibrium, inflation would show up in the indexed currency, the main ingredient of the Larida proposal, harming its stability and credibility. In addition, the economic environment has changed much since these discussions first took place: The budget deficit has increased and the trade surplus has decreased.

Partial deindexation or heterodox gradualism is the most recent route selected by the government to cope in the short run with the risk of hyperinflation. Price adjustments can occur only once a month and are limited to 80% of the previous month's rate of inflation. The lack of general consistency of this policy, as wages, the exchange rate, and monetary corrections pass along 100% of past inflation, suggests that it will be short-lived. Also, the new rule for price adjustments can only be enforced on a restricted set of products because the control agencies were dismantled with the liberalization. At present, the only prices over which the government exerts some control are public and a few administered prices. These are exactly the same prices that were left lagging behind costs during the last freeze and that are strong candidates for an eventual second freeze. To use them at this point as part of an antihyperinflationary policy could further aggravate the budget deficit and distort relative prices. Possibly it is for these reasons that the partial deindexation has been announced but not yet implemented, having just a short-run favorable impact on inflationary expectations.

There is little doubt that, if and when inflation stabilizes, a new attempt to eliminate the inertial component of inflation will be carried. A D day for prices and wages alignments and coordinated deindexation cannot be avoided because a gradual increase in public tariffs and administered prices in preparation for the freeze could provoke an additional inflationary shock with unpredictable consequences. Before this D day, however, the government should take severe steps to cut the budget deficit and reach an agreement with foreign creditors in order to create a favorable environment for successful price stabilization. The experience with the Cruzado Plan has shown that the political will to take such steps is weakened once inflation rates start responding to the price freeze. Given the recent failure of the Cruzado Plan, it is reasonable to assume that any new price and wage freeze would have to be limited in scope and time. After approximately three months the government should set up an active incomes policy to start lifting the freeze and to escape from automatic short-run reindexation.

At present the government is under considerable political pressure to determine immediately a new price freeze and to revive the Cruzado Plan. Without fiscal adjustment, with low foreign exchange reserves, and under an accelerating inflation rate, the chances of successful stabilization are small. However, if political convenience should dominate technical considerations, as has been the case during the entire time of the Cruzado Plan, it may be asserted that a new Cruzado Plan is not far away.

## Postscript

Two days after this paper was presented, on June 12, 1987, the Brazilian government announced the New Cruzado Plan, a less ambitious version of the original plan. At the onset public tariffs and administered prices were raised and the cruzado was devalued by 9.5%. The program imposes a wage and price freeze limited to ninety days and announces a cut in the budget deficit from 7.0% to 3.5% of GDP and positive real interest rates during the first months. For the period following the freeze, a new wage policy was introduced: monthly adjustments preset every quarter based on the average rate of inflation of the previous quarter.[16] The price basis of the consumer price index was displaced to June 15 for wage indexation purposes. Except for the wage sliding scale, most of the indexation rules of the economy, such as the daily cruzado minidevaluations, were maintained.

# Appendix

**Table 5A.1**
Main economic indicators of the Brazilian economy. 1980–86

| Economic indicator | 1980 | 1981 | 1982 | 1983 | 1984 | 1985 | 1986 |
|---|---|---|---|---|---|---|---|
| GDP, rate of growth (%) | 9.1 | −3.4 | 0.9 | −2.5 | 5.7 | 8.3 | 8.2 |
| Industry, rate of growth (%) | 9.2 | −9.2 | −0.1 | −6.6 | 6.1 | 9.0 | 12.1 |
| Implicit deflator of GDP (%) | 91.7 | 102.5 | 92.9 | 151.9 | 210.5 | 225.5 | 143.5 |
| General price index, FGV (annual variance, %) | 110.2 | 95.2 | 99.7 | 211.0 | 223.8 | 235.1 | 65.0 |
| Consumer price index, FIBGE (annual variance, %) | 99.2 | 95.6 | 104.8 | 164.0 | 215.0 | 242.2 | 75.5 |
| Exchange rate devaluation, end of period (%) | 54.0 | 95.1 | 97.7 | 289.4 | 223.1 | 229.5 | 42.4 |
| Exchange rate, annual average (Cz$/US$) | 0.053 | 0.093 | 0.179 | 0.573 | 1.836 | 6.169 | 13.580 |
| Trade balance surplus (billions of US dollars) | −2.8 | 1.2 | 0.8 | 6.5 | 13.1 | 12.5 | 8.3 |
| Net interest on foreign debt (billions of US dollars) | 6.3 | 9.2 | 11.4 | 9.6 | 10.2 | 9.7 | 9.1 |
| Gross foreign debt, medium and long term (billions of US dollars) | 53.8 | 61.4 | 69.7 | 81.3 | 91.1 | 95.9 | 101.0 |
| International reserves (billions of US dollars) | 6.8 | 7.5 | 7.0 | 4.6 | 12.0 | 11.6 | 6.8 |
| Monetary base, end of period (billions of cruzados) | 0.7 | 1.1 | 2.2 | 3.5 | 12.7 | 45.5 | 178.9 |
| Money supply, end of period (billions of cruzados) | 1.4 | 2.6 | 4.2 | 9.2 | 27.7 | 112.0 | 452.1 |
| Public sector borrowing requirement, nominal (% of GDP) | n.a. | n.a. | n.a. | n.a. | 23.3 | 27.5 | 10.8 |
| Public sector borrowing requirement, operational (% of GDP) | n.a. | n.a. | n.a. | n.a. | 2.7 | 4.3 | 3.7 |
| National treasury, revenue (billions of cruzados) | 1.2 | 2.2 | 4.6 | 11.3 | 33.8 | 134.5 | 394.0 |
| National treasury, expenditures (billions of cruzados) | 1.2 | 2.2 | 4.6 | 11.3 | 33.8 | 121.2 | 500.2 |

Sources: National Accounts of Brazil, Central Bank of Brazil.
n.a. = not applicable.

**Table 5A.2**
Consumer price index, monthly change (%)

| Date | Total | Foodstuffs | Residential articles | Personal expenses | Housing | Personal Health care | Transport, communication | Clothing |
|---|---|---|---|---|---|---|---|---|
| March 1985 | 12.8 | 11.5 | 13.4 | 15.8 | 14.7 | 8.5 | 13.9 | 10.1 |
| April | 8.8 | 8.7 | 11.9 | 4.3 | 9.4 | 16.6 | 5.0 | 15.3 |
| May | 6.8 | 5.2 | 11.3 | 6.4 | 4.5 | 9.8 | 5.7 | 15.4 |
| June | 7.7 | 6.5 | 11.1 | 8.0 | 4.2 | 7.5 | 9.4 | 13.4 |
| July | 9.3 | 10.9 | 11.6 | 6.5 | 6.3 | 7.2 | 11.1 | 9.1 |
| August | 12.1 | 16.0 | 12.8 | 9.4 | 11.1 | 9.0 | 9.2 | 10.7 |
| September | 12.0 | 12.2 | 11.4 | 19.6 | 7.2 | 10.5 | 11.0 | 12.9 |
| October | 9.6 | 9.3 | 11.3 | 6.4 | 11.4 | 6.5 | 9.1 | 14.8 |
| November | 11.1 | 11.5 | 11.9 | 11.1 | 9.9 | 14.0 | 9.6 | 11.7 |
| December | 13.4 | 17.3 | 11.0 | 11.5 | 10.4 | 11.3 | 12.6 | 10.7 |
| January 1986 | 16.2 | 17.2 | 11.9 | 14.5 | 15.6 | 8.9 | 22.9 | 11.3 |
| February | 14.4 | 17.6 | 10.4 | 15.8 | 13.1 | 11.4 | 13.3 | 7.9 |
| March | −0.1 | −3.5 | 2.0 | 1.2 | 0.1 | 1.9 | 1.4 | 6.3 |
| April | 0.8 | −0.7 | 1.6 | 0.5 | 0.7 | 1.4 | 1.7 | 4.4 |
| May | 1.4 | 0.2 | 2.3 | 1.1 | 0.8 | 0.5 | 1.9 | 7.0 |
| June | 1.3 | 0.5 | 2.1 | 0.9 | 0.6 | 0.5 | 2.2 | 4.1 |
| July | 1.2 | 0.1 | 1.9 | 1.1 | 0.8 | 0.3 | 3.4 | 2.0 |
| August | 1.7 | 0.4 | 2.2 | 2.1 | 1.0 | 0.3 | 4.2 | 2.3 |
| September | 1.7 | 0.3 | 1.2 | 1.1 | 0.6 | 0.7 | 4.0 | 5.4 |
| October | 1.9 | 5.7 | 2.4 | 1.8 | 0.6 | 0.6 | 3.5 | 5.5 |
| November | 3.3 | 3.1 | 1.5 | 1.3 | 4.1 | 0.6 | 5.5 | 5.8 |
| December | 7.3 | 4.9 | 3.6 | 7.4 | 8.0 | 2.0 | 25.7 | 5.0 |
| January 1987 | 16.8 | 16.5 | 5.6 | 48.0 | 3.7 | 8.2 | 22.1 | 7.0 |
| February | 13.9 | 16.8 | 16.5 | 9.2 | 18.4 | 12.2 | 7.2 | 9.8 |
| March | 14.4 | 8.6 | 36.9 | 13.5 | 24.8 | 27.6 | 12.6 | 13.9 |
| April | 21.0 | 21.0 | 17.4 | 8.7 | 43.3 | 39.6 | 9.6 | 14.7 |

Source: Fundacao Instituto Brasileiro de Geografia e Statistica (FIBGE).

**Table 5A.3**
Inflation rates, monthly change (%)

| Date | General price index | Consumer price index | Consumer price index, foodstuffs | Wholesale prices | | |
| --- | --- | --- | --- | --- | --- | --- |
| | | | | Industry | Agriculture | General |
| March 1985 | 12.7 | 12.8 | 11.5 | 14.8 | 10.8 | 13.6 |
| April | 7.2 | 8.8 | 8.7 | 7.3 | 7.0 | 7.3 |
| May | 7.9 | 6.8 | 5.2 | 4.2 | 11.0 | 6.5 |
| June | 7.8 | 7.7 | 6.5 | 5.7 | 13.6 | 7.1 |
| July | 8.9 | 9.3 | 10.9 | 8.0 | 5.6 | 7.6 |
| August | 14.0 | 12.1 | 16.0 | 12.9 | 22.6 | 14.5 |
| September | 9.1 | 12.0 | 12.2 | 9.5 | 10.1 | 9.1 |
| October | 9.0 | 9.6 | 9.3 | 12.4 | 4.6 | 9.5 |
| November | 14.9 | 11.1 | 11.5 | 12.9 | 29.7 | 15.1 |
| December | 13.2 | 13.4 | 17.3 | 12.1 | 6.1 | 12.3 |
| January 1986 | 17.8 | 16.2 | 17.2 | 17.0 | 27.1 | 19.0 |
| February | 22.4 | 14.4 | 17.6 | 19.5 | 19.6 | 22.2 |
| March | −0.9 | −0.1 | −3.5 | −1.3 | 0.0 | −1.0 |
| April | −0.6 | 0.8 | −0.7 | −1.8 | −0.2 | −1.5 |
| May | 0.3 | 1.4 | 0.2 | −0.7 | 0.7 | 0.1 |
| June | 0.5 | 1.3 | 0.5 | 0.3 | 0.7 | 0.4 |
| July | 0.6 | 1.2 | 0.0 | 0.2 | 1.2 | 0.6 |
| August | 1.3 | 1.7 | 0.4 | 0.9 | 2.5 | 1.3 |
| September | 1.1 | 1.7 | 0.3 | 0.0 | 2.4 | 0.7 |
| October | 1.4 | 1.9 | 5.7 | 0.2 | 3.6 | 1.2 |
| November | 2.5 | 3.3 | 3.1 | 1.5 | 3.2 | 2.1 |
| December | 7.6 | 7.3 | 4.9 | 7.7 | 6.3 | 7.7 |
| January 1987 | 12.0 | 16.8 | 16.5 | 8.3 | 16.2 | 10.5 |
| February | 14.1 | 13.9 | 16.8 | 12.8 | 3.0 | 10.4 |
| March | 15.0 | 14.4 | 8.6 | 17.3 | 2.7 | 14.1 |
| April | 20.1 | 21.0 | 21.0 | 24.7 | 7.7 | 21.0 |

Source: FIBGE, Fundacao Getulio Vargas (FGV).

**Table 5A.4**
Industrial production, index (1981 = 100)

| Date | Total | Capital goods | Intermediate goods | Consumer goods | Durables | Nondurables |
|---|---|---|---|---|---|---|
| March 1985 | 103.0 | 87.9 | 112.1 | 98.9 | 110.7 | 96.4 |
| April | 92.7 | 73.0 | 102.2 | 90.4 | 75.2 | 93.6 |
| May | 104.5 | 80.3 | 114.7 | 102.6 | 91.1 | 105.0 |
| June | 107.9 | 83.0 | 117.9 | 103.9 | 103.2 | 104.1 |
| July | 119.1 | 94.8 | 126.6 | 119.3 | 129.2 | 117.2 |
| August | 121.4 | 96.6 | 129.5 | 119.8 | 125.7 | 118.6 |
| September | 119.3 | 98.5 | 126.0 | 117.8 | 136.8 | 113.8 |
| October | 130.3 | 105.4 | 136.1 | 132.1 | 153.1 | 127.7 |
| November | 118.0 | 97.3 | 122.6 | 120.9 | 140.2 | 116.9 |
| December | 108.6 | 88.5 | 117.1 | 108.0 | 106.9 | 108.2 |
| January 1986 | 111.5 | 91.9 | 120.1 | 110.6 | 119.1 | 108.8 |
| February | 104.7 | 91.2 | 111.7 | 102.9 | 123.0 | 98.7 |
| March | 107.3 | 94.9 | 116.5 | 102.8 | 135.0 | 96.0 |
| April | 111.6 | 105.5 | 117.9 | 108.9 | 139.4 | 102.6 |
| May | 116.5 | 102.5 | 123.3 | 116.8 | 149.8 | 109.9 |
| June | 123.0 | 116.5 | 128.7 | 120.1 | 145.9 | 114.7 |
| July | 133.3 | 117.4 | 138.6 | 131.7 | 133.7 | 131.3 |
| August | 132.2 | 113.5 | 139.3 | 128.3 | 136.2 | 126.7 |
| September | 138.5 | 123.1 | 143.5 | 135.5 | 161.5 | 130.0 |
| October | 144.5 | 127.3 | 149.7 | 141.9 | 162.0 | 137.7 |
| November | 128.0 | 114.7 | 132.2 | 126.4 | 134.5 | 124.7 |
| December | 116.2 | 97.3 | 124.7 | 112.7 | 108.3 | 113.7 |
| January 1987 | 118.1 | 100.6 | 126.7 | 115.1 | 121.8 | 113.8 |
| February | 117.5 | 103.5 | 123.0 | 116.1 | 133.0 | 112.5 |
| March | 122.1 | 108.5 | 129.9 | 117.4 | 131.9 | 114.3 |
| April | 120.9 | 108.8 | 127.6 | 117.0 | 137.8 | 112.6 |

Source: FIBGE.

**Table 5A.5**
Growth of industrial production, accumulated over twelve months (%)

| Date | Total | Capital goods | Intermediate goods | Consumer goods | Durables | Nondurables |
|---|---|---|---|---|---|---|
| March 1985 | 8.1 | 16.1 | 9.6 | 3.1 | −1.2 | 4.1 |
| April | 8.0 | 14.5 | 9.0 | 4.1 | −0.4 | 5.2 |
| May | 7.6 | 12.9 | 8.4 | 4.3 | −0.6 | 5.4 |
| June | 7.1 | 12.6 | 7.4 | 4.4 | 1.1 | 5.2 |
| July | 6.9 | 12.6 | 6.8 | 4.9 | 3.2 | 5.4 |
| August | 7.0 | 12.0 | 6.7 | 5.6 | 4.4 | 6.0 |
| September | 7.7 | 12.8 | 6.8 | 7.1 | 9.3 | 6.7 |
| October | 7.8 | 12.3 | 6.9 | 7.5 | 12.5 | 6.6 |
| November | 8.0 | 12.0 | 6.9 | 8.0 | 14.0 | 6.9 |
| December | 8.5 | 12.3 | 7.2 | 9.0 | 15.1 | 7.9 |
| January 1986 | 8.3 | 11.4 | 7.1 | 9.4 | 14.2 | 8.3 |
| February | 9.2 | 12.8 | 7.8 | 10.7 | 17.1 | 9.2 |
| March | 8.6 | 11.7 | 7.3 | 10.3 | 17.4 | 8.6 |
| April | 9.9 | 15.1 | 8.5 | 11.4 | 23.7 | 8.7 |
| May | 10.7 | 17.8 | 8.5 | 12.6 | 30.4 | 8.9 |
| June | 11.6 | 20.8 | 9.1 | 13.7 | 33.2 | 9.6 |
| July | 11.9 | 21.3 | 9.3 | 13.4 | 30.3 | 9.8 |
| August | 11.9 | 21.9 | 9.3 | 13.2 | 29.8 | 9.6 |
| September | 12.2 | 22.3 | 9.8 | 13.2 | 27.7 | 9.9 |
| October | 12.0 | 22.5 | 9.7 | 12.4 | 24.5 | 9.6 |
| November | 11.9 | 22.7 | 9.8 | 11.6 | 21.7 | 9.3 |
| December | 11.5 | 22.1 | 9.4 | 10.8 | 20.4 | 8.5 |
| January 1987 | 11.0 | 21.7 | 8.9 | 9.9 | 19.1 | 7.9 |
| February | 10.9 | 21.0 | 8.9 | 9.7 | 17.4 | 8.0 |
| March | 11.6 | 21.4 | 9.5 | 10.5 | 15.2 | 9.4 |
| April | 10.8 | 18.2 | 9.0 | 9.6 | 10.2 | 9.4 |

Source: FIBGE.

**Table 5A.6**
Trade balance (billions of US dollars)

| Date | Exports | | | Imports | | | Balance |
|---|---|---|---|---|---|---|---|
| | Primary | Manufactured | Total | Oil | Other | Total | |
| March 1985 | 672 | 1262 | 1957 | 514 | 546 | 1060 | 897 |
| April | 827 | 1272 | 2124 | 462 | 584 | 1046 | 1078 |
| May | 860 | 1349 | 2239 | 347 | 654 | 1001 | 1238 |
| June | 747 | 1422 | 2195 | 442 | 523 | 965 | 1230 |
| July | 791 | 1371 | 2185 | 351 | 606 | 957 | 1228 |
| August | 770 | 1379 | 2170 | 460 | 613 | 1073 | 1097 |
| September | 796 | 1583 | 2404 | 484 | 615 | 1099 | 1305 |
| October | 677 | 1667 | 2370 | 516 | 740 | 1256 | 1114 |
| November | 607 | 1664 | 2292 | 501 | 713 | 1214 | 1078 |
| December | 834 | 1802 | 2665 | 458 | 997 | 1455 | 1210 |
| January 1986 | 542 | 1353 | 1910 | 444 | 765 | 1209 | 701 |
| February | 590 | 1145 | 1751 | 363 | 760 | 1123 | 628 |
| March | 832 | 1309 | 2157 | 226 | 795 | 1021 | 1136 |
| April | 820 | 1334 | 2172 | 139 | 741 | 880 | 1292 |
| May | 831 | 1441 | 2292 | 204 | 747 | 951 | 1341 |
| June | 644 | 1345 | 2000 | 167 | 762 | 929 | 1071 |
| July | 698 | 1506 | 2209 | 181 | 1009 | 1190 | 1019 |
| August | 622 | 1446 | 2099 | 174 | 966 | 1140 | 959 |
| September | 560 | 1290 | 1858 | 193 | 1117 | 1310 | 548 |
| October | 390 | 947 | 1340 | 205 | 1205 | 1410 | − 70 |
| November | 365 | 899 | 1277 | 222 | 1078 | 1300 | − 23 |
| December | 457 | 852 | 1329 | 268 | 1272 | 1540 | − 211 |
| January 1987 | 305 | 934 | 1259 | 276 | 1029 | 1305 | − 46 |
| February | 397 | 1046 | 1451 | 271 | 957 | 1228 | 223 |
| March | 482 | 932 | 1427 | 392 | 829 | 1221 | 206 |
| April | 629 | 1025 | 1663 | 288 | 855 | 1143 | 520 |

Source: Fundacao Comercio Exterior (FUNCEX), Gazeta Mercantil.

**Table 5A.7**
Monetary aggregates, balance (billions of cruzados)

| Date | MBª | M1ᵇ | M2ᶜ | M3ᵈ | M4ᵉ | M5ᶠ |
|---|---|---|---|---|---|---|
| March 1985 | 14.4 | 31.0 | 109.6 | 198.4 | 255.5 | 282.6 |
| April | 14.6 | 34.3 | 128.1 | 228.9 | 290.8 | 320.2 |
| May | 16.5 | 37.2 | 149.4 | 259.4 | 329.1 | 361.2 |
| June | 17.8 | 44.3 | 173.2 | 294.3 | 375.0 | 409.5 |
| July | 19.6 | 49.1 | 201.0 | 329.7 | 417.8 | 456.1 |
| August | 22.4 | 56.0 | 227.1 | 261.6 | 459.8 | 503.4 |
| September | 25.8 | 65.0 | 251.2 | 403.0 | 507.2 | 554.6 |
| October | 26.8 | 67.5 | 283.8 | 452.4 | 568.7 | 621.8 |
| November | 32.1 | 83.9 | 319.0 | 504.7 | 629.2 | 689.4 |
| December | 45.5 | 112.0 | 370.5 | 588.1 | 737.3 | 803.7 |
| January 1986 | 45.9 | 102.1 | 395.4 | 660.6 | 829.6 | 906.9 |
| February | 51.5 | 116.5 | 448.3 | 760.2 | 966.1 | 1050.7 |
| March | 70.0 | 209.8 | 580.0 | 880.5 | 1085.2 | 1171.4 |
| April | 94.8 | 250.6 | 617.0 | 900.6 | 1098.3 | 1186.9 |
| May | 109.0 | 288.5 | 656.5 | 939.6 | 1133.1 | 1224.6 |
| June | 120.6 | 334.2 | 689.1 | 977.8 | 1174.3 | 1272.9 |
| July | 137.6 | 333.5 | 678.2 | 973.1 | 1182.2 | 1282.1 |
| August | 145.8 | 356.2 | 705.1 | 1005.1 | 1244.4 | 1342.1 |
| September | 149.9 | 376.4 | 734.6 | 1046.9 | 1313.3 | 1413.0 |
| October | 157.6 | 402.0 | 739.7 | 1055.4 | 1364.4 | 1473.2 |
| November | 172.5 | 422.4 | 741.8 | 1059.1 | 1396.6 | 1505.1 |
| December | 178.9 | 452.1 | 811.4 | 1139.5 | 1493.2 | 1598.5 |
| January 1987 | 172.4 | 347.2 | 764.9 | 1130.5 | 1524.6 | 1630.9 |
| February | 164.3 | 371.9 | 882.5 | 1338.7 | 1766.2 | 1869.3 |
| March | 169.2 | 412.5 | 997.2 | 1570.1 | 1990.1 | 2147.6 |
| April | 187.0 | 363.4 | 1073.4 | 1756.0 | 2195.0 | 2352.4 |

Source: Banco Central do Brasil.
a. Monetary base.
b. Means of payments.
c. M1 + federal public debt net of holdings by monetary authority.
d. M2 + savings deposits.
e. M3 + time deposits.
f. M4 + state and municipal bonds and bills, bills of exchange, and housing bonds.

**Table 5A.8**
Monetary aggregates, rates of growth, monthly changes (%)

| Date | MB[a] | M1[b] | M2[c] | M3[d] | M4[e] | M5[f] |
|---|---|---|---|---|---|---|
| April 1985 | 1.2 | 10.7 | 16.9 | 15.4 | 13.8 | 13.3 |
| May | 13.2 | 8.4 | 16.7 | 13.3 | 13.2 | 12.8 |
| June | 7.8 | 19.0 | 15.9 | 13.5 | 13.9 | 13.4 |
| July | 10.1 | 10.9 | 16.0 | 12.0 | 11.4 | 11.4 |
| August | 14.0 | 14.1 | 13.0 | 9.7 | 10.1 | 10.4 |
| September | 15.1 | 16.0 | 10.6 | 11.4 | 10.3 | 10.2 |
| October | 4.1 | 3.8 | 13.0 | 12.3 | 12.1 | 12.1 |
| November | 19.7 | 24.3 | 12.4 | 11.6 | 10.6 | 10.9 |
| December | 41.6 | 33.4 | 16.1 | 16.5 | 17.2 | 16.6 |
| January 1986 | 1.0 | −8.8 | 6.7 | 12.3 | 12.5 | 12.8 |
| February | 12.2 | 14.1 | 13.4 | 15.1 | 16.4 | 15.9 |
| March | 35.9 | 80.1 | 29.4 | 15.8 | 12.3 | 11.5 |
| April | 35.3 | 19.4 | 6.4 | 2.3 | 1.2 | 1.3 |
| May | 15.0 | 15.1 | 6.4 | 4.3 | 3.2 | 3.2 |
| June | 10.6 | 15.8 | 5.0 | 4.1 | 3.6 | 3.9 |
| July | 14.1 | −0.2 | −1.6 | −0.5 | 0.7 | 0.7 |
| August | 6.0 | 6.8 | 4.0 | 3.3 | 5.3 | 4.7 |
| September | 2.8 | 5.7 | 4.2 | 4.2 | 5.5 | 5.3 |
| October | 5.2 | 6.8 | 0.7 | 0.8 | 3.9 | 4.3 |
| November | 9.4 | 5.1 | 0.3 | 0.4 | 2.4 | 2.2 |
| December | 3.7 | 7.0 | 9.4 | 7.6 | 6.9 | 6.2 |
| January 1987 | −3.6 | −23.2 | −5.7 | −0.8 | 2.1 | 2.0 |
| February | −4.7 | 7.1 | 15.4 | 18.4 | 15.9 | 14.6 |
| March | 3.0 | 10.9 | 13.0 | 17.3 | 12.7 | 14.9 |
| April | 10.5 | −11.9 | 7.6 | 11.8 | 10.3 | 9.5 |

Source: Banco Central do Brasil.
a. Monetary base.
b. Means of payments.
c. M1 + federal public debt net of holdings by monetary authority.
d. M2 + savings deposits.
e. M3 + time deposits.
f. M4 + state and municipal bonds and bills, bills of exchange, and housing bonds.

**Table 5A.9**
Nominal rates of return (%)

| Date | Rio de Janeiro stock exchange index (IBV) | Sao Paulo stock exchange index (IBOVESPA) | Parallel market dollars | Certificates of deposit | Savings deposits | Overnight deposits |
|---|---|---|---|---|---|---|
| March 1985 | − 1.2 | − 5.2 | 7.2 | 14.1 | 13.3 | 11.8 |
| April | 1.7 | 0.4 | 8.7 | 13.2 | 12.4 | 11.9 |
| May | 30.9 | 44.8 | 13.6 | 11.2 | 10.6 | 11.1 |
| June | 34.0 | 46.7 | 12.6 | 10.5 | 9.8 | 9.7 |
| July | 26.2 | 20.9 | 18.0 | 8.8 | 8.1 | 8.8 |
| August | 28.3 | 23.2 | 12.7 | 9.4 | 8.7 | 8.3 |
| September | 22.1 | 31.2 | 7.2 | 10.1 | 9.7 | 9.2 |
| October | 41.5 | 27.9 | 4.9 | 9.9 | 9.6 | 9.4 |
| November | 12.9 | 12.5 | 17.1 | 12.0 | 11.7 | 9.2 |
| December | − 11.8 | − 15.5 | 18.5 | 14.3 | 13.9 | 12.3 |
| January 1986 | 6.3 | 1.4 | 7.7 | 17.3 | 16.8 | 15.0 |
| February | 13.7 | 24.0 | 11.3 | 15.4 | 14.9 | 13.1 |
| March | 34.4 | 52.4 | 0.8 | 0.9 | 1.2 | 0.7 |
| April | 19.2 | 23.5 | 8.7 | 0.7 | 1.2 | 0.7 |
| May | − 2.0 | − 11.0 | 6.9 | 1.1 | 1.2 | 0.7 |
| June | − 0.4 | − 9.6 | 1.5 | 1.2 | 1.7 | 0.8 |
| July | − 5.8 | 1.7 | 6.8 | 1.4 | 1.7 | 1.1 |
| August | − 12.4 | − 17.7 | 8.1 | 1.8 | 1.9 | 1.5 |
| September | − 23.2 | − 23.8 | − 2.2 | 2.6 | 2.0 | 1.8 |
| October | 14.9 | 20.4 | 13.6 | 2.5 | 2.3 | 1.9 |
| November | − 22.1 | − 21.1 | 8.0 | 3.7 | 3.2 | 3.8 |
| December | − 7.6 | − 2.3 | − 4.0 | 8.2 | 2.8 | 5.5 |
| January 1987 | − 19.4 | − 23.3 | − 0.4 | 13.1 | 17.4 | 11.0 |
| February | − 8.7 | − 3.7 | 3.2 | 17.2 | 20.2 | 19.6 |
| March | − 0.7 | − 3.0 | 8.4 | 14.9 | 15.0 | 12.3 |
| April | 26.2 | 29.3 | 2.2 | 15.6 | 17.6 | 15.3 |

Source: Associacao Nacional das Instituicoes do Mercado Aberto (ANDIMA).

**Table 5A.10**
Average exchange rate

| Date | Official Cz$/US$ | Parallel Cz$/US$ | Premium (%) |
|---|---|---|---|
| March 1985 | 4.16 | 5.15 | 23.8 |
| April | 4.72 | 5.48 | 16.1 |
| May | 5.24 | 6.20 | 18.3 |
| June | 5.74 | 6.98 | 21.6 |
| July | 6.22 | 8.24 | 32.5 |
| August | 6.71 | 9.28 | 38.3 |
| September | 7.46 | 9.95 | 33.4 |
| October | 8.19 | 10.44 | 27.5 |
| November | 8.93 | 12.23 | 37.0 |
| December | 9.91 | 14.49 | 46.2 |
| January 1986 | 11.31 | 15.60 | 37.9 |
| February | 13.03 | 17.37 | 33.3 |
| March | 13.84 | 17.50 | 26.4 |
| April | 13.84 | 19.03 | 37.5 |
| May | 13.84 | 20.35 | 47.0 |
| June | 13.84 | 20.65 | 49.2 |
| July | 13.84 | 22.06 | 59.4 |
| August | 13.84 | 23.85 | 72.3 |
| September | 13.84 | 23.34 | 68.6 |
| October | 13.97 | 26.51 | 89.8 |
| November | 14.11 | 28.64 | 103.0 |
| December | 14.55 | 27.50 | 89.0 |
| January 1987 | 15.70 | 27.39 | 74.5 |
| February | 18.14 | 28.27 | 55.8 |
| March | 21.01 | 30.64 | 45.8 |
| April | 23.71 | 31.32 | 32.1 |

Source: Gazeta Mercantil.

**Table 5A.11**
Other variables, monthly changes (%)

| Date | Average exchange rate | Nominal wages | Open unemploy-ment rate | Sales[a] |
|---|---|---|---|---|
| March 1985 | 10.6 | 6.3 | 6.5 | 8.6 |
| April | 13.5 | 14.5 | 6.1 | 8.8 |
| May | 11.0 | 24.1 | 5.9 | 10.8 |
| June | 9.5 | 9.5 | 5.6 | 11.4 |
| July | 8.4 | 12.4 | 5.4 | 14.1 |
| August | 7.9 | 8.4 | 5.3 | 15.7 |
| September | 11.2 | 3.6 | 5.4 | 16.0 |
| October | 9.8 | 19.4 | 4.7 | 17.9 |
| November | 9.0 | 21.0 | 3.9 | 18.0 |
| December | 11.0 | 7.0 | 3.5 | 18.0 |
| January 1986 | 14.1 | 19.8 | 4.2 | 13.1 |
| February | 15.2 | 12.9 | 4.4 | 15.1 |
| March | 6.2 | 11.9 | 4.4 | 13.7 |
| April | 0.0 | 0.9 | 4.2 | 19.1 |
| May | 0.0 | 2.5 | 4.1 | 21.4 |
| June | 0.0 | 0.6 | 3.8 | 22.8 |
| July | 0.0 | 3.6 | 3.6 | 23.6 |
| August | 0.0 | 3.1 | 3.5 | 22.8 |
| September | 0.0 | 2.4 | 3.2 | 24.2 |
| October | 0.9 | 3.6 | 3.0 | 26.5 |
| November | 1.0 | 6.5 | 2.6 | 26.7 |
| December | 3.1 | 4.5 | 2.2 | 26.7 |
| January 1987 | 7.9 | 5.8 | 3.2 | 17.9 |
| February | 15.5 | 11.1 | 3.4 | 15.7 |
| March | 15.8 | 23.7 | 3.3 | 8.6 |
| April | 12.9 | 15.8 | 3.4 | 1.3 |

Source: FIBGE, Federacao das Industrias do Estado de São Paulo (FIESP), FGV.
a. Accumulated over the year, compared to same period in previous year.

## Notes

1. This section draws heavily on Modiano (1985a, 1985b).

2. For a nonanalytical exposition of the relation between conflict and inertia, see Bacha (1986).

3. Equation (5.3) is a discrete time version of the expression for the average real wage earlier derived by Simonsen (1984) and Modiano (1985b). The discrete time version is adopted here for consistency with the conversion rules of the Cruzado Plan.

4. This section draws heavily on Modiano (1986). The data used in this section can be found in the appendix.

5. The full compensation for the loss in real wages during the month would require the substitution of $p_{T-j}$ for $p_{T+1-j}$ in equation (5.4).

6. In terms of figures 5.1 and 5.2 the introduction of the wage bonus meant that the Cruzado Plan established a new peak real wage (the vertical intercept of the $IE$ curve) above the prevailing average real wage but below the cruzeiro peak real wage.

7. An effective income redistribution toward wage earners would also require an upward movement of the $DE$ curve in figure 5.1.

8. As the link between the average real wage and the inflation rate had not been eliminated, the $IE$ curve in figure 5.1 rotated counterclockwise without becoming horizontal.

9. By substituting 0.0167 for $p$ and 12 for $h$ in equation (5.3), the peak-to-average wage ratio is 1.094.

10. In the limit, when $p$ approaches 0 in equation (5.5), it can be shown that $w = w^*$.

11. The expressions for the average real wage under twelve-month and six-month adjustments are derived in Modiano (1985b).

12. With the introduction of the wage sliding scale the $IE$ curve in figure 5.1 becomes discontinuous for annual rates of inflation above 20% and, according to table 5.2, flatter than under the six-month adjustments for annual rates of inflation above 40.4%.

13. The data used in this section are presented in the appendix.

14. Carneiro (1987), Franco (1986), and Marques (1987) discuss in greater detail the first ten months of the plan.

15. The academic contribution of present Finance Minister Bresser Pereira to the discussions concerning inflation inertia and the heterodox shock is summarized in Bresser Pereira and Nakano (1984, 1986).

16. The advantages and disadvantages of this new indexation rule are discussed in Modiano (1985b, 1986).

# References

Arida, P., and A. Lara-Resende. 1985. "Inertial inflation and monetary reform in Brazil," in *Inflation and Indexation: Argentina, Brazil and Israel*, J. Williamson, ed. (Cambridge, Mass.: MIT Press), 27–45.

Bacha, E. L. 1982. *Macroeconomic Analysis. An Intermediate Text*. Rio de Janeiro: IPEA/INPES. (In Portuguese.)

Bacha, E. L. 1986. *On Inertia and Conflict: The Cruzado Plan and Its Challenge*. Discussion Paper 131. Department of Economics, Catholic University, Rio de Janeiro. (In Portuguese.)

Bresser Pereira, L., and Y. Nakano. 1984. *Inflation and Recession*. São Paulo: Editora Brasiliense. (In Portuguese.)

Bresser Pereira, L., and Y. Nakano. 1986. "Inertial inflation and heterodox shocks in Brazil," in *Inertial Inflation, Theories of Inflation and the Cruzado Plan*, J. M. Rego, ed. (Rio de Janeiro: Editora Paz e Terra). (In Portuguese.)

Carneiro, D. D. 1987. *The Cruzado Experience: An Untimely Evaluation after Ten Months*. Discussion Paper 152. Department of Economics, Catholic University, Rio de Janeiro. (In Portuguese.)

Dornbusch, R., and M. H. Simonsen. 1987. *Inflation Stabilization with Incomes Policy Support: A Review of the Experience in Argentina, Brazil and Israel*. New York: Group of Thirty.

Franco, G. H. B. 1986. *The Cruzado Plan: Diagnosis, Performance, and Perspectives on November 15*. Discussion Paper 144. Department of Economics, Catholic University, Rio de Janeiro. (In Portuguese.)

Lopes, F. L. 1982. "Inflation and the level of activity: An econometric study." *Pesquisa e Planejamento Econômico* 12(3):639–670. (In Portuguese.)

Lopes, F. L. 1984a. "Inertial inflation, hyperinflation, and disinflation: Notes and conjectures." *Revista da ANPEC* (November), 9. (In Portuguese.)

Lopes, F. L. 1984b. "Only a heterodox shock can cure inflation." *Economia em Perspectiva*. (In Portuguese.)

Lopes, F. L. 1986. "Problems of the price index on the transition to stability." Rio de Janeiro. Mimeo. (In Portuguese.)

Lopes, F. L., and A. Lara-Resende, 1981. "On the causes of the recent acceleration of inflation." *Pesquisa e Planejamento Econômico* 11(3):599–616. (In Portuguese.)

Marques, M. S. B. 1987. *The Cruzado Plan: Theory and Practice.* Paper 4/87. Centro de Estudos Monetários e de Economica Internacional, IBRE/FGV, Rio de Janeiro. (In Portuguese.)

Modiano, E. M. 1983. "The dynamics of salaries and prices on the Brazilian economy: 1966–81. *Pesquisa e Planejamento Econômico* 13(1):39–68. (In Portuguese.)

Modiano, E. M. 1985a. *"On Argentine Shocks and the Brazilian Dilemma.* Discussion Paper 112. Department of Economics, Catholic University, Rio de Janeiro. (In Portuguese.)

Modiano, E. M. 1985b. "A gradual review of past inflation and future prices." *Pesquisa e Planejamento Econômico* 15(3):513–536. (In Portuguese.)

Modiano, E. M. 1985c. "Salaries, prices, and exchange: The multiplying of shocks and an indexed economy." *Pesquisa e Planejamento Econômico* 15(1):1–32. (In Portuguese.)

Modiano, E. M. 1986. *Inflation of the Cruzado: Economic Policy in the First Year of the New Republic.* Rio de Janeiro: Editora Campus. (In Portuguese.)

Modiano, E. M., and D. D. Carneiro. 1984. *The Magic of the New Cruzeiro and the Generation of New Inflation.* Discussion Paper 78. Department of Economics, Catholic University, Rio de Janeiro. (In Portuguese.)

Ocampo, J. A. 1987. "A comparative evaluation of four recent anti-inflation plans." Fedesarollo, Bogota. Mimeo. (In Portuguese.)

Simonsen, M. H. 1984. "Deindexation and monetary reform." *Conjuntura Econômica* 28(11):101–105. (In Portuguese.)

Taylor, L. 1983. *Structuralist Macroeconomics.* New York: Basic Books.

# 6

# Price Stabilization and Incomes Policies: Theory and the Brazilian Case Study

## Mario Henrique Simonsen

That aggregate demand discipline is a necessary condition for sustained price stability has long been known by economists and well-advised policymakers. Yet it may not be sufficient to stop a big inflation under conditions of tolerable unemployment, as evidenced by the failure of a number of orthodox programs that overlooked inflationary inertia. Not surprisingly incomes policies have often been brought on stage to tackle the supply side of inflation and to ease the side effects of stabilization programs.

An adequate theoretical framework is needed to explain what causes inflationary inertia and how incomes policies can break the dependence of the inflation rate on its past behavior. The traditional explanation of the late 1960s, which combined the natural unemployment rate hypothesis with adaptive expectations, was a benchmark in terms of interpreting inflation as an autoregressive process, although it never made clear how incomes policies might affect expectations. In any case it was soon eclipsed by the rational expectations revolution that dismissed adaptative expectations as an "ad hoc" assumption usually inconsistent with optimal decision making.

Under the aegis of the new classic economics, inertial inflation can only spring from two sources: autoregressive expected rates of monetary expansion and outstanding contracts based on previous inflationary expectations. The first source can be dried up by a credible monetary rule, once money supply is put under the control of a respectable and independent Central Bank. The second source can only be responsible for temporary and dampened inertia, the so-called Fischer-Taylor inertia. Hence a painless inflation cure with no incomes policy support appears as a strong possibility, perhaps not in a shock treatment but at least in a gradualistic approach to price stability in line with the maturity of old contracts. Because the length of nonindexed contracts is a decreasing function of the inflation rate, the transition from high to zero inflation could be quite rapid. For instance, if money wages are reset once a year, with adjustment dates for different labor groups being uniformly distributed over time, inflation rates can be brought down from 20% in year 0 to 9% in year 1 and to 0% in year 2 with no recession at all.[1]

Anti-inflationary policies in the early 1980s were painful enough to suggest that inflation rates might be held back by a force ignored in rational expectations models, namely, inertia caused by strategic interdependence among private economic agents. Here I identify this source of inertia by bringing inflation and price setting into the realm of game theory. The central arguments of my analysis can be summarized by the following five points.

1. To avoid the fiction of the Walrasian auctioneer, markets should be described as an $(n + 1)$-person noncooperative game, where players are $n$ private participants and the government.

2. The key equilibrium concept of the theory of noncooperative games, that of Nash equilibrium, means nothing but ex post wisdom, as stressed in section 6.1. Whether it also corresponds to what really matters, namely, ex ante rationality, is a highly debatable issue. Players must choose their strategies before knowing other participants' choices, and in many instances a player can be severely damaged if he chooses a Nash strategy and the others do not. Cautious players may prudently prefer a maximin strategy, which guarantees the best possible yield in the worst conceivable scenario.

3. Rational expectations macroeconomics implicitly assumes that intelligent participants of a noncooperative game immediately locate a Nash equilibrium, as shown in section 6.2. This assumption is often justified by bringing on stage an auctioneer who prevents any transaction so long as any participant can improve his payoff by unilaterally changing his strategy. That the outcome is a Nash equilibrium is nothing but a tautology. Yet there is no place for the auctioneer, either in game theory or in the real world.

4. Prudent playing, namely, choosing maximin rather than Nash strategies, yields price and inflation inertia, as suggested by the price-setting model developed in section 6.3. In short, let us assume that after prolonged inflation the Central Bank announces that it will stop printing money so as to keep nominal GNP unchanged. Even if the general perception is that nominal GNP will be immediately stabilized by a new monetary constitution (an extreme hypothesis, because monetary austerity is not usually backed by a constitutional reform), prudent price setters should not take

the lead in stopping price increases so long as they consider the possibility of further price increases in other sectors. In fact, the first to jump has little to gain if he is followed by the remaining participants in the game and much to lose of he jumps alone. In the latter case the penalty is concrete, a real income cut, and the reward is abstract: additional customers' orders that cannot be met because the day has only twenty-four hours. The fact that excess demand does not mean additional effective demand or additional income helps to explain why prudent price setters should stick to something such as a maximin strategy.

5. In a repeated game with a large number of small players, leaving virtually no space for coalitions, threats, signaling, or Stackelberg dominance, maximin strategies that do not yield a Nash equilibrium are not likely to be indefinitely repeated. The price-setting model of section 6.3 indicates how prudent players in a repeated game may gradually narrow the conceivable range of other participants' strategies, triggering a "tatônnement approach" to a Nash equilibrium. Little can be said, however, about convergence speeds, which may be painfully slow after a prolonged period of high inflation rates.

The rationale for incomes policies is presented in section 6.4. Governments should play the role of the Walrasian auctioneer, speeding up the location of the Nash equilibrium, namely, using the visible hand to achieve what rational expectations models assume to be the immediate performance of the invisible hand. As such, the central function of incomes policies is not to constrain individual decision making but to tell each actor how others will play. That the temporary success of incomes policies may lead policymakers to ignore that price stability cannot be sustained without aggregate demand discipline is a true risk. In fact, the list of incomes policy failures is too long to be neglected. Yet the converse is also true. Trying to fight a big inflation from only the demand side may lead to such dismal stagflation that policymakers may well conclude that life with inflation is preferable to life with an orthodox stabilization program. Moreover, successful incomes policies combining a concerted approach to price stabilization from both the demand and the supply side should not be treated as exceptions. Inspiring examples are Brazil, Argentina, and Uruguay in the mid-1960s, France, Spain, and Italy in the early 1980s, and Israel since 1985.

A true failure was the Brazilian Cruzado Plan, discussed in section 6.6. Chronic inflation was already part of the Brazilian way of life and led to widespread indexation, as explained in section 6.5. As a consequence, inflationary inertia became strongly rooted, so that an orthodox stabilization program could hardly succeed. The big mistake of the government was to confound necessary with sufficient conditions and to diagnose inflation as a purely inertial problem. Demand inflation took its revenge.

## 6.1   Nash versus Maximin Strategies

What is rational behavior under strategical interdependence, that is, when each individual's payoff depends not only on his actions but also on other people's decisions? This is the central question that game theory proposes to answer. Since the pioneering work of von Neumann and Morgenstern, much light has been thrown on how to approach a number of problems involving conflict and interdependence. Yet, except for a limited class of games, a convincing concept of rationality has never been established. Game theorists are not to be blamed for that. One must simply recognize that their program was too ambitious.

Let us concentrate on noncooperative games, which describe how a market economy works in the absence of a Walrasian auctioneer. The key equilibrium concept was established by Nash and is an extension of Cournot's solution to the oligopoly problem. A Nash equilibrium is defined as a set of strategies, one for each player, such that no player can improve his expected utility by unilaterally changing his strategy. At first glance it sounds like a satisfactory description of rational behavior in noncooperative games. Yet some reflection shows that rational behavior, pragmatically understood as how intelligent people do behave and not how game theorists would like them to behave, is a much more intriguing issue. In fact, Nash equilibria are defined for games in normal form, which are defined as games of imperfect information: Players must choose their strategies before knowing other participants' choices. Once this point is made explicit, the true meaning of a Nash equilibrium is apparent: Except as far as the states of nature are concerned, this equilibrium is nothing but ex post wisdom in the sense of nonrepentance.

To what extent a Nash equilibrium also corresponds to what really matters, namely, ex ante rationality, is a much more intricate question. In most games with incomplete information, where each player knows his own payoff but ignores the payoffs of other participants, players simply have no means of immediately locating a Nash equilibrium. And even in games with complete information and with one unique Nash equilibrium, choosing a Nash strategy may seriously harm some player should the others fail to choose Nash strategies. Because decisions must be made before knowing other people's decisions, prudence may be a serious obstacle to the prompt location of a Nash equilibrium.

Extreme risk aversion relates to another game-theoretic concept: maximin strategies. A maximin strategy guarantees the best possible yield in the worst conceivable scenario in terms of other players' choices.

What is ex ante rational behavior in noncooperative games with imperfect information? Choosing a Nash strategy, a maximin strategy, or something in between? The question may be easily skipped for that class of games, which I call A-games, in which any Nash equilibrium is a combination of maximin strategies and in which, conversely, any combination of dominant maximin strategies yields a Nash equilibrium. These can be viewed as easy games, in the sense that playing defensively is the route to ex post wisdom. Zero-sum two-person games with a saddle point and games in which a dominant strategy is available for each player (such as the prisoners' dilemma) belong to this class, where Nash equilibria can be accepted as describing ex ante rationality. As another example, let us take the bimatrix game:[2]

|             | $Y_I$   | $Y_{II}$ | $Y_{III}$ |
|-------------|---------|----------|-----------|
| $X_I$       | (3; 7)  | (0; 4)   | (3; 2)    |
| $X_{II}$    | (2; 3)  | (3; 5)   | (4; 1)    |
| $X_{III}$   | (5; 7)  | (1; 9)   | (3; 5)    |

This is a variable-sum two-person game with no dominant strategy for either player. Yet it is an A-game because the combination $(X_{II}; Y_{II})$ of maximin strategies yields the unique Nash equilibrium.

Complications emerge in B-games, in which Nash equilibria are not the outcome of maximin strategic choices. Here, prudence must be left aside to hit a Nash equilibrium. Let us start with games of complete information and one unique Nash equilibrium. To act as a Nash strategist, every player must bet that all others will also behave as Nash strategists. Whether taking such a bet should be classified as rational behavior or as irresponsible decision making depends on two issues: (1) to what extent each player can trust the others as Nash strategists and (2) how much each player can lose if he chooses a Nash strategy and some others do not. The question is intricate enough to have no definite answer. Yet common sense suggests that players will act defensively, except perhaps in games involving a small group of experts that trust each other as Nash strategists. As an example of a B-game, let us examine the following bimatrix game:

|         | $Y_I$    | $Y_{II}$    | $Y_{III}$   |
|---------|----------|-------------|-------------|
| $X_I$   | $(3; 2)$ | $(-10; 8)$  | $(-3; 5)$   |
| $X_{II}$| $(8; 3)$ | $(5; 5)$    | $(-10; 4)$  |
| $X_{III}$| $(4; 6)$| $(5; -8)$   | $(4; 4)$    |

Maximin strategies are $X_{III}$ and $Y_{III}$, ensuring each player a minimum gain equal to 4. Yet the unique Nash equilibrium is $(X_{II}; Y_{II})$.

To hit the Nash equilibrium in the first move in this game, each player must firmly believe that the other is going to behave as a Nash strategist. One should note that each player has much to lose if he chooses the Nash strategy and the other cautiously prefers the maximin route. In fact, with $(X_{II}; Y_{III})$, player X would lose 10. Similarly, with $(X_{III}; Y_{II})$, player Y's loss would be 8. It seems plausible, therefore, to assume that in the first move both players will choose their maximin strategies.

As a more striking example let us examine the game of half of the average. In a classroom with $n$ students, each student is asked to write on a slip of paper a real number in the closed interval $[0; 1]$. Indicating by $x_i$ the number chosen by the $i$th student, her payoff will be, in dollars,

0        if $x_i > s$,

100     if $x_i = s$,

$-100$   if $x_i < s$,

where

$$s = \frac{1}{2n} \sum_{i=1}^{n} x_i,$$

namely, half of the average.

If each student could guess the average choice $y_i$ of the remaining students, namely,

$$(n-1)y_i = \sum_{j \neq i} x_j,$$

each would be able to collect \$100 by choosing

$$x_i = \frac{n-1}{2n-1} y_i. \tag{6.1}$$

The problem, of course, is that each student must choose $x_i$ before knowing $y_i$. In the unique Nash equilibrium all students would write $x_i = 0$, and each of them would receive $100. Yet $x_i = 0$ is a highly imprudent strategy, at least in a large classroom. In fact, if somebody else makes a different choice, the Nash strategist, instead of collecting $100, will have to pay a $100 fine.

Because in equation (6.1) $0 \leqslant y_i \leqslant 1$, any choice

$$x_i \geqslant \frac{n-1}{2n-1}$$

is a maximin play. The best maximin strategy is to turn the inequality into an equality, because it guarantees that the student will suffer no loss and still allows the possibility of a $100 premium should all other students choose $x_j = 1$.[3]

The foregoing discussion stresses an essential point: There is no reason to believe that rational players in a noncooperative B-game should immediately locate a Nash equilibrium. Whether they will stick to maximin strategies or take some further risks is a debatable issue, depending on individual psychology and risk aversion. In any case, acting as a Nash strategist without the assurance that all other players will do the same cannot be taken as a paradigm of rationality but rather one of imprudent behavior.

## 6.2   Rational Expectations and Nash Equilibria

Rational expectations macroeconomics is based on a particular game-theoretic framework developed by Lucas and Sargent in the following way. They let $h$ denote a collection of decision rules of private agents. Each element of $h$ in itself a function that maps some private agent's information about his state at a particular point in time into his decision at that point in time. Consumption, investment, and demand functions for money are all examples of elements of $h$. Lucas and Sargent let $f$ denote a collection of elements that forms the "environment" facing private agents. Some elements of $f$ represent rules of the game or decision rules selected by the government that map the government's information at some date into its decisions at that date. For example, included among $f$ might be decision rules for fiscal and monetary policy variables. The principle of strategic interdependence establishes that $h$ is a function of $f$:

$$h = T(f). \tag{6.2}$$

The mapping $T$ represents cross-equation restrictions because each element of $h$ and of $f$ is itself a decision rule or equation determining the choice of some variable under some agent's control.

Under Lucas and Sargent's principle of strategic interdependence (Lucas and Sargent 1981; Sargent 1985), economics can be viewed as a two-person game in which government and private agents interact. Active economic policies mean that the government acts as a dominant Stackelberg player: To maximize a social utility function $U(h, f)$, the government chooses strategies to maximize $U(T(f), f)$. The possibility of Stackelberg warfare between government and private sector is ruled out because private agents are assumed to be numerous and dispersed. [Sargent (1985) argues, nevertheless, that, once government is disaggregated between monetary authorities and fiscal authorities, Stackelberg warfare becomes a true possibility. In fact, this is how he views the policy mix of the Reagan administration, combining tight monetary with loose fiscal policies.][4]

Treating the private sector as a single player clearly involves an aggregation process. The assumption that, as opposed to government, the private sector cannot assume the role of a Stackelberg dominant player because private agents are numerous and dispersed clearly reveals that the principle of strategic interdependence summarized by equation (6.2) transforms what should be described as an $(n + 1)$-person game into a two-person game. The underlying aggregation assumptions are worth discussing.

Let us assume that there are $n$ private agents, and let us denote by $h_i$ the optimum set of decision rules by the $i$th agent. Aggregate private sector decisions are obviously a function of each individual agent's choices:

$$h = G(h_1, h_2, \ldots, h_n). \tag{6.3}$$

Optimum decision making by each private agent depends on his perception $f_i$ of the environment as well as on the strategies chosen by the other private agents:

$$h_1 = H_1(h_2, \ldots, h_n, f_1),$$

$$h_2 = H_2(h_1, h_3, \ldots, h_n, f_2),$$

$$\vdots$$

$$h_n = H_n(h_1, \ldots, h_{n-1}, f_n). \tag{6.4}$$

Equations (6.3) and (6.4) provide the microeconomic foundations for the principle of strategic interdependence. To derive the Lucas and Sargent equation (6.2) three assumptions are needed:

1. The environment vector is common knowledge, namely, $f_1 = f_2 = \ldots = f_n = f$. This means that, besides sharing the same perception of how the

government will act, all private agents acknowledge that their expectations for government policies are shared by all other private agents.

2. With $f_1 = f_2 = \ldots = f_n = f$, there exists one unique solution $(\hat{h}_1, \hat{h}_2, \ldots, \hat{h}_n)$ to equation system (6.4).

3. Private sector agents are able to solve equation (6.4) under the assumption $f_1 = f_2 = \ldots = f_n = f$ and choose their decision vectors by making $h_i = \hat{h}_i$ $(i = 1, \ldots, n)$.

The correspondence between rational expectations macroeconomics and Nash equilibria now becomes evident: For each environment vector $f$ private agents solve their internal strategic interdependence problem by immediately locating a Nash equilibrium. Under this assumption the original $(n + 1)$-person game is then transformed into a two-person game.

The assumption that the environment vector $f$ is to be treated as common knowledge may be challenged on the grounds that information is not a free good. Traditional criticism of rational expectations macroeconomics has focused on this point. Yet this is nothing but a convenient hypothesis for simple modeling, one that can be relaxed in more complex rational expectations exercises. The central weakness of the rational expectations macroeconomic hypothesis is to be found in a much more sophisticated point. It implicitly assumes that rational participants in a noncooperative game with millions of players promptly move to a Nash equilibrium. As stressed in section 6.1, in B-games this is nothing but a confusion between ex ante and ex post rationality.[5]

## 6.3  A Price-Setting Game

Let us assume an economy with a continuum of nonstorable goods, each one produced by an individual price setter, in which the nominal output $R$ is controlled by the government. In line with monetary theory, one may assume that the Central Bank controls some monetary aggregate that determines $R$. The nominal output is preannounced by a credible administration, but prices must be set simultaneously, each agent ignoring how others will decide, except for the fact that no good is expected to be priced above $P_{max}$. This means that both $R$ and $P_{max}$ are common knowledge.

Production starts after prices have been set, according to consumers' orders. Because goods cannot be stored, this rules out the possibility of excess supplies. Supply shortages may indeed occur but are not anticipated by consumers.

All individuals have the same utility function:

$$U_x = L_x^b \left\{ \int_0^1 q_{xy}^a \, dy \right\}^{1/a} \qquad (0 < a \leqslant \tfrac{1}{2}; b > 0), \tag{6.5}$$

where $U_x$ stands for utility, $L_x$ for leisure time, and $q_{xy}$ for the consumption of good $y$ by individual $x$ $(0 \leqslant x \leqslant 1)$.

The supply of good $x$ equals the number of daily working hours by individual $x$:

$$S_x = 24 - L_x. \tag{6.6}$$

Hence, by indicating by $P_x$ the price of good $x$ and by $R_x$ the nominal income of individual $x$, we obtain

$$R_x = P_x S_x. \tag{6.7}$$

Individual $x$'s budget constraint is expressed by

$$\int_0^1 P_y q_{xy} \, dy = R_x. \tag{6.8}$$

Because nominal output equals the sum of individual incomes,

$$\int_0^1 R_x \, dx = R. \tag{6.9}$$

Let us first determine demand for good $y$ by individual $x$. Because utility function (6.5) leaves no room for corner equilibria, marginal utilities must be proportional to prices:

$$a q_{xy}^{a-1} = \lambda_x P_y.$$

Taking into account budget constraint equation (6.8), we obtain

$$q_{xy} = R_x P^m / P_y^{m+1}, \tag{6.10}$$

where

$$m = \frac{a}{1-a} \tag{6.11}$$

and the consumer price index $P$ is determined by

$$P^{-m} = \int_0^1 P_y^{-m} \, dy. \tag{6.12}$$

It should be noted that, because $0 < a \leqslant \frac{1}{2}$,

$$0 < m \leqslant 1. \tag{6.13}$$

Taking into account equation (6.9), the total demand for good $y$ is given by

$$Q_y = RP^m / P_y^{m+1}. \tag{6.14}$$

By combining equations (6.5), (6.10), and (6.11) and by leaving aside supply shortages, we can express individual $x$'s utility by

$$U_x = L_x^b(R_x/P), \tag{6.15}$$

or, by introducing equations (6.6) and (6.7),

$$U_x = (P_x/P)S_x(24 - S_x)^b. \tag{6.16}$$

Let us now determine the supply $S_x$ of good $x$. According to the hypotheses of the model, individual $x$ first sets $P_x$ and then receives consumers' orders. The latter may be fully met or not, according to individual $x$'s preferences. That is, $S_x$ is chosen to maximize the right-hand side of equation (6.16), taking $P_x$ and $P$ as given and under the constraint $S_x \leqslant Q_x$. Easy calculations, combined with equation (6.14), yield

$$S_x = \min\left(\frac{RP^m}{P_x^{m+1}} ; \frac{24}{1 + b}\right). \tag{6.17}$$

Market clearing requires

$$\frac{RP^m}{P_x^{m+1}} \leqslant \frac{24}{1 + b} \tag{6.18}$$

for all $0 \leqslant x \leqslant 1$. One cannot guarantee a priori that this inequality will hold for all markets, ruling out the possibility of supply shortages. The fact, however, is that no individual considers the hypothesis of having his possible consumption being restricted by such shortages. Hence equation (6.16) stands as individual $x$'s notional utility, namely, the function he will try to maximize in the price-setting game. By introducing equation (6.17), we obtain

$$U_x = \begin{cases} \dfrac{RP^{m-1}}{P_x^m}\left(24 - \dfrac{RP^m}{P_x^{m+1}}\right)^b & \text{if } \dfrac{RP^m}{P_x^{m+1}} < \dfrac{24}{1+b}, \\[3ex] \dfrac{P_x}{P}b^b\left(\dfrac{24}{1+b}\right)^{1+b} & \text{if } \dfrac{RP^m}{P_x^{m+1}} > \dfrac{24}{1+b}. \end{cases} \tag{6.19}$$

Individual $x$ is assumed to know these expressions, and, as easy calculations show, for a given $P$ the optimum price-setting rule gives

$$P_x^{m+1} = cRP^m,$$                                                      (6.20)

where

$$c = \frac{m + b(m + 1)}{24m}.$$                                            (6.21)

Let us now determine the Nash and the maximin pricing strategies. In a Nash equilibrium all price setters should follow equation (6.20) with perfect foresight on $P$. Taking into account equation (6.12), one immediately concludes that there exists a unique Nash equilibrium where

$$P_x = P = cR.$$                                                           (6.22)

To determine the maximin strategy, let us observe in equations (6.19) that, because $0 < m \leqslant 1$, $U_x$ is a decreasing function of $P$. Hence the maximin strategy takes $P = P_{max}$ in equation (6.20), namely,

$$P_x^{m+1} = cRP_{max}^m.$$                                                (6.23)

Let us now revisit the problem of inertial inflation. The starting point is a chronic inflation at a constant rate per period. For $t \leqslant 0$ the government has been expanding the nominal output at a constant rate $r$, namely,

$$R_t = R_0(1 + r)^t \qquad \text{for } t \leqslant 0.$$

Price setters have already adjusted for chronic inflation and its moving Nash equilibrium by using equation (6.22) with $P_t = cR_t$ for $t \leqslant 0$. At the end of period $t = 0$ a new administration, whose credibility is beyond any doubt, announces nominal output stabilization, namely, that it will make $R_t = R_0$ for $t \geqslant 1$.

In rational expectations models inflation would immediately stop because new Nash equilibria would make $P = cR_0 = P_0$ for $t \geqslant 1$. The problem is that, even if all price setters are convinced that the government will actually stabilize the nominal output at $R_0$, they may suspect that other prices will continue to increase. In fact, the only available information is that $P_1$ will fall in some point of the closed interval $P_0 \leqslant P_1 \leqslant P_0(1 + r)$.

If we assume that price setters are prudent enough to behave as maximin strategists, prices in period 1 will be set according to equation (6.23) with $R = R_0$ and $(P_{max})_1 = P_0(1 + r)$. Hence, taking into account equation (6.20), we obtain

$$P_1^{m+1} = cR_0[P_0(1 + r)]^m,$$

or, equivalently,

$$P_1 = P_0(1 + r)^{m/(m+1)}. \tag{6.24}$$

To describe the price dynamics further, we need an additional hypothesis on how $P_{max}$ is estimated for $t \geqslant 2$. If we assume that $R$ is kept unchanged, then a possible revision rule is provided by

$$\frac{(P_{max})_t}{P_{t-1}} = \frac{P_{t-1}}{P_{t-2}}, \tag{6.25}$$

which assumes that, as a result of nominal output stabilization, economic agents estimate a nonincreasing path for the inflation rate. Because $cR = cR_0 = P_0$, the maximin price-setting rule (6.23) combined with equation (6.12) yields

$$P_t^{m+1} = P_0(P_{max})_t^m. \tag{6.26}$$

By combining equations (6.25) and (6.26) and by making $p_t = \log P_t$, we can describe the price dynamics by the difference equation

$$(m + 1)p_t - 2mp_{t-1} + mp_{t-2} = p_0,$$

where $p_t$ converges to the Nash equilibrium $p_0$.

The preceding discussion provides a compromise between adaptive and rational expectations. Formally the described price dynamics is similar to that of an old-fashioned adaptive expectations model. Yet the economic hypotheses that lead to a gradual approach to Nash equilibrium are completely different from those of a traditional model of backward looking expectations, insensitive to changes in policy rules. First, the whole discussion skips the idea of expectations, a somewhat vague concept often used to escape a much more complex issue, namely, how strategic interdependence problems should be dealt with. Second, inflation falls below the historical rate $r$ in period 1, not because of recession but simply because price sellers actually believe that the government will stabilize nominal output at $R_0$. The reason why this is not enough to promote immediate price stabilization is that price setters have no guarantee that other prices will stop increasing.

## 6.4   The Role of Incomes Policies

The foregoing discussion provides the rationale for incomes policies: Governments should play the role of the Walrasian auctioneer, speeding up the location of Nash equilibria, that is, using the visible hand to achieve what rational expectations models assume is achieved by the invisible hand. In the price-setting model given in section 6.3, if the government, besides stabilizing the nominal output at $R_0$, decides to freeze all prices at their levels in period $t = 0$, inflation would stop immediately, with no recession or shortages, simply because price setters would be assured that the government would not expand nominal output and other agents would not continue to increase prices. In short, price setters would behave like Nash strategists because they would be assured that other players would act in the same way.

As previously noted, the central function of incomes policies is not to constrain individual decision making but to clear up uncertainties in a B-game, telling each actor how the others will play. This, incidentally, dismisses a traditional argument against incomes policies—that governments are not better equipped than free markets to identify individual Nash strategies. In fact, the central problem in a B-game is not to discover such strategies but to coordinate their simultaneous playing.

This also explains why, in a second stage of a stabilization program, wage and price controls should be removed gradually in successive sectoral steps and not in a one-shot manner. In fact, even if incomes policies are successful enough to bring the economy to a Nash equilibrium, there is no way of conveying such information to the participants in the game. Each player finds himself in equilibrium but does not know if the same applies to other players. If controls are lifted sector by sector, players will realize that no participant in the game will increase prices even when allowed to do so. On the other hand, the one-shot approach would simply bring back the uncertainty of individual players as to what other players will do, perhaps triggering large defensive wage and price increases.

Of course, the chances of hitting a Nash equilibrium through incomes policies are extremely remote. Staggered wage and price setting may be a formidable obstacle to a wage-price freeze, because it implies that there is no calendar date at which relative prices are in equilibrium. That is, before being frozen, wages and prices must be realigned. Yet, even if the synchronization problem is solved, the fact that wage and price controls yield some supply shortages should not come as a surprise. In fact, policymakers can easily detect when relative prices are visibly out of equilibrium but can never perfectly identify when the equilibrium has been reached. Even if they could and then decree a wage and price freeze, the following week they would be wrong, because equilibrium prices move up and down with shifts in demand and supply over time.

The central question in a program intended to fight a big inflation is to choose what is preferable in terms of welfare costs: a few product shortages, which eventually may be overcome by imports, or massive unemployment, which is nothing but a shortage of jobs. From this point of view, objections to incomes policies should not be taken too seriously, at least when the problem is to fight a big inflation with strong inertial roots. This is all the more so because incomes policies can be managed with appropriate flexibility, substituting price administration for price freezes.

A more fundamental contention is that the temporary success of incomes policies may lead policymakers to forget that price stability can be sustained only with aggregate demand discipline. The temptation is to misread price stability and produce a boom. The misleading signals are a true risk, as is known from uncountable examples in history.

The model presented in section 6.3 indicates where these misleading signals may come from. Let us assume that in period $t = 0$ the government freezes prices at $P_{x0} = P_0 = rR_0$ without preventing further expansion of nominal output. Shortages will not emerge immediately but only when

$$\frac{RP^m}{P_x^{m+1}} = \frac{R}{cR_0} > \frac{24}{1+b},$$

violating the market-clearing condition (6.18). If we take into account equation (6.21), shortages will show up only once:

$$\frac{R}{R_0} > 1 + \frac{b}{m(1+b)}.$$

The fact that after a price freeze some nominal output expansion is possible without yielding supply shortages helps to explain why price controls are usually so successful in the short run. Price setters are converted into price takers, thus being forced to accept some squeeze in their profit margins. So long as the profit margins do not fall below perfect competition margins, nominal output expansion leads to both output growth and increased welfare. Yet this euphoric start is nothing but an incomes policy trap. In fact, once price controls are lifted, producers will restore their previous margins by increasing prices and reducing quantities. Moreover, one ominous possibility is that policymakers, misinterpreting price signals, might become convinced that, once prices have been frozen, price stability can be reconciled with sustained economic growth through relentless aggregate demand expansion. The rise and fall of the Cruzado Plan should serve as a case study on how naive policymakers backed by highly sophisticated economic advisers can fall into the incomes policy trap.

## 6.5    Staggered Wage Setting, Indexation, and Inflationary Inertia

That staggered wage setting is a source of inflationary inertia even under rational expectations has been known since the pioneering work of Taylor (1979). Here I extend Taylor's model and analyze the inertial complications introduced by strategic interdependence among different groups of workers.

In the following discussion, although labor is assumed to be homogeneous, workers are uniformly distributed among a continuum of classes, one for each real number $0 \leqslant x < 1$. Nominal wages of class $x$ are reset at time $x + n$ for every positive, zero, or negative integer $n$. That is, individual nominal wages move by steps of time length $T = 1$ [the step curve below $S(\tau)$ in figure 6.1] but adjustment dates for different classes are uniformly spread over time.

Under these assumptions the average nominal wage at time $t$ is given by the shaded area in figure 6.2:

$$W(t) = \int_{t-1}^{t} S(\tau)\, d\tau. \tag{6.27}$$

$S(\tau)$ indicates the individual nominal wage of the class with resetting date $\tau$ ($t - 1 \leqslant \tau < t$). To make sure that the integral on the right-hand side of equation (6.27) does exist, we assume that $S(\tau)$ is a continuous function of $\tau$.

Let us further assume that the price level $Q(t)$ is determined by multiplying unit labor costs by a constant markup factor:

$$Q(t) = (1 + m)bW(t),$$

where $m$ is the profit margin and $b$ is the labor input per unit output. In the following discussion I overlook supply shocks and both cyclical and long-term changes in productivity, thus treating $b$ as a constant. This makes the average real wage $W(t)/Q(t)$ a constant:

$$W(t) = zQ(t), \tag{6.28}$$

where $z^{-1} = (1 + m)b$.

Staggered wage setting in an inflationary economy introduces two different real wage concepts, the peak and the average. The peak $k(\tau) = S(\tau)/Q(\tau)$ ($OP$ in figure 6.3) is the individual purchasing power of the class

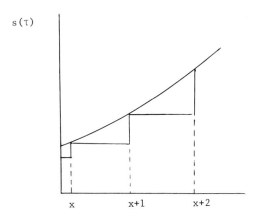

**Figure 6.1**
Individual nominal wage paths.

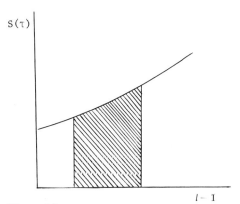

**Figure 6.2**
Nominal wage structure at time $t$.

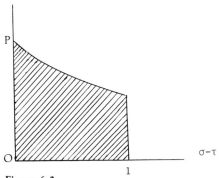

**Figure 6.3**
Individual real wage cycle.

with resetting date $\tau$, immediately after the nominal wage increase. The average

$$z(\tau) = k(\tau) \int_{\tau}^{\tau+1} Q(\tau)/Q(\sigma)\, d\sigma, \tag{6.29}$$

indicated by the shaded area in figure 6.3, is the worker's average real wage in the period where the nominal wage remains fixed. For example, if $Q(\sigma) = Q(0)e^{\pi\sigma}$, that is, if the inflation rate $Q'(\sigma)/Q(\sigma)$ is a constant $\pi$, the peak-average ratio is given by

$$k(\tau)/z(\tau) = \frac{\pi}{1 - e^{-\pi}}, \tag{6.30}$$

an increasing function of $\pi$ that for small inflation rates can be approximated by

$$k(\tau)/z(\tau) = 1 + \pi/2.$$

The converse is also true: If all labor groups set their wage peaks at $k(\tau) = rz$, where $r$ is a constant greater than 1, then the inflation rate will converge to $\pi$, where[6]

$$r = \frac{\pi}{1 - e^{-\pi}}. \tag{6.31}$$

What really matters for both employers and employees is the average real wage $z(\tau)$. Yet the only objective element in each wage contract is the real wage peak $k(\tau)$. That $k(\tau)$ should be set to achieve a target average $z(\tau)$ seems pretty obvious. If the economy remains at full employment with a constant inflation rate $\pi$, there is no reason why workers should accept any reduction in the real wage peaks. In practice this is achieved by periodic nominal wage increases for cost-of-living escalation:

$$S(\tau) = S(\tau - 1)\frac{Q(\tau)}{Q(\tau - 1)},$$

making $k(\tau) = k(\tau - 1)$.

Now, equation (6.31) proves the converse. Because indexation periodically resets real wage peaks above the real average, the economy can afford to pay and inflation becomes predominantly inertial, no longer being the result of too much money chasing a few goods. The problem at this stage is no longer explaining why prices actually increase but explaining how inflation can accelerate or decelerate.

Excess demand for labor is one possible source of inflation acceleration by making $k(\tau) > k(\tau - 1)$, namely, by substituting indexation-plus for simple cost-of-living escalation. Increased inflationary expectations can do the same, either because economic agents anticipate more expansive monetary policies or because each labor group expects other labor groups to move from simple indexation to indexation-plus. Adverse supply shocks, which lower the equilibrium real wage average $z$, are another cause of inflation acceleration in an indexed economy. Recomposing the same real wage peaks now means increasing the coefficient $r$ in equation (6.31), thus lifting the equilibrium inflation rate. Finally, if labor unions manage to reduce the wage adjustment interval, say, from twelve to six months, what was previously the annual inflation rate will become the six-month cost-of-living increase. This, once again, results from equation (6.31), where $\pi$ is the equilibrium inflation rate for the wage-resetting time interval.

In the model inflation can be cured only if workers accept a cut in their real wage peaks. If workers behaved as Nash strategists, a wage cut could be achieved without unemployment, provided that a credible administration announced a monetary policy leading to falling rates of growth of nominal output.[7] The point is that one should not expect workers to behave as Nash strategists. Under full employment there is no reason why they should accept any cut in their real wage peaks except if they are assured that the same cut will apply to all other labor groups and actually lower the inflation rate.[8]

Summing up, to break wage indexation, there are only two alternatives, massive unemployment or incomes policies. Two incomes policy models should be mentioned: the Bulhões-Campos wage formula and synchronization.

The Bulhões-Campos wage formula was adopted in Brazil between 1964 and 1968. Real wage peaks were set according to

$$k(\tau) = z\left(1 + \frac{\pi^*}{2}\right),$$

where $z$ is the average real wage observed in the previous twenty-four months adjusted for productivity growth and $\pi^*$ is the expected inflation rate for the following twelve months. Wage-resetting intervals were fixed at twelve months and were announced by the government. As previously seen, $1 + \pi^*/2$ is the first-order approximation for the peak/average ratio. Because expected inflation rates were substantially below the past ones, real wage peaks were substantially reduced.

Synchronization is decreed monetary reform in which all wages are converted from an old currency into a new currency by an average equilibrium value. This involves increasing the nominal wages of some labor groups and decreasing those of other groups, depending on how recent the last adjustment was. The idea was used in the Cruzado Plan, but a political softener was introduced at the last moment: Wages were converted from cruzeiros into cruzados using the average purchasing power of the last six months (then the wage-resetting interval) plus an 8% bonus. This actually meant increasing average real wages by 8%, perhaps the original sin of the Cruzado Plan.

## 6.6   Inflation, Indexation, and Incomes Policies in Brazil[9]

The Bulhões-Campos Reforms

In the late 1950s and early 1960s annual inflation rates in Brazil escalated from 17% in 1958 to 92% in 1964, first as a consequence of the Kubitschek expansionary policies and then as a result of the populist engagements of the Goulart administration. Between 1964 and 1967 the Bulhões-Campos reforms, backed by military president Castello Branco, successfully brought down the inflation rate to 24% per year and restored both external equilibrium and Brazil's access to foreign credit markets. The side effects on output were tolerable and short-lived because the 5% industrial recession of 1965 was followed by a 10% industrial recovery in 1966. Moreover, the road was paved for a seven-year period of high growth and declining inflation.

The reforms were a skillful mix of a budget deficit cut, incomes policies, exchange rate devaluation, and capital markets indexation. By cutting government consumption and subsidies and by raising taxes, the public sector deficit was reduced from 4% to 1% of GDP. Exchange rate devaluations replaced the commercial arrears of early 1964 with a comfortable reserve position in 1965 and 1966. Indexed capital market instruments encouraged private savings and restored the mortgage market, which was virtually killed in the early 1960s by the 12% per year usury ceiling on nominal interest rates. Tax indexation, besides stimulating private savings by no longer taxing inflation adjustments, was also helpful in reducing tax evasion. (In 1963, when the inflation rate was running at 80% per year, the penalty on tax arrears was no more than 32% a year.)

The incomes policy part of the plan, which played a major role in fighting inflation, was the Bulhões-Campos wage deindexation formula, described in section 6.5. A problem with the formula is that it actually squeezed the real wages whenever future inflation rates were underestimated by the government. The problem was felt in 1965, 1966, and 1967, when the cost of living increased 45%, 41% and 24%, respectively, compared to forecast inflation rates of 25%, 10%, and 15%. The outcome, a 25% real wage decline in manufacturing industry between 1964 and 1968, can be partly explained by the weakened position of the labor unions under the military regime.

A more consistent view, however, is that a substantial decline in real wages was inevitable, given the policy objectives of increasing indirect taxes, real rents, and real public utility rates, cutting subsidies, and promoting a strong exchange rate devaluation. It could have been the result of prolonged stagflation; it could have been achieved by higher inflation rates, but still it was inevitable. The Bulhões-Campos wage formula helped to reconcile this inevitable real wage cut with declining inflation rates and low output losses.

## Widespread Indexation

Imaginative as they might have been, the Bulhões-Campos reforms involved a major asymmetry that could not last for long. Most incomes and financial assets, but not wages and the exchange rate, were indexed. The almost inevitable extension came in 1968. For the exchange rate a crawling peg adjusted the dollar/cruzeiro rate at small and irregular time intervals according to a basic guideline consisting of the inflation rate differential between Brazil and the United States. For wages a complicated formula was used to offset the effects of unanticipated inflation in the Bulhões-Campos wage rule. In practice, this meant that nominal wages were adjusted every twelve months in proportion to the cumulative increase in the cost of living plus a productivity gain. This indexation rule was a backward-looking one that restored every twelve months the real wage peak adjusted for productivity growth.

Because the average/peak ratio is a decreasing function of the inflation rate, the new wage rule implied that inflation could decline only so long as average real wages grew faster than the officially determined productivity gain. Moreover, because the law determined a floor rather than a ceiling to changes in labor compensation, it introduced an asymmetry between inflation acceleration and inflation deceleration. In fact, markets were free to increase the real wage peak but not to reduce it, except through labor turnover, the only way to escape the law. Yet this was a costly device in the case of skilled labor and largely ineffective in the case of nonskilled workers, because unskilled labor is protected by minimum wage levels adjusted by the same indexation rule.

In short, backward-looking wage indexation introduced highly adverse short-run inflation-output trade-offs, discouraging quick anti-inflationary policies and favoring monetary accommodation. The problem was not perceived until 1973, because during the golden years of the Brazilian miracle real wages rose much faster than the officially determined productivity increases, with annual inflation rates gradually falling from 25% in 1967 to 16% in 1973. Yet the expansionary monetary policies of 1972 and 1973 combined with the first oil shock lifted the annual inflation rate to 35% in 1974. Tight monetary policies were then tried, but it was soon perceived that indexation had anchored the wage-price spiral. Eventually monetary accommodation was accepted, and annual inflation rates were kept in the 35–40% per year range until 1978.

Escalation

Two imprudent policy steps in late 1979 were to lead to further escalation of inflation rates. First, the government decided to control interest rates, accepting high increases in the money supply. Then a new wage law, besides introducing a number of complications, reduced the nominal wage adjustment interval from twelve to six months. As theory could predict, what was previously the annual rate of inflation became the six-month inflation rate. Tight monetary policies implemented in 1981 and 1982 had to face the adverse trade-offs created by backward-looking indexation. The country experienced its first major industrial recession since 1965, but inflation rates only declined from 110% in 1980 to 95% in 1981 and then rose to 100% in 1982.

A dramatic balance of payments adjustment in response to the debt shock was imposed in 1983. Key policy changes were a 30% real exchange rate devaluation and, following IMF advice, substantial indirect tax increases and subsidy cuts. This, of course, implied a significant real wage cut that under the prevailing indexation rules could only be achieved by accelerating the inflation rate to squeeze the average/peak ratio to the proper level. In fact, inflation leaped to 210% per year, and tight monetary policies produced an unprecedented recession. Eventually, in mid-1984, the government decided to turn once again to monetary accommodation.

In March 1985 the passing of power to a civilian president opened the way to increased wage demands by labor unions. The government first tried to reconcile substantial increases in real wages with reduced inflation rates by tightening price controls and increasing the real interest rate on treasury bills to 21% per year. In August Dilson Funaro replaced Francisco Dornelles as minister of finance. Some price controls were lifted, interest rates were substantially lowered, and real wages continued to increase at unprecedented rates. As a result, by the end of 1985 and in January and February of 1986, the inflation rate escalated to almost 15% per month. President Sarney, under the risk of losing all political support, decided to react with a bold announcement, the heterodox shock.

The Cruzado Plan

The Cruzado Plan was intended to stop inflation by halting all indexation. The key measures were the following:

1. Prices were frozen and the exchange rate was fixed at 13.80 Cz/$US. The public was enlisted to defend the controls, and the government was committed to a zero-inflation target.

2. Wages were converted into cruzados by computing their average purchasing power in the last six months with an increase of 8% in general and with a 15% bonus in the case of the minimum wage; a trigger point indexation clause was introduced with a threshold of 20%.

3. The same rule, except for the 8% increase, was extended to rents and mortgage payments.

4. Cruzeiro bills and demand deposits were immediately converted into cruzados, without write-offs, by a cut of three zeros. Conversion rates for cruzeiro-denominated liabilities with future maturities were set to decline by a daily factor, starting on February 28, of 1.0045 until maturity. This conversion rule did not apply to indexed liabilities.

5. Indexation clauses were prohibited in short-term contracts and capital market instruments (less than twelve months), except for savings accounts.

The immediate success of the program was overwhelming. Consumers could compare supermarket prices with the listed official maximum prices and denounce violators to the police. The fact that nominal wages were cut in some cases and adjusted substantially below past inflation in all cases did not cool off the popular support for the program.

Yet technical weaknesses in the plan were evident. First, the Cruzado Plan was announced as a pure incomes policy because it was believed that fiscal adjustment had already been promoted in late 1985 and that the

Brazilian inflation of January and February was purely inertial. Second, there was no reason to believe that there was room for the 8% real wage bonus and the 15% real minimum wage increase. Third, although the plan tried to solve the problem of wage synchronization, it did nothing to meet the staggered price-setting issue. Prices were frozen at their level of February 27, when the relative price structure had no reason to be close to equilibrium. Some sectoral prices, including milk, automobiles, pharmaceutical products, and electric power, were clearly frozen below their equilibrium point. Hence the success of the Cruzado Plan was contingent on a short-term replacement of price freezes by price administration.

A trump card for the Brazilian authorities was that the Cruzado Plan was implemented under highly favorable external conditions. In 1984 and 1985 Brazil had already scored trade surpluses in the range of $12.5–$13.0 billion per year, bringing its external current account to equilibrium despite the huge interest payments on the foreign debt. The Cruzado Plan was implemented when the decline in oil prices, the decline in international interest rates, and the depreciation of the dollar implied a $4 billion annual improvement in Brazilian external accounts.

Until late May the Cruzado honeymoon was incredibly happy—too happy to be sustainable, as the authorities should have suspected. Not only did inflation stop immediately with no recession, but also retail sales expanded by 25% in real terms, real estate prices doubled, and stock prices experienced an unprecedented boom. In the wave of optimism Brazil was described by the minister of finance as a country with Swiss inflation and twice the Japanese growth rate, and the president decided that the price freeze that brought him so much popularity should be kept until the memory of inflation was definitely erased. As for the business community, its few concerns with low profit margins and with the political management of the price system were largely superseded by the euphoria arising from higher sales.

That this was a situation ripe for demand inflation to take off was the lesson ignored by Brazilian policymakers. They did not even react to some disquieting signals, such as the steep increases in commodity futures and the rapid growth of the black market exchange rate premium. Plainly demand was overheated because of real wage increases, because the public sector deficit actually remained at 4.7% of GDP and because interest rate controls led not only to generous increases of M1 but also to a sizable expansion of M4. In short, money was created much faster than required to compensate for the decline in other financial assets held by the public.

Shortages, black markets, and a drop in quality were visible in early June

1986. In July and August the government announced a small-scale fiscal package and decided to liberalize imports and increase nominal interest rates while trying to keep the price freeze at any cost, including subsidies to producers. The net outcome was a reignition of inflationary expectations that aggravated shortages and black market premiums. Worse than that, despite all favorable external shocks, the trade balance deteriorated and external reserves fell sharply because of export losses resulting from both increases in domestic costs and expansion of domestic demand. Warnings given by economic advisers were largely ignored by President Sarney, who firmly believed that the sustained price freeze was his trump card to win the elections on November 15.

As conceived by its intellectual authors, the Cruzado Plan should have been an improved version of the Bulhões-Campos reforms. Its central mistake, as diagnosed by Daniel Valente Dantas, was to create a jumbo jet piloted by a taxi driver. In fact, under the command of President Sarney and Minister Funaro, the plan became one more attempt to promote economic welfare by combining a price freeze with relentless increases in nominal output.

Why such attempts are highly successful in the short run and bound to fail after a few months was explained in section 6.4. In fact, inflation rates fell from the previous 15% per month to an average 1.8% per month between March and October 1986. Even taking into account sectoral shortages and black market premiums the decline of the inflation rate was impressive. Real wages increased 15%, and the consumption boom convinced President Sarney that 30 million new consumers had been added to the domestic market. Moreover, increased consumption led to an 8.2% rate of growth of GNP in 1986 (despite the poor performance of agriculture), and unemployment rates receded to 3%, the lowest level since 1980.

That the plan was to collapse at some point was plainly obvious. Oddly enough the trigger was a new austerity fiscal package announced six days after the November elections [when the Partido Movimento Democratico Brasileiro (PMDB) scored an overwhelming victory], the so-called Cruzado II. The package was particularly unfortunate because it skipped both expenditure cuts and income tax increases. Once again, economic advisers convinced President Sarney that, in order to spare the lower income groups, additional tax revenues should be provided exclusively by excise tax increases on automobiles, cigarettes, beverages and liquor, gasoline, and electricity. This actually meant that a few products were submitted to price increases so high that the inflation rate in November soared to 5.5% per month. Inflationary expectations were now reignited to the point of transforming the end of the price freeze into a self-fulfilling prophecy. The government still tried to substitute price administration for the previous price freeze, threatening violators with strong penalties. However, at this point government threats were no longer credible, especially because the promise to keep prices unchanged had been broken by Cruzado II. The general perception of the business community was that the costs of violating price controls were substantially lower than the benefits because violations were the rule and no longer the exception.

Whether a more adequately designed fiscal package might have rescued the Cruzado Plan is a controversial issue. Not only were relative prices plainly out of equilibrium, but also nominal wages had already expanded too much to provide the necessary credibility to support the zero-inflation target. Moreover, the balance of payments had already been ruined. In any case the remote possibilities of managing an unstable equilibrium became still more remote with Cruzado II.

The price explosion forced the government to reintroduce short-term indexation, first on the exchange rate (to prevent a further collapse in external reserves) and then on capital market instruments (to prevent capital flight). As for wages, the trigger threshold of the Cruzado Plan became effective in January 1987, forcing nominal wage adjustments every two months until June.

Loose monetary and fiscal policies combined with reindexation lifted monthly inflation rates to the 20–30% range in April, May, and June of 1987. In short, the Cruzado Plan failed to tackle the demand side of inflation, being nothing but a replay of the Chilean experience under Allende in 1971 or the Argentine experience after the return of Peron in 1973.

In April 1987 Minister of Finance Funaro was replaced by Luis Carlos Bresser Pereira. A new stabilization program, the so-called Bresser Plan, was announced on June 12; it combined a new round of incomes policies with a promised fiscal reform. Whether the plan will be a success or another failed incomes policy experiment depends on adequate aggregate demand management based on a substantial budget cut.

## Notes

1. For a proof, see Simonsen (1970).

2. In a bimatrix game player $X$ must choose a row and player $Y$ a column, each ignoring the other's choice. The entries $(a_i, b_j)$ indicate the payoffs of $X$ and $Y$, respectively.

3. How students actually play the game of "half of the average" can be easily tested in a classroom.

4. The previous description of the principle of strategic interdependence is based on Sargent (1985), chapters 1 and 2.

5. The connection between rational expectations equilibria and Nash equilibria was first established by Townsend (1978) for a particular market model. That the correspondence holds generally, at least in an economy with a large number of small participants, was shown by Evans (1983). The principle of strategic interdependence makes the proof much easier and much more general because it naturally maps strategies into expectations.

6. For a proof, see Simonsen (1986), appendix 1.

7. An optimum stabilization path consistent with staggered wage setting was proposed by former Brazilian Finance Minister Octávio Gouveia de Bulhões. For a detailed analysis, see Simonsen (1986).

8. Except for the game-theoretic framework, the argument is essentially the same as that used by Keynes to explain why workers resist money wage cuts (Keynes 1936, chs. 2 and 19).

9. Part of this section was borrowed from Dornbusch and Simonsen (1987).

## References

Arida, P., and A. Lara Resende. 1985. "Inertial inflation and monetary reform in Brazil," in *Inflation and Indexation*, John Williamson, ed. (Washington, D.C.: Institute for International Economics), 27–45.

Dornbusch, R. and M. H. Simonsen. 1987. *Inflation Stabilization with Incomes Policy Support* New York: Group of Thirty.

Evans, G. 1983. "The stability of rational expectations in macroeconomic models," in *Individual Forecasting and Aggregate Outcomes*, Roman Frydman and Edmund S. Phelps, eds. (Cambridge: Cambridge University Press), 69–93.

Fellner, W. 1976. *Towards a Reconstruction of Macroeconomics*. Washington, D.C.: American Enterprise Institute.

Fischer, S. 1977. "Long term contracts, rational expectations and the optimal money supply rule." *Journal of Political Economy* 85(1):479–513.

Jones, A. J. 1980. *Game Theory*. Chichester: Ellis Horwood; New York: Halsted Press.

Keynes, J. M. 1923. *A Tract on Monetary Reform*. Reprinted by the Royal Economic Society (London) in 1971.

Keynes, J. M. 1936. *The General Theory of Employment Interest and Money*. New York: Harcourt Brace.

Lopes, F. 1986. *On Heterodox Shock*. Rio de Janeiro: Editora Campus. (In Portuguese.)

Lucas, R. 1976. "Econometric policy evaluation: A critique," in *The Phillips Curve and Labor Markets*, K. Brunner and A. Meltzer, eds. (Amsterdam: North Holland), 19–46.

Lucas, R., and T. Sargent. 1979. "After Keynesian macroeconomics." *Federal Reserve Bank of Minneapolis, Quarterly Review* 3:1–16.

Lucas, R., and T. Sargent, eds. 1981. *Rational Expectations and Econometric Practice*. Minneapolis, Minn.: University of Minnesota Press.

Modiano, E. 1986. *Inflation and the Cruzado*. Rio de Janeiro: Editora Campus. (In Portuguese.)

Modigliani, F. 1977. "The monetarist controversy, or should we forsake stabilization policies?" *American Economic Review, Papers and Proceedings*, 1–19.

Sargent, T. 1979. *Macroeconomic Theory*. New York: Academic Press.

Sargent, T. 1985. *Rational Expectations and Inflation*. New York: Harper & Row.

Schelling, T. 1982. *Micromotives and Macrobehavior*. New York: Norton.

Simonsen, M. H. 1970. *Inflation: Gradualism versus Shock Treatment*. Rio de Janeiro: APEC. (In Portuguese.)

Simonsen, M. H. 1986. "Rational expectations, incomes policies and game theory." *Revista de Econometria* 6(2):7–46.

Taylor, J. B. 1979. "Staggered wage setting in a macro model." *American Economic Review, Papers and Proceedings*, 108–118.

Townsend, R. M. 1978. "Market anticipations, rational expectations and Bayesian analysis." *International Economic Review* 19:481–494.

*Comment by Eliana A. Cardoso*

The February 1986 Cruzado Plan stopped inflation dead, and for the next six months inflation remained low. Less than a year later inflation exploded again. By June 1987 Brazil faced an annualized inflation rate of 800%, twice as large as inflation when the plan was first implemented. Policymakers had emphasized inertia as the most important component of inflation. They had thus chosen a shock treatment centered around an uncompromising price freeze. But they paid insufficient attention to the need for fiscal restraint. The Brazilian plan is now seen as the most obvious example of the failure of heterodox programs to stop inflation and thus forces us to look at fundamentals.

My comments emphasize two points. First, there are the problems of fiscal consolidation in the presence of a large public debt. What is missed in many analyses is precisely the particular debt situation and the role of foreign exchange availability in successful versus nonsuccessful programs. Second, I discuss the role of budget deficits in the inflationary process in Brazil.

**Debt and Inflation Stabilization**

In the past twenty-two years Brazil has experimented with two stabilization programs, in 1964 and in 1986. Seen in conjunction, they teach a number of lessons. One of them is that the size of the public debt may stand in the way of viable fiscal consolidation. The high inflation that preceded the 1964 stabilization plan reduced the public debt/GDP ratio to less than 4% because of the lack of any indexation. For the 1986 stabilization, by contrast, the prevailing indexation of government debt and high real interest rates had left a debt/income ratio (combining foreign and domestic debt) of 50%. There is a limit to the amount of taxes the government can raise to finance growing interest payments on its debt. No wonder, in 1986, the large debt and insufficient budget improvement led to the expectation that the government might seek to reduce the debt burden by inflation. This expectation pushed up nominal interest rates and the black market premium.

Another important difference between the two programs concerns the availability of foreign resources. The military government that took power in 1964 found a favorable international reception. Debt rescheduling was facilitated, and new loans from the Agency for International Development (AID) and the International Monetary Fund (IMF) were made available. Debt relief did not prevent a stabilization-induced recession as a result of contractionary monetary and fiscal policies. Import demand fell because of the reduction in aggregate demand; combined with a recovery of exports, this produced trade surpluses in 1964–66 and the elimination of arrears and other short-term debts. The supportive international environment, however, did help to prevent an even steeper decline in income and permitted import growth in the early stages of recovery in 1967.

In 1986, by contrast, the position of the public sector was badly compromised by the need to extract resources from the private sector for the service of the external debt. Domestic adjustment can only go so far, and real resource transfers abroad of 4% to 5% GDP cannot continue indefinitely. Any analysis of the sad denouement of late 1986 and early 1987 is incomplete without reference to the risky adjustment policy using external debt of the late 1970s. One lesson of the Brazilian experience is that external debt quickly turns from being part of the solution to disequilibrium to being part of the problem.

Fiscal consolidation was made difficult by the size of the debt, but the policymakers also did not make an honest effort to reduce the deficit. Some among them argued that Brazilian inflation was different from that in other countries, and the budget deficit did not have a role in it; inflation was purely inertial, and all that was needed to stop it was a price freeze and some formulas to recalculate wages, rents, and future installments on existing contracts. Others denied the existence of the problem by putting numbers together that showed a zero budget deficit.

## The Budget Deficit

Table 1 shows the available information concerning the budget deficit. In 1982 the budget deficit of the consolidated public sector, corrected for

**Table 1**
Different measures of the budget deficit as a share of GDP

| Year | Increase in total debt/ GDP | Deficit corrected for inflation/ GDP | FGV[a] measure/ GDP | BRPS[b]/GDP | Operational[c] deficit/GDP |
|------|------|------|------|------|------|
| 1982 | 25.9 | 8.4 | 3.7 | 15.8 | 6.6 |
| 1983 | 60.5 | 15.2 | 4.1 | 19.9 | 3.0 |
| 1984 | 60.7 | 4.6 | 4.7 | 23.3 | 2.7 |
| 1985 | 65.6 | 6.1 | n.a. | 27.8 | 4.3 |

Sources: E. Cardoso and E. Reis, "Deficits, debt, and inflation in Brazil," *Pesquisa e Planejamento Economico* (December 1986), 16:575–598 (in Portuguese). Central Bank, *Brazil: Economic Program*, February 1987 (in Portuguese).
a. Calculated on a cash-flow basis; excludes the monetary authorities' deficit.
b. Calculated on an accrual basis; excludes the monetary authorities' deficit.
c. Subtracts monetary correction from BRPS.

inflation exceeded 8% of GDP. An agreement with the IMF [whose staff calculated the borrowing requirement of the public sector (BRPS) as 15.8% of GDP in 1982] was reached in December. The following year, rather than decelerating, inflation more than doubled. The public sector deficit exceeded its targets regularly, not merely because of the difficulty of controlling noninterest expenditures and increasing tax receipts but also because of rapidly growing internal and external interest payments.

All data, except perhaps for the numbers under the "operational deficit" column, indicate the existence of large deficits.[1]

## Can Budget Deficits Explain Inflation in Brazil?

If increasing money-financed budget deficits are to explain the ever increasing inflation between 1979 and 1985, one would expect seigniorage as a share of GDP to rise. This does not happen. Between 1970 and 1985 seigniorage as a share of GDP is fairly constant at around 2%. Seigniorage models as an explanation of inflation in Brazil have thus been dismissed on the grounds that seigniorage as a share of GDP shows absolutely no correlation with inflation.

The money-goods model of monetarism is inappropriate to the Brazilian economy because it fails to account for changes in deficits not financed by money creation. It predicts that seigniorage drives the system. But the Brazilian experience has to be interpreted in light of the institutional reality of financial markets and growing external debt.

There is yet another reason why a more complete model is necessary to account for inflation in Brazil. It concerns the dynamics of inflation. Fully flexible prices imply equality between seigniorage and the inflation tax on the monetary base all the time, but the Brazilian data rule out this possibility. An increase in inflation increases the inflation tax but also increases velocity and reduces seigniorage.

If full price flexibility is ruled out, different assumptions about price dynamics yield unattractive models of seigniorage. The reason is that money holders are assumed to build up disequilibrium levels of real balances under the control of monetary authorities. This establishes the need for the introduction of financial markets in the model.

## Seigniorage Models for the Open Economy with a Financial Market

Consider an economy in which the current account is financed by either commercial loans or changes in foreign reserves. All external borrowing is done by the public sector. The government finances the budget deficit by borrowing abroad and by creating both money and domestic debt.[2] We can combine the government budget constraint and the balance of payments equation to obtain an equation for the growth rate of the real money base:

$$\mu = x/m - \pi, \tag{1}$$

where $m$ is the real money base, $\mu$ is its growth rate, $\pi$ is inflation, and $x$ is the sum of the domestic component of the budget deficit financed by money creation plus the noninterest current account.

The next question concerns the inflation dynamics. The nominal interest rate adjusts to clear the money market all the time. We also assume that there is inflation inertia: Inflation increases whenever the level of activity exceeds full employment, that is, whenever the actual real interest rate $i - \pi$, defined by goods and money market equilibrium, is below the full-employment real interest rate $r$:

$$\dot{\pi} = a[r(G, T) - (i - \pi)], \tag{2}$$

where $G$ and $T$ are permanent government expenditure and the trade surplus, respectively.[3]

The model described by equations (1) and (2) is represented in figure 1, where the adjustment path for an increase in government expenditure financed by money creation is shown.

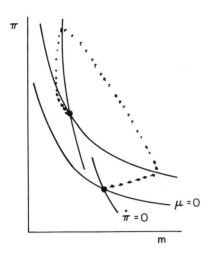

**Figure 1**
A money-financed increase in government expenditure.

A larger budget deficit financed by money creation shifts the schedule $\mu = 0$ to the right. Increased government expenditure requires a higher full-employment real interest rate, thus shifting $\dot{\pi} = 0$ to the left. The economy moves from the initial low inflation equilibrium to the new equilibrium with a higher inflation rate through oscillations. As money increases, the nominal interest rate falls, as does the real interest rate, stimulating activity and pushing up the inflation rate. Gradually inflation catches up with money growth and then exceeds it, reducing real cash balances and increasing the real interest rate.

This story might fit the post–Cruzado Plan data, shown in figure 2, but it certainly does not fit the period of increasing inflation between 1979 and 1985 shown in figure 3. The inflationary process in figure 3 can be explained better by a different story.

Figure 4 shows the adjustment of inflation and real balances in the presence of unchanged seigniorage and rising equilibrium real interest rates. Seigniorage is unchanged so long as the increased sum of budget deficits and noninterest current account surpluses does not get monetized but is financed by larger domestic debt. The increase in the equilibrium real interest rate can be attributed to crowding out (growing government expenditures financed by debt) or to increased trade surpluses, made necessary to finance interest payments on the foreign debt.

Consider a situation in which a balance of payments crisis, such as the halting of capital inflows at the end of 1982, requires a real devaluation,

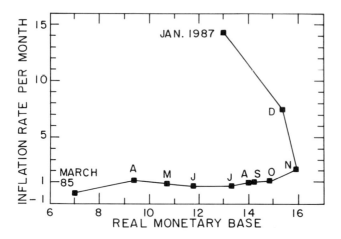

**Figure 2**
The inflation rate and the real monetary base in Brazil, March 1986 to January 1987.

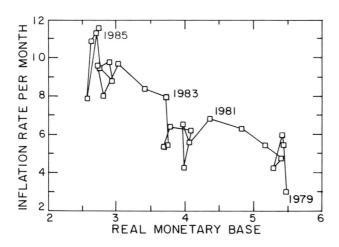

**Figure 3**
The inflation rate and the real monetary base in Brazil from the second quarter of 1979 to the fourth quarter of 1985 (monthly averages during the quarter).

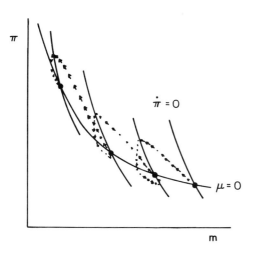

**Figure 4**
Successive increases in the full-employment real interest rate.

which induces growing trade surpluses. Monetary targets imposed by the IMF program bring about a change in domestic finance from money to debt. The sum of the budget deficit and noninterest current account financed by money creation is left unchanged. The higher real exchange rate and trade surplus are counterbalanced by a higher equilibrium real interest rate.

How do we move from one equilibrium to another with higher inflation? The higher real exchange rate brings about increased activity in the tradable goods sector, thus raising employment and inflation. As inflation increases and money growth lags behind, the real interest rate increases. The economy adjusts in a cyclical fashion.

Figure 4 shows a leftward looping pattern of adjustment for inflation and real balances, induced by successive increases of the equilibrium real interest rate. This matches the Brazilian data in figure 3 extremely well.

## Concluding Remarks

Between 1979 and 1985 Brazilian inflation doubled three times. From 45% in mid-1979 it jumped to 100% in 1980–82 and to 200% in 1983–84. At the end of 1985 and the beginning of 1986, the annualized inflation rate grew to 400%. The Brazilian inflationary process cannot be explained by increasing budget deficits financed by money creation. This does not mean that Brazilian budget deficits were not large or that they did not have an important role in sustaining inflation. That process has to be understood in light of changing sources of financing the budget and the economy. The inflation acceleration between 1979 and 1985 is linked to the switch from external to domestic finance and to the larger trade surpluses that pushed up interest rates and inflation.

The Cruzado Plan failed to pay attention to the debt problem and the need for budget consolidation (probably through debt relief and a capital levy). In the absence of an integrated approach the plan pushed the economy into a classic inflationary finance situation.

## Notes

I thank Rudi Dornbusch for comments and suggestions.

1. The Central Bank calculates the operational deficit by eliminating the payments of monetary correction on domestic debt from the borrowing requirement of the public sector (BPRS). Part of the debt has an exchange clause. In years such as 1983, when the devaluation rate far exceeded the inflation rate, government capital losses are important.

2. For a more detailed version of the model discussed here, see E. Cardoso and A. Fishlow, *The Macroeconomics of the Brazilian External Debt* (Cambridge, Mass.: National Bureau of Economic Research, 1988), ch. 5.

3. The real exchange rate is kept constant through a policy of minidevaluations, which take place in response to the existing inflation rate. Maxidevaluations can occur and are defined as an increase of the real exchange rate to a higher level.

## *Comment by Roberto Macedo*

Eduardo Modiano provides us with a useful review of the theoretical foundations of the Cruzado Plan, the implementation of the plan itself, which was basically an anti-inflationary policy package, and the difficulties that followed and eventually defeated it. Modiano emphasizes a major aspect of the plan, namely, the mechanics of the real wage adjustment following the average taken from the six preceding months. This feature of the plan was itself Modiano's contribution.

I do not wish to argue about my disagreement with Modiano's analysis, which is in fact over just a few details here and there. Given the limited space available, I prefer to direct my comments to (1) the reasons for the failure of the plan, (2) the present economic scenario vis-à-vis the expectation of a new shock, and (3) the economic and political difficulties that will surround this new shock. My comments thus add to Modiano's points, but they also reflect that at this point my major concern is what comes next.

In retrospect, the Cruzado Plan is an example of a heterodox shock that failed utterly and went on to define what is worst in an anti-inflationary policy, both in the heterodox and orthodox contexts.

I start with the heterodox context of the plan. To begin with, the price freeze, which should have limited itself only to breaking quickly the inflationary inertia, went beyond its useful limits. This decision, or indecision, led in the end to a remarkable price explosion and to serious distortions with regard to the exchange rate and the rate of interest, because in administering the freezes the government followed unrealistic estimates of the rate of inflation. On top of that there was no incomes policy of the type that one would normally expect to follow a price freeze. Quite the opposite, together with the price freeze there was a nominal wage increase that by itself was one of the causes of the collapse of both the price freeze and the whole plan.

In the orthodox context there was excessive remonetization of the economy, low real interest rates, and exaggerated credit expansion. On the fiscal side it was wrongly assumed that the deficit had been drastically reduced by the fiscal package of December 1985. It was also assumed that there always existed a positive effect of the price stabilization on tax revenues. In reality, the Cruzado Plan was adopted without a previous readjustment of prices and tariffs charged by the public enterprises, which were then lagging behind inflation. This aggravated the government deficit. Moreover, the initial impact of the plan reduced significantly the financial sector operations from which the government derived much of its tax revenues. If we combine this with a lack of control of public expenditure at the federal, state, and local government levels—1986 was an election year—the result is a serious increase in the public deficit.

In a nutshell, the increase of nominal wages together with a price freeze plus lower interest rates that by themselves made consumers and firms leave financial assets and move to expenditures in the real side of the economy plus the increase of public deficit were the most important ingredients that boosted the aggregate demand and caused the plan to fail. In June 1987 most predictions point to a monthly rate of inflation well above 20%, that is, worse than at the start of the Cruzado Plan.

There is a widespread belief in Brazil that the major responsibility for the failure lies with the politicians, because they insisted that lifting the price freeze be postponed until after the elections. They are also blamed for refusing to take needed but unpopular measures in order to control the growth of the aggregate demand, which in the second quarter of 1986 was already showing signs of overheating. But there were also mistakes made by the team that was responsible for managing the economy. The team recognizes now that it neglected the excessive remonetization of the economy and failed to perceive that demand was overheating and that the public deficit was much higher than originally expected. Particularly disastrous was the fiscal package of November 1986 (made soon after the elections), when a last attempt was made to save the plan by restraining aggregate demand. This package, prepared by the economic team of the Ministry of Finance, established a steep increase in indirect taxes, which in turn caused a sharp increase in inflation, paradoxically by the government's own initiative.

With inflation soaring above the 20% monthly mark, there now exists enormous pressure for the government to intervene. Thus we can expect that a new shock is in the making, only this time under more unfavorable conditions than those of February 1986, when the Cruzado Plan was born. Inflation is now higher, and relative prices are in disarray. On top of that, foreign trade surplus and reserves have fallen deeply, necessitating an exchange rate devaluation, which by itself will add to inflation. It is also important to understand that now the indexation mechanisms are more agile, with daily exchange rate indexation and nominal wages subject to a new readjustment every time inflation reaches the 20% mark. It is also important to note that the government deficit is much higher now and that government agencies in charge of price controls are in trouble because most members of their staff have left. It is doubtful that they will pull themselves together on short notice in order to impose an efficient price freeze, even one of smaller scope than the one that characterized the Cruzado Plan. Finally, this time we see that the population, which was so supportive of the Cruzado Plan price freeze, is now disillusioned and will respond less positively or may not cooperate at all.

Even if the government does somehow implement a shock, this time with a short-lived price freeze consistently articulated with wage, exchange rate, and interest rate policies, the difficulties of controlling the public deficit will be much larger. After two decades of military governments, the politicians who have taken over belong to the old populist tradition that refuses to adhere to even a few principles of economic rationality. Their proposals always tend to an increase in public expenditures, no matter how they are to be financed. Besides that, President Sarney was not elected by the popular vote, and this alone makes him lack political legitimacy; for his own support he counts on state governors who were elected in 1986, but this support is costly because it is achieved with extra funds from the federal government so these governors can fulfill election promises regarding public works and expansion of government services.

Given these limitations, in all likelihood a new shock will have to accept more modest objectives. It is extremely improbable to imagine something similar to the Cruzado Plan, that is, to bring inflation down to zero. The strong initial success of the plan had made this possible, so long as the government dared to make tough decisions to complement the whole package. These decisions did not materialize, and the failure of the Cruzado Plan brought about a gamut of difficulties that by themselves make a new attempt much more complex. This is the challenge facing the Brazilian policymakers: promoting a new shock given that the previous one failed and that the conditions are worse now.

With this in mind, it is right to expect a new attempt, but this time one not aimed at bringing about zero inflation and thus not following the examples set by Bolivia and Israel. More likely, Brazil will follow the direction of the Austral Plan, the goal of which was to prevent hyperinflation, not bring inflation down to zero. It will be enough if we can maintain a monthly inflation rate between 5% and 10%.

We can also see in retrospect that both Brazil and Argentina have learned with the Cruzado and Austral plans how to break inflation inertia by making use of the heterodox component of the shocks, in particular price freezes and *tablitas*. The Brazilian experience also tells us that wages were treated wrongly and that renewed shocks will have to pay attention to this. It is also worth stressing that, once inertial inflation has been broken, the old problems do reappear, in particular, how to face changes in the relative prices in an indexed economy and how to make use of the right fiscal and monetary policies.

Another major problem in Brazil is that both public opinion and politicians wrongly believe that heterodoxy and orthodoxy are mutually exclusive, with a heterodox plan thereby dispensing the consistent use of monetary and fiscal policies. I think economists are to blame for this semantic confusion when they imprecisely name a shock "orthodox" or "heterodox." I suggest much more care in the advertising of heterodox plans by stressing that economists cannot dispense with traditional policies. Perhaps we should call the shocks "orthodox" so as not to leave any doubts that *tablitas*, price freezes, and various forms of incomes policies are not sufficient to curb inflation of the Brazilian and Argentine type.

With the high rates of inflation that Brazil is facing and the return of indexation, the fight against inflation does require an orthodox plan. This will have to combine measures to break the inertia of inflation with consistent monetary and fiscal policies. However, we should not be under any illusions if we want to bring inflation to below the 10% or 20% annual mark. In order to achieve this, we need time, because society as a whole and politicians in particular will have to accept a reorganization of the public sector and find more rational ways to finance it.

What is actually happening in Brazil is that the public sector is overburdened by overwhelming external and internal debts. On top of this there is the ever present attempt by the central government and the state enterprises to raise more resources to spend or invest. In order to obtain resources, the state enterprises raise prices and tariffs for their products and services and the central government relies mostly on indirect taxes and still resorts to increases in the money supply, all of which brings high inflationary pressures. The privatization of some state enterprises and/or having them raise equity capital would reduce these pressures. At the same time, the tax structure should increase direct taxes in order to achieve the same purpose and to make taxes more equitable; the money supply should no longer be used to finance government expenditures.

It is not an easy task to convince politicians of the need for these changes. To make matters worse, they are fond of raising nominal wages and of freezing prices.

If these attitudes are maintained in Brazil, we will continue to face the risk, typical of Latin American countries, of the pendular movement in which a military government is succeeded by a populist one that brings chaos to the economy and the return of a military government. Economists in Brazil should bear in mind that, for their plans and ideas to succeed, they will have to first grasp the "politics of the economic policy" by trying to instill in the politicians' and the public's minds that economic rationality is badly needed. To have a chance at success, any stabilization plan cannot dispense with this effort of persuasion, which thus far has been neglected.

### Comment by Guillermo Ortiz

It may be useful to recall briefly the rationale for the Cruzado Plan. The basic idea was that in Brazil inflation was largely inertial. Inertia means that inflation in the current period is essentially a reproduction of inflation in the previous one, and the reason why this occurs is the existence of widespread formal or informal indexation interacting with the staggered setting of wages and other important prices and/or contracts. There are two important points that should be noted in connection with the design of stabilization programs in the context of high, largely inertial inflations. The first is that indexation arrangements, and especially backward-looking wage settlements, are asymmetric with respect to external shocks, in the sense that these represent a floor to inflation, but there is no upper limit to price increases in response to excess demand or to supply-induced price hikes. The second point, obviously related to the first, is that, as noted by Simonsen, reducing inflation through demand restraint is exceedingly difficult because the short-run output/inflation trade-off becomes steep.

Once these points are recognized, it is clear that an effective anti-inflationary strategy—and by this I mean one that is socially tolerable—must include some form of incomes policy to shift to a new reference inflation rate in setting prices and establishing contracts. The Cruzado Plan included a system of wage, price, and exchange rate controls as the co-ordinating device and zero inflation as the reference rate. The Cruzado Plan certainly went far beyond a mere deindexation exercise.

From a conceptual viewpoint there is no disagreement on the rationale behind the heterodox disinflation strategy or on the conditions that must be secured for its successful implementation. Controls (or other forms of income policies) are the essential coordinating device, which must be combined with adequate deindexation measures to homogenize present values of overlapping contracts. However, these issues, which are quite transparent at the theoretical or conceptual level, become difficult to resolve at the operational level, posing serious difficulties for the imple-mentation of these types of plans because of, at a minimum, measurement problems, especially in the case of Brazil.

With the benefit of hindsight, it seems clear that among the basic important elements that must be in place for a heterodox program to work are (1) initial conditions that procure the existence of aggregate equilibrium in the goods market (or preferably some degree of excess supply); (2) a minimum dispersion of relative prices so that the initial price freeze will not produce excessive windfall profits or losses in a context of staggered price setting and thus will avoid the appearance of shortages that could threaten the effectiveness of price controls; (3) adequate conversion rules for the valuation of existing wage contracts, financial operations, and other types of transactions that need to be synchronized; (4) a sufficient level of foreign exchange reserves to lend credibility to the maintenance of a fixed exchange rate in the relevant horizon (and hopefully a sustainable external position over the medium term); and (5) a perception of political commitment on the part of the government to eliminate inflation, which should be reflected in actions tending to break inflationary expectations.

In the case of Brazil, it appears that some of the important "objective" necessary conditions were met, whereas others were wrongly perceived to be in place. Among the former, as Modiano and Simonsen point out, the external environment was favorable for the implementation of the plan; the price of oil and interest rates were falling, and the dollar was being depreciated against the yen and other European currencies. International reserves were at reasonably high levels. One of the major miscalculations, however, was the size of the fiscal deficit; instead of being close to equilibrium, as it was thought when the Cruzado Plan was launched in February 1986, the deficit is now believed to have remained in the range of 4–5% of GDP. A second controversial element—and one that is somewhat confusing in the sense that there are various methods for calculating its magnitude—was the size of the wage increases following the conversion of wages into cruzados (an 8% wage bonus and a 15% increase in the minimum wage). A third feature of the program operating against the objective of breaking inflationary expectations and one that ultimately contributed to its failure was the automatic wage increase clause that was to be triggered when inflation reached a cumulative 20%.

There is no controversy on the diagnosis of the failure of the Cruzado Plan—plain, old-fashioned demand overheating—or on the inappropriate design of the fiscal package included in Cruzado II, which had an immediate large impact on the price level, ultimately precipitating the surge of inflation. However, the technical sophistication of the plan plus its auspicious beginning seem to indicate a particularly fortunate and relevant application of academic insight. The failure of the plan has thus been especially frustrating, and to some extent the postmortem discussion has focused on whether the flaws were mostly made in the design of the plan or in its implementation. Simonsen concludes that the fault lies entirely on the side of the implementation, whereas Modiano attributes some of the blame to problems of design.

The line between where the problems of design end and where those associated with implementation begin can be argued endlessly. In practice, of course, it is difficult to draw the line. But one fundamental issue is the fact that, although incomes policy should, in theory, play the essential role of a coordinating device to tackle the inertial component of inflation, in the Cruzado Plan this policy came to be viewed as an objective in itself. Furthermore, this objective turned out to be incompatible with that of economic stabilization. On a general level it appears that the central problem was an attempt to distribute more than 100% of the pie. As Simonsen concludes, the Cruzado Plan should not be considered as a stabilization plan with incomes policy support. In fact, it could be argued that the way in which the plan was implemented is more consistent with the view of a populist distributional scheme disguised as an economic stabilization program.

A related point that Modiano clearly leads to is the conceptual difficulty of designing a "neutral shock" (that is, a set of incomes policies and conversion rules that would preserve the pattern of income distribution existing before the implementation of the plan). One problem is that, at the time the program was launched, inflation was on the rise and consequently the pattern of income distribution was changing to the extent that indexation mechanisms were not being uniformly applied to all income sources. In this sense the objective of "neutrality" in income distribution remained elusive because it lacked a fixed reference point. On the other hand, the supposed objective of neutrality is not easy to reconcile with the handling of wage policy because the Cruzado Plan provided for real wage gains well in excess of the gains observed in productivity.

There is no question that the conversion schemes (which together with the controls constituted the basic instrument of incomes policy) were quite ingenious and elaborate; but, again, the size of the pie was badly miscalculated, as evidenced by the notions prevailing at the outset regarding the magnitude of the public sector's claim on resources and the handling of wage policy. As mentioned by Simonsen, one of the crucial aspects of the success of the earlier Bulhões-Campos reforms was the drastic decline in real wages (25% between 1964 and 1968).

What are some of the conclusions to be drawn from the Cruzado Plan experiment? First, in the context of a heterodox program, *incomes policies* should be regarded as an instrument of the stabilization strategy, not as a policy target. It seems clear that a separate income distribution objective may be in conflict with the inflation target of the authorities.

Second, regarding *pricing policies*, it is evident that one of the most important problems in the implementation of these programs is precisely when and how the price freeze should be lifted. One obvious lesson from Brazil is that this is not possible in the presence of excess demand, but then in that situation it is also difficult to maintain them. It seems important then to keep in mind that an initial reduction in demand (and possibly some contraction in economic activity) may have to be accepted. The "political fear of recession" turned out to be clearly unjustified in Brazil; in fact, the experience of Argentina and Israel indicates that the initial response of economic activity is rather more expansionary than expected.

Third, it may be necessary to generate at the outset a *fiscal overshooting*, that is, a temporary reduction in the fiscal deficit (or perhaps even a fiscal surplus) that should go beyond the perceived desirable or sustainable level in the medium term. This seems important to help establish the conditions of excess supply necessary to sustain the price freeze at the first stages and to lift it eventually. In addition, the provision for some margins or reserves that may eventually be distributed in the context of incomes policies would seem particularly important.

Finally, regarding monetary policy, it is important to monitor carefully the process of monetization; excessively large increases in the monetary aggregates, even if responding mostly to higher demand for money, will probably have an adverse effect on expectations.

### Comment by Miguel Urrutia

I have prepared my comments by reading what the authors of the Cruzado Plan have said in the past about inflation and stabilization in Brazil. In particular, I read the proceedings of the Institute for International Economics Inflation and Indexation Conference (December 1984) on the heroic assumption that the analysis of Brazilian inflation in that volume would contain many of the elements that Modiano and Simensen presented.

First, let me state that this exercise in the history of economic thought is not embarrassing for my colleagues. Nevertheless, one message of Arida and Lara-Resende in 1984 was that Brazilian inflation was primarily inertial. The fundamentals were close to being right, although Arida and Lara-Resende did admit that the data were scanty and that it was difficult to measure the level of the fiscal deficit.

The failure of the Cruzado Plan suggests that the "fundamentals" were not right and that there was probably a serious fiscal problem. In a world with such imperfect economic information, a good case can be made for Stan Fischer's idea of overshooting, that is, designing a policy package based on pessimistic assumptions about the degree of excess demand in the economy.

I have four additional points to make. First, given the apparent failure of the first heterodox shock, a valid question to ask is, What does one failure imply for future policy packages? It is obvious that expectations are crucial in stabilization plans. An interesting question is whether the failure of one heterodox package improves the chances of success of the next one. It is suggested that this was the case in Israel, where the failure of simple wage and price freezes convinced politicians that a more ambitious austerity package was necessary to stop inflation. Will the Cruzado Plan have the same political benefits?

At present, it seems that economic agents in Brazil expect a new freeze, and this has led to larger than necessary price increases that include an insurance premium against the next freeze. Because in Brazil there is no evidence that the Cruzado Plan failure improved the political support for fiscal orthodoxy, failure of the first stabilization package may in fact accelerate inflation.

Second, the experience of the Cruzado Plan suggests that the high parallel exchange rate generated pessimistic expectations about the success of the stabilization effort. In a future heterodox package, could dollar-indexed savings instruments avoid excessive pressure on the parallel rate? (I assume foreign capital flows remain controlled in Brazil).

Third, I find that Modiano's and Simonsen's discussions of Brazilian inflation oversimplify the functioning of labor markets; they usually assume that all wages are indexed. Nevertheless, much labor is not unionized in the formal urban sector, and I suspect that wages move at different rhythms in a fairly free labor market. I found, for example, that real wages in agriculture and large industry moved in opposite directions in Colombia during the 1970s. I suspect that indexation is not as uniform in different sectors of the economy as suggested by the models.

Finally, I also feel that there is insufficient discussion of the role of agriculture in inflation. Agricultural product variations affect inflation rates, and agricultural prices are hard to control. Can measures be taken to avoid the *destabilizing* shocks of agricultural price changes during a stabilization package? For example, one could include agricultural product import policies in such packages.

# IV          Bolivia

# 7 Inflation Stabilization in Bolivia

## Juan-Antonio Morales

Between the first quarter of 1982 and the fourth quarter of 1985 Bolivia experienced the highest inflation in the history of Latin America. High inflation, but not at hyperrates, had been present since the early months of 1982. Hyperinflation, if one uses Cagan's (1956) criterion, started approximately in April 1984 and ended in early September 1985. In the seventeen months of hyperinflation, prices increased by a factor of 623, and the average monthly inflation rate was 46%. Sachs (1986) ranks the Bolivian hyperinflation as the seventh largest in the twentieth century.

The stabilization program initiated on August 29, 1985, put a dramatic end to the plight: The March 1986 to March 1987 (annual) inflation rate was 21% or, equivalently, an average monthly rate of 1.6%. Inflation came to an end in two steps after the program began. In the first step the growth rate of prices fell rapidly to the point of becoming negative but this was followed by a strong upsurge in inflation three months later; this called for additional measures that, in the second step, effectively stopped the process.

As a background to hyperinflation and stabilization, the following factors have to be taken into account. Bolivia is a poor country with a per capita GNP of around $500 and a very small industrial base (manufacturing was 12% of GDP in 1985). Bolivia is an export economy that relies on two major exports: tin, which is subject to strong price fluctuations in world markets, and natural gas, the earnings of which depend on complex political considerations because it is a bilateral monopoly (Argentina is the only export market). Among Bolivia's legal exports (that is, excluding cocaine), tin and natural gas accounted for 58% of merchandise exports in the 1970s and 79% in the first half of the 1980s. This composition of exports makes Bolivia's foreign trade vulnerable and also reflects on internal stability because of the weight of taxes bearing on the external sector. Taxes related to the foreign trade sector constituted on average 55% of government revenue between 1981 and 1985.

I should mention the cocaine trade in this background discussion. Bolivian economics and politics are significantly affected by the presence of trade in cocaine. Conservative estimates give about the same value for cocaine exports as for legal exports, and value added in cocaine and cocaine-related activities may represent around 12% of legal GNP. These and higher figures appear in Doria Medina (1986). With regard to inflation and stabilization, there is some evidence that cocaine producers are major suppliers of foreign exchange to the black market. It may be conjectured that with a stable demand for foreign exchange the characteristic price jerks in the black market are caused by supply shocks derived from the vagaries of the cocaine trade. It should be stressed that failure to take strong action against the production of coca and cocaine has hindered the flow of external resources needed to support the several stabilization attempts between 1982 and 1985.

Bolivia was not a country of chronic inflation before high inflation erupted in 1982, nor did it have an abundance of built-in mechanisms that tended to perpetuate inflation, as has happened in other Latin American countries. Indexation was confined to the financial market. Between 1957 and 1981 the inflation rates were generally low, except when following a devaluation—and there were only two of them over the period. The genesis of inflation in Bolivia is somewhat different from other experiences discussed in this book. Untreated fiscal ailments, hidden transitorily by access to foreign credit, were more clearly the culprit. When the net flow of external resources became negative, inflation jumped upward. High inflation interacted with the chronic Bolivian political instability, which in turn can be partly explained by the acute distributive claims on the national income of a poor country. Bolivian inflation also had two other distinctive characteristics. First, the rates were much higher than in Argentina, Brazil, or Israel. Second, long-term peso contracts were nonexistent, and the short-lived wage indexation mechanisms were in shambles by the final months of hyperinflation. The economy had become indexed to the dollar to a significant extent, although not completely, when the stabilization program was initiated in August 1985.

Note also that the smallness of the Bolivian manufacturing and modern mining sections and, more generally, the lack of industrial tradition have important bearings on the economics and politics of stabilization. First, there are fewer markets with rigid prices in an economy of this type than in ones in which the industrial sector, with all its price-setting mechanisms, is large. Second, wage earners constitute only a small fraction of the labor force, and their eventual opposition to stabilization measures may not be shared by the population at large. In Bolivia strong militancy and mobilization made up for the small numbers, but in the long run continuous confrontation with the government weakened the endurance of labor. Third, in most cases before the installation of indexation in 1982, labor contracts did not carry well-defined periods of validity. Money wages were negotiated by the unions, either individually or collectively in the Confederation of Bolivian Workers (in both instances with government-provided arbitration), whenever the unions felt the need to recoup past losses in real wages. A prudent waiting interval was, however, always observed between wage readjustments.

The Bolivian stabilization program is closer to the orthodox IMF package than to the heterodox approaches discussed in other chapters of this book. It is a shock program whose main thrust is fiscal correction. It was accompanied by an ample program of market liberalization.

I have organized my discussion as follows. The features and accomplishments of the program and some remarks on the nature of Bolivian hyperinflation are discussed in section 7.1. Details of the stabilization program are given in section 7.2. I devote significant space in section 7.3 to the description of how the program has worked until now: its intended and unintended results. In that section I include a preliminary evaluation of the achievements and the costs. In section 7.4 I present the policy issues as of June 1987. My conclusions make up section 7.5.

## 7.1 The Immediate Conditions: Open Hyperinflation

The means of stopping Bolivian hyperinflation can be better evaluated after a description of the inflationary process itself. This section includes a short background. More complete accounts can be found in Sachs (1986), Kharas and Pinto (1986), and Morales (1986).

### Accelerating Inflation

High inflation was preceded by intense political turmoil. The four years from 1978 to 1982 witnessed several interim presidents, coups, and stalemated elections; there were nine heads of state. The political chaos of the period had a paralyzing effect on the economy as the surrounding uncertainty delayed the recognition of the nature of the impending crisis, the symptoms of which were already present, and obstructed the decision-making process. Quite unfortunately for Bolivia the internal political chaos and the onset of the world recession of 1981–82 overlapped. The political conditions impaired the necessary corrections in the fiscal front and delayed the adjustments to redress the disequilibrium in the external accounts that had been aggravated by the international conditions. Indeed, by December 1981 the exchange rate was grossly overvalued, the fiscal deficit was large, the extent of external indebtedness relative to GDP was high, and new and expensive short-term foreign loans had been added to the large debt to sustain consumption levels. The shaky political situation precluded the corrections out of fear of implications for income distribution. Furthermore, Bolivia remained largely isolated from the discussions in international academic and official circles on the ways to cope with the crisis; many macroeconomic mistakes can be attributed to this.

Fatigue along with the deterioration of the economy and the political instability forced the military to reconvene the Bolivian Congress elected in 1980, which in turn, acting as an electoral college, named the civilian Hernán Siles-Zuazo as president in October 1982. Siles-Zuazo governed with a coalition of center-left and leftist parties, including, as a junior partner, the Communist Party of Bolivia. The composition of Siles-Zuazo's cabinet had indeed far-reaching implications for the economics of inflation. The aggravation of inflation, culminating in hyperinflation, occurred during his term.

The sudden reversal in the net flow of external resources in the first months of 1982 as a consequence of the international debt crisis can be identified as the proximate cause of the high inflation rates. At the onset of the crisis Bolivia found itself with a large foreign debt. Moreover, the debt was heavily concentrated in the public sector. In the second half of the 1970s foreign credits had been the main source of financing for public investment projects and for fiscal current account deficits. At the end of 1981 the ratios of total external debt to GDP and exports of goods and nonfactor services were 81% and 306%, respectively, the same ratios for the public long-term debt (outstanding and disbursed) were 69% and 268%, respectively.[1] Bolivia was already experiencing difficulties honoring its debts when the international crisis broke. For instance, arrears on amortizations to private creditors had built up between the third quarter of 1980 and the second quarter of 1981.[2]

The reversal in external resource flows came with this background of indebtedness. It should be underscored that Bolivia did not suffer a terms of trade shock, as other countries in the region did when the crisis began. Unanticipated increases in the average interest rate during 1981–82 and a shortening of maturities had a more important impact than the terms of trade deterioration, but the most important shock came when Bolivia suddenly could no longer borrow.

As foreign exchange reserves dwindled, Bolivia had to, first, devalue significantly. Then speculation against the peso forced the monetary authorities to abandon in March 1982 the regime of unified fixed exchange rates for a while in favor of a dual regime, with an official rate reserved for wheat imports and public foreign debt servicing and a parallel free market rate for all other transactions. Exporters had to surrender 40% of their export proceeds to the Central Bank at the official rate.[3] The peso depreciated rapidly in the parallel market between March and October 1982 (see table 7A.1 in the appendix). In the public sector the negative net external resource flow was met with a substitution of foreign sources by internal financing. The rapid peso depreciation in the parallel market worsened the fiscal deficit, which in turn was financed by issuing money, and this led to more depreciation. The situation clearly became unstable by September 1982.

The process of inflation was already well on its way when the new government of President Siles-Zuazo was installed in October 1982. A few weeks after his inauguration a stabilization plan was announced—the first of at least six attempts during his term. It is worth discussing this program briefly for two reasons. First, the Bolivian press tends to attribute the failure of economic policy during the Siles-Zuazo administration to the aftereffects of this initial move. Second, some important lessons can be drawn from its developments.

This first stabilization program was indeed the most heterodox of all, containing on the one hand standard measures to correct relative prices (including a strong devaluation of the official exchange rate by 78% and hikes in the prices of publicly provided goods and services) and, on the other hand, a return to a fixed exchange rate with controls, a set of ceilings for the prices of essential goods and interest rates, and the establishment for the first time in Bolivia of wage indexation with a "trigger" device of automatic readjustment of the minimum wage whenever cumulative inflation since the last wage correction hit 40%.[4] Foreign exchange controls were accompanied by "dedollarization" of contracts among Bolivian residents.[5]

The program of 1982 failed quite rapidly. Although the consumer price index grew at relatively low rates for two months, telltale signs of forthcoming trouble appeared almost immediately in the by now flourishing black market for foreign exchange.[6] Indeed the premiums increased to more than 100% by the end of February 1983 (see table 7A.3 in the appendix).

After March 1983 inflation accelerated. The foreign exchange and price controls to check inflation proved themselves to be futile over the medium run and, worse, pernicious, with welfare costs and unbearable fiscal costs. A situation of excess demand at the controlled prices appeared with severe shortages and thriving black markets (including the one for contraband exports) of staples provided by the private sector. With reference to the fiscal sector, in addition to the familiar Olivera-Tanzi effect on the real tax base, the severe overvaluation of the official exchange rate had strongly negative repercussions on both public enterprises producing for export and the central government, given the importance of foreign trade for tax revenues.[7] Similarly, prices of publicly provided goods and services lagged behind inflation significantly, further contributing to the deterioration of public sector finances. The extent of the fiscal catastrophe is shown in table 7.1.

The public sector deficits were increasingly financed by the Central Bank and by the building up of arrears on the public external and internal debt. The private sector producers facing controlled prices diverted goods to black markets and knocked on the door of the government for subsidies. The most important mechanism of subsidization was that of Central Bank loans to the banking system and ultimately to producers at negative real interest rates. In many markets private producers were compensated with cheap credit for selling their products at the controlled prices, which were below equilibrium prices. Money creation was as much the result of loans to the private sector, needed because of incorrect administered prices, as of financing the public sector deficits (see table 7.2).

In the beginning months of Siles-Zuazo's administration, the labor unions lent support to the government in exchange for significant wage increases. As inflation accelerated and austerity measures had to be taken, the original labor support became bitter opposition. The unchecked "wage race" in the public sector curtailed the many attempts to reduce real public expenditures. Public expenditures needed to fall in the face of falling revenues.

The financing of the fiscal deficits and of the subsidized loans to the private sector (which I call "quasi-fiscal deficits") with the issuance of money by the Central Bank lost its effectiveness rapidly as the demand for money decreased.

**Table 7.1**
Summary of public sector operations (% of GDP)

| Operation | 1980 | 1981 | 1982 | 1983 | 1984 | 1985 |
|---|---|---|---|---|---|---|
| 1. Current revenues, general government | 13.1 | 15.3 | 10.9 | 6.9 | 4.6 | 11.1 |
| a. Tax revenues[a] | 8.7 | 8.9 | 4.9 | 2.8 | 2.8 | 8.8 |
| 2. Current expenditures of general government | −16.5 | −17.9 | −21.6 | −26.0 | −25.4 | −18.8 |
| 3. Current account balance of general government (1 + 2) | −3.4 | −2.7 | −10.7 | −19.2 | −20.7 | −7.7 |
| 4. Current account balance of public enterprises | 1.2 | 2.1 | 3.0 | 1.3 | −2.4 | 2.1 |
| 5. Current account balance of consolidated public sector (3 + 4) | −2.2 | −0.6 | −7.7 | −17.9 | −23.1 | −5.6 |
| 6. Capital revenue of consolidated public sector | 0.2 | 0.5 | 0.6 | 4.5 | 0.3 | 0.3 |
| 7. Capital expenditure of consolidated public sector | −6.9 | −7.4 | −7.4 | −5.7 | −4.6 | −3.8 |
| 8. Net lending of consolidated public sector | −0.1 | −0.3 | −0.2 | 0.0 | 0.0 | 0.0 |
| 9. Overall surplus (+) or deficit (−) of consolidated public sector (5 + 6 + 7 + 8) | −9.0 | −7.8 | −14.7 | −19.1 | −27.4 | −9.1 |
| 10. Financing of consolidated public sector deficit | 9.0 | 7.8 | 14.7 | 19.1 | 27.4 | 9.1 |
| a. External net | 4.9 | 4.9 | −1.0 | −1.6 | 2.3 | 0.2 |
| b. Internal net | 3.9 | 3.0 | 16.6 | 20.7 | 25.1 | 8.9 |
| c. Short-term foreign loans | 0.2 | −0.2 | −0.9 | 0.0 | 0.0 | 0.0 |

Source: Unpublished IMF data.
a. Tax revenue of the central administration and nonfinancial public enterprises.

**Table 7.2**
Sources of expansion of the money base, 1982–August 1985 (% of GDP)[a]

| Year | (1) Net foreign exchange reserves | (2) Net credit to public sector | (3) Credit to banks | (4) Other | (5) = (1) + (2) + (3) + (4) Money base |
|------|------|------|------|------|------|
| 1982 | −8.9 | 11.4 | 2.6 | 4.7 | 9.8 |
| 1983 | 8.2 | 8.9 | 1.6 | −10.8 | 7.9 |
| 1984 | 3.3 | 3.3 | 3.4 | 0.5 | 10.4 |
| 1985[b] | 1.4 | −1.1 | 2.6 | 6.5 | 9.5 |

Source: Author's estimates based on Central Bank of Bolivia data.
a. Annual averages based on quarterly changes divided by quarterly GDP.
b. From January 1985 to August 1985.

## Transition to Hyperinflation

The situation degenerated in the second quarter of 1984 in a clear case of hyperinflation.[8] Between March 1984 and August 1985 prices increased by a factor of 623. This gives an average monthly rate of inflation of 46%. In February 1985 inflation beat all Latin American records: 182%.

Hyperinflation was the most visible element in a picture of general economic decline. Between 1982 and 1985 GDP fell by 18%, and investment rates diminished steadily to reach an all-time low of 5.7% in 1985. The accumulation of external debt continued mostly in the form of conversion of short-term loans into medium- and long-term loans and unilateral capitalization of interest (see table 7.3). There is no doubt that inflation, especially government attempts to suppress its symptoms, and the surrounding uncertainty had important real supply-side effects. The real costs were compounded by the fact that a significant part of the economy went underground to escape the government controls. Inflation and controls were not of course the only culprits of the chaos; the external adjustment needs and the attendant foreign exchange constraints were as pernicious.[9]

With regard to real wages, it should be mentioned that between 1982 and 1985 the trend was one of deterioration but with seesaw movements in the short run. The trigger mechanism of indexation was abandoned in April 1984 and replaced by a system with a fixed periodicity of four months. In the final months of hyperinflation, the adjustment interval was changed to one month. It must be said, however, that the wage regime was in shambles after the second quarter of 1984, with the government trying to buy time before any due adjustment and the unions obtaining concessions outside

**Table 7.3**
Bolivia: Key indicators, 1980–86

| Key indicator | 1980 | 1981 | 1982 | 1983 | 1984 | 1985 | 1986[g] |
|---|---|---|---|---|---|---|---|
| **Prices, exchange rates, and wages (1980 = 100)[a]** | | | | | | | |
| Consumer price index | 100.0 | 132.2 | 295.4 | 1,109.4 | 15,324.7 | 1,815,918.7 | 6,833,885.5 |
| Official exchange rate | 100.0 | 100.0 | 260.3 | 1,007.8 | 11,389.9 | 1,844,462.1 | 8,395,124.4 |
| Parallel market exchange rate | 100.0 | 128.5 | 587.6 | 2,635.9 | 33,814.4 | 2,932,866.5 | 9,140,008.2 |
| Nominal wage | 100.0 | 120.7 | 210.4 | 812.0 | 17,366.0 | 1,082,814.6 | 3,865,232.0 |
| Annual inflation rate (%)[b] | 47.2 | 32.2 | 123.5 | 275.6 | 1281.4 | 11749.6 | 276.3 |
| **Monetary indicators** | | | | | | | |
| Annual rate of growth of base money (%)[c] | — | 11.4 | 125.2 | 242.5 | 585.1 | 7820.4 | 355.6 |
| Base money (% GDP)[d] | 9.6 | 8.6 | 7.6 | 7.5 | 3.6 | 2.6 | 3.9 |
| M1 (% GDP)[d] | 9.5 | 8.8 | 7.4 | 6.4 | 3.4 | 2.6 | 3.9 |
| M2 (% GDP)[d] | 15.8 | 15.4 | 14.3 | 11.0 | 4.7 | 4.9 | 7.7 |
| Interest rate[e] | 28.0 | 45.0 | 45.0 | 62.0 | 150.0 | 231.1 | 65.16 |
| **Relative price levels (1980 = 100)** | | | | | | | |
| Real effective official exchange rate[e,i] | 100.0 | n.a. | 135.4 | 162.6 | 281.3 | 78.3 | 84.3 |
| Terms of trade | 100.0 | 99.7 | 98.1 | 99.3 | 104.1 | 104.3 | 81.9 |
| Real wage[e] | 100.0 | 91.3 | 66.6 | 63.3 | 61.0 | 59.3 | 55.7 |
| **Consolidated public sector deficit (% GDP)** | 9.0 | 7.8 | 14.7 | 19.1 | 27.4 | 9.1[g] | 4.0 |
| **External sector** | | | | | | | |
| Exports FOB (millions of US dollars) | 942.2 | 912.4 | 827.7 | 755.1 | 724.5 | 623.4 | 543.4 |
| Imports CIF (millions of US dollars) | 678.4 | 975.4 | 577.5 | 589.1 | 491.6 | 551.9 | 717.5 |
| Current account balance (% GDP) | −1.5 | −12.7 | −5.6 | −5.5 | −5.1 | −9.2 | −10.7 |
| Debt outstanding and disbursed (% GDP)[f] | 62.9 | 69.2 | 71.2 | 82.3 | 84.1 | 86.2 | 88.4 |
| Debt outstanding and disbursed (% exports of goods and NF services)[f] | 217.7 | 268.0 | 306.2 | 364.4 | 394.5 | 457.2 | 511.0 |
| Total debt service (% GDP)[f] | 8.2 | 7.3 | 7.4 | 7.6 | 8.4 | 6.6 | 4.5 |
| Total debt service (% exports of goods and services)[f] | 28.4 | 28.1 | 31.7 | 33.3 | 39.5 | 34.8 | 26.2 |

**Table 7.3** (continued)

| Key indicator | 1980 | 1981 | 1982 | 1983 | 1984 | 1985 | 1986[g] |
|---|---|---|---|---|---|---|---|
| **Output, investment, savings, and employment** | | | | | | | |
| GDP per capita (US dollars) | 825 | 799 | 733 | 662 | 664 | 588 | 555 |
| Annual rate of growth of real GDP | 1.2 | −0.4 | −5.6 | −7.2 | −2.4 | −4.0 | −2.9 |
| Gross fixed capital formation (% GDP)[h] | 13.9 | 13.0 | 7.9 | 3.1 | 10.0 | 5.7 | 6.1 |
| Gross national savings (% GDP)[h] | 13.4 | 4.2 | 7.4 | 4.0 | 6.9 | 0.8 | 0.9 |
| Unemployment rate (%)[e] | 5.8 | 9.7 | 10.9 | 13.0 | 15.5 | 18.0 | 20.0 |

Sources: Prices, exchange rates, wages, real wages, unemployment rates, and monetary indicators from UDAPE, *Anexo Estadístico* (La Paz: UDAPE, December 1986); unpublished UDAPE data; and Banco Central de Bolivia, *Boletín Estadístico* (various issues). Real exchange rates from unpublished IMF and UDAPE data. Terms of trade from CEPAL, *Statistical Yearbook for Latin America and the Caribbean* (various issues) and unpublished World Bank data. Balance of payments from IMF, *International Financial Statistics, Yearbook* (February 1986); and unpublished UDAPE data. External debt figures from World Bank, *World Debt Tables* (1986 edition). Fiscal budget figures from IMF unpublished data and author's estimates. National accounts from Banco Central de Bolivia, *Boletín Estadístico* (various issues) and unpublished World Bank data.

a. Annual averages.

b. Year-to-year changes of annual average price levels.

c. Year-to-year change of annual average base money stock.

d. Based on annual average money stocks.

e. End of year.

f. Based on end-of-year debt values; only public and publicly guaranteed long-term debt are included.

g. Preliminary estimates.

h. Derived from figures at current prices.

i. Increasing values indicate appreciation.

the legally defined indexation interval. It is interesting to note that the unions never demanded reductions in the pay periods, as happened with hyperinflationary experiences in other countries. Dollarization and the development of a vigorous retail market for dollars probably explain this.

Inflation interacted with serious political instability. Numerous strikes and other forms of work stoppages marred both production and policy-making. Cabinet reshuffles were frequent: Over the thirty-three months of the Siles-Zuazo presidency there were seven ministers of finance and an equal number of Central Bank presidents.

There were six attempts at stabilization between November 1982 and August 1985, and all of them failed. Each stabilization package contained a devaluation (open or concealed), other corrections of relative prices, and increasing liberalization of markets, except the first package. Two attempts, in April 1984 and February 1985, were fairly orthodox and close to the standard IMF package. In February 1985 a fiscal rescue operation was undertaken in the form of indexation of taxes and interest rates, but to no avail.[10] General strikes organized by the Confederation of Bolivian Workers were the fatal blow to the April 1984 and February 1985 stabilization attempts.

Stabilization

The worsening of the situation obliged President Siles-Zuazo to call for early elections in 1984. The elections were won by center and center-right parties, with the left suffering a heavy defeat that also weakened the labor unions. Victor Paz Estenssoro succeeded Siles Zuazo as president in August 1985. Paz rules with the support of center-right and rightist parties in Congress, and several prominent businessmen hold key posts in his cabinet.

By August 1985 the situation was economically and politically ripe to try to stabilize once again. The low real value of the money base gave a favorable precondition for a new attempt. Long-term peso contracts had almost completely disappeared, the wage indexation mechanisms (and the labor unions) were discredited, and the economy had become extremely (but not fully) dollarized to the point of using dollars alongside pesos in small transactions.[11] At the same time there was a strong social demand for stabilization, even for a shock treatment. Any new government could have enjoyed a long honeymoon if it implemented suitable policies incorporating some imagination. The new government (and the public) became rapidly convinced that hyperinflation had to be stopped, even at the cost of a full but hopefully short recession.

Supreme Decree 21060, announced on August 29, 1985, contained the main elements of the stabilization program and the underlying rationale. The decree and the complementary measures included in the so-called New Economic Policy (NEP) have stopped inflation. Details of the program, its achievements, and unresolved problems appear in the following sections.

## 7.2 Features of the Stabilization Program

The core of the stabilization program (and of the NEP) is given by drastic measures of fiscal correction, a unification of exchange rates, and a return to full convertibility. A full liberalization of markets has accompanied the program. As a side comment it should be mentioned that the Bolivian Congress approved a monetary reform in 1986, changing the national currency unit from the peso to the boliviano. One boliviano equals one million pesos. The intention of the reform was to facilitate the accounting and day-to-day operations. This reform does not have a major role in the stabilization program.

The Fiscal Package

The fiscal measures deal with the revenue and expenditure sides of the accounts of central government and the public enterprises. When it was announced, the program did not state explicitly a target on the fiscal deficit. There was, however, a declared intention that it be as close to zero as possible. Quantitative targets came later, in April 1986, when the budget was passed and followed by a standby agreement with the IMF.

With regard to revenue, a key measure was to raise the price of gasoline and other petroleum products [which are provided by the state enterprise Yacimientos Petroliferos Fiscales Bolivianos (YPFB) and were grossly under-valued at border prices] to levels slightly above the international ones. (Gasoline prices increased overnight by a factor of 7 in real terms.) This quickly benefited YPFB and the central government with the collection of excise taxes. As important, the government called for immediate payment of the substantial back taxes, revalued at the new prices, owed by YPFB. Given the new prices, YPFB was in a position to pay all tax liabilities. Taxes on gasoline and other oil products had two advantages when the program was unveiled: First, they could be collected rapidly, and evasion was almost nil; second, the initial prices were so low that a correction provided a once and for all significant jump in revenues. To prevent future lags in prices of oil derivatives (and other publicly provided goods and services), SD 21060 fixed them in dollar terms. Subsequently the government indexed taxes to the dollar as well.

The de facto devaluation (93%) that accompanied the unification of exchange rates (discussed later) also had an important net positive impact on fiscal revenues, given the importance of taxes on foreign trade and the presence of public enterprises in the export markets.

The steps taken to reduce expenditures were almost as dramatic. All wages in the public sector were frozen at their prestabilization (nominal) levels, after a consolidation of extra bonuses to the basic wage, with some ceilings that actually reduced the annual salaries of some specialized workers. The low wages induced, quite naturally, "voluntary" retirement from the public sector. In addition, the NEP called for a substantial reduction of employment in the public sector, in both public enterprises and the central government. Several state enterprises were dismembered and their parts transferred to local governments. The avowed intention in doing so was to facilitate their privatization.

The severe terms of trade shock suffered by Bolivia in the last quarter of 1985 soon after the stabilization program was announced was a strong reason for the government to reduce employment in the main export state enterprises. In the last quarter of 1986, 23,000 out of 30,000 miners of the state-owned mining enterprise Corporacion Minera de Bolivia (COMIBOL) were discharged. In YPFB, employment was also reduced but in less dramatic proportions than in COMIBOL. By March 1987 employment in the public sector had decreased by 10%.[12]

To sum up, the real wage bill in the public sector was reduced by lower real wages, by dismissals, and by a significant number of resignations.

The stabilization program enforced a temporary freeze on public sector investment. After two years of implementing the program, investment in the public sector is still parsimonious. In addition to the freeze on investment, the state enterprises have been subjected to a tightened grip on their current operations, which only recently has been loosening somewhat.

In 1986 and 1987 the consolidated public sector budgets were passed by the Bolivian Congress, and they have been used effectively as guidelines for fiscal behavior. Strict obedience to the budget is a cornerstone of the stabilization program. For the first time in many years the state enterprises are generally respecting their budget constraints. These are significant regime changes in Bolivia, in contrast to the frequent discretionary behavior in the past, particularly during the high-inflation period.

Bolivia has not been servicing its debt to private foreign creditors, mainly commercial banks, and arrears with them are currently substantial;

but Bolivia has been negotiating, with a high probability of success, a partial debt cancellation and repurchase. Bolivia has normalized its situation with lending governments and official multilateral banks.[13] It should be emphasized that during the first nine months virtually the only external source of financing the program was the accumulation of arrears on the debt to private foreign creditors.

In mid-1986 a new tax law was approved by the Congress. A value added tax of 10% and some wealth taxes are the core of the new legislation, and it can be easily verified that the tax incidence incorporated in the reform is essentially proportional to income, except for low incomes. Fiscal expediency has been the dominant factor in the design, and equity considerations seem to be absent.

Exchange Rate Unification

The unification of exchange rates was the other pillar of the stabilization package. This had been obtained through a rather ingenious mechanism of dirty floating that works as follows. Private agents are allowed to buy and sell foreign exchange at whatever price they agree, but the Central Bank sells foreign exchange to the public in a daily open auction. The Central Bank buys foreign exchange at the average price fixed in the last auction. The main suppliers to the Central Bank are public enterprises. In principle, exporters are obliged to surrender 100% of their foreign exchange proceeds to the Central Bank, but in fact this rule is binding only for the public sector exporters because private enterprises can repurchase their sales in the auctions of the Central Bank.

Intervention of the Central Bank in the auction has two prongs: (1) a base price for all bids to participate in the auction and (2) the amount that is offered in each auction. Bidders do not know beforehand either the base price or the amount offered by the bank, and thus they have to process the information provided by the previous auction. Since February 1986 the Central Bank has been intervening as another bidder. This poses the question of how flexible the exchange rate regime is in fact.

The Program of Liberalization

The stabilization program was accompanied by an ample program of liberalization of markets. Price ceilings, except for publicly provided goods and services and a handful of public utilities, have been eliminated. There are no quantitative restrictions or other barriers to domestic and international trade. Import tariffs have been fixed at a uniform rate of 20%, and there is an ongoing discussion in government circles over whether to lower them to a uniform level of 10%. To avoid anti-export biases in the tariff structure, almost all exporters are granted a uniform tax rebate on their inputs equal to 10% of the free onboard (FOB) value of their exports.

The extent of financial liberalization is also significant. All ceilings (and floors) on interest rates have been eliminated. Banks are allowed to participate without restriction in the financing of foreign trade operations and in transactions of the capital account of the balance of payments. Depositors can open dollar and dollar-indexed accounts, and banks can make dollar and dollar-indexed loans along with peso credits in any way they deem convenient. Moreover, dollar and dollar-denominated accounts have small legal reserve requirements. An ongoing profound reform of the Central Bank should also be placed in the financial liberalization package.

In the labor market legal restrictions to discharge workers in the private sector freely have been attenuated. The NEP has returned to the system of market adjustment in individual wage negotiations between employees and employers, eliminating the supervisory powers on labor contracts of the Ministry of Labor and the peculiar ways of collective bargaining that prevailed before in Bolivia. Moreover, compulsory across the board wage indexation and, at first, minimum wage provisions were eliminated. Subsequently a very low minimum wage was fixed [currently around $25 (US dollars) per month]. The only significant practical implication for such a low wage is for social security pensions, where it serves as a baseline. The reservation wage (or supply price) of all other workers in the labor force, even of unskilled teenagers, is presumably well above that minimum wage.

## The Anchors for Inflation

Although de facto stabilization started in the foreign exchange market, as is shown in section 7.3, the stabilization program did not initially seek to use the exchange rate to anchor inflation. In a somewhat rhetorical way SD 21060, which is the heart of the program, proposed the concept of a "real, unique and flexible exchange rate." "Real" meant "realistic" in the context of the decree. In the spirit of SD 21060 the exchange rate was intended to play a role as important for recovery as for stabilization. Notwithstanding the original position, after a short revival of inflation in December 1985–January 1986, stabilization has focused explicitly on the exchange rate.

At the start of the stabilization program the government committed itself to check the expansion of "monetary emission" drastically; however, no specific quantitative targets were fixed. The signal to the public was clearly on the rate of growth of money, and, given the nature of the fiscal correction, the commitment was credible. Monetary emission is of course a primitive concept, and after a short while it had to be qualified and changed to "inorganic monetary emission," that is, expansion of the money base unbacked by foreign reserves.

Last but not least, in a country such as Bolivia the freezing of wages in the large public sector and the tough stance on the labor unions of the state enterprises added a strong ingredient to the credibility of the commitment to check "inorganic" money growth and, ultimately, inflation. For a sizable fraction of the public the wage freeze became tantamount to controlled fiscal deficits and money creation.

## 7.3 Stabilization Results to Date

The Achievements

The most important achievement of the Bolivian stabilization effort has been the dramatic fall in inflation, as can be seen in figure 7.1 and in table 7A.2 in the appendix. Except for September 1985 and the period from

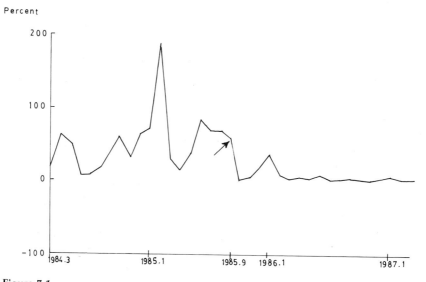

**Figure 7.1**
Month-to-month changes of average price levels, March 1984–March 1987. Arrow indicates beginning of stabilization.

December 1985 to February 1986, to which a reference is made later, the monthly inflation rate has been consistently lower than 4.3%. The annual inflation rate from March 1986 to March 1987 was 21%, or 1.6% per month. In regard to the unification of the exchange rates, it can be seen from table 7A.3 that after March 1986 the premiums have generally been below 3% (see also figures 7.2 and 7.3). This is in clear contrast to what happened during the high-inflation period.

The September 1985 change in the consumer price index (57%) was still very high but can be explained by the hitherto repressed component of inflation, which became open with the adjustments in the prices of the public sector goods and services, the de facto devaluation of the official exchange rate, and the elimination of the few price ceilings that were still active. In fact, after an initial jump, prices fell for some weeks, starting in the second week of September 1985, and then the inflation rate was stabilized at the low rates mentioned, except for a short-lived outburst, which is examined later Table 7.4 shows the rapid end to inflation.

The story of how inflation was stopped abruptly is more controversial. Stabilization started in the parallel market for foreign exchange, where quotations of the dollar decreased immediately after the plan was an-

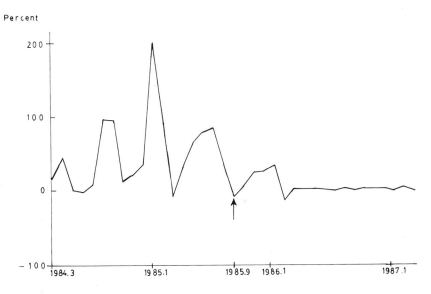

**Figure 7.2**
Month-to-month changes of average foreign exchange rates in the parallel market, March 1984–March 1987. Arrow indicates beginning of stabilization.

Percent

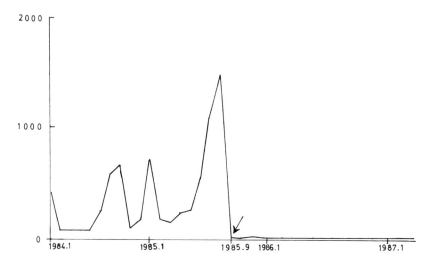

**Figure 7.3**
Premiums in the parallel market exchange rates, March 1984–March 1987. Arrow
indicates beginning of stabilization.

**Table 7.4**
Week-to-week percentage changes in prices and free market exchange rates, August
1985–September 1985

| Time period | CPI | Exchange rate |
| --- | --- | --- |
| August 5–11 | 18.37 | 4.91 |
| August 12–18 | 8.57 | 2.42 |
| August 19–25 | 6.15 | 9.26 |
| August 26–September 1 | 19.87 | 12.81[a] |
| September 2–8 | 36.82 | −12.96 |
| September 9–15 | −4.60 | −9.78 |
| September 16–22 | −0.84 | −3.15 |
| September 23–29 | −2.51 | 8.09 |
| September 30–October 6 | 0.74 | 1.87 |

Source: Unpublished data of the Bolivian National Institute of Statistics.
a. The stabilization program was announced on August 29.

nounced (see table 7.4). But this had also happened during the failed stabilization attempts of the previous government, when hyperinflation was alive and the real value of the stock of pesos was already low with regard to past patterns (see the May 1984, June 1984, and March 1985 figures in table 7A.2 in the appendix). My explanation for this phenomenon is rather simple: The strong devaluation of the official exchange rate and the steep hikes in public sector prices produced an additional contraction of the already low real money stock, measured in terms of domestic prices (and the official exchange rate). The once and for all high jump in administered prices and the official exchange rate caused a liquidity crunch. With the liquidity shortage, expectations of inflation or further depreciation over the short run abated, the demand for money increased, and the Central Bank started to build up foreign exchange reserves. Lower (peso) liquidity and lower expectations had their most immediate impact on the parallel foreign exchange market. Notice that in the previous stabilization attempts, for instance in April 1984 and February 1985, in the month immediately following the initiation of the stabilization programs, foreign exchange in the parallel market was stabilized and the real money stock, using the CPI deflator, initially diminished. In the following months the real money stock increased rapidly but only for a while, until inflationary expectations awoke again (see table 7A.4 in the appendix). These dynamics of the interaction between money creation, free market exchange rates, and big jumps in official exchange rates and administered prices explain transitory stabilization.

The stabilization kickoff given by supertight liquidity and how this affected expectations over the short run need to be emphasized. Notice the parallelism with other experiences, particularly the one in Germany (Dornbusch 1986b, c). Sachs (1986) has a somewhat different view. He analyzed in detail the features of short-run stabilization starting in the foreign exchange market and developed several models in which immediate cessation of inflation is consistent with no immediate change in inflationary expectations, even over the short term. In those interesting models stabilization could proceed even without a return of confidence.[14]

After initial stabilization the problem was sustaining the effort. It is here that the fiscal correction entered the scene. Tax revenues generated in the domestic market for oil products and payments of arrears on tax liabilities had started to replenish the government coffers already in October 1985. In the last quarter of 1985 taxes from the oil sector constituted 74% of all central government revenues and 8% of quarterly GDP. Table 7.5 shows the importance of revenues in the quarters before and after the announce-

**Table 7.5**
Quarterly central government tax revenue, 1985

| Tax revenue | First quarter | Second quarter | Third quarter | Fourth quarter |
|---|---|---|---|---|
| **Total tax revenue** (% of GDP) | 1.1 | 1.2 | 1.6 | 11.3 |
| Taxes on hydrocarbons (% of GDP) | 0.4 | 0.0 | 0.4 | 8.4 |
| Taxes on hydrocarbons (% of total tax revenue) | 39.0 | 2.2 | 22.1 | 74.1 |

Source: UDAPE (1986) and author's estimates.

ment of the program. The quick fiscal recovery was possible because of the discrete jump upward in public prices from the low initial levels. The combination of high prices for oil derivatives, high taxes, and tight control of current expenditures in YPFB and the freeze in its investments retired money from the public and made room for other sources of expansion for the monetary base, which then grew at a moderate pace (see figure 7.4 and table 7A.2 in the appendix). Notice the "crowding out" of credit on the public sector.

It should also be mentioned that speculation against the program when the government made public its preparation led to defensive price increases and supply shortages. [Compare this with what happened in Germany in the final months of hyperinflation, according to Cagan (1956) and LaHaye (1985).] When the program came to light, some prices actually decreased from their previous levels. This implied an immediate and crucial political capital gain for the program.

Last, although it may not seem clear at once, liberalization had a non-negligible role in disinflation because it provided natural checks to domestic speculative behavior and reduced the need to finance quasi-fiscal deficits. The latter effect was probably more important than the former.

The collapse of the tin market in the London Metal Exchange in the last days of October 1985 put a severe strain on the stabilization effort. Anticipation of shortages of foreign exchange awoke speculation against the peso. In addition, a clearly incorrect handling of the foreign exchange auctions in the Central Bank, with sudden strong reductions in the amounts offered, sent the wrong messages to the public, increasing speculation further. To this already unfavorable background, a one-step increase in the monetary base, resulting from the need to finance the traditional Christmas bonus of civil servants in December 1985, was added at the same time that the state petroleum company YPFB was trying to escape from the tight governmental control on its current expenditures. The confluence of all

Percent

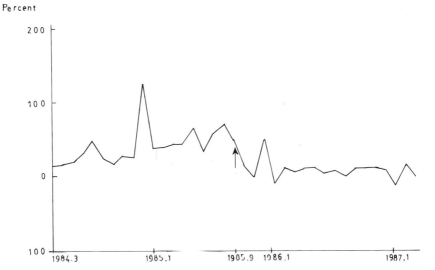

**Figure 7.4**
Monthly rates of growth of the money base, March 1984–March 1987. Arrow indicates
beginning of stabilization.

those factors reignited inflation in December 1985 and January 1986, at
high rates (see table 7.6). Those two months were the most dangerous ones
for the stabilization program.

To overcome the situation, the government took two steps, one rather
conventional and the other considerably riskier. First, it tightened even
more its fiscal and monetary policies. On the fiscal front more controls
were imposed on the current revenues and expenditures of state enterprises. Furthermore, the government delayed for almost a month the payment of wages and salaries due to its workers, hence increasing the floating
internal debt but diminishing the recourse to monetary emission. In fact,
public sector workers made an involuntary loan to the government that
lasted for several months. Another monetary measure was a temporary
increase in the legal reserve ratio of the banking system to 100% on in-
structions from the Central Bank. In January 1986 all nominal monetary
aggregates decreased (see table 7A.1 in the appendix).

Second, the government took the risky measure of increasing significantly the amount of foreign exchange offered in the auctions of the
Central Bank, announcing at the same time that it expected a fall in the
peso price of the dollar of around 35% in the following three weeks. The
announcement was credible, in view of the tightness of the monetary

**Table 7.6**
Week-to-week percentage changes in prices and free market exchange rates, November 1985–February 1986

| Time period | CPI | Exchange rate |
|---|---|---|
| November 11–17 | −1.19 | 10.97 |
| November 18–24 | 2.27 | 2.00 |
| November 25–December 1 | 2.98 | 20.73 |
| December 2–8 | 10.44 | 6.81 |
| December 9–15 | 0.51 | −2.41 |
| December 16–22 | 5.47 | −1.38 |
| December 23–29 | 3.83 | 10.39 |
| December 30–January 5 | 3.63 | 3.94 |
| January 6–12 | 13.32 | 23.90 |
| January 13–19 | 8.92 | 14.64 |
| January 20–26 | 10.38 | −18.30[a] |
| January 27–February 2 | −5.32 | −9.40 |
| February 3–9 | 0.14 | −3.65 |
| February 10–16 | 0.01 | −0.63 |
| February 17–23 | −0.34 | 0.92 |
| February 24–March 2 | −0.31 | 0.37 |

Source: Unpublished data of the Bolivian National Institute of Statistics.
a. Minister of Planning Sanchez de Lozada announced measures of disinflation in the foreign exchange market on January 18.

policy, and speculative bubbles disappeared. In fact, almost immediately the dollar fell in both the official and the parallel market at a percentage slightly lower than the target, and this was obtained with little loss in foreign reserves (see table 7.6). The peso appreciation penalized speculators in the foreign exchange market and made them more cautious than during the high-inflation period. This was an important explanatory factor of stabilization in the following months. In February 1986 stabilization was back on its feet. Note that, once again, stabilization started in the foreign exchange market.

The vicious circle was initiated: A budget was passed by the Bolivian Congress with a targeted ceiling for the overall consolidated public sector deficit equivalent to 6% of GDP. In fact, fiscal year 1986 ended with a deficit slightly below 4%. As stabilization continued, the government was able to regain credibility and access to foreign sources of finance. Bolivia has been able to secure new loans from official lending institutions for more than $1.2 billion (US dollars); however, the major part has not as yet been disbursed. In June 1986 the government reached a standby agreement with the IMF, followed by a compensatory finance loan and a structural adjustment loan.

The net international reserves of the Central Bank increased from a low of $30 million (US dollars) at the end of August 1985 to $350 million by December 1986.[15] A significant fraction of the increase in reserves was due to the repatriation of capital induced by the high rates of interest.

The growth in the money base has been sustained but at relatively low levels, as can be observed in table 7A.2 in the appendix and in figure 7.4. Data in table 7A.4 in the appendix show increases in the demand for (real) M1 but they are not spectacular, given the extreme demonetization of the economy suffered during hyperinflation. The expansion of the broader definition of money, M2, is significantly more important, but it should be recalled that dollar and dollar-denominated deposits constitute the major component. Short term deposits in dollar and dollar-indexed accounts have increased significantly, going from less than $28 million in September 1985 to an estimated $270 million in March 1987. High interest rates plus regained confidence explain this inflow. Most of the deposits are, however, thirty-day deposits.

The extreme tightness of money at the beginning of the stabilization program led to high real rates of interest (see table 7.7). Interest rates have come down since then but are still high, in part because of tight money and in part because of expectations. Interest rates are high not only in pesos but also in dollars. For instance, time deposits in the banking system as of June 1987 paid 15% per annum on dollar accounts and 18% per annum on dollar-indexed accounts.

The Costs

There is some evidence that the costs in foregone output and employment on the implementation of the program have been substantial. Unfortunately disturbances in the external sector impede reaching clear-cut conclusions.

Estimates of the decrease in GDP in 1986 range from 2.9% to 3.5%. The investment rate in 1986 reached one of its lowest values since data have been recorded (6.1%, as is shown in table 7.3). The open unemployment rate increased by 3 points, reaching 20% by the end of 1986.[16] Underemployment has also increased from 56% to 60%. Unemployment is highly concentrated in the highland cities, where the public sector is important.

**Table 7.7**
Interest rates, inflation, and premiums on dollars, September 1985–December 1986
(% per month; inflation refers to the following month)

| Month | Interest rate | Inflation | Premium |
|---|---|---|---|
| **1985** | | | |
| September | 32.0 | − 1.9 | 0.9 |
| October | 22.5 | 3.2 | 1.7 |
| November | 21.6 | 16.8 | 14.1 |
| December | 19.2 | 32.9 | 8.0 |
| **1986** | | | |
| January | 20.0 | 7.9 | 8.8 |
| February | 19.8 | 0.1 | 4.4 |
| March | 18.5 | 3.6 | 4.0 |
| April | 13.1 | 1.0 | 1.2 |
| May | 8.5 | 4.3 | 3.1 |
| June | 6.5 | 1.8 | 2.2 |
| July | 6.5 | 0.7 | 1.5 |
| August | 5.4 | 2.3 | 1.3 |
| September | 5.4 | 0.6 | 0.5 |
| October | 4.6 | − 0.1 | 0.7 |
| November | 4.6 | 0.7 | 0.7 |
| December | 4.5 | 2.4 | 1.3 |

Source: Data from UDAPE and Central Bank of Bolivia.

The picture on real wages is somewhat clouded. In the aftermath of the stabilization program, real wages fell substantially, even when measured net of the inflation tax, but they recovered quite rapidly until the second quarter of 1986 (see table 7.8). Since then they have been stagnant. Differences across sectors are also important: There has been slow growth in the sectors in which public activity is important, whereas increases in the personal services sector have been substantial.

The public sector services have received the severest blow: There is a noticeable deterioration in their scope and quality. Many middle-level civil servants have quit the sector, impairing the normal functioning of the government. In the education sector approximately 25% of rural teachers have abandoned their schools. The longer-run costs of this should be evident.

It is frequently argued that the losses in output, investment rates, and employment cannot be attributed to the stabilization program because the economy suffered severe external shocks in the last quarter of 1985 and in 1986, when sales of natural gas to Argentina declined significantly and the

**Table 7.8**
Real wage index, 1982−1986 (base: November 1982 = 100)

| Quarter | Wage in final month of quarter | Average wage over the quarter with one-month backward lag[b] |
|---|---|---|
| **1982** | | |
| I | 92.8 | 74.2 |
| **1983** | | |
| I | 103.4 | 87.3 |
| II | 88.2 | 93.5 |
| III | 80.9 | 79.5 |
| IV | 91.9 | 81.4 |
| **1984** | | |
| I | 65.5 | 72.3 |
| II | 69.5 | 67.2 |
| III | 65.5 | 65.4 |
| IV | 150.5 | 81.2 |
| **1985** | | |
| I | 122.0 | 139.0 |
| II | 100.5 | 102.3 |
| III | 34.0 | 49.2 |
| IV | 67.8 | 38.6 |
| **1986** | | |
| I | 71.1 | 59.6 |
| II | 70.1 | 72.0 |
| III[a] | 73.6 | 74.1 |

Source: Author's estimates based on data from UDAPE.
a. July−August.
b. The indicator approximates the real wage *net* of the inflation tax.

intervention of American troops curtailed (illegal) cocaine exports, and because hyperinflation disorganized production and hence some time had to be allowed for recovery. In this view the negative rate of growth of GDP means the continuation of the downward trend begun in 1980. Also, the stabilization program only substituted the inefficient inflation tax for more efficient taxes, leaving aggregate demand unchanged; hence its effects on the level of activity should be neutral (Sachs 1986).

It is indeed true that the terms of trade fall in 1986 amounted, ceteris paribus, to an income loss of 3.8%. But, on the other hand, the significant increase in external loans should have offset this loss, given the potential increase in the capacity to import that it furnished. In fact, the severe foreign exchange constraint that faced the (legal) economy between 1982 and 1985 was significantly lessened during 1986. As proof, for the first time in five years the Bolivian balance of trade was negative, and, interestingly enough, most imports were of consumer goods. The increase in the capacity to import, after stabilization, potentially removed one of the most important constraints on investment, and yet this has not been taking place. Higher investment, even with a high import content, would have had significant spillover effects on the demand for home goods. To be sure, the external shocks have important and relatively permanent repercussions on the economy and are not just a once and for all fall in the terms of trade. In addition, the collapse of traditional export markets, with its long-run consequences, impaired expected investment returns.

The argument concerning the trend of falling GDP growth rates is difficult to reconcile with some facts. First, although high inflation, the accompanying nonprice rationing of some goods, and the surrounding uncertainty were conducive to severe misallocations of resources, penalized production, and reduced aggregate supply, some expansionary factors on the aggregate demand side were simultaneously present, namely, government consumption and illegal exports. Actual trades were constrained on the supply side, but aggregate demand was strong; indeed there was a situation of excess demand. Second, it can be conjectured that the high inflation caused more than a fall in GDP, producing a process of the economy going underground with agents trying to escape foreign exchange and price regulations. Third, during the high inflation period the economy suffered a severe foreign exchange constraint, having been severed from international capital flows. This was an important determinant of the fall in output.

With the stabilization program most of the factors that hindered supply disappeared, and yet production is not recovering. The only, but important, remaining hindrance is the aftereffect of the low investment rates of the previous five years. The current low level of activity (and the fall in GDP last year) seems to be due to a conventional Keynesian demand insufficiency in both the goods and the labor markets. In other words, the nature of the factors determining low recorded output and employment has changed between the inflationary period and its aftermath.

That substitution of the inflation tax by more efficient taxes should entail no decrement of aggregate demand is not really the argument. Rather, the point is that the stabilization program has decreased government's real expenditure, and this has been done by and large by cutting expenses on nontraded goods, namely, on the real wage bill. The overall effect should be contractionary.

## 7.4 Outstanding Policy Issues

There are several outstanding issues to be addressed by Bolivia, namely, the consolidation of stabilization, reactivation of the economy, and resumption of growth.

Consolidation of Stabilization

However important the gains in stabilization, it is yet far from being completely solidified.[17] The fiscal sector continues to present some telltale weaknesses. On the revenue side shortfalls of taxes on the foreign sector may occur. Revenues for the state oil enterprise and government taxes are likely to suffer from the present situation on the sales of natural gas to Argentina. Moreover, implementation of the tax reform is facing more difficulties than expected. The fiscal problem clearly is to raise more revenues. There is not much room for more substantial cuts in expenditure. Additional layoffs in the public sector will lead to almost complete paralysis in the government and to social tensions in the public enterprises, some of which cannot be afforded. A symptom of the fiscal difficulties is the rapid increase of the internal floating debt, which is now around 5% of GDP.

A top priority for the government is to generate savings to be used as local counterpart funds to the disbursement of contracted foreign loans. This is a formidable challenge, given the circumstances and the difficulties ahead.

The current situation of low average real wages in the public sector is giving rise to a potentially unstable situation over the medium run. Many experienced functionaries have already left, badly needed middle managers cannot be attracted, and general unrest in the public sector labor force is hindering the work effort. Up to now strikes and other work stoppages have been controlled by the government with the threat—credible, given the high rate of unemployment—of dismissals. But this may not be sustainable.

The Recovery of Economic Activity and Growth

There is currently a strong social demand for economic reactivation and resumption of growth. The public believes that the fiscal and monetary equilibria have been obtained at a low level of activity. Top priorities in the reactivation agenda are to increase the investment rate from the current excessively low base and to expand exports.

The external shocks have positioned Bolivia in the uneasy situation of trying to stabilize and make structural adjustments simultaneously. In particular, the recovery of exports requires important shifts in resource allocation that in turn require "activist" fiscal policies, but stabilization places rigid constraints on their scope.

Bolivian authorities do not overlook the fact that public investment has to play a major role in the recovery, but the dismantling of the administration has lowered the resource absorption capacity of the public sector. Expansion of investment also calls for the unfreezing of the operations of the state enterprises. The tight central government grip on them needs to be unfastened if they are to behave as efficient enterprises. They also have to regain access to internal credit. Sensible as those prescriptions may seem, they involve heavy risks to the stabilization program. The treatment of the state enterprises poses difficult policy dilemmas, given the size of the public sector in the economy, even after the privatization impulse of SD 21060.

The persistently high interest rates are holding back economic activity in the private sector. The poor internal and external demand prospects have to be added to this feature, and that is not all. There are also the problems associated with the high domestic transportation and energy costs, which in turn result from the high domestic prices of oil and the high interest rates.

Exchange rate overvaluation crept in after the depreciation of the dollar after February 1986 (mentioned in section 7.3). Estimates range between 7% and 13%, taking as a base the last quarter of 1985.[18] Although the extent of overvaluation is not yet severe, a further and likely accumulation will hinder Bolivia's recovery prospects. Short-term capital inflows, attracted by the high interest rates, are contributing to this phenomenon. In fact, the Central Bank has had to intervene to avoid a greater revaluation of the peso.

The substantial balance of trade deficit in 1986, the first in five years, sent a warning signal (see table 7.3). The problem is not so much the trade deficit itself but the factors that have caused it. Imports of durable consumer goods were well above trend. Backlogs as well as expectations on the maintenance of the policy of openness and on the exchange rate may have played a role. This surge in imports of consumer durables may be transitory but could easily become more permanent, especially if overvaluation becomes more severe.

The health of the banking sector is also an outstanding issue and is partially behind the problem of high interest rates as well as a result of them. Banks benefited significantly from the inflation tax during the high-inflation years, but the rapid disinflation has removed this source of profits. The banks now find themselves overstaffed and with high operating costs. Worse, a problem of solvency has surfaced in some banks.

At the end of hyperinflation many banks were left with small portfolios of loans, most of them bad, but given their smallness, this was not a serious problem. The problem of conversion of loans (and other contracts), given the change in the inflationary environment, was not of major concern for debtors or for creditors. In fact, hyperinflation and dedollarization had liquidated most of the debt of the private nonbanking sector. However, with the persistent high interest rates there has been a rapid accumulation of debt in the nonbanking sector, and, as a result, the quality of the loan portfolio of the banks has deteriorated. Indeed, arrears have been building up rapidly in the last twelve months in many banks. The high volatility of the dollar and dollar-indexed deposits in the banking system compounds the dangers.

The weakness of the banking sector has fallout on the design of macroeconomic policy. The government has received several official development credits intended for the private sector that are not being used because of the state of the (public and private) banks. Disbursements of these development credits could, of course, lower interest rates across the board.

The foreign debt overhang with private creditors continues to be a major policy issue. This condition hurts even some day-to-day financing operations such as short-term trade loans. The situation with commercial banks has been, in addition, a source of strain with the IMF. Notwithstanding, at this point Bolivia cannot honor its commitments without risking the stabilization program. Fortunately Bolivia has found some degree of understanding among private creditors, and fruitful negotiations are under way.

The Political Prospects of the Program

Stabilization has imposed extreme austerity on several segments of the population (miners, teachers, pensioners, etc.). This has been taken rather calmly because there is the perception that despite the costs the situation has improved with regard to the last chaotic months of hyperinflation. However, the lasting recession is taking its toll, and an increase in worker restlessness has been observed in the last months: The number of strikes has been increasing, and the labor unions have been able to gather large (and angry) crowds in the streets to protest the economic policies. Those pressures may hinder the decision-making process and lead to premature excessively activist policies to reactivate a return to money printing as a temporary safety valve. If there are no indications of recovery soon, the government may not be able to withstand the pressures.

## 7.5    Concluding Remarks

The severity of inflation in Bolivia and the drastic stabilization steps have few parallels in this century. The preliminary results on stabilization are indeed impressive: low inflation, small budget deficits, and significant accumulation of foreign exchange reserves. There is also an attendant modest improvement in some sectors of the economy, in comparison with the hyperinflation situation.

Comparison with the past, however, constitutes a poor evaluation criterion for the stabilization program. Hence a more relevant question is, What would have been achieved with an alternative, less drastic, and more carefully designed program? After all, the stabilization program of August 1985 contains a heavy (and maybe unwarranted) dose of overkill.

The current program, in essence, has bought time for policymaking, and this is a substantial accomplishment, given the initial conditions, but it is not enough. Moreover, the program was probably too costly. The problem of a true and consolidated disinflation remains, for there are still deep unresolved problems that jeopardize the current stability. On the fiscal front the program initially benefited from the slack given by untaxed resources that could be and were drawn upon rapidly. But now the necessary increases in tax collections face more difficult problems related to the external sector, which the government cannot control, and to the low level of economic activity. Sustained stability requires indeed a recovery of the level of economic activity and economic growth. This is a difficult challenge, given the fact that the crucial external markets continue to be weak and their long-term prospects dim. Also, because inflation is being held back to a great extent by a tight monetary policy, this is causing more delays in the recovery than expected. In this context high interest rates continue to be a major problem.

Notwithstanding all the difficulties mentioned, Bolivia does not lack trump cards. Among the trump cards are the foreign loans secured by Bolivia—thanks to the stabilization effort—but not yet disbursed. Those credits, if correctly used, could play the role that similar loans had in the stabilization of the European hyperinflations after World War I. The road to consolidated stabilization and economic recovery is still full of obstacles, but it is not impassable. It must be also said that the Bolivian economy has shown more resilience than was expected by outside and inside analysts.

# Appendix: Statistical Tables

**Table 7A.1**
Prices, exchange rates, and money, second quarter of 1982 to first quarter of 1987[a]

| Quarter or month | Consumer price index (Base 1982 = 1) | Parallel market exchange rate (pesos per US dollar) | Official exchange rate (pesos per US dollar) | Money base (billions of pesos) | M1 (billions of pesos) | M2 (billions of pesos) |
|---|---|---|---|---|---|---|
| **1982** | | | | | | |
| II | 0.7 | 90 | 43[b] | 26 | 25 | 49 |
| III | 1.1 | 97 | 43 | 38 | 38 | 76 |
| IV | 1.7 | 144 | 145 | 68 | 57 | 99 |
| **1983** | | | | | | |
| I | 2.1 | 415 | 196[c] | 75 | 67 | 117 |
| II | 2.7 | 398 | 196 | 97 | 84 | 145 |
| III | 3.8 | 563 | 196 | 123 | 101 | 179 |
| IV | 6.4 | 1,108 | 399 | 195 | 175 | 266 |
| **1984** | | | | | | |
| I | 10.8 | 2,181 | 500 | 250 | 238 | 345 |
| April | 21.1 | 3,576 | 2,000 | 289 | 270 | 388 |
| May | 31.1 | 3,512 | 2,000 | 345 | 330 | 461 |
| June | 32.3 | 3,342 | 2,000 | 449 | 440 | 624 |
| July | 34.0 | 3,570 | 2,000 | 659 | 599 | 864 |
| August | 39.1 | 7,238 | 2,000[d] | 812 | 718 | 1,071 |
| September | 53.7 | 13,585 | 2,000 | 935 | 889 | 1,314 |
| October | 85.5 | 15,205 | 2,000 | 1,188 | 1,194 | 1,647 |
| November | 112.4 | 18,469 | 9,000[e] | 1,492 | 1,495 | 1,985 |
| December | 180.9 | 24,515 | 9,000 | 3,345 | 3,296 | 3,986 |

**Table 7A.1** (continued)

| Quarter or month | Consumer price index (Base 1982 = 1) | Parallel market exchange rate (pesos per US dollar) | Official exchange rate (pesos per US dollar) | Money base (billions of pesos) | M1 (billions of pesos) | M2 (billions of pesos) |
|---|---|---|---|---|---|---|
| **1985** | | | | | | |
| January | 305.3 | 73,016 | 9,000 | 4,570 | 4,630 | 5,635 |
| February | 863.3 | 141,101 | 50,000[e] | 6,375 | 6,455 | 7,734 |
| March | 1,078.6 | 128,137 | 50,000 | 9,084 | 9,089 | 10,971 |
| April | 1,205.7 | 167,428 | 50,000 | 13,036 | 12,885 | 16,438 |
| May | 1,635.7 | 272,375 | 75,000 | 21,500 | 21,309 | 26,612 |
| June | 2,919.1 | 481,756 | 75,000 | 28,558 | 27,778 | 37,804 |
| July | 4,854.6 | 885,476 | 75,000 | 45,042 | 47,341 | 60,952 |
| August | 8,081.0 | 1,182,300 | 75,000 | 76,503 | 74,306 | 98,701 |
| Stabilization begins | | | | | | |
| September | 12,647.6 | 1,087,440 | 1,077,890[f] | 111,746 | 103,272 | 138,862 |
| October | 12,411.8 | 1,120,210 | 1,102,060 | 128,550 | 132,550 | 184,600 |
| November | 12,809.1 | 1,366,720 | 1,197,370 | 128,090 | 140,400 | 216,325 |
| December | 14,961.5 | 1,715,870 | 1,588,610 | 190,078 | 198,678 | 290,318 |
| **1986** | | | | | | |
| January | 19,893.3 | 2,240,220 | 2,057,650 | 170,404 | 180,255 | 273,471 |
| February | 21,475.1 | 1,916,880 | 1,835,790 | 190,283 | 191,061 | 311,999 |
| March | 21,489.3 | 1,962,670 | 1,886,760 | 198,143 | 189,252 | 336,160 |
| II | 22,724.3 | 1,946,367 | 1,904,760 | 245,637 | 240,441 | 483,379 |
| III | 24,135.0 | 1,930,580 | 1,909,580 | 286,188 | 286,188 | 620,927 |
| IV | 24,732.1 | 1,940,823 | 1,923,860 | 373,310 | 384,633 | 816,566 |
| **1987** | | | | | | |
| I | 25,700.0 | 1,982,387 | 1,955,300 | 369,425 | 387,025 | 969,565 |

Source: Derived from Central Bank of Bolivia data in *Boletin Estadistico* (various issues from 1982 to 1987).

a. Prices and exchange rates are quarterly and monthly averages. Money data are outstanding stocks at end of period, month or quarter.

b. Effective rate higher for all imports and exports, except wheat.

c. Effective rate close to official rate for legal exports and imports.

d. Effective rate higher for nonessential imports.

e. Effective rate higher for exports.

f. Administered float.

**Table 7A.2**
Average month-to-month percentage changes in prices, exchange rates, and money, third
quarter of 1982 to first quarter of 1987

| Quarter[a] or month | Consumer price index | Parallel market exchange rate | Official exchange rate | Money base | M1 | M2 |
|---|---|---|---|---|---|---|
| **1982** | | | | | | |
| III | 14.9 | 29.6 | 0.0 | 12.7 | 14.0 | 15.7 |
| IV | 16.0 | 7.5 | 49.9 | 21.7 | 14.7 | 8.9 |
| **1983** | | | | | | |
| I | 7.4 | 19.4 | 10.6 | 3.2 | 5.6 | 5.8 |
| II | 8.9 | − 1.4 | 0.0 | 9.1 | 7.9 | 7.3 |
| III | 12.8 | 18.5 | 0.0 | 8.3 | 6.3 | 7.4 |
| IV | 18.8 | 18.7 | 26.6 | 16.6 | 20.3 | 14.1 |
| **1984** | | | | | | |
| I | 18.8 | 25.3 | 7.8 | 8.6 | 10.8 | 9.0 |
| April | 63.0 | 40.6 | 300.0 | 15.6 | 13.4 | 12.6 |
| May | 47.0 | − 1.8 | 0.0 | 19.5 | 22.4 | 18.7 |
| June | 4.1 | − 4.8 | 0.0 | 30.3 | 33.3 | 35.4 |
| July | 5.2 | 6.8 | 0.0 | 46.6 | 36.1 | 38.5 |
| August | 15.0 | 97.1 | 0.0 | 23.3 | 19.9 | 24.0 |
| September | 37.3 | 94.4 | 0.0 | 15.1 | 23.9 | 22.6 |
| October | 59.1 | 11.1 | 0.0 | 27.1 | 34.3 | 25.4 |
| November | 31.6 | 21.5 | 350.0 | 25.5 | 25.2 | 20.5 |
| December | 60.9 | 32.7 | 0.0 | 124.2 | 120.4 | 100.8 |
| **1985** | | | | | | |
| January | 68.8 | 197.8 | 0.0 | 36.6 | 40.5 | 41.4 |
| February | 182.8 | 93.2 | 455.6 | 39.5 | 39.4 | 37.3 |
| March | 24.9 | − 9.2 | 0.0 | 42.5 | 40.8 | 41.8 |
| April | 11.8 | 30.7 | 0.0 | 43.5 | 41.8 | 49.8 |
| May | 35.7 | 62.7 | 50.0 | 64.9 | 65.4 | 61.9 |
| June | 78.5 | 76.9 | 0.0 | 32.8 | 30.4 | 42.1 |
| July | 66.3 | 83.8 | 0.0 | 57.7 | 70.4 | 61.2 |
| August | 66.5 | 33.5 | 0.0 | 69.8 | 57.0 | 61.9 |
| Stabilization begins | | | | | | |
| September | 56.5 | − 8.0 | 1337.2 | 46.1 | 39.0 | 40.7 |
| October | − 1.9 | 3.0 | 2.2 | 15.0 | 28.4 | 32.9 |
| November | 3.2 | 22.0 | 8.6 | − 0.4 | 5.9 | 17.2 |
| December | 16.8 | 25.5 | 32.7 | 48.4 | 41.5 | 34.2 |

**Table 7A.2** (continued)

| Quarter[a] or month | Consumer price index | Parallel market exchange rate | Official exchange rate | Money base | M1 | M2 |
|---|---|---|---|---|---|---|
| **1986** | | | | | | |
| January | 33.0 | 30.6 | 29.5 | −10.4 | −9.3 | −5.8 |
| February | 8.0 | −14.4 | −10.8 | 11.7 | 6.0 | 14.1 |
| March | 0.1 | 2.4 | 2.8 | 4.1 | −0.9 | 7.7 |
| II | 2.7 | −1.6 | −0.4 | 9.7 | 8.8 | 16.3 |
| III | 2.0 | −0.3 | 0.1 | 5.2 | 6.0 | 8.7 |
| IV | 0.8 | 0.2 | 0.2 | 9.3 | 10.4 | 9.6 |
| **1987** | | | | | | |
| I | 1.3 | 0.7 | 0.5 | −0.3 | 0.2 | 5.9 |

Source: Derived from Central Bank of Bolivia data in *Boletin Estadistico* (various issues from 1982 to 1987).
a. Quarterly figures are monthly averages over quarter.

**Table 7A.3**
Premiums in the parallel market for foreign exchange, March 1982–March 1987 (percentage of parallel market over official exchange rate)

| Month | 1982 | 1983 | 1984 | 1985 | 1986 | 1987 |
|---|---|---|---|---|---|---|
| January | | 73.5 | 260.0 | 711.3 | 8.9 | 1.0 |
| February | | 119.3 | 340.0 | 182.2 | 4.4 | 3.1 |
| March | 11.8[a] | 142.0 | 408.6 | 156.3 | 4.0 | 0.2 |
| April | 84.1 | 102.3 | 78.8 | 234.9 | 1.2 | |
| May | 104.9 | 86.1 | 75.6 | 263.2 | 3.1 | |
| June | 139.1 | 119.9 | 67.1 | 542.3 | 2.2 | |
| July | 244.9 | 159.0 | 78.5 | 1080.6 | 1.5 | |
| August | 327.2 | 265.7 | 251.9 | 1476.4 | 1.3 | |
| September | 495.7 | 287.6 | 584.3 | 0.9[c] | 0.5 | |
| October | 405.5 | 341.0 | 660.3 | 1.7 | 0.7 | |
| November | 18.2[b] | 142.6 | 105.2 | 14.1 | 0.7 | |
| December | 44.1 | 148.8 | 172.4 | 8.0 | 1.3 | |

Source: Derived from Central Bank of Bolivia data.
a. Beginning of dual exchange regime.
b. Official end of dual regime, parallel market becomes black.
c. Stabilization begins and parallel market is legal again.

**Table 7A.4**
Real monetary aggregates, March 1982–March 1987[a]

| Quarter or month | M1 | | M2 | |
|---|---|---|---|---|
| | Billions of 1982 pesos | Millions of US dollars | Billions of 1982 pesos | Millions of US dollars |
| **1982** | | | | |
| I | 29.88 | 372.95 | 60.04 | 749.37 |
| II | 31.76 | 227.35 | 62.56 | 447.79 |
| III | 27.80 | 136.76 | 56.43 | 277.59 |
| IV | 27.75 | 181.74 | 49.54 | 324.48 |
| **1983** | | | | |
| I | 27.64 | 133.72 | 48.85 | 236.32 |
| II | 28.38 | 184.56 | 48.92 | 318.17 |
| III | 21.36 | 127.21 | 37.91 | 225.77 |
| IV | 18.61 | 118.85 | 29.36 | 187.49 |
| **1984** | | | | |
| I | 15.89 | 81.03 | 24.48 | 124.85 |
| April | 12.01 | 70.98 | 17.33 | 102.43 |
| May | 9.65 | 85.38 | 13.65 | 120.81 |
| June | 11.91 | 115.21 | 16.77 | 162.25 |
| July | 15.27 | 145.49 | 21.87 | 208.35 |
| August | 16.83 | 93.53 | 24.73 | 137.46 |
| September | 14.96 | 58.71 | 22.20 | 87.13 |
| October | 12.19 | 68.50 | 17.32 | 97.36 |
| November | 11.96 | 72.80 | 16.15 | 98.32 |
| December | 13.24 | 97.71 | 16.50 | 121.77 |
| **1985** | | | | |
| January | 12.98 | 54.27 | 15.76 | 65.88 |
| February | 6.42 | 39.28 | 7.74 | 47.37 |
| March | 7.21 | 60.65 | 8.67 | 72.99 |
| April | 9.11 | 65.62 | 11.37 | 81.85 |
| May | 10.45 | 62.77 | 13.16 | 79.03 |
| June | 8.41 | 50.95 | 11.03 | 66.86 |
| July | 7.74 | 42.42 | 10.17 | 55.76 |
| August | 7.53 | 51.45 | 9.88 | 67.52 |
| Stabilization begins | | | | |
| September | 7.02 | 81.65 | 9.39 | 109.23 |
| October | 9.50 | 105.26 | 13.03 | 144.38 |
| November | 10.65 | 99.86 | 15.65 | 146.67 |
| December | 11.33 | 98.81 | 16.93 | 147.63 |

**Table 7A.4** (continued)

| Quarter or month | M1 | | M2 | |
|---|---|---|---|---|
| | Billions of 1982 pesos | Millions of US dollars | Billions of 1982 pesos | Millions of US dollars |
| **1986** | | | | |
| January | 9.52 | 84.57 | 14.17 | 125.83 |
| February | 8.65 | 96.85 | 13.63 | 152.71 |
| March | 8.85 | 96.89 | 15.08 | 165.12 |
| II | 10.01 | 120.53 | 19.55 | 235.41 |
| III | 11.17 | 142.55 | 23.84 | 304.23 |
| IV | 14.46 | 184.18 | 31.33 | 398.47 |
| **1987** | | | | |
| I | 14.27 | 184.67 | 35.39 | 458.12 |

Source: Derived from Central Bank of Bolivia data in *Boletín Estadístico* (various issues from 1982 to 1987).
a. Real aggregates computed according to $(M + M(-1)/2P$, where $M$ is the end-of-month relevant monetary variable and $P$ is the relevant monthly average price. Dollar values are derived using the parallel market exchange rate. Quarterly data are outstanding stocks at end of quarter.

## Notes

I am grateful to Michael Bruno and Jeffrey Sachs for their useful suggestions on an earlier version. I remain responsible for errors and viewpoints.

1. The figures are derived from World Bank, *Debt Tables* (1986).

2. The resolution of the problem of arrears led to an onerous rescheduling of the Bolivian debt to private creditors in April 1981. On this point see, for example, Ugarteche (1986).

3. The collapse of the foreign exchange regime of March 1982 was an important proximate determinant in the emergence of inflation. See Morales (1986).

4. The Bolivian plan of November 1982 can probably be classified as in between heterodox and "poets" in the Dornbusch and Simonsen (1986) taxonomy.

5. Dedollarization converted de jure dollar-denominated contracts to peso contracts. In fact, the ultimate result, although unintended, was to nationalize the foreign debt held by the private sector. In the process some small depositors in the banking system were penalized. Dedollarization was one of the most controversial measures of the Siles-Zuazo administration.

6. The Siles-Zuazo administration never attempted to check seriously the expansion of the black market for foreign exchange. The market became semilegal in November 1983, when some foreign exchange deals were allowed to go there. In

February 1985 exporters were granted the right to sell between 20% and 30% of their proceeds, depending on the type of commodity exported, in the black (or parallel) market. This of course increased their effective exchange rate significantly.

During the final months of hyperinflation, the percentage (in value) of imports brought in with dollars at the official exchange rate was small. This feature facilitated unification of the exchange rates after the stabilization plan of August 1985.

7. References for the Olivera-Tanzi effect are, of course, Olivera (1967) and Tanzi (1977).

8. The monetary dynamics of the Bolivian hyperinflation can be fairly well represented by models akin to the ones in Bruno and Fischer (1985) and Dornbusch and Fischer (1985). On this point, see also Sachs (1986) and Morales (1986). Kharas and Pinto (1986) have an explicit open economy model of the Bolivian process.

9. As has been mentioned, foreign debt service was a heavy burden during the period, although in May 1984 the government, under strong pressure from the labor unions, decided to stop payments to foreign commercial banks. In addition, long delays in payments by Argentina for Bolivian natural gas sales frequently caused severe liquidity problems.

10. The failure of the stabilization attempts between 1982 and 1985 is examined in some detail by Morales (1987). Kharas and Pinto (1986) in a formal model show that the rule, typical in the packages of these years, of devaluing the official exchange rate toward the black market rate, led to a steady-state high inflation rate, exhibiting saddle-point stability. The result is indeed intriguing but depends on some strong assumptions.

11. Dollars have been used as a medium of exchange for domestic transactions for some large deals, for instance in real estate, since at least the early 1950s. Their use in ordinary transactions was rare before the high-inflation episode. In the final months of hyperinflation, dollar bills in small denominations were employed and accepted alongside pesos. There were also reports that in the eastern city of Santa Cruz, the second largest in Bolivia, pesos were no longer accepted in some hardware and grocery stores.

Domestic currency was substituted in a significant way, but substitution was far from complete. Payments to the government for taxes or goods and services, and wages and salaries with few exceptions were always made in pesos.

12. The dismissal of more than 60% of the employees of the Central Bank of Bolivia illustrates the will of the government to reduce the bank's size. Overall figures on the reduction in public sector employment reflect its impact incompletely because relatively few layoffs have taken place in the military and among public school teachers, where the bulk of public employment is found.

13. Bolivia renegotiated its debt with creditor governments in the Club of Paris in June 1986. Details on the agreement appear in Muller & Machicado Asociados (1986).

14. This view differs from Sargent's classic paper (1982).

15. Sources of information on monetary variables are the *Statistical Bulletin* of the Central Bank of Bolivia, the IMF *International Financial Statistics*, UDAPE (1986), and unpublished data from UDAPE.

16. Data on employment are notoriously bad in Bolivia; hence the numbers have to be interpreted with caution. The figures in the text are from UDAPE.

17. Muller & Machicado Asociados (1986) provide a good evaluation of the fiscal outlook.

18. There are indeed several examples in Latin America in which bringing down inflation with exchange rate manipulation led to destructive overvaluation. See Dornbusch (1986a). However, overvaluation may be unavoidable in the aftermath of extreme inflation.

## References

Banco Central de Bolivia. Various issues of *Boletin Estadistico*. La Paz: BCB, Publications Section. (In Spanish.)

Bruno, M., and S. Fischer. 1985. "Inflation and the expectation trap." Cambridge, Mass.: Massachusetts Institute of Technology.

Cagan, P. 1956. "The monetary dynamics of hyperinflation," in *Studies in the Quantity Theory of Money*, Milton Friedman, ed. (Chicago, Ill.: Chicago University Press), 25–117.

Doria Medina, S. 1986. *The Informal Economy of Bolivia*. La Paz: Editorial Offset Boliviana. (In Spanish.)

Dornbusch, R. 1986a. *Inflation, Exchange Rates, and Stabilization*. Essays in International Finance 165 (October). Princeton, N.J.: Department of Economics, Princeton University.

Dornbusch, R. 1986b. *Stopping Hyperinflation: Lessons from the German Experience in the 1920s*. Working Paper 1675 (revised). Cambridge, Mass.: National Bureau of Economic Research.

Dornbusch, R. 1986c. "Tight fiscal policy and easy money: The key to Argentine stabilization." Cambridge, Mass.: Massachusetts Institute of Technology.

Dornbusch, R., and S. Fischer. 1985. "Towards a survey of inflation stabilizations." Cambridge, Mass.: Massachusetts Institute of Technology.

Dornbusch, R., and M. H. Simonsen. 1986. *Inflation Stabilization with Incomes Policy Support*. New York: Group of Thirty.

International Monetary Fund. *International Financial Statistics*. Various issues. Washington, D.C.: IMF.

Kharas, H., and B. Pinto. 1986. "Exchange rate rules, black market premia and fiscal deficits: The Bolivian hyperinflation." Washington D.C.: The World Bank.

LaHaye, L. 1985. "Inflation and currency reform." *Journal of Political Economy* 93:537–560.

Morales, J. A. 1986. *Money Demand and Money Creation during the Bolivian High Inflation 1982–1985.* Working Paper 07/86. La Paz: Universidad Catolica Boliviana, Instituto de Investigaciones Economicas.

Morales, J. A. 1987. *Prices, Salaries, and Economic Policy during the Bolivian High Inflation of 1982–1985.* La Paz: Instituto Latinoamericano de Investigaciones Sociales. (In Spanish.)

Muller & Machicado Asociados. 1986. *Economic Evaluation 1986.* La Paz: Muller & Machicado Asociados. (In Spanish.)

Olivera, J. 1967. "Money, prices and fiscal lags: A note on the dynamics of inflation." *Banca Nazionale del Lavoro Quarterly Review* 20:258–267.

Sachs, J. 1986. *The Bolivian Hyperinflation and Stabilization.* NBER Working Paper 2073 (November). Cambridge, Mass.: National Bureau of Economic Research.

Sargent, T. J. 1982. "The ends of four big inflations," in *Inflation: Causes and Effects,* R. E. Hall, ed. (Chicago, Ill.: Chicago University Press), 41–98.

Tanzi, V. 1977. "Inflation, lags in collection and the real value of tax revenue." *IMF Staff Papers* 24:154–167.

Ugarteche, O. 1986. *The Debtor State. Economic Policy of Debt: Peru and Bolivia 1968–1984.* Lima: Instituto de Estudios Peruanos. (In Spanish.)

UDAPE. 1986. *The Process of Stabilization, New Economic Policy, and a Characterization of the Present.* La Paz: Unidad de Analisis de Politicas Economica, Ministerio de Planeamiento. (In Spanish.)

# Comments on Part IV

## Comment by Gail E. Makinen

My comments should be regarded as an addendum to or an elaboration of Morales's discussion, for I agree with his thesis on the proximate cause of hyperinflation. Arguing that it was set in motion when Central Bank advances were substituted for the foreign financing of the budget deficit does not tell us why this occurred, however. Many countries have faced dramatic shocks without recourse to hyperinflation.

## Why Did Bolivia Have Hyperinflation?

Did a political failure force the government to rely too heavily on seigniorage? If it did, it should not have (unless people forget their history or do not understand it). A bizarre aspect of Bolivia's hyperinflation is that the president of the republic during this episode, Hernán Siles-Zuazo, was the president whose stabilization efforts thirty years ago ended Bolivia's first bout of triple-digit inflation in the post–World War II era—an inflationary episode occurring during the first presidency of Victor Paz-Estenssoro, who is now carrying out the 1985 stabilization program!

Understanding the cause of Bolivia's hyperinflation and assessing the prospects for the success of the 1985 stabilization require a review of the 1952–56 inflationary episode.

Bolivia first encountered serious inflation after World War II when the National Revolutionary Movement (MNR), led by Paz-Estenssoro and Siles-Zuazo, came to power in 1952. The MNR's ambitious agenda to reduce poverty and accelerate economic growth involved the nationalization of tin mines, petroleum production, and a vast acreage of farm land; the institution of social insurance; wage increases and price suppression through controls; and constraints on the ability of employers to fire workers. Growth was to be encouraged through planning and government allocation of real resources and credit.

The MNR economic program resulted in a large budget deficit financed by US aid and advances from the Central Bank. The bank loans produced a dramatic increase in the rate of inflation, which, having averaged in the 20% range for the three years before the MNR, rose to 100% in 1953, 124% in 1954, and to almost 180% in 1956. The boliviano, which had traded at an official rate of 60 to the dollar and a blackmarket rate of 210 in 1952, had by 1956 reached an official rate of 190 and a blackmarket rate of 14,000. In addition, Bolivia ceased paying its foreign debt.

The United States persuaded Bolivia to invite a stabilization delegation headed by George Jackson Eder. Eder judged that Bolivia's inflation was caused by a chronically unbalanced public sector budget financed largely by advances from the Central Bank. The government was reluctant to accept this assessment, maintaining that the fall in tin prices after the Korean War was to blame.[1]

Eder proposed an orthodox stabilization plan calling for a balanced public sector budget and an end to Central Bank lending to the government. He wanted a change in fiscal and monetary regimes similar to those that ended the hyperinflations after World War I. He drew on this experience and the successful stabilization of the Greek economy after its hyperinflation during World War II, especially the functioning of the Currency Control Committee, a supracentral bank whose unanimous consent was required before currency could be issued.

An important aspect of Eder's plan was to free the economy from state control, especially imports, exports, foreign exchange, interest rates, and the prices of various domestic products (it was the deficit of the state petroleum monopoly rather than the nationalized tin mines that contributed most heavily to the deficit of the public sector).

Eder was careful to explain the consequences of setting a low price for petroleum, of artifically holding down the foreign exchange rate and rationing the available supply, and of price controls in general. These practices did not restrain inflation but, instead, by increasing government expenditures and reducing tax revenue, led to a greater reliance on money financing. They also encouraged criminal behavior (notably smuggling), reduced domestic output (especially argriculture), diverted labor from production to queuing, created false incentives for production, encouraged corruption among public officials, and caused wasteful expenditures by state enterprises, which in response to preferential exchange rates diverted purchases abroad.

Following implementation of the Eder plan, Bolivia enjoyed a long period of relative price stability during the 1960s and most of the 1970s, but only because of special and precarious circumstances. Eder's principal recommendation was a balanced budget for the public sector. For the first stabilization year, this was to be achieved by substantial US aid—equal to 40% of revenue. The dependence on US aid was to be a temporary expedient until basic reforms could be enacted. This unfortunately did not occur. US aid became a way of life. Eder provides data (1968, p. 596) for the period 1954–64 that shows that except for two years the United States provided more revenue for the Bolivian budget than did Bolivian taxpayers—in 1964, 50% more! When the revenue constraint was removed from the budget, there was little need to carry out Eder's suggested reforms, and those burdensome for the government's supporters were relaxed in what President Siles-Zuazo euphemistically called "concessions to reality." When the United States reduced aid in the 1970s, Bolivia borrowed abroad to live beyond its means.'

Bolivia has an amazing history. For nearly thirty years it appeared to be stable, but its situation was actually precarious. Whenever US aid ceased or foreign lending dried up, Bolivia faced grave consequences. When this occurred in the early 1980s, the Siles-Zuazo government repeated the errors of Paz-Estenssoro thirty years earlier with the same consequences. The events described by Morales on Bolivia's hyperinflation could just as easily have been taken from Eder's narrative of Bolivia's earlier experience. Somehow in the interim the wisdom of George Eder was forgotten.

Bolivia, therefore, had a democratically elected government that not only failed to amend its policies but implemented others it should have known would produce severe inflation, economic dislocations, and criminal behavior. Had the government realized it was levying an inflation tax, it would have understood that it was shifting the major tax burden to its own supporters.

Unless we understand why and how this failure took place, we have little basis to assess whether Bolivia can carry out the fiscal and monetary regime changes necessary for long-run stabilization.[3]

## The Dynamics of the Collapse of Public Finances

An alarming aspect of hyperinflation is the rapidity of its development, especially when accelerated by misguided public policies. The Bolivian government's decision to raise a larger fraction of revenue from the inflation tax need not have produced hyperinflation. This tendency was accelerated when the government held down prices of services it sold, including foreign exchange. The foreign exchange decision was especially crucial because a significant portion of Bolivian revenue comes from customs duties. Morales's analysis could benefit from a description of the Bolivian tax system, its elasticity with respect to inflation, and the reason for the shift in 1982 to a greater reliance on the inflation tax. The collapse of revenue from explicit taxation should also be traced in greater detail with a discussion of when it might have been averted: Here is the key to the inevitability of hyperinflation.

## Aftermath of Stabilization

Morales is rightly concerned about wanting to arrest the fall in Bolivian GNP with its resulting rise in unemployment, serious problems for any country. Before policy recommendations are made, the nature and causes of unemployment should be clarified, something Morales has not done.

Unemployment in Bolivia has three primary causes. The first is due to stabilization and arises because events differ from what economic agents expect.[4] Consequently these agents temporarily price themselves out of the market and are voluntarily unemployed. If subsequent events confirm their expectations or if their expectations adjust to the new lower inflation rate, they will once again be employed and unemployment will tend to settle to about its natural rate.

The second and third causes are structural in nature and imply a change in the natural rate itself. The second was identified and measured for Germany by Garber (1982). This cause of unemployment will occur even if economic agents correctly anticipate actual events and behave accordingly. Unemployment arises because hyperinflation causes distortions in the composition of output, the techniques of production, and the structure of industry. In Bolivia this could have occurred because the government held down both exchange and interest rates and used the proceeds of the inflation tax to subsidize state and some private enterprises. Laying off a large number of miners and civil servants and cutting the bloated staffs of private banks are indications of this type of unemployment. As industry and productive techniques are rationalized in the new stable price environment, the natural rate of unemployment should rise.[5]

The third reason for unemployment resulted from the drastic fall in Bolivia's export earnings from tin, hydrocarbons, and cocaine during 1986, estimated at 10–15% of GNP in a single year (Sachs 1986).

Until the reasons for unemployment can be apportioned among these causes, the government would be ill advised to use deficit financing or new credit creation to stimulate aggregate demand. If unemployment is due primarily to structural factors, which raise the natural rate of unemployment, demand stimulation will reignite inflation and threaten the fragile stabilization.

## Has Stabilization Succeeded?

Morales should distinguish the slowdown in the rate of price increases from the occurrence of regime changes identified by Sargent (1982), Bomberger and Makinen (1983), and Makinen (1984) as essential to the long-run success of the European stabilizations that ended hyperinflations after World Wars I and II. Inflation can be ended in the short run without fundamental changes in fiscal and monetary regimes. Bolivia appears to have accomplished the former but perhaps not the latter.

The budget deficit that remains would be larger if foreign debts were serviced. The deficit is being covered by foreign credits, not a reassuring development given the experience of the last thirty years. Most of the revenue comes from a single tax on hydrocarbons. It is not clear what other taxes have been instituted, the revenue they produce, or what their potential is to raise revenue—or what the elasticity of that revenue is with respect to inflation. The privatization of state enterprises, the activities of which have been responsible for past budget problems, remains incomplete. Finally, Bolivia has failed to establish an independent Central Bank capable of refusing the government's demand for accommodation.

An examination of real money balances subsequent to stabilization offers encouragement that public confidence is returning. In the first eighteen months of stabilization (September 1985 through March 1986), real money balances approximately doubled.[6] These increased holdings are, however, less than for a comparable period following the European stabilizations, and the Bolivian economy remains substantially unmonetized.[7]

Is it true that a nation that forgets its history is forced to relive it? Perhaps President Paz-Estenssoro learned a great deal from the tireless efforts and wisdom of George Eder. If he did, Bolivia is on its way to a future of stable prices and growth dependent on its own resources and will. At the least, the work of Eder ought to be required reading for the political leaders of Bolivia.

## Notes

The views expressed here are those of the author and do not reflect the views of the Congressional Research Service or the Library of Congress.

1. For a discussion of the stabilization mission to Bolivia and its work, see Eder (1968).

2. Temporary foreign assistance played an important role in the stabilization programs in Austria, Hungary after World War I, Germany, Greece, and Taiwan. For details, see Sargent (1982), Makinen (1986), and Makinen and Woodward (1987).

3. Capie (1986) suggests that hyperinflation follows internal social disorder. This theory may be appropriate to Bolivia, for hyperinflation followed shortly after the military government was overthrown. One might argue, however, that throughout much of its modern history Bolivia has been in a state of social disorder. My explanation suggests that Bolivia's hyperinflation followed from ignorance of or a lack of concern over government policies.

4. This can occur because, as rational agents, economic agents do not believe that stabilization will succeed or because they need time to learn about the new policies or because they form their expectations adaptively.

5. Eder (1968, p. 503) provides evidence that this type of unemployment was important following the 1956 stabilization. It was concentrated in the textile industry and the public sector.

6. Real money balances are computed using the monetary base as the measure of the money supply. The data and method of computation are taken from Morales.

7. For the first year following stabilization, real money balances rose 4-fold in Greece, Germany, and Hungary (after World War II), 2.6-fold in Austria and Hungary (after World War I), and 2.5-fold in Poland. Makinen and Woodward (1987) explain that the mere rise in real balances does not necessarily provide discriminating evidence in favor of a public perception that a genuine regime change has occurred.

## References

Bomberger, W. A., and G. E. Makinen. 1983. "The Hungarian hyperinflation and stabilization of 1945–46." *Journal of Political Economy* 91(5):801–824.

Capie, F. 1986. "Conditions in which very rapid inflation has appeared." *Carnegie-Rochester Conference Series on Public Policy* 24:115–168.

Eder, G. J. 1968. *Inflation and Development in Latin America: A Case History of Inflation and Stabilization in Bolivia.* Michigan International Business Studies 6. Ann Arbor: The University of Michigan School of Business Administration.

Garber, P. M. 1982. "Transition from inflation to price stability." *Carnegie-Rochester Conference Series on Public Policy* 16:11–42.

Makinen, G. E. 1984. "The Greek stabilization of 1944–46." *American Economic Review* 74(3):1067–1074.

Makinen, G. E. 1986. "The Greek hyperinflation and stabilization of 1943–46." *Journal of Economic History* 46(3):795–806.

Makinen, G. E., and G. T. Woodward. 1987. "The Taiwanese hyperinflation and stabilization of 1945–1952." Washington, D.C.: Congressional Research Service, Library of Congress. Mimeo.

Sachs, J. 1986. *The Bolivian Hyperinflation and Stabilization.* NBER Working Paper 2073. Cambridge, Mass.: National Bureau of Economic Research.

Sargent, T. J. 1982. "The ends of four big inflations," in *Inflation: Causes and Effects,* R. E. Hall, ed. (Chicago, Ill.: University of Chicago Press), 41–96.

### Comment by Joseph Ramos

Morales has presented a stimulating account of Bolivia's stabilization program (NEP). I would like to address two questions of special interest: (1) What explains the program's success in bringing inflation down abruptly without producing the acute recession that all forms of adaptive expectations augmented Phillips curve analysis would expect? (2) Why was there no need for the wage and price controls that heterodox programs consider essential to bring price setters' expectations rapidly and simultaneously into line with the inflationary target implicit in macroeconomic policy? The response to both questions hinges on the nature of expectations during hyperinflations and the *way* (not the fact) that the fiscal deficit is closed.

### Expectations: Orthodox versus Heterodox Stabilization Programs

Even if inflationary expectations are forward looking (rational), recession can ensue if expectations in fact fail to anticipate correctly the inflation implicit in macroeconomic policy. Such a sluggish response of expectations, even to technically sound macroeconomic policies, cannot be ruled out, for no one can guarantee how lasting such a policy change will be or consequently how credible it will be to economic agents. Hence there is the insistence of heterodox stabilization programs on temporary wage and price controls to complement needed demand constraint policies (the orthodox approach) to ensure credibility, to overcome price setters' fears of being alone in abiding by the new inflationary target, and to coordinate their price behavior with each other and with policy.

Yet the heterodox position is especially relevant for cases in which high and persistent inflation make expectations relatively stable and thus rigid, but not for hyperinflations, where expectations, although extreme, are hardly consolidated. Moreover, because in hyperinflation prices must be set daily, indexing and price setting are increasingly based on the free price of foreign exchange, which is the only parameter with a broad impact on costs whose price varies daily or hourly and is rapidly and widely known (such "dollarization" was abetted in Bolivia by the widespread availability of dollars resulting from cocaine production). Consequently, if the exchange rate can be stabilized, all other prices will automatically and synchronously fall into line. Stabilizing the exchange rate is thus, during hyperinflation, the equivalent of generalized wage and price controls. Additional wage and price controls are then indeed redundant.[1]

What it takes to stabilize the exchange rate is a different matter. Certainly the exchange rate cannot be set arbitrarily at any old rate;[2] nor will it hold if unaccompanied by appropriate demand constraint policies (as in most of the previous stabilization programs tried in Bolivia between 1982 and 1985). But it cannot be conclusively determined whether the exchange rate along with all other prices stabilized because the NEP had gained widespread credibility (the "spontaneous" rational expectations view) or whether other prices stabilized because the exchange rate stabilized (as Sachs[3] and the heterodox supporters argue). Nevertheless, what evidence there is points in this latter direction. For example, despite the fall in the price of oil and the collapse of the tin market at the end of 1985, the *real* effective exchange rate since the inception of the NEP has actually declined (making Bolivia less competitive); indeed the nominal rate has remained virtually fixed since January 1986. Such exchange rate stability, in the face of a blatant need to adjust, is suggestive more of short-run confidence in its maintenance over the short run (arising from the immediate availability of $800 million in credits from bilateral and multilateral agencies) than of credibility in the long-run success of the stabilization program.

Because of this ambiguity in determining the cause of price stability and because in hyperinflation price and wage controls collapse into exchange rate control, the more adequate testing ground of the validity of the spontaneous (orthodox) versus guided (heterodox) rational expectations approach to stabilization is persistent inflation, not hyperinflation.

## The Fiscal Deficit: The Way It Was Closed

A secondary, albeit important, reason why recessive costs were not acute is that Bolivia's fiscal deficit was cut by increased revenues far more than by reduced expenditures.[4] Even though the reduction of fiscal expenditures has the same effect on aggregate demand as an increase in revenues, it is far more likely to lead to undesired quantity adjustments, not price adjustments, for except for subsidies expenditure reduction is necessarily and entirely focused on only a fraction of GNP (the 20% or so in the public sector), whereas increased revenues as a rule affect demand across the board (and hence are more likely to be fully compensated by the similarly across the board expansionary effects of the reduced inflation tax). Moreover, because a reduction in the deficit through expenditure reduction tends to concentrate cuts on a few items (public investment especially), the probability of quantity adjustment is accentuated.

The NEP was, in fact, able to increase revenues readily because Bolivia's public sector normally enjoys a large surplus in foreign exchange (earnings from the gas and tin exports of state firms are greater than public sector imports and annual interest payments on foreign debt). Thus one policy instrument, a devaluation, tends not only to improve external equilibrium but also to reduce the fiscal deficit. This is in contrast to other countries (for example, Brazil and Argentina) whose public sectors chronically have a foreign exchange deficit (because of interest payments and, in Brazil, petroleum imports). Hence every time they need to devalue to improve their external situation, their fiscal sector peso deficit increases, requiring far greater demand constraint policies to transfer resources from the private to the public sector.

The NEP's devaluation increased revenues by 5% of GNP, alone accounting for 40–50% of the closing of the fiscal deficit (depending on whether or not one includes debt arrears as expenditure reduction). Roughly another $2\frac{1}{2}\%$ of GNP came from the NEP's setting of domestic fuel prices at international levels. Thus, unlike most stabilization programs, Bolivia was able to close the deficit largely on the basis of revenue increases.

But not fully. Indeed what costs Bolivia did experience—a relatively modest 3% fall in output (possibly understated as Morales argues)—and especially the highly skewed distribution of such costs can largely be attributed to the expenditure reduction that took place in public sector investment, employment, and wages. In fact, none of these had grown markedly during 1982–85. Rather it was the collapse of tax revenues (nonpetroleum taxes amounting to 3−4% of GNP in mid-1985 versus 8% in 1980) that set off and produced the hyperinflation. Yet the NEP's inability to restore significantly nonpetroleum fiscal revenues meant that the burden of closing the remaining deficit fell on generally labor-intensive fiscal expenditures: The central government's wage bill fell from $6\frac{1}{2}$% of GNP in 1981−84 to around 5% in 1986, and public sector investment virtually ceased. Because these cuts were effected in the midst of already existing high unemployment, real wages throughout the economy fell over 40% (and still hover some 10−20% below the prehyperinflation period).

In short, the burden of closing the deficit is dependent on the way it is closed. Recession, unduly low wages, and virtually zero public sector investment in infrastructure are thus the counterpart of unduly low taxes.

## Were Other Options Possible?

We finally come to the central question raised by Morales—whether an alternative stabilization program could have been designed to reduce inflation but with less recession and certainly at a lesser distributive cost. Because hyperinflation had left tax administration in a shambles, the ideal policy of increasing income taxes, rather than cutting quantity-adjustment-prone fiscal expenditures, was not a realistic alternative in late 1985. Yet a feasible second best would have been to focus the effort on more easily collectible taxes, such as those on gasoline. Given its inelastic demand and its widespread use, an additional energy tax, leaving domestic energy prices well above international ones, could have been levied to close the remaining deficit until normal tax collection increased to replace it over time, for high as domestic petroleum prices seem to Bolivians, they are in fact 25% higher in Chile and Peru, 50% higher in Argentina, and over 100% higher in Brazil.

Not only could this form of closing the deficit have minimized the recession and its sharply regressive distributive impact, but it also would have made the program more credible. The durability of the current program is in doubt so long as its success is seen as resting on its keeping wages and public investment at artificially and intolerably low levels (even for Bolivia). Even today, as Morales insists, consolidation of the stabilization program and economic recovery require that Bolivia shift from expenditure reduction to revenue collection. If it fails in this regard, the program's eventual success will be in jeopardy, for effective sovereignty is ultimately measured by a government's capacity to raise revenues, not by how well it cuts expenditures.

## Notes

1. Nor need it lead to exchange rate lag as in exchange-rate-led stabilization programs in the southern cone of Latin America in recent years, for in persistent inflation (but not hyperinflation) the exchange rate is only one of several factors influencing expectations. Hence, even though the budget deficit is closed (as in Chile and Uruguay), prices often decelerate far less rapidly than the exchange rate, resulting in a balance of payments crisis, recession, and a renewed outburst of inflation. See Joseph Ramos, *Neoconservative Economics in the Southern Cone of Latin America, 1973–83* (Baltimore, Md.: Johns Hopkins University Press, 1986).

2. Thus the NEP's free float of the exchange rate, before fixing it, made sense. All the more so because by August 1985 less than $100 million was held as M2 (roughly the same as international reserves); thus it was not difficult to withstand a speculative attack on the exchange rate.

3. Jeffrey Sachs, "The Bolivian hyperinflation and stabilization" (Cambridge, Mass.: Harvard University, October 1986), mimeo.

4. A further reason is that those sectors especially sensitive to inflationary expectations and thus subject to aggregate demand variations (manufacturing and construction) account for less than 20% of GNP. Most other important segments of the Bolivian economy are largely free of the inertia and rigidities arising from mistaken inflationary expectations, for they are clear price takers domestically (agriculture) or internationally (mining, energy, and coca).

# V  Lessons from Mexico

# 8 Lessons from Mexico

### Francisco Gil Diaz and
### Raul Ramos Tercero

The notion that price stabilization may sometimes require not only the elimination of the fundamental cause of inflation—an excessive budget deficit—but also the simultaneous implementation of a price freeze has achieved theoretical respectability in a remarkably short time. Heterodox stabilization plans have been justified by the existence of multiple inflation equilibria (that is, a situation that implies that the economy may remain at a high-inflation equilibrium although the underlying fiscal stance could in principle sustain a much lower rate) and/or inertia in price formation. Bruno (1986) examined multiple equilibria and showed that the likelihood that a heterodox strategy will be necessary in order to reach a low-level inflationary equilibrium is greater the lower the elasticity of inflation revenue and the higher the responsiveness to inflation of key prices, such as the wage rate and the exchange rate.

Such conditions are likely to be satisfied in countries that have experienced high inflation for a prolonged period. Mexico, on the other hand, lacks a history of chronic inflation but has been experiencing gradually increasing price instability for the last fifteen years and currently faces for the first time in its modern history the prospect of suffering three-digit inflation rates for two consecutive years.

Our main objective here has three parts. First, we attempt to measure the parameters mentioned by Bruno in order to assess the relevance of heterodox stabilization plans for Mexico. Second, we examine the fiscal fundamentals of inflation; and third, we try to show that, in general, price stabilization is incompatible with an exchange rate policy aimed at pegging the real exchange rate.

In section 8.1 we describe the current Mexican economic situation and previous stabilization episodes. In section 8.2 we examine how the rates of growth of wages, public prices, and the exchange rate have changed their responsiveness to inflation since the early 1970s. We analyze the net fiscal contributions of inflation and the real exchange rate in section 8.3, and in section 8.4 we consider the fiscal gap that remains to be closed before a return to price stability is feasible. We discuss the compatibility between price stabilization and exchange rate management aimed at pegging the real exchange rate in section 8.5 and present our conclusions in section 8.6.

## 8.1  The Mexican Experience with Price Stabilization

The Mexican experience with three-digit inflation is recent. As figure 8.1 shows, until 1982 prices had never risen at annual rates above 30% for more than two consecutive quarters. Before the oil price collapse of 1986 the implementation of stabilization policies in Mexico had usually followed major devaluations: in 1954, 1976, and 1982.

Whether the strategies of 1954 and 1976 should be considered "orthodox" is a moot question, but an important feature of the current heterodoxy (namely, the fixing of the nominal exchange rate) was present in those episodes. Partly as a result, both stabilization attempts (especially the first one) can be judged as fairly successful: In 1954 inflation fell below 20% per annum one quarter after the devaluation, and in 1976 it decreased below 20% after two quarters. On the other hand, although the devaluation of 1954 signaled the beginning of a period of financeable budget deficits that lasted until 1971, the 1976–77 stabilization was characterized by a rather mild deficit cut. Thus the public sector's primary deficit (that is, the difference between total noninterest public spending and total public revenues), which in the period 1965–71 averaged 0.7% of GDP, fell to only 2.7% in 1977–80 (table 8.1). Inflation also remained at a new, higher plateau of 21.7% per annum in the same period (table 8.2).

Another feature of the stabilization episodes of 1954 and 1976 is that, contrary to the notion that disinflation reduces economic activity, in both cases in important recovery accompanied the reduction of inflation. The aftermath of the 1983 adjustment would confirm this behavior (albeit more protractedly because of the persistent decline in the terms of trade).

As pointed out by van Wijnbergen (1986) and others, this output pattern reflects the contractionary effect that the real depreciation that follows a discrete jump in the exchange rate has on output. In general, however, this contraction, which operates through several channels on both the demand and supply sides, is transitory because the impact of the devaluation on domestic prices pushes the real exchange rate back to its original level.

The devaluation of 1982 differed from preceding episodes in two main aspects. First, by 1982 the vulnerability of the Mexican economy to exter-

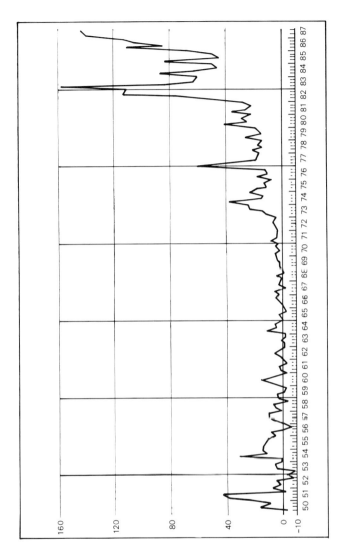

**Figure 8.1**
Quarterly inflation (at annual rates) for Mexico. 1950–1963: Wholesale prices. 1969–1987: Consumer prices.

**Table 8.1**
Main indicators of public finances (% of GDP)

| Year | Financial requirements of public sector | Total interest payments | Public sector primary deficit |
|------|------|------|------|
| 1965 | 0.9 | 0.8 | −0.0 |
| 1966 | 1.2 | 0.9 | 0.3 |
| 1967 | 2.4 | 1.2 | 1.0 |
| 1968 | 2.2 | 1.1 | 0.8 |
| 1969 | 2.2 | 1.1 | 0.8 |
| 1970 | 3.8 | 2.0 | 1.5 |
| 1971 | 2.5 | 1.6 | 0.5 |
| 1972 | 4.9 | 1.9 | 2.4 |
| 1973 | 6.9 | 1.9 | 3.8 |
| 1974 | 7.3 | 2.0 | 4.0 |
| 1975 | 10.0 | 2.3 | 6.5 |
| 1976 | 9.9 | 3.3 | 4.9 |
| 1977 | 6.7 | 3.0 | 2.3 |
| 1978 | 6.7 | 3.2 | 2.4 |
| 1979 | 7.4 | 3.4 | 2.9 |
| 1980 | 8.5 | 3.7 | 3.2 |
| 1981 | 13.5 | 5.2 | 8.4 |
| 1982 | 17.2 | 8.6 | 7.5 |
| 1983 | 12.1 | 12.9 | −4.2 |
| 1984 | 9.7 | 12.2 | −4.9 |
| 1985 | 10.5 | 12.1 | −3.7 |
| 1986 | 16.2 | 17.4 | −2.3 |

**Table 8.2**
Main indicators of output, prices, exchange rates, and wages

| Year | Real GDP[a] | Consumer price index (%)[b] | Wholesale price index (%)[b] | Controlled exchange rate (%)[b] | Free exchange rate (%)[b] | Real wage index[c] | Real exchange rate indexes[d] | | Terms of trade index |
|---|---|---|---|---|---|---|---|---|---|
| | | | | | | | Consumer prices | Wages | |
| 1965 | 6.5 | n.a. | 0.0 | 0.0 | — | 90.7 | 102.6 | 92.3 | 84.1 |
| 1966 | 6.9 | n.a. | 2.7 | 0.0 | — | 91.7 | 103.4 | 94.2 | 85.2 |
| 1967 | 6.3 | n.a. | 1.9 | 0.0 | — | 95.2 | 100.4 | 92.6 | 83.9 |
| 1968 | 8.1 | n.a. | 2.2 | 0.0 | — | 97.1 | 98.4 | 95.1 | 89.0 |
| 1969 | 6.3 | 4.3 | 4.0 | 0.0 | — | 100.7 | 100.6 | 96.3 | 88.0 |
| 1970 | 6.9 | 4.8 | 5.2 | 0.0 | — | 100.0 | 100.0 | 100.0 | 96.7 |
| 1971 | 4.2 | 5.2 | 3.0 | 0.0 | — | 100.5 | 100.8 | 104.0 | 100.0 |
| 1972 | 8.5 | 5.5 | 5.1 | 0.0 | — | 106.4 | 104.5 | 106.6 | 103.3 |
| 1973 | 8.4 | 21.3 | 25.3 | 0.0 | — | 103.5 | 106.5 | 114.3 | 115.2 |
| 1974 | 6.1 | 20.7 | 13.4 | 0.0 | — | 106.1 | 97.0 | 101.3 | 100.1 |
| 1975 | 5.6 | 11.2 | 13.5 | 0.0 | — | 110.7 | 94.4 | 98.0 | 97.8 |
| 1976 | 4.2 | 27.2 | 45.7 | 59.7 | — | 122.7 | 103.5 | 100.0 | 113.0 |
| 1977 | 3.4 | 20.7 | 18.1 | 14.0 | — | 125.1 | 129.6 | 127.3 | 113.0 |
| 1978 | 8.2 | 16.2 | 15.8 | −0.1 | — | 121.8 | 126.9 | 131.3 | 104.1 |
| 1979 | 9.2 | 20.0 | 19.9 | 0.3 | — | 119.9 | 120.6 | 126.7 | 113.1 |
| 1980 | 8.3 | 29.8 | 26.4 | 2.0 | — | 114.7 | 108.0 | 115.0 | 127.6 |
| 1981 | 7.9 | 28.7 | 27.2 | 12.8 | — | 125.6 | 91.0 | 87.9 | 124.3 |
| 1982 | −0.5 | 98.8 | 92.6 | 267.5 | 466.2 | 124.0 | 124.7 | 129.0 | 108.2 |
| 1983 | −5.3 | 80.8 | 88.0 | 49.2 | 8.7 | 84.2 | 133.9 | 202.8 | 98.8 |

**Table 8.2** (continued)

| Year | Real GDP[a] | Consumer price index (%)[b] | Wholesale price index (%)[b] | Controlled exchange rate (%)[b] | Free exchange rate (%)[b] | Real wage index[c] | Real exchange rate indexes[d] | | Terms of trade index |
|---|---|---|---|---|---|---|---|---|---|
| | | | | | | | Consumer prices | Wages | |
| 1984 | 3.7 | 59.2 | 63.2 | 33.8 | 30.1 | 77.3 | 111.2 | 185.9 | 97.1 |
| 1985 | 2.8 | 63.7 | 63.4 | 92.9 | 113.1 | 81.2 | 106.9 | 174.8 | 91.9 |
| 1986 | −3.8 | 105.7 | 104.0 | 148.5 | 104.5 | 73.0 | 156.3 | 303.2 | 65.6 |

a. Rate of growth.
b. December–December rate of change.
c. Average wages in manufacturing sector.
d. Average of monthly values.

nal shocks had increased because oil exports, which before 1975 had been negligible, became a major source of public revenue in 1978. Furthermore, the public sector's external debt had increased by a whopping 56.6% ($18 billion) in 1981 (for external accounts, see table 8.3). A second major difference in the 1982 episode was the absence of a deficit correction following the first devaluation in February. As a result, the economy became extremely unstable, and by the end of the year the free and the controlled peso-to-dollar exchange rates had depreciated by 458% and 262%, respectively, with respect to the end-of-January parity.

The devaluations had an immediate inflationary impact, and the CPI increased 99% in 1982. Nevertheless, the average real exchange rate rose 37% with respect to the previous year, and the merchandise account exhibited a surplus for the first time in thirty-nine years. On the other hand, real GDP fell 0.5%, but the recession did not reach its trough until 1983, when GDP diminished 5.3%

In 1983 and 1984 the new administration implemented a drastic fiscal correction, and the primary deficit fell from 7.5% of GDP in 1982 to −4.2% in 1983 and −4.9% in 1984. As a result the current account yielded a surplus in both years, and foreign reserves rose continuously, albeit at a decreasing rate. Because inflation exceeded exchange rate depreciation, the real exchange rate measured in terms of prices diminished 22% from December 1982 to December 1984.

In 1985 the public primary surplus fell from 4.9% to 3.7% of GDP, reinforcing the decline of the current account surplus that the real appreciation of 1983–84 had initiated through its stimulating effect on output and imports. Furthermore, the reduction of the primary surplus coincided with a strong surge in private credit demand. In 1983 and 1984 real banking credit to the private sector had fallen precipitously, thereby freeing resources to finance both the deficit and a sizable accumulation of international reserves. On the other hand, the coincidence in 1985 of higher public and private financial requirements reduced foreign reserves.

In order to counteract this decline and the speculation that had arisen as internal credit expansion became excessive, banking reserve requirements were increased and the controlled exchange rate underwent a discrete devaluation of 20% in July and depreciated from September to December at an annual rate of 142%. As a result inflation increased again and by the fourth quarter of 1985 was higher than in 1984. Similarly, by the end of 1985 the real exchange rate had increased to a level similar to that of December 1982 (129, with 1970 = 100).

In 1986 the Mexican economy suffered the most severe terms of trade

**Table 8.3**
Main indicators of the balance of payments (millions of dollars)[a]

| Year | Current account | | | Capital account | | | Errors and omissions | Change in Banco de Mexico's gross reserves[b] |
|---|---|---|---|---|---|---|---|---|
| | Total | Public sector | Private sector | Total | Public sector | Private sector | | |
| 1965 | −442.9 | −120.2 | −322.7 | 342.3 | −1.7 | 344.0 | 79.7 | −21.0 |
| 1966 | −477.8 | −210.0 | −267.8 | 527.0 | 233.2 | 303.8 | −43.1 | 6.1 |
| 1967 | −603.0 | −317.6 | −285.4 | 647.3 | 569.1 | 78.1 | −4.4 | 39.8 |
| 1968 | −775.4 | −402.4 | −373.0 | 513.8 | 382.5 | 131.3 | 310.6 | 49.0 |
| 1969 | −708.4 | −430.0 | −278.4 | 665.4 | 462.0 | 203.5 | 90.7 | 47.9 |
| 1970 | −1,187.9 | −747.4 | −440.5 | 848.6 | 443.0 | 405.6 | 396.1 | 102.1 |
| 1971 | −928.9 | −611.6 | −317.3 | 895.7 | 420.6 | 475.2 | 193.5 | 200.0 |
| 1972 | −1,005.7 | −769.4 | −236.3 | 432.5 | 149.4 | 283.1 | 798.7 | 264.7 |
| 1973 | −1,528.8 | −1,429.9 | −98.9 | 2,051.2 | 1,624.2 | 427.0 | −400.2 | 122.3 |
| 1974 | −3,226.0 | −2,432.5 | −793.5 | 3,822.5 | 2,921.6 | 900.9 | −559.6 | 36.9 |
| 1975 | −4,442.6 | −2,938.8 | −1,503.8 | 5,458.9 | 4,347.8 | 1,111.1 | −851.2 | 165.1 |
| 1976 | −3,683.3 | −2,825.6 | 857.7 | 5,070.0 | 5,092.7 | −22.7 | −2,390.6 | −1,004.0 |
| 1977 | −1,596.4 | −2,468.8 | 872.4 | 2,276.0 | 2,922.7 | −646.6 | −22.5 | 657.1 |
| 1978 | −2,693.0 | −2,567.9 | −125.1 | 3,254.1 | 2,573.8 | 680.3 | −127.0 | 434.1 |
| 1979 | −4,870.5 | −2,072.9 | −2,797.6 | 4,533.3 | 3,352.2 | 1,181.1 | 686.2 | 348.9 |
| 1980 | −10,739.7 | −489.8 | −10,249.9 | 11,442.3 | 3,323.7 | 8,118.6 | 245.1 | 1,108.6 |
| 1981 | −16,052.1 | −124.7 | −15,927.3 | 26,357.5 | 17,541.8 | 8,815.1 | −9,030.1 | 1,012.2 |
| 1982 | −6,221.0 | 3,066.7 | −9,287.7 | 9,752.7 | 7,907.9 | 1,844.8 | −6,831.8 | −3,184.7 |
| 1983 | 5,418.4 | 5,572.2 | −153.8 | −1,416.4 | 2,301.9 | −3,718.3 | −884.0 | 3,100.9 |
| 1984 | 4,238.5 | 4,759.2 | −520.8 | 38.9 | 4,217.6 | −4,178.7 | −924.3 | 3,200.9 |
| 1985 | 1,236.8 | 4,313.2 | −3,076.4 | −1,526.7 | 1,226.4 | −2,753.1 | −2,133.5 | −2,328.4 |
| 1986 | −1,270.4 | −1,856.4 | 586.0 | 2,270.5 | 3,109.3 | −838.8 | −210.3 | 985.0 |

a. The concepts included in the table may not add up to zero as a result of the omission of SDR allocations and other minor concepts.
b. The change in Banco de Mexico's gross reserves would appear with an opposite sign in conventional balance of payments accounts.

deterioration in its modern history, when the average dollar price of its crude oil exports fell 53.4%, thereby reducing oil export revenues by 58% (from $14.7 to $6.2 billion). As a result, the current account of the public sector's balance of payments turned to a deficit for the first time since 1982, and GDP fell 3.8%.

Despite the efforts to counteract the fiscal effects of the oil shock, the primary surplus fell to 2.3% of GDP in 1986 and public financial require-ments jumped to 15.1% of GDP because of the increase in both nominal and real domestic interest rates that followed the terms of trade deteriora-tion. However, notwithstanding this budget deterioration and a lack of foreign financing for most of the year, reserves fell only transitorily in the first semester and by December had increased by almost a billion dollars. This was a result of the continuation of the credit freeze that had been introduced in the latter part of 1985 and of a 148% depreciation of the controlled exchange rate in 1986, which increased the real exchange rate to a level of 173 (with 1970 = 100) in the fourth quarter of 1986. On the other hand, the increasing trend of inflation became more acute, and by the first quarter of 1987 consumer prices were rising at an annual rate of 139%.

The economic situation in the aftermath of the oil shock raises several issues related to the design of a disinflation strategy. First, the recent experience of high inflation in Mexico has presumably increased the speed with which economic agents react to changes in the price level, a condition that, as pointed out by Bruno (1986), would increase the desirability of a heterodox scheme. Second, the need for further adjustment of the fiscal fundamentals has been questioned because the public sector has been running a primary surplus since 1983. Third, once the real amortization of peso-denominated public debt (including currency) resulting from inflation is deducted from the total public financial requirements, the resulting inflation-corrected deficit or operational deficit (see table 8.5) is only slightly higher in the period 1983–86 than in the price stability era. Fourth, although the real depreciation of 1986 was indispensable to accommodate the oil price collapse in the short run, it is unclear whether the real exchange rate prevailing at the end of 1986 represents a long-run equilibrium or whether further realignment is necessary before a heterodox strategy can be con-sidered. The following sections examine these questions.

## 8.2   The Responsiveness of Key Prices to Inflation

An important determinant of the stability of an economy subject to infla-tionary shocks is the responsiveness of key prices to inflation. To gauge the

**Table 8.4**
Indicators of the responsiveness of key prices to inflation[a]

| Period | Rate of growth of exchange rate | Rate of growth of nominal wages in manufacturing industries | Rate of growth of public prices |
|---|---|---|---|
| January 1972–August 1976 | 0 | 0.640 | n.a. |
| September 1976–January 1982 | −0.921 | −1.924 | 0.519[b] |
| January 1982–March 1987 | 0.829 | −1.762 | 1.064[c] |

a. Sum of coefficients of the contemporaneous value and three lags of monthly rate of growth of the CPI.
b. Coefficients estimated for the period January 1981–December 1982.
c. Coefficients estimated for the period January 1983–March 1987.

importance of this factor in the Mexican case, we ran regressions of the rate of increase of three key prices (the nominal wage rate in the manufacturing industry, the exchange rate, and the price index of goods and services sold by the public sector) on current and lagged values of the inflation rate for three sample periods.[1] The first regression runs from the end of the price stability era to the eve of the 1976 devaluation (January 1972–August 1976), the second from the aftermath of the 1976 devaluation to the eve of the 1982 devaluation (September 1976–January 1982), and the third from the aftermath of the 1982 devaluation to the most recent available data (February 1982–March 1987). The results of these regressions appear in table 8.4.

Our estimates show that the Mexican experience conforms only broadly to the expectation of a generally increasing responsiveness of key prices to inflation. Consider first the exchange rate. The responsiveness of its monthly rate of growth to monthly inflation (measured by the sum of the regression coefficients of three lags of the monthly rate of growth of the CPI) is obviously nil in the first subperiod; in the second subperiod it becomes negative (a result that agrees with the notion that the exchange rate was used to stabilize the price level at that time), and in the third it increases drastically. This jump reflects an important difference between the current stabilization strategy and previous episodes, because, although a crucial element in the 1954 and 1976 stabilization programs was a prompt fixing of the exchange rate after the initial devaluation (notwithstanding the ensuing real appreciation), the exchange rate followed inflation closely after the real depreciation of 1986, thereby preserving the initial real exchange rate increase. The fall in the dollar against other currencies strengthened this rise in the real exchange rate.

Consider next that the responsiveness of the rate of growth of public prices to inflation increases from 0.5 to 1.0. However, these estimates are not strictly comparable to those of the exchange rate and of nominal wages because, as a result of restrictions on data availability (see table 8.4), the regressions for public prices were estimated for periods different from those used for the other variables.

Finally, the pattern of nominal wage inflation responsiveness to price inflation is broadly similar to that of the exchange rate (falling from the first to the second subperiod and then increasing in the third). However, it is outstanding in this case that the sum of regression coefficients in all the subperiods churns out a negative value, including the third, highly inflationary period. This result suggests that the burden of the short-run stabilizing role played by the exchange rate and the nominal wage rate in the second subperiod fell only on the nominal wage rate in the third subperiod. Thus a comparison of our result with the patterns of generally increasing and positive responsiveness found by Bruno (1986) for Israel points to the conclusion that wage adjustment was not a cause of inflation inertia in the last few years. Of course, this is not evidence that less than full indexation is possible today, after the real wage cuts of 1986 and 1987 (see table 8.1).[2]

## 8.3   The Role of Inflation and the Real Exchange Rate in Mexican Public Finance

It is now more or less generally understood that, in assessing the impact of fiscal policy on aggregate demand, conventional deficit figures should be corrected for the real debt amortization resulting from inflation. Otherwise, how can we make sense of the fact that a country whose public sector deficits have run above 10% of GDP has nevertheless been able to generate balance of payments current account surpluses? And, indeed, once the real amortization of the peso-denominated public debt resulting from inflation is deducted in order to get the operational deficit (OD) (see table 8.5), the behavior of the budget meshes better with that of the current account. Furthermore, once one inspects the behavior of the OD, it is no longer surprising to find that the ratio of the peso-denominated public debt to GDP remained more or less constant from 1983 to 1985.

However, the OD figures do not show the magnitude of the deficit that (in the absence of changes in tax rates and spending patterns) would remain if inflation were eliminated.[3] A price freeze would not only do away with the inflation-coupon payments on the peso-denominated public debt (which is the effect that the OD concept takes into account) but would also eliminate, among other things, both the Olivera-Tanzi effect and the inflation tax. It is important to account for these and other effects in order to measure, however approximately, the gap of resources (if any) that would remain after a price freeze and to gauge how the net contribution of inflation to public revenues has evolved in the last few years. Table 8.5 shows the figures of a full-inflation-corrected budget deficit, which we call the adjusted operational deficit (AOD). This concept takes into account the following five effects:[4] (1) the Olivera-Tanzi effect, (2) the effect of inflation on financial subsidies, (3) the effect of inflation on the composition of the peso public debt (because in an environment of price stability the demand for non-interest-bearing public debt would increase relative to the demand for interest-bearing debt, thereby reducing the average cost of funds to the public sector), (4) the inflation tax on non-interest-bearing public debt, and (5) the inflation tax on the peso-denominated interest-bearing public debt.

The concept of the AOD is equal to the algebraic sum of the aforementioned effects and the OD. Three features of table 8.5 bear emphasis. In all the years under consideration inflation made a positive net contribution to public revenues. Thus, had a price freeze been implemented in any given year, an increase in explicit taxation and/or a reduction in spending would have been necessary to maintain the sans-freeze rate of growth of public debt. Second, the two years in which the total contribution of inflation is highest (1976 and 1982) correspond to years of discrete devaluations of the peso-to-dollar exchange rate. However, whereas in 1982 a very high tax on the peso-denominated public debt (6.7% of GDP) offset relatively high real revenue losses by means of the Olivera-Tanzi and the financial subsidies effects (1.1% of GDP), in 1976 both the inflation tax and the latter effects were much more modest (2.7% and 0.3% of GDP, respectively). Third, a sizable reduction in the inflation elasticity of total inflation revenue is apparent. Using the average values of both total inflation revenue (column of table 8.5) and the inflation rate (column 9) and taking percentage changes with respect to the average values of the period 1965–72, we calculate that the implicit inflation elasticity of total net inflation revenue diminished from 0.67 for the period 1973–81 to 0.42 in 1981–83 to 0.17 in 1984–86.

Perhaps even more impressive in this respect is the comparison of 1986 with the preceding years. Although 1986 has the highest inflation rate on record, we estimate that the net contribution of inflation to public revenues in that year is only the fifth largest for the period 1965–86 and, in particular, that it is smaller than in years with much lower inflation, such as

**Table 8.5**
Public sector deficit adjusted for inflation (% of GDP)

| Year | (1) Operational deficit | Inflation tax (2) On non-interest-bearing debt | (3) On interest-bearing debt | (4) Olivera-Tanzi effect | (5) Financial subsidies | (6) Debt composition effect | $(7)=(2)+(3)-(4)-(5)-(6)$ Total effect of inflation | $(8)=(1)+(7)$ Adjusted operational deficit | (9) Average monthly Inflation rate | (10) Inflation and real exchange rate corrected deficit |
|---|---|---|---|---|---|---|---|---|---|---|
| 1965 | 0.9 | 0.0 | 0.1 | 0.0 | 0.0 | 0.0 | 0.1 | 0.9 | 0.0 | 1.0 |
| 1966 | 1.0 | 0.2 | 0.2 | 0.0 | 0.0 | 0.0 | 0.3 | 1.3 | 0.2 | 1.3 |
| 1967 | 2.2 | 0.1 | 0.2 | 0.0 | 0.0 | 0.0 | 0.2 | 2.4 | 0.2 | 2.4 |
| 1968 | 1.9 | 0.1 | 0.2 | 0.0 | 0.0 | 0.0 | 0.3 | 2.1 | 0.2 | 2.2 |
| 1969 | 1.6 | 0.2 | 0.2 | 0.1 | 0.0 | 0.0 | 0.3 | 1.9 | 0.4 | 1.9 |
| 1970 | 3.2 | 0.3 | 0.3 | 0.1 | 0.0 | 0.0 | 0.5 | 3.6 | 0.4 | 3.6 |
| 1971 | 1.8 | 0.3 | 0.3 | 0.2 | 0.0 | 0.0 | 0.4 | 1.4 | 0.4 | 1.4 |
| 1972 | 4.2 | 0.3 | 0.4 | 0.1 | 0.0 | 0.0 | 0.6 | 4.8 | 0.5 | 4.7 |
| 1973 | 3.9 | 1.2 | 1.1 | 0.3 | 0.0 | 0.0 | 2.0 | 6.0 | 1.6 | 5.8 |
| 1974 | 4.5 | 1.1 | 0.9 | 0.3 | 0.0 | 0.1 | 1.6 | 6.2 | 1.6 | 6.2 |
| 1975 | 8.3 | 0.6 | 0.5 | 0.2 | 0.0 | 0.1 | 0.9 | 9.2 | 0.9 | 9.4 |
| 1976 | 6.2 | 1.6 | 1.1 | 0.3 | 0.0 | 0.0 | 2.3 | 8.6 | 2.0 | 8.5 |
| 1977 | 4.3 | 1.2 | 0.7 | 0.2 | 0.0 | 0.1 | 1.5 | 5.8 | 1.6 | 5.2 |
| 1978 | 4.7 | 0.9 | 0.5 | 0.2 | 0.0 | 0.1 | 1.1 | 5.8 | 1.3 | 5.3 |
| 1979 | 5.0 | 1.1 | 0.6 | 0.2 | 0.1 | 0.1 | 1.4 | 6.5 | 1.5 | 6.2 |
| 1980 | 5.2 | 1.6 | 0.8 | 0.3 | 0.2 | 0.1 | 1.7 | 6.9 | 2.2 | 6.9 |
| 1981 | 10.0 | 1.6 | 0.3 | 0.3 | 0.5 | 0.1 | 1.0 | 11.0 | 2.1 | 11.0 |
| 1982 | 6.5 | 4.4 | 2.3 | 0.8 | 0.3 | 0.2 | 5.5 | 12.0 | 5.9 | 12.5 |

**Table 8.5** (continued)

| Year | (1) Operational deficit | Inflation tax (2) On non-interest-bearing debt | (3) On interest-bearing debt | (4) Olivera-Tanzi effect | (5) Financial subsidies | (6) Debt composition effect | (7) = (2)+(3)−(4)−(5)−(6) Total effect of inflation | (8) = (1)+(7) Adjusted operational deficit | (9) Average monthly Inflation rate | (10) Inflation and real exchange rate corrected deficit |
|---|---|---|---|---|---|---|---|---|---|---|
| 1983 | 2.4 | 2.8 | 0.6 | 0.8 | 0.2 | 0.3 | 2.1 | 4.5 | 5.1 | 5.4 |
| 1984 | 2.1 | 2.0 | 0.3 | 0.6 | 0.2 | 0.2 | 1.4 | 3.5 | 4.0 | 3.7 |
| 1985 | 2.1 | 2.3 | 0.1 | 0.7 | 0.3 | 0.2 | 1.3 | 3.4 | 4.2 | 3.6 |
| 1986 | 2.7 | 3.2 | −0.0 | 0.8 | 0.2 | 0.2 | 1.9 | 4.6 | 6.2 | 4.2 |
| **Averages** | | | | | | | | | | |
| 1965–72 | 2.1 | 0.2 | 0.2 | 0.1 | 0.0 | 0.0 | 0.3 | 2.3 | 0.3 | 2.3 |
| 1973–81 | 5.8 | 1.2 | 0.7 | 0.2 | 0.1 | 0.1 | 1.5 | 7.3 | 1.6 | 7.2 |
| 1982–83 | 4.5 | 3.6 | 1.5 | 0.8 | 0.3 | 0.2 | 3.8 | 8.3 | 5.5 | 9.0 |
| 1984–86 | 2.3 | 2.5 | 0.1 | 0.7 | 0.2 | 0.2 | 1.5 | 3.8 | 4.8 | 3.8 |

1973 and 1976. Although the patterns of spending and taxation changed considerably between 1986 and, for instance, 1982, the fall in the net contribution of inflation to public revenue between those years (more than 3.5 percentage points of GDP) is wholly due to a reduction in the inflation tax revenue (about one-third to the tax on non-interest-bearing debt and two-thirds to the tax on interest-bearing debt). This is all the more remarkable when one considers that from 1982 to 1986 the banking reserve/ deposit ratio increased from 57% to 71%, thereby forcing an increase in the share of peso-denominated non-interest-bearing public debt.

Thus table 8.6 shows that the reduction of inflation tax revenue from 1982 to 1986 reflects a continuous erosion both in the absolute inflation tax base and in the effective tax rate on interest-bearing public debt holdings. Consider that in 1986 the ratio of M1 to GDP was about 50% lower than in the late 1960s and early 1970s and that the real interest rate payable on the peso denominated interest bearing public debt has been increasing since 1982, rising for the first time above 10% in 1986.

The AOD figures should also be corrected for the effect of transitory real exchange rate fluctuations on the budget deficit. Maintaining a high real exchange rate in order to enhance the international competitiveness of the domestic economy effects the budget deficit not only through its impact on inflation but also through other channels to which not much attention is commonly paid.[5] When there is a surplus in the public sector's balance of payments current account, a transitorily high real exchange rate amounts to an improvement in the terms of trade of the public sector vis-à-vis the rest of the domestic economy. Given a certain pattern of taxing and spending, this improvement in the public sector's terms of trade reduces its deficit by increasing the internal purchasing power of its net external revenues. In column 10 of table 8.5 we present estimates of an inflation and real exchange rate corrected deficit (IRECD). The real exchange rate related gains for the public sector are calculated as the public sector's current account surplus times the difference between the actual exchange rate and the PPP exchange rate.

The IRECD figures show that from 1982 to 1985 a high real exchange rate made a significant contribution to public revenues, especially in 1983, when the difference between the actual and the PPP exchange rates was relatively large and the public sector's current account surplus increased as a result of the reduction in its imports. This situation was reversed in 1986 as the public sector's current account turned to a deficit. Thus in 1986 a high real exchange rate compounded the fiscal problem created by the fall in oil prices by generating a net loss to the public sector of 0.4% of GDP.

**Table 8.6**
Inflation tax parameters

| Year | M1/GDP (%) | Real interest rate paid on peso-denominated nonmonetary public debt (%) | Banking reserve/deposit ratio (%) |
|------|------|------|------|
| 1965 | 10.0 | 7.3 | 38 |
| 1966 | 9.7 | 4.8 | 39 |
| 1967 | 9.7 | 6.3 | 37 |
| 1968 | 9.7 | 6.0 | 37 |
| 1969 | 9.6 | 3.5 | 35 |
| 1970 | 9.5 | 4.9 | 34 |
| 1971 | 9.3 | 3.8 | 33 |
| 1972 | 9.3 | 2.3 | 36 |
| 1973 | 9.5 | − 10.2 | 36 |
| 1974 | 8.8 | − 8.1 | 40 |
| 1975 | 8.8 | 0.3 | 45 |
| 1976 | 8.7 | − 10.1 | 47 |
| 1977 | 8.2 | − 5.5 | 51 |
| 1978 | 8.7 | 0.1 | 47 |
| 1979 | 9.0 | − 1.8 | 47 |
| 1980 | 8.6 | − 4.7 | 48 |
| 1981 | 8.3 | 3.5 | 48 |
| 1982 | 7.5 | − 23.9 | 57 |
| 1983 | 6.0 | − 1.0 | 59 |
| 1984 | 5.6 | 3.7 | 60 |
| 1985 | 5.5 | 9.2 | 61 |
| 1986 | 4.9 | 10.5 | 71 |

More generally, because the real exchange rate is (the inverse of) a broadly defined terms of trade index of the domestic economy vis-à-vis the rest of the world, in judging the desirability of improving the competitiveness of domestic producers through a real exchange rate depreciation,[6] we must take into account the potential real income losses, which in the case of a net debtor country such as Mexico can be enormous. This is readily apparent when one compares the ratios of the external debt evaluated at both the actual and the PPP exchange rate to GDP.

## 8.4   What Government Budget Effort Is Necessary to Attempt a Chichimeca Plan?[7]

Although the AOD figures in table 8.5 may look "small" in relation to the conventional budget deficit, it is necessary to put them into proper perspective. From a short-run point of view it is necessary to determine whether the growth rate of the demand for financial assets at price stability would be sufficient to accommodate the observed AOD.

To reach a tentative answer we estimated the difference between the domestic financial savings that would be available in the short run under price stability and the funds that would have to be used to finance the private sector and foreign reserve accumulation, taking the end-of-1986 values of these variables as initial conditions. Our admittedly crude estimates attempt to capture the notion that a higher rate of output growth augments domestic savings by increasing the demand for financial assets and, on the other hand, reduces the availability of funds for the public sector to the extent that output growth is an increasing function of real banking credit to the private sector.[8] The resulting figures of the financeable deficit under price stability (table 8.7) are based on the additional assumptions that no external resources are available and that the foreign reserves accumulation goal is to keep the ratio of foreign reserves to M5 at the value observed at the end of 1986 (22.1%).[9]

Our estimates in table 8.7 indicate that in the short run the flow of real credit required by the private sector to achieve higher rates of output growth rises more rapidly than the demand for financial assets. As a result the public deficit that could be financed in the short run under price stability diminishes rather quickly as the target rate of growth increases. Thus, for a real rate of growth of GDP of 1%, the financeable deficit is smaller than the 1986 AOD figure by more than 2.5 percentage points of GDP. Although the closing of this gap may seem to entail a minor fiscal effort, it should be considered that during the 1965–86 period only twice

**Table 8.7**
Estimates of the financeable deficit under price stability (% of GDP)

| Target rate of growth of real GDP (%) | (1) Nominal flow of M1 | (2) Nominal flow of quasi-money | (3) Nominal flow of other banking liabilities | (4) Nominal flow of foreign reserves | (5) Nominal flow of banking credit to private sector | (6) = (1) + (2) + (3) − (4) − (5) Financeable deficit |
|---|---|---|---|---|---|---|
| −2 | 0.78 | 1.41 | 0.64 | 0.81 | −1.04 | 3.07 |
| −1 | 0.83 | 1.49 | 0.68 | 0.83 | −0.53 | 2.70 |
| 0 | 0.87 | 1.57 | 0.71 | 0.85 | −0.01 | 2.31 |
| 1 | 0.90 | 1.64 | 0.75 | 0.87 | 0.53 | 1.89 |
| 2 | 0.94 | 1.71 | 0.78 | 0.89 | 1.09 | 1.45 |
| 3 | 0.98 | 1.78 | 0.81 | 0.92 | 1.67 | 0.99 |
| 4 | 1.02 | 1.85 | 0.84 | 0.94 | 2.27 | 0.50 |
| 5 | 1.05 | 1.92 | 0.87 | 0.96 | 2.89 | −0.01 |

(in 1976 and 1986) was the AOD reduced by more than 2.5 percentage points of GDP—and those reductions started from high deficit levels.

From a long-run perspective the need to resume a satisfactory permanent rate of economic growth should bear heavily on the determination of an appropriate target for the AOD. Even a zero AOD ensuring an unchanged public debt at zero inflation might be insufficient if, for given noninterest public expenditures, the servicing of the resulting constant public debt requires a level of taxation that adversely affects capital accumulation.

An in-depth examination of this problem is beyond the scope of this chapter. However, some recent trends in the budget may have to be changed in order to reach a structure and a level of taxing and spending more conducive to growth. In the first place, although the economic significance of some classifications of public expenditure is debatable, there is little doubt that, in the course of the adjustment process of the last years, public investment has suffered a greater proportional decrease than public consumption. Thus the data in table 8.8 show that, whereas the share of public capital spending in GDP was 1.2 percentage points lower in 1986 than in 1970, the corresponding share of noninterest current spending was more than 9 percentage points higher. This trend is undesirable from a long-run point of view because theoretical considerations indicate that an optimal adjustment to a permanent shock such as the fall in oil prices should involve basically a reduction in consumption, leaving investment

**Table 8.8**
Public sector spending and revenues (corrected for inflation; % of GDP)

| Year | (1) External revenues | (2) Non-PEMEX internal tax revenues | (3) Other internal revenues | (4) Capital spending | (5) Non-interest current spending | (6) External interest | (7) Internal interest |
|------|------|------|------|------|------|------|------|
| 1965 | 1.8 | 6.5 | 9.7 | 3.7 | 15.0 | 0.2 | 0.9 |
| 1966 | 1.5 | 7.7 | 8.7 | 3.5 | 14.1 | 0.2 | 1.0 |
| 1967 | 1.6 | 7.2 | 8.7 | 5.0 | 13.4 | 0.3 | 1.1 |
| 1968 | 1.3 | 7.7 | 8.7 | 5.1 | 13.4 | 0.3 | 1.2 |
| 1969 | 1.3 | 7.9 | 9.0 | 5.4 | 13.4 | 0.3 | 1.3 |
| 1970 | 1.0 | 7.9 | 10.1 | 7.0 | 13.4 | 0.4 | 1.5 |
| 1971 | 1.1 | 8.0 | 9.5 | 5.2 | 13.7 | 0.4 | 1.6 |
| 1972 | 1.2 | 8.0 | 9.6 | 6.8 | 14.3 | 0.3 | 1.5 |
| 1973 | 1.2 | 8.9 | 10.3 | 6.7 | 17.2 | 0.4 | 1.4 |
| 1974 | 1.4 | 9.0 | 10.9 | 6.4 | 18.7 | 0.5 | 1.2 |
| 1975 | 1.5 | 9.8 | 12.1 | 8.2 | 21.4 | 0.5 | 1.1 |
| 1976 | 1.5 | 10.3 | 12.2 | 8.4 | 20.2 | 0.7 | 1.0 |
| 1977 | 2.2 | 10.3 | 12.3 | 7.6 | 19.4 | 0.8 | 0.8 |
| 1978 | 3.1 | 10.7 | 12.3 | 8.7 | 19.6 | 1.2 | 1.0 |
| 1979 | 4.4 | 11.1 | 11.5 | 9.8 | 19.8 | 1.3 | 1.0 |
| 1980 | 6.8 | 11.2 | 10.4 | 10.0 | 21.0 | 1.2 | 1.0 |
| 1981 | 7.2 | 11.0 | 10.0 | 13.4 | 22.2 | 2.1 | 1.1 |
| 1982 | 10.0 | 9.8 | 11.1 | 10.6 | 26.9 | 3.4 | 1.0 |
| 1983 | 3.0 | 9.8 | 12.3 | 7.8 | 21.8 | 4.8 | 0.9 |
| 1984 | 11.4 | 9.6 | 12.6 | 6.9 | 20.9 | 4.0 | 0.9 |
| 1985 | 10.3 | 9.7 | 13.0 | 6.2 | 22.2 | 3.9 | 1.1 |
| 1986 | 7.4 | 10.2 | 14.0 | 5.8 | 22.6 | 4.4 | 1.0 |

largely untouched.[10] Second, there is also the need to redesign the structure of public investment, the overall social profitability of which tended to decline as it leaned heavily toward the industrial sector in the late 1970s and early 1980s. Third, transitory elements loom large in the recent budget adjustment. The size of the federal bureaucracy has increased, and the nonfederal public sector (mostly enterprises) has seen a reduction in the number of entities concerned but not significantly in its size. Also, real current spending reductions have been mostly achieved through falls in real wages, and the question remains as to at what level wages will settle in the long run.

On the other hand, the need to foster economic growth implies that the effort to reach a desirable long-run fiscal deficit will have to be concentrated on reducing spending. On the revenue side the ratio of nonoil internal tax revenues to GDP fell almost continuously from 1981 to 1984. However, the peaks of 1980 and 1981 are probably an inappropriate basis for comparison because of the abnormally high levels of economic activity of those years, and in any case the reduction in nonoil tax revenues was partially reversed in 1985 and 1986. Furthermore, as a result of an improved public pricing policy, the share of nontax internal revenues in GDP increased by almost 4 percentage points with respect to 1981, so the ratio of total noninflation internal revenues to GDP has increased since that year.

## 8.5   Is Price Stabilization Compatible with Real Exchange Rate Pegging?

Much has been made of the need to align relative prices and in particular the real exchange rate before undertaking a price freeze. This is certainly a crucial question for heterodox strategies, especially when an economy is undergoing sizable real shocks. Nevertheless, real exchange rate alignment can degenerate into real exchange rate targeting, a procedure that generally leads to the failure of a stabilization strategy even if the fiscal fundamentals are "right." As pointed out by Adams and Gros (1986):

The adoption of real exchange rate rules serves to index both the nominal exchange rate and, through the balance of payments, the money supply to the price level. Under these conditions, a real exchange rate rule in combination with a target for domestic credit implies that there is no exogenous nominal anchor that can tie prices down. A real exchange rate rule represents therefore a policy of complete monetary accommodation; an increase in domestic inflation from any source is automatically accommodated by a faster rate of exchange rate depreciation and by a faster rate of monetary growth. (p. 2)

**Table 8.9**
Estimates of equation (8.1)[a]

| Rates of growth calculated for: | Group I | Group II | Group III | Group IV |
|---|---|---|---|---|
| One month | 0.637 | 0.799 | 0.841 | 0.673 |
| | (57.93) | (45.42) | (44.80) | (39.02) |
| Three months | 0.624 | 0.749 | 0.745 | 0.408 |
| | (55.84) | (43.94) | (37.31) | (26.62) |
| Six months | 0.592 | 0.667 | 0.592 | 0.218 |
| | (52.18) | (40.35) | (30.87) | (18.16) |
| Twelve months | 0.554 | 0.517 | 0.350 | 0.082 |
| | (44.78) | (35.31) | (25.10) | (12.48) |
| Three years | 0.389 | 0.244 | 0.138 | 0.004 |
| | (31.44) | (23.62) | (20.68) | (6.82) |
| Five years | 0.308 | 0.161 | 0.081 | 0.0005 |
| | (21.62) | (20.36) | (25.57) | (25.27) |
| Ten years | 0.227 | 0.074 | 0.023 | −0.00004 |
| | (7.79) | (8.10) | (8.72) | (−1.02) |

a. *t*-statistics appear in parenthesis.

In order to test the hypothesis that an exchange rate policy cannot permanently affect the real exchange rate without leading to a continuous price acceleration or deceleration, we examined the relationship between the real and the nominal exchange rates in four groups of countries that during 1975−85 experienced various degrees of inflation (see appendix A for a description of the four groups).[11] Table 8.9 shows the least-squares estimates of the following regressions:

$$G_{RER}(i, t) = \alpha_0 + \alpha_1 G_{NER}(i, t) + u_t, \qquad (8.1)$$

where $G_{RER}(i, t)$ and $G_{NER}(i, t)$ represent rates of growth in month $t$ of the real and nominal exchange rates, respectively, and the rates of growth are calculated with respect to the values in month $t - i$. According to a strong version of the exchange rate neutrality hypothesis, we would expect the rates of growth of the nominal and the real exchange rates to be uncorrelated at all time horizons. According to a weaker version we would expect that their correlation would tend to 0 for longer time horizons.

Three patterns and a major puzzle are readily apparent in our estimates. First, for all four groups the relation between the rates of growth of the nominal and the real exchange rates diminishes as one considers longer time horizons. Second, except for the shortest time horizons, the relation is generally smaller for more inflationary groups. Third, the coefficients for more inflationary groups fall more rapidly. On the other hand, from a theoretical point of view a puzzle in our results is that the positive relation between the rates of growth of the nominal and the real exchange rates for the least inflationary group (group I) is numerically significant, even for a horizon as long as ten years.[12] However, the fact that the coefficients for higher-inflation countries are much lower suggests that group I's positive coefficients do not imply the existence of a stable long-run trade-off exploitable for policy purposes.

Do we have another candidate for the numerous and growing family of vertical Phillips curves? Just as trade-offs between unemployment (or real interest rates or real wages or real output) and inflation can be expected to be transitory, inflation seems to emerge as victorious sooner or later when the nominal exchange rate is increased to achieve a real depreciation. Because the trade-off is transitory, longer-run attempts at achieving real depreciation by means of exchange rate management can succeed only at the cost of accelerating inflation.

This result severely restricts the usefulness of exchange rate policy to improve the current account. However, not much attention has been paid to it in current trade promotion discussions. Curiously economists who regularly teach their students about the hypothesis of the invariance of real to nominal variables and who would not dare to suggest targeting monetary policy on the real wage or on the rate of unemployment have no compunction in recommending that a "high" real exchange rate be maintained, even though such a target may differ from the "non-inflation-accelerating" real exchange rate.

Admittedly, although one may reject in principle the possibility of fixing the real exchange rate without destabilizing the price level, in practice the need to smooth fluctuations of the real exchange rate about its non-inflation-accelerating level (a concept that is, if anything, as elusive as that of the natural rate of unemployment) is bound to remain.

In the Mexican case this issue is complicated by the wild behavior exhibited by various real exchange rate indexes in recent years. Figure 8.2 depicts both a wage-based real exchange rate, which compares the foreign and domestic costs of the archetypical nontraded good (labor) and a CPI-based index, which compares baskets with both nontraded and traded goods.

A feature of figure 8.2 bearing particular emphasis is that, although the CPI-based index slipped back toward its historical average value after the 1982 devaluation, the wage-based index remained at an extremely high level by historical standards. This result suggests that, even though the

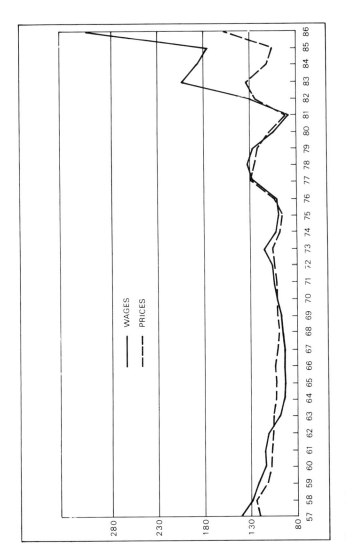

**Figure 8.2**
Real exchange rate indexes for Mexico.

wage-based index is the appropriate measure of export competitiveness, a broadly based index is what most people associate with notions such as under- or overvaluation of the real exchange rate. The CPI-based index, as shown by Mexico's and others' experiences, tends to converge to some stationary equilibrium value because international arbitrage is a major determinant of its behavior, and therefore its deviations from a central tendency can be expected to be mostly transitory.

In order to get a rough idea of the long-term depreciation of the CPI-based real exchange rate that could be explained by the terms of trade deterioration of 1986, we estimated a regression relating the CPI-based real exchange rate to the terms of trade, per capita real GDP, the internal real public sector deficit, the flow of external credit to the public sector, and a dummy variable to capture the effect of discrete devaluations of the nominal exchange rate. The model was estimated with annual data for the period 1965–85 (see appendix B). The results of the estimation generally agree with what theory would lead us to expect: The real exchange rate is increased by a terms of trade deterioration, by reductions in the flow of external credit to the public sector, by decreases in the public sector's internal real deficit, and by discrete devaluations.

One would expect that a terms of trade deterioration as severe as the one observed in 1986 would drastically increase the CPI-based real exchange rate and that this effect would be reinforced by the 1986 reduction in the public sector's internal deficit. Indeed, the value forecasted by the regression for 1986 in the absence of a discrete devaluation is 17% above the median value of the CPI-based real exchange rate for the period 1950–85. This is a relatively high level because only 6% of the observations in that period are higher than this estimate and because they correspond to years coinciding with or immediately following a major devaluation. On the other hand, the estimate is 24.2% and 30.6% lower than the 1986 average and end-of-year values of the real exchange rate, respectively.

This result leads us to believe that the inordinately high level that the real exchange reached in 1986 is to some extent a transient result of the nominal depreciation that occurred that year. Thus we conjecture that, in the absence of further nominal exchange rate shocks, the real rate would tend to fall. If this conjecture is correct, keeping the real exchange rate at its 1986 level could lead to an acceleration of inflation, and the current account improvement resulting from such a policy would be in part a consequence of the internal savings that originate in an increase in inflation taxation.

## 8.6   Conclusions

Heterodox policies have emphasized issues in price stabilization to which no appropriate attention had been given, such as the importance of co-ordinating disinflationary expectations and the endogeneity of the budget under inflation. However, as the proponents of these policies have repeatedly emphasized, except in rather extreme cases the heterodox part of the program cannot substitute for the "fundamental" adjustments (the short-run and structural reduction of the deficit).

The evidence we have presented here suggests three conclusions. First, despite the sizable adjustment of the Mexican budget in 1982–86, further corrections remain, from a long-run point of view but also from a short-run perspective, once the private sector's credit needs are taken into account. Second, the reduction in the elasticity of net revenue from inflation coupled with increased exchange rate and public prices indexation implies that future adverse deficit shocks could generate sharp increases in inflation and create adverse conditions for stabilizing prices by the sole means of a budget deficit reduction. And third, pegging the price-measured real exchange rate at the level it reached in the aftermath of the oil shock could be incompatible with price stabilization. If this is correct and the real exchange rate has to appreciate before price stability becomes feasible, further fiscal adjustment will be necessary to sustain the current account correction of recent years, which is probably related in part to the negative effect of a high real exchange rate on the private sector's investment-savings balance.

Assuming that the fundamental fiscal roots of inflation are in fact eliminated and that no attempt is made at keeping the real exchange rate at a level incompatible with price stability, we could pose the following hypothetical question: Will the fiscal adjustment suffice to stabilize prices, or will it be necessary to complement it with heterodox measures such as a price freeze, the fixing of the exchange rate, and the introduction of a new currency and of debt-rescaling clauses?

When one recalls that one of the components of the heterodox package, namely, the fixing of the exchange rate, was also a crucial ingredient in the price stabilizations of 1954 and 1976, it becomes apparent that the successful old-fashioned strategies applied in Mexico in the past were not so different from the new stabilization plans as they are sometimes construed to have been. Indeed the Mexican experience indicates that, as a result of the unavoidable openness of the economy, a fixed nominal exchange rate can be an effective anchor for nominal magnitudes—if the fundamental fiscal conditions for its maintenance exist.

Other ingredients of the heterodox package are more problematic. The introduction of a new currency and of mandatory debt-rescaling clauses seeks to avoid the emergence of unexpected wealth transfers from debtors to creditors and as such may be indispensable when inflation is reduced to zero from high levels. However, when inflation is lower initially, the welfare gains of avoiding more moderate wealth redistributions should be weighed against the loss of confidence in the financial system and the legal costs that the introduction of debt-rescaling clauses can entail. Apparently the latter complications were not negligible in Argentina, and in the Mexican case they would have to be carefully considered.

Finally, the role of a general price freeze, given the appropriate fundamentals, has been the subject of much inconclusive speculation. How to avoid letting the freeze become a straitjacket on the economy remains an unsolved dilemma. On the other hand, the usefulness of the freeze seems to hinge on intangibles, such as the existence of a nearly unanimous will to try for at least a short reprieve from inflation. This condition is likely to exist in chronic high-inflation environments but is more questionable in economies experiencing their first contacts with triple-digit inflation. Besides, the freeze may serve some purposes in economies sheltered from foreign competition, but, given the current uncertainty concerning the equilibrium values of relative prices, it is clearly an inferior alternative to simply fixing the nominal exchange rate and letting international price arbitrage take care of price stabilization. As Mexico's previous stabilization efforts have shown, output will rebound shortly, not because price freezing prevents an overshooting of inertia-dominated prices—we have not instituted programs of that sort—but because a lower real exchange rate will stimulate a recovery. Finally, whether correct or not, the perception that the Brazilian and Argentine freezes have by and large failed has created adverse conditions for other freezes.

# Appendix A

**Table 8A.1**
Annual rates of inflation for selected countries (1975–85)

| Group | Average annual inflation | Coefficient of variation of annual inflation (%) |
|---|---|---|
| **Group 1** | 6.98 | 43.7 |
| Austria | 5.09 | 26.1 |
| Canada | 8.12 | 34.0 |
| France | 10.06 | 23.7 |
| Japan | 4.65 | 59.8 |
| West Germany | 3.97 | 36.0 |
| Sweden | 9.77 | 24.8 |
| Switzerland | 3.32 | 55.7 |
| United Kingdom | 10.86 | 47.7 |
| **Group II** | 16.92 | 28.1 |
| Spain | 15.19 | 29.7 |
| Greece | 18.53 | 24.9 |
| Italy | 15.10 | 24.8 |
| Portugal | 22.53 | 23.4 |
| South Korea | 12.42 | 70.9 |
| Colombia | 23.45 | 23.5 |
| Venezuela | 11.23 | 46.1 |
| **Group III** | 22.18 | 49.9 |
| Ecuador | 19.99 | 65.5 |
| Philippines | 16.55 | 84.0 |
| Indonesia | 12.73 | 45.4 |
| Iran | 16.15 | 47.6 |
| Nigeria | 18.51 | 62.7 |
| Sudan | 25.75 | 55.0 |
| Turkey | 45.56 | 59.5 |
| **Group IV** | 121.98 | 79.0 |
| Argentina | 306.92 | 78.7 |
| Brazil | 101.83 | 62.3 |
| Chile | 54.83 | 120.4 |
| Peru | 77.52 | 49.7 |
| Uruguay | 51.40 | 32.4 |
| Israel | 139.38 | 84.8 |

## Appendix B

In order to get a rough idea of the long-term real exchange rate deprecia-tion that could be explained by the terms of trade deterioration of 1986, we estimated the following model:

$$RER_t = \beta_0 + \beta_1 TOT_t + \beta_2 PCGDP_t + \beta_3 IICD_t + \beta_4 FISP_t$$
$$+ \beta_5 DUM_t + u,$$

where $RER_t$ is the real exchange rate in year $t$, $TOT_t$ is the terms of trade in year $t$, $PCGDP_t$ is per capita real GDP in year $t$, $IICD_t$ is the internal real public sector deficit in year $t$ (as a proportion of GDP), $FISP_t$ is the flow of external credit to the public sector in year $t$ (as a proportion of GDP), and $DUM_t$ is the dummy variable that takes a value of 1 for years in which the nominal exchange rate undergoes a discrete devaluation and is 0 otherwise.

The model was estimated with annual data for the period 1965–85. The results of the estimation are the following (see note 1):

$\beta_0 = 80.181\ (7.5)$

$\beta_1 = -0.383\ (-2.9)$

$\beta_2 = 0.007\ (4.7)$

$\beta_3 = -1.863\ (-2.2)$

$\beta_4 = -2.736\ (-3.6)$

$\beta_5 = 22.891\ (7.7)$

$\bar{R}^2 = 87.67$

$F(5, 15) = 29.45$

Number of observations $= 21$

$DW = 2.39$

## Notes

1. The regressions for the nominal exchange rate and public prices also included a constant and dummies for periods in which the monthly rate of growth of the cor-responding price was higher than 20% and 15%, respectively. The regression for the rate of growth of nominal wages included dummies for March and December.

2. We are indebted to Rudiger Dornbusch for this point.

3. The OD is the concept to use if one wishes to measure the real change in government debt. It is also the concept to apply if one wants to look at the real excess demand the government is applying to the economy, but it is not the concept that would show the fiscal imbalance that would remain under stable prices. The reason is that there are several other components of government income and expenditures besides interest payments whose real values depend on the rate of inflation. Thus under inflation the whole deficit will become endogenous. Furthermore, because of changes in the inflation tax, the OD may look better when public finances have worsened and bad when they have improved. Thus the OD may not even indicate the true direction of fiscal policy.

4. A complete description of the calculation of these effects is available from the authors on request.

5. There are exceptions, however, in Fernández and Trigueros (1986) and Buiter (1984).

6. We ignore for the time being the transitory nature of most such attempts, which rely almost exclusively on the artificial boost of the real exchange rate

7. The often repeated reference to an Aztec Plan has probably disqualified this label as a name for a heterodox scheme for Mexico. On the other hand, the Chichimecas were a primitive, fierce, bloody, and sometimes suicidal people.

8. Clearly any estimate of the financeable deficit under price stability will be highly sensitive to the assumptions concerning the inflation and income elasticities of money demand, the real credit elasticity of output supply, and the initial conditions for the calculations. We used Lago's (1982) estimates of the demand functions for M1 and quasi-money and his estimates of the aggregate supply function. A complete description of the method used in the computation of the results in table 8.6 is available from the authors on request.

9. The flow of "other banking liabilities" was calculated on the assumption that its ratio to M5 would remain constant at its end-of-1986 value.

10. See, for example, Blanchard (1983).

11. Real exchange rates are measured in terms of the CPI, using a world price index of 133 countries weighted by dollar GDP (*International Financial Statistics*).

12. Statistically all coefficients (except the one for the most inflationary group for a ten-year horizon) are significantly different from 0 with a probability of 99%.

## References

Adams, C., and D. Gros. 1986. *Some Illustrative Examples of the Consequence of Real Exchange Rate Rules for Inflation*. Mimeo DM/86/7. Washington, D.C.: International Monetary Fund.

Blanchard, O. 1983. "Debt and the current account deficit in Brazil," in *Financial Policies and the World Capital Market: The Problem of Latin American Countries*, P. Aspe, R. Dornbusch, and M. Obstfeld, eds. (Chicago, Ill.: University of Chicago Press), 187–197.

Bruno, M. 1986. "Israel's stabilization: The end of the lost decade?" Jerusalem: Hebrew University. Mimeo.

Buiter, W. 1984. *Measurement of the Public Sector Deficit and Its Implications for Policy Evaluation and Design*. IMF Staff Papers. Washington, D.C.: International Monetary Fund.

Fernández, A., and I. Trigueros. 1986. "Public finance and the role of exchange rate policy in the adjustment to exogenous shocks." Mexico City: Instituto Tecnológico Autónomo de México. Mimeo.

Lago, R. 1982. *Financial Programming and Macroeconomic Policy: A Financial Model of the Mexican Economy*. Discussion Paper 1. Mexico City: Finance Ministry, Cuadernos de Planeación Hacendaria. (In Spanish.)

van Wijnbergen, S. 1986. "Exchange rate management and stabilization policies in developing countries," in *Economic Adjustment and Exchange Rates in Developing Countries*, S. Edwards and L. Ahamed, eds. (Chicago, Ill.: University of Chicago Press), 17–38.

# Comment on Part V

*Comment by Herminio Blanco*

Gil and Ramos's purpose is to assess the relevance of heterodox stabilization plans for Mexico. They approach this task by first evaluating if Mexico is in the high and stable inflation equilibrium of the multiple inflation equilibria model of Bruno (1986). This is an important step in their assessment because a heterodox stabilization program with a price freeze could move an economy from a high- to a low-inflation equilibrium. Bruno showed that the existence of a high stable inflation equilibrium depends on the reaction speed of key nominal prices (for example, the exchange rate, wages, and the prices of public goods) to the rate of actual or expected inflation.

The estimation of these reaction functions does not lead Gil and Ramos to a definite conclusion about the existence of such an equilibrium in the Mexican case. However, apart from the potential specification errors of these functions, it is important to point out that the sensitivity of these prices for the relevant future depends on government decisions. These prices could become extremely sensitive to the inflation rate if there is a decision to prevent any further drop in the real exchange rate, real wages, or the real prices of public goods.

Gil and Ramos then proceed to compute the public sector deficit for a zero-inflation rate. This is a crucial part of their elvaluation of the feasibility of a heterodox program for Mexico because recent experiences show that the chances of success of these programs are null if the "fundamentals" are not "right" (for example, in the case of Brazil). Although one could disagree with some of the details of their computations, Gil and Ramos present a meticulous methodology to filter the budget deficit from the effects of inflation. For any potential "user" of heterodox stabilization programs, this is definitely the main contribution that Gil and Ramos make.

Gil and Ramos conclude their evaluation of the feasibility of the zero-inflation equilibrium by computing the maximum amount of resources that the public sector could collect in such an equilibrium for different growth rates of output. Although the methodology is appropriate in principle, one would have to inquire about the robustness of their results to some alternative specifications of the estimated functions. The need to check the robustness of their results becomes particularly important given the pessimistic conclusions about the maximum rate of output growth that could support a noninflationary equilibrium in Mexico.

Although the section on the determinants of the real exchange rate is only peripherally related to Gil and Ramos's objective, this section contains some further evidence on the long-run independence of the real exchange rate from the nominal exchange rate. Additional econometric work is required in this section because Gil and Ramos present in the same section two specifications of the real exchange rate determination that are inconsistent. One specification has a set of explanatory variables plus a dummy variable to account for changes in the nominal exchange rate, and the other specification includes only the changes in the nominal exchange rate.

In the final section Gil and Ramos raise a set of important issues that constitute a fertile field for further research: Is the present Mexican real exchange rate a "non-inflation-accelerating" rate? How relevant for the success of the present administration's stabilization program is the fact that the reduction in public expenditures has been concentrated on capital expenditures while current expenditures have increased? How useful for the evaluation of stabilization programs is it to characterize a reduction in expenditures as permanent or transitory? How important would wealth redistributions be in the case of a substantial unexpected decrease of inflation in Mexico?

I would like to conclude by stating that there is a good deal of uncertainty about the potential success of heterodox stabilization programs. We still ignore some combination of the following elements that could warrant the success of these programs: (1) the "right fundamentals," (2) the external sector balance, (3) the propaganda campaign, (4) the required excess supply in the goods market at the moment that the program is applied, and (5) the design of the price control program. Learning what is the "right" combination of these elements may imply that success in stopping inflation requires several attempts at applying these programs (for example, the case of Israel).

## References

Bruno, M. 1986. "Israel's stabilization: The end of the 'lost decade'?" Jerusalem: The Hebrew University.

# VI

How to Restore Growth

# Three Views on
# Restoring Growth

## Comment by Domingo Cavallo

I want to emphasize two aspects of a growth strategy for highly indebted countries, especially those of Latin America. The first aspect is the need for changes in domestic economic institutions. The second aspect is the need for support from the leading nations of the world economy.

### The Current Situation

The 1980s have witnessed serious worsening of the climate of frustration, disorientation, and lost hopes in Latin America. The standard of living in the region has fallen because of the drastic adjustments that were necessary to maintain an only apparent normality in international financial relations.

The endless and exhausting process of debt renegotiation has consumed the largest part of the time of the various government economic officials. The adjustments have been painful and costly as a result of the uncertainties in the future of the world economy. These uncertainties have obstructed Latin America's progress toward a greater and more effective participation in international trade.

The powerful interests created within the domestic economy, which is excessively protected and oriented toward import substitution, have argued in favor of maintaining the status quo. They point to the growing level of protectionism in the industrial countries not only for agriculture but also for industry. They also allude to the risks of a breakdown in the world economy. Among the leaders of Latin America it is common to hear pessimistic prognostications about the future of the world economy in view of the difficulties Europe is having in reducing unemployment, the United States in reducing its fiscal deficit, and Japan in maintaining its growth with lower trade surpluses.

Therefore the adjustment process has been made to a degree through greater restrictions on imports and a decrease in Latin American purchases abroad. The process has been more oriented toward significant decreases in the level of consumption and investment than toward a reallocation of resources, which would lead to a sustained increase in foreign trade. In terms of growth this strategy implies serious risks for each of the countries as well as for the world and is truly worrisome.

## Latin America Is Prepared for a New Global Strategy

Latin American leaders are aware that the resolution of these problems contains heavy dose of self-criticism and that schemes of thought and rules of the game that have been wrong or at least inefficient must be replaced. Latin America is realizing that in practice their ideological nonalignment, far from leading to a fruitful combination of the best aspects of socialism and capitalism, has led to an almost chaotic economic system that can be characterized as socialism without a plan and capitalism without a market.

It is also recognized that the abuse of the state, its budget, and its regulations as instruments for development has led to neglect of the provision of essential services, such as justice, security, public health, education, and social assistance for the poor and disabled. Similarly, price and wage controls have not been an adequate substitute for explicit income redistribution policies. They have led to a distorted allocation of resources, depriving the countries of the utilization of their comparative advantages.

There is also a growing awareness of the need to increase the level of integration between Latin America and the rest of the world and to avoid the misuse of the intelligence of business executives who have concentrated their efforts in the political arena to obtain monopoly rents deriving from restrictions on domestic and foreign competition. On the contrary, Latin American leaders are now advocating the efficient use of the region's physical and human resources in a demanding and competitive world.

It is also understood that the "sweet money" of one day is the bitter debt of the next, and consequently the transient fiancial capital wandering around the world markets is no longer of interest. Most Latin American countries are interested only in direct investment or long-term loans that can help build the future. They have abandoned the prevalent prejudices of the 1960s and 1970s that favored indirect investment and loans that supposedly allowed them to maintain their capacity for sovereign national economic decision making.

But all of these changes in attitudes and behavior are not in and of themselves sufficient. A question arises as to whether Europe would have experienced its extraordinary postwar economic growth if it had relied only on overhauling the ideas and attitudes of its leaders. The implementation of a reconstruction plan for the economies devastated by the war and the creation of a climate of understanding for the reestablishment of an expanding world economy, with the total backing and commitment of the United States, was undoubtedly the indispensable complement of the renovation of political and economic ideas.

Latin America and other regions of the third world now need the United States, Europe, and Japan to support their transformation and growth within the framework of a thorough integration of their national economies with the world economy. A strategy such as the one that permitted the reconstruction of Europe and Japan in the 1950s and 1960s will not only have benefits now, as it did then, for the countries for which the aid is intended but will also allow for a sustained recovery of growth in the overall world economy.

## The Benefits for the United States, Europe, and Japan

The enormous adjustment effort made by the highly indebted countries has been reflected in a reduction of their current deficits from $53 billion in 1982 to $11 billion in 1986. This has run parallel to the imbalances in the current accounts of the industrial countries. Thus the current account deficit of the United States went from $2 billion to $132 billion during that period, whereas the overall surplus of Europe and Japan grew from $3 billion to $127 billion.

A policy of direct investment and long-term financing would permit an increase in the level of investment and growth in the highly indebted countries, allowing them to become integrated with the world economy. This would greatly facilitate the correction of the imbalances in trade among the industrialized countries. The other two alternative methods for correcting these imbalances, domestic expansion in Japan and Europe and fiscal and monetary restraint in the United States, may have dangerous price effects.

The first alternative, a more rapid European monetary and fiscal expansion in order to stimulate domestic consumption, could decrease the savings rate. Over the long run this would lead to a decrease in the rate of investment and economic growth. The second alternative, a rapid decrease in the US fiscal deficit or, even worse, a strong monetary contraction, could have a recessionary effect on the world economy, which since 1985 has been fluctuating.

In contrast, a strategy to promote an increase in foreign investment in the highly indebted countries offers none of these risks. In addition, to the extent that these countries integrate themselves into the world economy—and most of Latin America is prepared to do so—the efficiency gains resulting from the utilization of underutilized natural and human resources would ensure a rapid increase in the supply of goods. This would decrease the risk of inflation that always threatens when there is a rapid expansion in overall demand.

Many of the industries within the industrial countries that have experienced low levels of demand in recent years are precisely those that were affected by the severe decrease in demand for their products by highly indebted countries in the third world. The reversing of this tendency would help to alleviate the problem of unemployment in Europe, but the most important remedy for this chronic problem could be reached by a strong expansion of employment in services, the sector that has offered many new jobs in the United States.

A rapid expansion of the world economy and trade would increase the demand for services related to transportation, insurance, commercial intermediation, technology, communication, and other areas in which Europe has considerable experience that is highly valued in Latin America. For their part the indebted countries would be especially encouraged to reduce their obstacles to the service industries of the industrial countries; in return, the industrial countries would reduce their agricultural and industrial protectionism and, above all, contribute the capital that is so necessary for growth.

Another great benefit for all involved would be derived from the concentration of the efforts of governments, banks, and businesses to reduce the obstacles to trade and to encourage expansion of investment. This would lead to a more effective utilization of the comparative advantages of each country rather than the maintenance of an appearance of international financial normality while the risks of world economic fragmentation increase. The foreign debt and its servicing cannot be sustained by the highly indebted countries, regardless of the financial alchemy invented to put off the problem if conditions are not created within the world economy for rapid expansion in trade, direct investment, and long-term financing that would permit the debtors to readjust their economies by means of growth.

## Conclusion

The United States, Europe, and Japan could facilitate the coordination of their policies and reduce the imbalances in their current accounts if they decide to help the indebted countries increase their levels of investment and encourage their growth within the framework of integration with the world economy. Most of Latin America is prepared to welcome enthusiastically this type of initiative.

It is necessary that the leaders of the countries responsible for world economic leadership see that we are living with the vision that predominated at the end of World War II and avoid the post–World War I myopia written into the Treaty of Versailles. In favor of this initiative are the accumulated experiences of this century, the real progress that industrial countries have made toward coordinating their national economies, and the much more favorable third world attitudes toward multilateral integration.

### Comment by Manuel Guitián

The presentations and ensuing discussions of the various stabilization programs undertaken recently in Israel, Argentina, Brazil, and Bolivia were both interesting and insightful. They focused mainly on stabilization issues and served as a setting for an assessment of the relative effectiveness of the various policy programs in bringing inflation under control. Comparatively less attention was devoted, however, to questions related to growth. This seemed paradoxical in a conference centered on the so-called heterodox policy approach to stabilization that had been heralded for its ability to control inflation at little or no expense in terms of economic activity and growth.

Growth is the main subject of my remarks. During the discussion of country experiences, it was noted that last year Argentina bounced back from a deep recession, Brazil's economy continued to proceed on a strong real expansion path, and in Israel, although growth slowed down, it remained significant. It could be expected, therefore, that the relationship between economic policies and the growth process would be at the center of the discussions, particularly because a number of statements with an important bearing on the issue of economic growth were made in the context of those country cases. For example, references were made to the prevalence of historically high real rates of interest, the related subject of faltering investment levels, and growing trends in consumption demand as well as of rising real wages. In themselves none of these factors would appear to augur well for growth, but the issue was not pursued to its logical conclusion. This could have been an acknowledgment of the complexities of the growth process and of our incomplete understanding of the transmission mechanism between economic policy and real economic activity. Or it could have been an implicit recognition that last year's growth results might not be sustained. Whatever the reason, it seems clear from the experiences under review that the link between economic policy and growth warrants further investigation.

## Is Restoration of Growth Enough?

Against this background a discussion on how to restore growth cannot be more opportune. In fact, the scope of the subject could be expanded to the broader issue of how to restore and *maintain* growth: The challenge to policy is not restoring growth as an isolated, "flash in the pan" event but rather setting an economy on a sustained growth path.

From this vantage point the country experiences examined in this book give rise to a number of interesting questions that need to be placed in the appropriate time framework. This is critical because the choices confronting the economic policymaker often amount to a selection of intertemporal trade-offs. These involve, for example, growth today versus growth tomorrow, price stability now at the expense of inflation later, and favorable price and output performance in the short run at the cost of balance of payments problems in the future. These are hard choices that require analysis and public emphasis. Frequently the divergence between conclusions derived from politicial and economic analyses can be traced to different perceptions of these intertemporal trade-offs. This should not be surprising because the time horizon of practitioners of politics rarely coincides with that of practitioners of economics.

These considerations bring forth certain issues in the cases under review: Can the growth rates recorded in Argentina and Brazil in 1986–87 be regarded as sustainable? How is the growth rate in Israel to be stepped up? Is Bolivia now poised to move into a positive growth path? Some light on these questions has been provided by Stanley Fischer in a recent paper on economic policy and growth.[1] Fischer referred to thirteen lessons listed by Harberger on growth policy, including three prescriptions of particular relevance for the cases at hand:

Keep budget deficits under adequate control.

Keep inflationary pressures also under reasonable control.

Use price and wage controls sparingly, if at all.

With respect to the first prescription, the discussion of Brazil showed how important budget control is; indeed, it underscored that there was hardly any room for incurring deficits. On the positive side a similar message was provided by the experience of Israel, where fiscal consolidation proved essential for the effectiveness of the adjustment effort. On the second prescription both Argentina and Brazil illustrate amply the difficulty of keeping inflation under control. As for the third prescription, it does not seem to have been heeded, because a trademark of the heterodox approach to stabilization is price and wage controls. But it has to be recalled that the approach envisaged them as strictly transitory devices. Thus the problem was in implementation, not in concept; that is, the problem was ensuring the temporariness of the controls.

In view of this record the fourteenth prescription Fischer added to Harberger's lessons could not be more opportune: Do not allow the exchange rate to become overvalued. Indeed, this most necessary recommendation may well be the only means of safeguarding a measure of efficiency whenever the other prescriptions are not observed.

## Which Are the Fundamentals?

Basically two factors are critical to attain and maintain a sound growth rate in an economy: the *amount* of resources available and the *efficiency* of their use.[2] Arguments stressing the importance of the first factor are the most frequent and focus essentially on the financing aspect of the growth process. Although important, these arguments should not be exaggerated, as they amount to stating that "more is needed" for an economy to grow, a peculiar line of economic reasoning, particularly in situations of severe and rigid resource limitations. The constraint imposed by lack of resources will not vanish by arguing that the arrival of plenty is the best means to overcome scarcity.

Furthermore, the difficulties recently confronted by many debtor countries have made it evident that resource availability alone is not sufficient to ensure sustained growth. On the contrary, the foreign resources that in the form of debt flows moved across national borders—which could have served to promote growth—are often described now as a constraint to current and prospective growth. Inevitably, therefore, attention must be focused on the other engine of growth: efficiency in resource use, which is all the more imperative the more limited resources are.

## Which Are the Policy Implications?

Efficiency requirements tend to narrow the range of policy mixes available to policymakers. For example, the process of stabilization in an economy often requires a reduction in the budget deficit. Such a reduction can be effected in a variety of ways, not all of which are compatible with efficiency and growth. Efficiency and growth call for the reduction to be achieved in a specific fashion, for example, by lowering consumption outlays rather than productive public investment spending. In general, stability-*cum*-growth will require durable policy measures that raise efficiency in the economy. Yet the discussion of country experiences makes clear that fiscal adjustment, to the extent that it has been undertaken, has tended to rely on expedients of a nonrecurring character and did not always conform to efficiency requirements. Similar observations apply to actions taken in other policy areas.

Against this background a question that can be raised is whether policy approaches that overlook efficiency considerations can lead to sound and sustained growth rates. Efficiency in resource use is not an esoteric notion but one that has wide acceptance, as in the abstract hardly anybody disagrees with it. In practice, however, rare are the instances when policy actions give reality to the consensus. And let us be clear: efficiency is just as necessary when capital is flowing internationally as when it is not. This much has been made evident by the experience of the last decade.

Growth mainly spurred by consumption trends that rely unduly on foreign savings can hardly be expected to continue indefinitely. Indeed, such growth will have to be reduced in the process of adjustment, and the reduction will constitute part of the solution, not, as it is often contended, a manifestation of the problem. Similar considerations apply to situations of demand-pull growth based on unproductive investment outlays.

In sum, the *amount* of available resources matters for growth, but it cannot substitute for *efficiency* in their use, without which growth, even if attained, is unlikely to be sustained.

## What Can Policy Do?

The task of restoring and sustaining growth in an economy is indeed complex. One thing is clear, though: There is much that economic policy can do to impair and stunt growth. The degree of symmetry in this assertion is limited, and less can be said about what economic policy alone can do to ensure growth.

From the policymaking standpoint a clear course of action consists in avoiding policy measures likely to hamper growth. This is in line with what Fischer earlier called the "distortion removal" approach to policy management. This deceptively modest suggestion often turns out to be more ambitious than it appears: Policy actions required to remove distortions to growth are difficult to adopt and call for resolve and determination on the part of the policymaker. Typically such actions have generally unpopular sectoral and distributional impacts than can be felt rapidly. Their benefits, in contrast, frequently lie too far into the future or are diffused so that those likely to reap them (the economy as a whole) do not rise in their defense. The merits of allowing for an appropriate waiting period noted earlier by Rudiger Dornbusch cannot be overstressed in this context: Economic policies must be given time to yield results.

**Are There Any Lessons?**

At a minimum a lesson to be drawn is that undue claims regarding what can be achieved by policy action alone are best avoided. Yet a measure of balance between "realistic" and "ambitious" policy objectives or targets is needed. Some time ago I argued that a degree of realism in setting policy objectives was necessary to avert a lack of credibility.[3] I contended at the same time that an element of ambitiousness was also required lest progress in economic performance go unnoticed. I wonder now whether it would not have been better to cast the argument in terms of policy actions and policy objectives. If so, the appropriate combination would involve relatively *ambitious policy actions* (to ensure that results are attained) and relatively *realistic policy objectives* (to contain undue expectations).

In sum, there is much yet to be learned about the link between economic policy and growth. The experiences of the countries discussed can provide useful insights not only on growth itself but also on the sustainability of the stabilization effort.

**Notes**

The views expressed here are the author's and not necessarily those of the International Monetary Fund.

1. Stanley Fischer, "Economic growth and economic policy," in *Growth-Oriented Adjustment Programs*, V. Corbo, M. Goldstein, and M. Khan, eds. (Washington, D.C.: International Monetary Fund and World Bank, 1987), 151–178. See also Arnold C. Harberger, *World Economic Growth* (San Francisco: Institute for Contemporary Studies, 1984).

2. See Manuel Guitián, "Adjustment and growth: Their fundamental complementarity," in *Growth-Oriented Adjustment Programs*, V. Corbo, M. Goldstein, and M. Khan, eds. (Washington, D.C.: International Monetary Fund and World Bank, 1987), 63–94. A summary of this paper has been published recently under the title "The fund's role in adjustment" [*Finance and Development* (June 1987), 24(2):3–6].

3. See Manuel Guitián, *Fund Conditionality: Evolution of Principles and Practices*, IMF Pamphlet Series 38 (Washington, D.C.: Internatioal Monetary Fund, 1981).

## Comment by Rosemary Thorp

I first consider the different potential for resuming growth among the different case studies considered in this volume. I then discuss to what degree heterodox policies are compatible with the measures desirable for long-run growth. The comparative discussion incorporates Peru because Peru also implemented a heterodox shock in August 1985.

## Growth Potential

I suggest two vectors as appropriate to begin a differentiation of the case studies. The first vector considers the degree to which there were real supply-side costs in the preceding inflation—and therefore the degree to which growth can be expected from the simple act of stabilization of prices alone. The second vector considers the degree of "structural crisis" underlying short-run macroeconomic problems and thus the degree to which resuming growth must incorporate not simply stimulus to investment but also structural change.

   Table 1 provides an intuitive ranking of the studies, running from the most to the least favorably placed. Real supply-side costs are clearly most extreme when hyperinflation is reached. Bolivia far outshines the others in this one respect. The costs can be divided into static (misallocations resulting from inflation itself) and dynamic (a reduced rate of investment). The first category reaches absurd heights when inflation reaches 20,000%, vividly illustrated by the Bolivian bus example: A seat had to be removed to allow the driver space to handle his cash! Static costs are a function of the degree of relative price distortion, which diverts activity to speculative

**Table 1**
Ranking of countries

| Extent of real supply-side costs in preceding inflation | | Degree of underlying structural crisis | |
|---|---|---|---|
| High | Bolivia | Low | Israel |
| | Argentina | | Brazil |
| | Peru | | Mexico |
| | Brazil | | Argentina |
| | Israel | | Peru |
| Low | Mexico | High | Bolivia |

lines and generates inefficiencies within productive use. Indexation reduces static costs, which are partly why the more highly indexed economies (Brazil and Israel) have low rankings. But even with indexation (in part because of it?) the banking system overexpands, thus placing even Israel significantly above the relatively low inflation case of Mexico.

The second category of supply-side costs concerns the reduction in investment. This is complex to analyze, and each case has its own characteristics. In part the investment reduction is a function of the static costs because inflation deters more the more it leads to distortions. The core element is uncertainty, leading easily to capital flight at the cost of domestic investment (the Argentine case). Often the causal connection is the *fear* of stagnation caused by the recessive measures seen as appropriate to deal with inflation. For years Brazilian investors were remarkably undeterred by high rates of inflation because they believed both in the government's commitment to growth and in its feasibility. The level at which this confidence breaks down appears to vary with time and with country-specific circumstances.

The postshock growth potential given by these real supply-side costs varies with their nature. The benefits from ending "Alice in Hyperland" situations come fast and easy and explain why after 1956 Bolivian output actually increased and why today in Bolivia aggregate output levels have fallen rather little. The benefits from being able to reduce an inflated banking sector are harder to reap, requiring tough political bargaining and compensation.

Turning to the second column of table 1, to develop the story behind the ranking of course requires several books and cannot be done here. Again, intuitively my argument is that for the Latin American economies there are at least three important strands in the structural change required if growth is to proceed in the 1990s. First is a more adequate form of integration into the international economy, providing more autonomy as well as, on average, less constraint. This pinpoints the impossibility of separating "growth resumption" from (1) resolving debt, (2) tackling protectionism in developed countries, (3) finding new lines of nontraditional exports, (4) rationalizing and further promoting import substitution, and (5) possibly even taking seriously economic integration.

Second is the problem of the quality of the state. Perhaps even more fundamental than and certainly lying behind the issue of macroeconomic disequilibrium caused by budget deficits is the whole issue of poor quality of management, particularly of public investments. The issue affects every other concern and certainly affects the first concern because, given the importance of state enterprises in such countries as Bolivia and Peru, rationalizing and promoting import substitution means largely changing behavior and management patterns in the state sector.

Third is the issue of distribution. If democracy is to become more real, distribution is not only essential to resolve on welfare grounds but also crucial on political grounds. It relates to growth because in several of the case studies, Argentina in particular, distributive tensions are at the heart of inflation; and if stability is needed for growth, some resolution must be found.

Impressionistically, then, these elements explain my ranking. Bolivia moves firmly to the bottom as severely disadvantaged; Brazil and Israel move firmly to the top; Argentina, Peru, and Mexico all suffer in different ways related to their specific histories and intense problems in relation to both the external sector and the quality of the state. The severity of the distribution problem in Argentina puts it closer to Peru than one might otherwise expect, given Argentina's size and greater level of development.

**Heterodoxy and Growth**

Having set out in this impressionistic fashion the situation in respect of growth potential, what of heterodoxy and the transition? The overwhelmingly striking conclusion from reviewing the cases and listening to the debate is that heterodox policies in practice unfortunately tend to lead to measures that conflict *directly* not just with resuming growth but with just about every likely goal of structural change. At the "simple" end of the scale comes Israel, where the issue can reasonably be simplified into restimulating investment: As Bruno has emphasized, high taxation and high interest rates have been integral to the heterodox shock and now oppose growth. At the more complex end of the scale the conflicts are far worse. The programs have typically involved a freeze on public sector prices and thus falling real prices, a tendency to overvalued exchange rates, a freeze on food prices, and thus again falling real prices. In the Peruvian case real interest rates have been negative, in the others positive and high.

If we return now to the elements of structural crisis, the conflicts are clear. The exchange rate is too obvious to need further comment, but public sector prices are equally problematic. A key element of health for the medium term is a rationalization of state enterprise investments and purchasing policies to increase the local component and reduce imports, in part by more suitable technology and size of projects. This requires the creation of motivated, committed, and imaginative teams of people to develop and execute bright ideas: This is unthinkable in a context of acute and growing budget crisis caused by falling real prices.[1] Each plan has involved a slackening, if not a fall, in public investment, again counterproductive.

A further level of conflict also concerns me—the level of policymaking. Heterodoxy is by nature complex and interventionist. One of the chief costs of the debt crisis in Latin America has been the imposed preoccupation with the short term: *cortoplacismo* in the expressive Spanish term. This is liable to persist in the new and innovative phase if we do not fight it consciously.

Such conflicts of course do not imply that heterodox policies should not be followed. In my view orthodoxy is no solution whatsoever, and we have to walk this path. But it is important to *highlight* the extent of these contradictions: *Concientización* is itself of value.

## Note

1. Juan-Antonio Morales made the relevant point that orthodoxy is every bit as bad in relation to this goal because public enterprises are somehow branded as the culprit of the preceding process, and, even though revenues may be increased, still increased spending and revitalization are unthinkable.

# Contributors

Herminio Blanco
Comite de Asesores Economicos
Mexico City, Mexico

Michael Bruno
Bank of Israel
Jerusalem, Israel

Alfredo Canavese
University of Buenos Aires
Buenos Aires, Argentina

Eliana A. Cardoso
Fletcher School of Law and
  Diplomacy
Tufts University
Medford, Massachusetts

Domingo Cavallo
Fundacion Mediterranea
Cordoba, Argentina

Alex Cukierman
Department of Economics
Tel Aviv University
Tel Aviv, Israel

Juan Carlos de Pablo
Catholic University of Argentina
Buenos Aires, Argentina

Francisco Gil Diaz
Banco de Mexico
Mexico City, Mexico

Guido Di Tella
Instituto Torcuato Di Tella
Buenos Aires, Argentina

Rudiger Dornbusch
Department of Economics
Massachusetts Institute of
  Technology
Cambridge, Massachusetts

Jose Maria Fanelli
Banco Central de Argentina
Buenos Aires, Argentina

Stanley Fischer
Department of Economics
Massachusetts Institute of
  Technology
Cambridge, Massachusetts

Peter Garber
Department of Economics
Brown University
Providence, Rhode Island

Manuel Guitián
International Monetary Fund
Washington, D.C.

Elhanan Helpman
Research Department
International Monetary Fund
Washington, D.C.

Daniel Heymann
CEPAL
Buenos Aires, Argentina

Nissan Liviatan
Graduate School of Business
University of Chicago
Chicago, Illinois

Roberto Macedo
USP-Economia
São Paulo, Brazil

Jose Luis Machinea
Banco Central de Argentina
Buenos Aires, Argentina

Gail E. Makinen
Congressional Research Service
Library of Congress
Washington, D.C.

Eduardo M. Modiano
Departmento de Economica
Catholic University
Rio de Janiero, Brazil

Juan-Antonio Morales
Universidad Catolica Boliviana
La Paz, Bolivia

Guillermo Ortiz
International Monetary Fund
Washington, D.C.

Sylvia Piterman
Bank of Israel
Jerusalem, Israel

Joseph Ramos
UN ECLA
Santiago, Chile

Carlos Alfredo Rodriguez
CEMA
Buenos Aires, Argentina

Mario Henrique Simonsen
Fundacao Getulio Vargas
Rio de Janeiro, Brazil

Raul Ramos Tercera
Banco de Mexico
Mexico City, Mexico

Rosemary Thorp
St. Anthony's College
Oxford, England

Miguel Urrutia
Economic and Social Development
  Department
Inter-American Development Bank
Washington, D.C.

# Index

Adjusted operational deficit (AOD) in Mexico, 372
Agency for International Development (AID), 288
Aggregate demand and supply curves, for Israel, 20–21
Agriculture
  in Argentina, effect of on inflation, 129, 131
  in Brazil, supply shock in, 220–221
  in Israel, effects of stabilization program on, 35–36
Alfonsin (President), and Austral Plan, 197
"Alfonsin effect," 229
Argentina
  avoidance of hyperinflation in (see Austral Plan for avoidance of hyperinflation in Argentina, 1985–1987)
  balance of payments crisis in, 209–210
Aridor (Treasury Minister), policies of, 49
Asset(s), balance of shekel-dominated, rise of, 24
Austral Plan for avoidance of hyperinflation in Argentina, 1985–1987, 111–148, 153–187
  balance of payments disequilibrium, 125
  behavior of economy, 120–123
  changes in monetary policy, 131, 134
  contractual duration and uncertainty, 122
  credibility tests of, 128–129
  deindexation of economy and, 159–162
  dollarization of economy, 121
  domestic transfer, 120–121
  economy before plan, 111–120
  external economy under, 145–146
  first economic program, 118–120
  first stage of, 159–162
  four stages of, 157
  fourth stage of, 166–168
  freeze effects on inflation, 129, 131
  heterodox shock, 125–126
  imbalances under, flexibility and management of, 141–146
  implementation of, 123–128
  initial conditions for, 155–157
  introduction of, 127–128, 156
  investment decline, 122–123
  main points of, 156
  monetary crunch and, 164–166
  monetary reform, 127–128
  1981–1983 adjustment process, 112–113, 118
  price expectations, 121–122
  price freeze under, 144–145
  quasi-fiscal deficit and, 206, 208–209
  real interest rates, 134
  reindexation and, 162–164
  relative price adjustments, 123–125
  second stage of, 162–164
  second wave of measures of, 142, 144
  shock policy and, 128–141
  structural pressures in, 205–206
  tax measures under, 204
  third stage of, 164–166
  wage and price freeze and, 166–168
  wage and price freeze, 126–127

BAGON, 203
Balance-of-payments
  disequilibrium of in implementation of Austral Plan, 125 and heterodox stabilization in Israel, 59–60, 103–104
Balance-of-payments in Argentina, cause of acceleration in inflation, 209–210

Balance-of-payments in Israel
 crises in, 4–11
 deterioration in, 103–104
 effect of stabilization program on, 59
Balance of trade
 in Argentina, 113, 118
 in Brazil under Cruzado II, 237
Bank credit, total, in Israel, decrease in,
  53–54
Bank of Israel
 and bank credit restrictions, 7, 26
 and lowering of interest rate(s), 26–27
 and prime rate, 1986, 27
 and real interest rates, 26–27
 reserve requirements of, 26
 role of in stabilization program, 26–28
Bank share arrangement in Israel, 5
Banking system in Israel, effects of stabilization program on, 36
BARRA, 203
Barro-Gordon dynamic inconsistency
  problem, 52
Bolivia
 acceleration of inflation, 309–312
 achievements of stabilization plan, 322–
   323, 325–329
 aftermath of inflation in, 350–351
 background on inflation in, 307–309
 costs of stabilization plan, 329–332
 exchange rate unification, 320
 features of inflation in, 318–322
 fiscal deficit, closing of, 355–356
 fiscal package, 318–320
 future of inflation in, 333–336
 growth of economy, 333–335
 hyperinflation, causes of, 347–349
 industrial base of, 307–308
 inflationary anchors, 321–322
 liberalization of markets, 320–321
 open hyperinflation, 309–318
 orthodox vs. heterodox programs for,
   353–354
 political prospects, 335–336
 public finances, collapse of, 349–350
 stabilization consolidation, 333
 stabilization of inflation, 317–318
 transition to hyperinflation, 314, 317
Boliviano, introduction of, 318
BONIN, 203
BONOR, 203
Branco, Castello, 278

Brazilian case study of incomes policies
  and price stabilization, 259–284
Brazilian New Republic, 220
 first phase of economic policy of, 220–
   221
 increase in inflation under during 1985,
   222
 second phase of economic policy of,
   221–223
Brazilian stabilization program, and Cruzado Plan, 215–255. See also Cruzado Plan
Bresser Plan, 284
Budget deficit, decrease in, 8–9
Budget deficit in Brazil, 288–289
 effect of on inflation, 289–290
Budget deficit in Israel
 increased in 1984, 49
 reduction of, 53
Bulhões-Campos reforms, 278–279
Bulhões-Campos wage formula, 277
Business sector in Israel, effects of high
  inflation on, 35

Capital market, and inflation stabilization in
  Israel, 7
Central Bank of Argentina
 decline in losses of, 127
 growth of monetary base and, 203
 liabilities as cause of quasi-fiscal deficit,
   206, 208–209
 performance of during first stage of Austral Plan, 160
Certainty in Argentina during first stage
  of Austral Plan, 161
Chichimeca Plan
 government budget effort and, 377–378,
   380
 and price stabilization in Mexico, 377–380
Cocaine trade in Bolivia, 308
Communist Party in Bolivia, 310
Confederation of Bolivian Workers, 309
 strikes by, 317
Conflict inflation model of Brazilian economy, and Cruzado Plan, 216–220
Construction industry in Israel, effects of
  stabilization program on, 35
Consumer price index in Brazil (IPCA)
 deindexation and use of, 221–222
 modification of under Cruzado Plan, 229
 purge of automobile and gasoline price
  increases from, 236–237, 238

Consumption in Israel
  effect of on imports, 18
  effect of stabilization program on, 60
  expansion of, 17–18
  and inflation stabilization, 17–18, 20–23
Contract(s)
  in Bolivia, "dedollarization" of, 311
  future, in Brazil, conversion of under
    Cruzado Plan, 236
Controlled goods, relative prices of in Israel,
    effect of stabilization program on, 65
"Controlled rates of inflation" in Argentina,
    163
Conversion problem in Argentina, 168–170
Corporacion Minera de Bolivia
    (COMIBOL), 319
Cost-of-living adjustment under Cruzado
    Plan, 225
Cournot, solution of for oligopoly problem,
    262
Credit, consumer, in Israel, increase in, 36–
    37
Cruzadinho, 236
Cruzado, establishment of, 223
Cruzado Plan, 281–284. See also Cruzado II
  Brazilian stabilization program, 215–255
  conflict inertial model of Brazilian econ-
    omy and, 216–220
  cost-of-living adjustments under, 225
  disinflation under, March–June 1986,
    233–236
  distortion in relative price(s), 234
  exchange rate, 230
  failure of, 294–298
  failure of heterodox portion of, 295
  failure of orthodox portion of, 295
  failure of social pact, 239
  fiscal policies under, 232–233
  future of, 241–244
  future contract conversions under, 231
  and incomes policies, 281–284, 300–
    301
  increase in consumption, 234
  increase in money supply, 235
  increase in public deficit, 235–236
  inertial model of Brazilian economy and,
    216–220
  inflation stabilization and, 287–288
  key measures of, 281
  lifting of price controls, 239
  monetary policies under, 232

New, 244
  policies of, 223–233
  preconditions for, 220–223
  price conversions, 228–230
  price increases under, 238
  and pricing policies, 301–302
  reinstitution of restricted consumer price
    index (INPC), 238
  rent conversions under, 230–231
  results of, 233–241
  return of indexation, 239
  seigniorage model for open economy and,
    290
  shortage under, 234–235
  sliding scale for wages, 225–226
  slowdown in economic activity, 240
  "technical moratorium" on foreign debt,
    240
  wage conversion under, 223–224
  weaknesses in, 281–283
Cruzado Plan II, July–October 1986, 236–
    238. See also Cruzado Plan
  balance of trade under, 237
  failure of, 282–284
  increase in industrial output under, 237
Currency in Israel
  devaluation of, 15
  real appreciation of, 12

Decree Law 2283 for wage conversion in
    Brazil, 224
Defense expenditure, cut in, in Israel, effect
    of on exports, 18
Deficit in fiscal accounts in Argentina,
    reduction of, 127
Deficit reduction in Israel, 6–7
Deindexation (desagio) in Argentina, 156
Deindexation in Brazil, and use of consumer
    price index (IPCA), 221–222
DENOR, 203
Devaluation, increase in rate of in Israel,
    49
Devaluation of shekel, 7
Disinflation and inflation stabilization in
    Israel, 33–37
  business sector and, 35–36
  consumer credit and, 36–37
  and government revenue and expenditure,
    33–35
Disinflation in Brazil, March–June 1986,
    233–236

"Dollarization" of economy in Argentina, 121
Domestic transfer in Argentina, 120–121

Easy monetary policy and reindexation of key prices in Argentina, 163
Economic growth
  benefits to industrial countries, 397–398
  in Bolivia, reactivation of, 333–335
  current situation, 395–396
  fundamentals of, 400–402
  heterodoxy and, 406–407
  in Latin America, 396–397
  policies for, 402–403
  potential for, 404–406
  restoration of, 395–407
  weakness of banking sector and, 334–335
Economy in Argentina
  adjustment process in, 1981–1983, 112–113, 118
  evolution of under Austral Plan, 128–129, 131, 134, 136, 138, 141–142, 144–146
  external shocks to, 145
  state of, 1975–1985, 111–112
  structural issues of, 141
Economy of Israel, institutional structures of importance for use of heterodox program, 81
Eder, George Jackson, stabilization plan for Bolivia, 348–349
Exchange rate(s)
  under Cruzado Plan, 230
  pegging of to five-currency basket, 11
  and synchronization of nominal anchors, 28–33
Exchange rate(s) in Argentina, 113
  pegging of, 126
Exchange rate(s) in Bolivia, devaluation of, 311
Exchange rate(s) in Israel
  freezing of, 7
  and inflation stabilization, 11
  pegging of, 53, 54
  real, effect of stabilization program on, 59–60
  use of as nominal anchor, 82–84
Exchange rate policy in Israel
  and heterodox stabilization, 104–105
  inflation stabilization and, 28–33
  and synchronization of nominal centers, 28–33

Expectations, inflationary, orthodox vs. heterodox programs and, 353–354

Fiscal consolidation, public debt and, 287, 288
Fiscal deficit in Argentina
  decline in, 134
  drop in during first stage of Austral Plan, 159
  reduction of, 156
  regression analysis of, 205–206
Fiscal deficit in Bolivia, closing of, 355–356
Fiscal policy under Cruzado Plan, 232–233
Fischer-Taylor inertia, 259
Foreign aid, importance of to Bolivia, 349
Foreign debt
  in Argentina, impact of on stabilization, 166
  in Israel, increase in, 49

Game theory of inertial inflation, 260–261
Game theory of inflation
  noncooperative game, 262–265
  price-setting, 267–271
  rational expectations and, 265–267
General Price Index in Brazil (IGP-DI), increase in, 220–221
Goulart, populist engagements of, 278
Government revenue and expenditure in Israel
  effects of stabilization program on, 34–35
  effects of high inflation on, 33–34
Gradualism, failure of in Brazilian economy, 222
Gross domestic investment in Israel, effect of stabilization program on, 63

Heterodox gradualism, 243
  partial deindexation, 243
Heterodox measures in Argentina, 157
Heterodox stabilization, key elements of program, 299–300
"Historical price vector," use of in price controls, 199–202
Hyperinflation in Argentina, 1985–1987, Austral Plan for avoidance of, 111–148, 153–187. See also Austral Plan for avoidance of hyperinflation in Argentina, 1985–1987
Hyperinflation in Bolivia, 314, 317
  cause of, 347–349

IMF
  Argentina's negotiations with, 119–120
  standby agreement between Argentina
    and, 125
Import(s), surplus in, and inflation stabilization in Israel, 21–23
Incomes Policies
  aggregate demand discipline in, 273–274
  attempt to set in Argentina, 119
  Brazilian case study of, 259–284
  Bulhões-Campos reforms, 278–279
  Cruzado Plan and, 281–284, 300–301
  escalation, 280–281
  indexation, 274–278
  inflationary inertia, 274–278
  Nash equilibria, 262–267
  price-setting game, 267–271
  rationale for, 271–274
  role of, 271–274
  staggered wage setting, 274–278
  usefulness of in Brazil, 300–301
  widespread indexation, 279–280
Indexation, 274–278
  in Argentina, effect of during second phase
    of Austral Plan, 164
  in Brazil, and "indexed currency" proposal,
    221
  widespread, 279–280
Indexed currency (Larida) proposal, 215
  indexation in Brazil and, 221
Inertial model of Brazilian economy, and
  Cruzado Plan, 216–220
Inflation
  double-wage setting and inertial, 274,
    276–278
  escalation of in Brazil, 280–281
  features of inertial, 121–122
  game theory of inertial, 260–261
  increase in, in Israel, 1983–1984, 5
  inertial, 260–261, 274–278
  and real exchange rate corrected deficit
    (IRECD), 375
  sources of inertial, 259
  staggered wage setting and inertial, 274,
    276–278
  strategic interdependence and inertial, 274,
    276–278
  threshold of, 205
Inflation in Argentina history of, 153–154
Inflation in Bolivia
  acceleration of, 309–312

background of, 308–309
Inflation in Israel
  as wartime economy, 95–98
  end to high rate of, 48–88
  excess supplies and, 101–102
  exchange rate policies for, 100–101
  expectations in, 55, 59
  inconsistencies in reactions to, 99–101
  main features of July 1985 stabilization
    program for, 53–55
  preconditions for July 1985 stabilization
    program for, 49–53
  shock treatment and, 101–102
Inflation rate(s) in Argentina
  drop in, 129
  inertial mechanisms affecting, 191
  rise of, 142, 144
Inflation rate(s) in Israel
  current, 3
  drop in, 55, 8
  1983–1984, 49
  1979–1983, 49
  public opinion of, 49
  Treasury Minister Aridor's policies and, 49
Inflation variance in Israel, 63
INPC (restricted consumer price index), 222
Interest rate(s) in Argentina
  during first stage of Austral Plan, 160–161
  increase in, 118
  real, 134
Interest rate(s) in Israel
  fiscal policy and, 8–11
  and inflation stabilization, 9–11
  real, effect of stabilization program on, 61,
    63
Investment in Argentina, decline of, 122–
  123
Investment in Israel, effect of stabilization
  program on, 60
Israel
  background of stabilization program in,
    4–11
  balance-of-payment crises, 4–11
  balance of payments in heterodox stabili-
    zation, 59–60, 103–104
  bank share arrangement in, 5
  budget in, 6–7
  capital market in, 7
  consumption and investment in heterodox
    stabilization, 60
  credibility of program for, 55–59

Israel (cont.)
current financial problems in, 3—4
devaluation in, 7
disinflation in, 33—37
excess supplies and inflation in, 101—102
exchange rate(s) in, 11, 28—33
exchange rate in heterodox stabilization, 74—78, 82—84, 100—101, 104—105
government revenue and expenditure in, 33—35
government-union interaction in, 105—107
gross domestic investment and, 63
heterodox stabilization and package deals, 81—82
inconsistencies in reactions to inflation in, 99—101
inflation in as wartime economy, 95—98
inflation variance in heterodox stabilization, 63
interest rate(s) in, 9—11
monetary control in, 24—28
monetary velocity in heterodox stabilization, 60—61
multiple nominal anchors, 7
net debt in heterodox stabilization, 59—60
net domestic credit in, 27
net seigniorage in heterodox stabilization, 60—61
preconditions for heterodox stabilization, 49—53
price control(s) in, 11
private consumption in, 17—18, 20—23
private savings squeeze in, 12—24
qualification of model for heterodox stabilization, 78—81
rate of unemployment and heterodox stabilization, 65
real decrease in bank credit and heterodox stabilization, 53—54
real exchange rate and heterodox stabilization, 59—60, 61—63
real wage overshooting in, 12—24
relative price of controlled goods and heterodox stabilization, 65
relative price variability and heterodox stabilization, 65
renewed growth in, 37—41
results of heterodox stabilization, 102—105
role of external factors in heterodox stabilization, 82

shock treatment and inflation in, 101—102
stabilization in, two-year review of, 3—41
surplus in import(s) in, 21—23
synchronization of nominal anchors, 28—33
tax revenues and heterodox stabilization, 63
unemployment in heterodox stabilization, 68—71
wage increase(s) in, causes for, 12, 15—17
wage policy in, 8

Key prices
exchange rate in Mexico, 370
nominal wage inflation, 371
rate of growth of public prices
reindexation of in Argentina, easy monetary policy and, 163
responsiveness of to inflation, 369—371
Kibbutzim, effects of stabilization program on, 35
Kubitschek expansionary policies in Brazil, 278

Larida (indexed currency) proposal, 215
Larida Plan, 243
Letras do Banco Central (LBC), link of financial contracts to returns on, 238
Lucas and Sargent's principle of strategic interdependence, 266

Maximin strategies
described, 263
Nash equilibria vs., 262—265
in price-setting game, 270—271
Memorandum of Strategic Understanding, 96
Mexico, price stabilization in, 361—368
Chichimeca Plan and, 377—380
history of, 362—369
key prices, responsiveness of, 369—371
pegging to real exchange rate, 380—384
public finance, real exchange rate and, 371—377
Monetary control and inflation stabilization in Israel, 24—28
net domestic credit and, 27
Monetary crunch in Argentina, 164—166
Monetary expansion in Argentina, cause of during first stage of Austral Plan, 160
Monetary policy, use of net domestic credit in, 27—28

Monetary policy under Cruzado Plan, 232
Monetary velocity in Israel, effect of stabilization program on, 60
Money, increased demand for in Argentina, 131, 134
Money aggregates in Israel, real expansion of, 25–26
Money supply in Argentina, increase in, 163–164
Moshavim, effects of stabilization program on, 35–36
Multiple inflation equilibria:
  defined, 361
  heterodox stabilization plans and, 361
Multiple nominal anchors, and inflation stabilization in Israel, 7

Nash equilibrium, defined, 262
Nash strategy
  in price-setting game, 270
  and rational expectations, 265–267
  vs. maximin strategies, 262–265
National Revolutionary Movement (MNR), 347–348
New Cruzado Plan, 244
New Economic Policy in Bolivia, 318
  achievements of, 322–323, 325–329
  cost of, 329–332
  effect of collapse of tin market on, 326
  effect of increase in monetary base on, 326
  exchange rate as anchor under, 321–322
  exchange rate under, 320
  expenditures under, 319
  financial liberalization under, 321
  fiscal package of, 318–320
  foreign debt under, 319–320
  impact of supertight liquidity on, 325
  importance of revenues under, 325–326
  market liberalization under, 320–321
  petroleum prices under, 318–319
Nominal anchors
  effect of crawling peg on, 32
  effect of dollar peg on, 30, 32
  effect of on prices in Israel, 30
  exchange rate and synchronization of, 28–33
  in stabilization program in Israel, 28
Nominal variables, freezing of in Israel, 7
  Histadrut (General Federation of Labor) and nominal wage agreement, 7

Obrigações Reajustaveis do Tesouro Nacional (ORTN), 215
Oligopolistic industrial structure and orthodox stabilization program, 167–168
  effect of on economy, 168
Olivera-Tanzi effect, 52, 118, 204
  in Bolivia, 312
  elimination of in Argentina, 156
  in Mexico, 372
Open economy with financial market, seigniorage models for, 290–291, 293
Operational deficit (OD) in Mexico, 371
Orthodox stabilization in Israel, monetary policy game describing, 74–76
ORTN (Obrigações Reajustaveis do Tesouro Nacional), 221
Oscillation of relative prices, defined, 168

Patam, abolishment of, 61
Paz Estenssoro, Victor, 317
Peso, devaluation of, 124
Plano de Metas, 236
Political instability in Bolivia, effect of on stabilization, 317
Price(s) in Argentina
  during second phase of Austral Plan, 164
  guidelines for during third stage of Austral Plan, 164–165
Price control(s)
  in Argentina, 142
  gradual removal of, 272
  and inflation stabilization in Israel, 11
  problems of, 192–193
Price control system in Israel, relaxation of, 11
Price conversion under Cruzado Plan, 228–230
Price freeze in Argentina, 126, 156–157
  discontinuation of, 163
  1987, 166–168
  problems with, 159
Price freeze in Brazil, 220
  and price conversion, 228–230
Price freeze in Israel, 53, 54
Price level in Israel, total direct fixing of, 66–67
Price shock in Israel, 1983, 5
Price stabilization, real exchange rate and pegging of, 380–382, 384
Price stabilization in Brazil case study of, 259–284

Price stabilization in Mexico, 361–368
Chichimeca Plan and, 377–380
history of, 362–369
key prices, responsiveness of, 369–371
oil shock, effect on, 367, 369
pegging to real exchange rate, 380–384
public finance, real exchange rate and, 371–377
Pricing policies, Cruzado Plan and, 301–302
Private savings squeeze, and inflation stabilization in Israel, 12–24
Production in Argentina, effect of shock on, 136, 138

Quasi-fiscal deficit(s)
in Argentina, Central Bank liabilities as cause of, 206, 208–209
in Bolivia, 312

Rational expectations, Nash strategy and, 265–267
Real exchange rate
pegging to, and price stabilization in Mexico, 380–384
role of in Mexican public finance, 371–372, 375, 377
Real wages in Argentina
effects of, 126
during first stage of Austral Plan, 161
Real wages in Israel, rise of, 12–17
cause of, 12, 15
employment sectors affected, 16–17
Relative price(s) in Argentina, adjustment of, 123–125
Relative price variability in Israel, effect of stabilization program on, 64–65
Rent(s) in Brazil
commercial, 230–231
conversion of under Cruzado Plan, 230–231
residential, 230
Restricted consumer price index (INPC), 222
Revenue in Argentina, increase in, 134, 136

Sarney, José, and declaration of Cruzado Plan, 223
Seigniorage, total, in Israel, effect of stabilization program on, 60–61
Seigniorage model for open economy and Cruzado Plan, 290

Siles-Zuazo, Hernán
election of, 310
hyperinflation during presidency of, 317
Solel Boneh, effects of stabilization program on, 35
Stackelberg player, government as, 266–267
Stackelberg warfare, 266
Strategic interdependence, Lucas and Sargent's principle of, 266
Supreme Decree 21060, 318
Synchronization, 277
defined, 278

Tax revenues in Israel
decline in, 5
effect of stabilization program on, 63
Tax structure in Israel, effect of on budget deficit, 49, 52
Taylor's model of staggered wage setting, extension of, 274, 276–278
TCD, 203
Threshold of hyperinflation, 170–171
TIDOL, 203
Tripartite wage agreement(s) (package deals), 52, 81, 100
failure of, 54–55
in Israel, 1984–1985, 5–6, 8
1987, 11

Unemployment in Bolivia, causes of, 350–351
Unemployment in Israel
effect of stabilization program on, 65
rate in Israel's occupied territories, 98
United States aid to Israel, 8
United States aid to Israel
importance of, 97
increase in, 54

VAVIS, 203

Wage(s)
in Argentina, during second phase of Austral Plan, 164
in Bolivia, during hyperinflation, 314
in Brazil, conversion of to cruzados, 223–224
sliding scale for, under Cruzado Plan, 225–228
Wage adjustments in Brazil, lack of synchrony in, 219

Wage bonus under Cruzado Plan, 225
Wage contracts in Argentina, duration of
    before Austral Plan, 122
Wage conversion in Brazil, Decree Law
    2283 for, 224
Wage costs in Israel, compensations for, 11
Wage freeze
  in Argentina, 126–127, 156–157
  1987, 166–168
  gradual removal of, 272
  in Israel, 53, 54
Wage increase(s) in Israel, causes for, 12,
    15–17
Wage indexation
  in Bolivia, 311
  in Brazil, backward-looking, 279–280
Wage policy
  in Brazil, during second phase of Brazilian
    New Republic economic policy, 221
  and inflation stabilization in Israel, 8
"Wage race" in Bolivia, 312
Walrasian auctioneer, economy in absence
    of, 262–265
War reparations, effect of on economy, 167
Wartime economy
  in Israel, 95–98
  in United States, 95–96

Yacimientos Petroliferos Fiscales Bolivianos
    (YPFB), 318